YOUNG J.
EDGAR

YOUNG J. EDGAR

HOOVER, THE RED SCARE, AND THE ASSAULT ON CIVIL LIBERTIES

KENNETH D. ACKERMAN

CARROLL & GRAF PUBLISHERS
NEW YORK

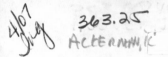
YOUNG J. EDGAR
Hoover, the Red Scare, and the Assault on Civil Liberties

Carroll & Graf Publishers
An Imprint of Avalon Publishing Group, Inc.
245 West 17th Street
11th Floor
New York, NY 10011

AVALON
publishing group incorporated

All illustrations are courtesy of the Library of Congress
except those on the following pages:

p. 163: Ellis Island Library
p. 38 (Edgar with bicycle and with parents): Hoover Center
frontispiece, p. 38 (Edgar as cadet), and p. 47: NARA
pp. 72, 74, and 104: Anthony Collection

Library of Congress Cataloging-in-Publication Data is available.

ISBN-13: 978-0-78671-775-0
ISBN-10: 0-7867-1775-0

9 8 7 6 5 4 3 2 1

Designed by Pauline Neuwirth and Maria E. Torres
Printed in the United States of America
Distributed by Publishers Group West

Congress shall make no law . . . abridging the freedom
of speech. . . .

—United States Constitution,
First Amendment

The right of the people to be secure in their persons, houses,
papers, and effects, against unreasonable searches and seizures,
shall not be violated, and no Warrants shall issue, but upon
probable cause, supported by Oath or affirmation, and particularly describing the place to be searched, or the person or
things to be seized.

—Fourth Amendment

No person shall . . . be deprived of life, liberty, or property,
without due process of law. . . .

—Fifth Amendment

YOUNG J.
EDGAR

Edgar Hoover in 1924.

CONTENTS

· 1 ·
DENIALS

Washington, D.C., May 10, 1924, four years after the Palmer Raids.

THE DOOR CLOSED and J. Edgar Hoover found himself alone with his boss, Harlan Fiske Stone, the new attorney general of the United States. "He told me brusquely to sit down and looked at me intently over the desk," Edgar recalled years later, telling the story for the hundredth time. He snapped to the command. Stone cut an imposing figure. He stood six and a half feet tall, weighed 250 pounds, was almost twice Edgar's age of twenty-nine, and a full head higher. Stone loved fishing, and proudly displayed a medal he'd won from the Long Island Country Club for hauling in a 36-ounce trout.

Stone wasted no time on small talk. Edgar tried to raise administrative odds and ends, but Stone cut him off. "Then he said to me 'Young man, I want you to be acting director of the Bureau of Investigation.'"

J. Edgar Hoover still had boyish good looks in 1924: wavy dark hair, a bright face, and flashy brown eyes. He was a smart dresser in the latest fashions, double-breasted suits, vests, spats, cashmeres and tweeds, crisp white shirts, like any other up-and-coming child of the Jazz Age. He spit out his words in a confident fast staccato, a delivery he had forced on himself as a teenager to stop stuttering. He had to be thrilled at the offer. The new attorney general was paying him a stunning compliment and offering a rare career opportunity. He looked back across the desk at Stone and studied the older man's brown eyes peering back over his glasses, the bushy eyebrows, the massive forehead, the receding brown hair.

"I'll take the job, Mr. Stone, but only on certain conditions," he answered. Harlan Stone gave a quizzical look. It took a rare cockiness for anyone, certainly a youngster like J. Edgar Hoover, to play coy at a moment like this, on being offered a top federal post.

Stone had spent weeks trying to decide whom to pick as the new chief for the Bureau of Investigation. Scandal engulfed Washington in 1924, the notorious "Teapot Dome," named for the stretch of Wyoming desert that held one of the United States Navy's principal oil reserves. Interior Secretary Albert B. Fall faced prison for leasing these lands to oil industry friends in 1922 in exchange for bribes, prompting a criminal prosecution that made headlines across the country. But the scandal went deeper. Senate hearings that spring had uncovered a sewer of corruption at the Department of Justice and its Bureau of Investigation: graft and kickbacks from gangsters and bootleggers, agents with criminal records, badges being issued to private provocateurs (called "dollar-a-year men") who grew rich on extortion, and Bureau agents assigned to harass members of Congress. As the details came out, insiders tagged Justice with a new name: the Department of Easy Virtue.

In March 1924, a new president, Calvin Coolidge, brought in a new attorney general to clean up the mess, an old-line reformer and long-time dean of New York's Columbia University Law School. This new man was Harlan Fiske Stone.

Reaching Washington in April 1924, Stone barely knew where to start. "When I became attorney general, the Bureau of Investigation was . . . in exceedingly bad odor," he recalled. Reaching the Justice Department building on Vermont Avenue, Stone found himself an outsider, surrounded by strangers. "I don't know whom to trust; I don't know any of these people," he lamented.

Installing a new chief at the Bureau of Investigation would be his biggest step yet. The day before, on May 9, 1924, he had fired the Bureau's corrupt sitting director, a cigar-chomping, wisecracking former private detective named William J. Burns. Now, to replace him—at least temporarily—he had sent for J. Edgar Hoover.

Edgar had no social pedigree and no Ivy League diploma. He had earned his law degree from George Washington University, and his father had been a mere government clerk, a map printer at the U.S. Coast and Geodetic Survey. And he was so young, younger than most of the Bureau agents he'd be expected to supervise. Would they respect him? Would he have the backbone to stand up to older entrenched powers? Oddly, Harlan Stone thought yes. Who could miss the hard work, the professional polish, the competence of the young man? Stone frequently saw Edgar working long hours at the office, staying well past dinner each night and routinely working on weekends. Edgar had a command of detail, an ability to decide questions, and a willingness to give orders. He seemed to have no social life, no girlfriends, and few close office buddies. Other than belonging to a handful of men's clubs like the Masons, the Sigma Delta and Kappa Alpha fraternities, and the University Club, he made his job his life.

And now, this latest wrinkle—the fact that this young J. Edgar Hoover had the composure and confidence to set his own conditions on the job as Bureau chief—only deepened Harlan Stone's growing respect.

"What are they?" the attorney general asked.

Edgar had come prepared. As Stone studied him from across his polished desktop, he proceeded to lay out an agenda of ideas that couldn't help but impress even the most zealous reformer. "The Bureau must be divorced from politics and not be a catch-all for political hacks. Appointments must be based on merit. Promotions will be made only on proven ability. And the bureau will be responsible only to the attorney general."

Despite his age, Edgar already counted himself a Justice Department veteran by 1924, having worked there for seven years since starting in 1917 as a twenty-two-year-old clerk. It had been Edgar's first job after earning his law degree, and he'd made the most of it.

America had entered World War I during that spring of 1917, and Edgar should have topped any list for military service. He was smart, fit, and well-trained, valedictorian of his high school graduating class, captain of its cadet corps and leader of its track and debate teams. He even led the school's cadets marching down Pennsylvania Avenue in Woodrow Wilson's 1913 inaugural parade. Born and raised in Washington, D.C., in a modest neighborhood near the U.S. Capitol, a few boyhood friends still called him "Speed," a nickname he earned as a ten-year-old when he carried grocery bags for a few nickels for old ladies in the neighborhood. A typical high school report card gave him good grades for English, French, History and Physics, but perfect grades, straight E's, for Neatness.

His mother raised him Lutheran, and he once sang soprano in the church choir, though he switched and joined a Presbyterian church as a teenager, drawn by a charismatic local preacher who organized baseball games and got Edgar to teach Sunday school.

But family duty had squelched any thought of his joining the army in 1917. That spring, Edgar's father had been forced by higher-ups to quit his job as a federal government clerk after forty-two years, losing his pension and leaving the family with no income. Earlier, his father had been committed to an asylum in Laurel, Maryland, for chronic depression—what his doctors called "melancholia," a little-understood, debilitating condition marked by dejection, self-loathing, lack of interest in the outside word, and suicidal thoughts. Edgar, the youngest of three children, became his parents' main financial support. So as America went to war in 1917 and he watched school friends ship off to face death in European trenches, Edgar stayed home and used a family tie to win a draft-exempt desk job at the Justice Department.

At Justice, Edgar had engineered a meteoric rise. During the War, he went to work for the newly formed War Alien Enemy Bureau, responsible for tracking German residents on U.S. soil. He earned repeated promotions and, after the Armistice, won a spot on the attorney general's staff, then another series of promotions in the department's Bureau of Investigation. By 1924, Edgar had climbed the ladder to become one of Justice's top officials.

He had mostly kept his nose clean during Teapot Dome. As the scandals worsened, he avoided them by burying himself in the Bureau's routine paperwork and a few special cases that caught his eye. By the time the new attorney general called him in for a talk, he had prepared himself to deliver a perfect pitch. Harlan Stone found Edgar's conditions very appropriate; in fact, they were exactly what he wanted to hear. "I wouldn't give [the job] to you under any other conditions," Stone told him from across the desk. Then, just as abruptly, he ended the conversation. "That's all. Good day."

Edgar followed Stone's lead in executing a catalog of new reforms. He fired scores of incompetents, hacks, and dollar-a-year men, raised standards for new recruits, and directed his agents to stop the political witch hunts and keep the Bureau's activities "limited strictly to investigations of violations of law," as Stone put it. In applying the rules, Edgar refused to be bullied by politicians, and Stone consistently backed him. Stone was delighted with his protégé. He praised Edgar as "a man of exceptional intelligence, alertness, and executive ability" who gave "far greater promise than any other man I had heard of."

Stone took only seven months to declare his experiment a success. In December 1924, he named Edgar the permanent director of the Bureau of Investigation, later renamed the FBI.

J. Edgar Hoover would hold the directorship for forty-eight years, until the day he died in 1972 as the most controversial law enforcement figure of the twentieth century. He would achieve mythic status in America, building the FBI into a pillar of government, with over 8,600 agents and a budget of $336 million. His reorganization of the Bureau in the 1920s under Harlan Fiske Stone drew wide praise. In the 1930s, he made headlines solving the Lindbergh baby kidnapping case and capturing or killing gangsters like John Dillinger, George "Machine Gun" Kelly, and Lester "Baby Face" Nelson. He introduced scientific crime fighting, an FBI National Academy and Crime Laboratory, Uniform Crime Reports, and a Fingerprint Division whose files by 1974 held a staggering 159 million sets of prints. In the 1940s and 1950s, boys across the country dreamed of growing up to be G-Men, portrayed on screen by movie and television stars like James Cagney, Jimmy Stewart, and Efrem Zimbalist Jr.

But all these achievements came with a cost. By the 1960s, his abusive probes of leftists, Vietnam War protestors, and civil rights leaders like Martin Luther King Jr. made him a figure to be feared. Stories abounded about Hoover's power, how he could blackmail presidents, senators, and movie stars with voluminous, secret sex files that he kept on so many. Even after death, his legend grew. Congressional probes would reveal decades of FBI abuses: black bag jobs, covert wiretaps, and systematic violations of law. Later biographies cast him in surprising roles, some doubtful, some plausible, from stories of cross-dressing to suggestions of his being one of America's highest ranking gay men, or the descendant of an African-American ancestor.*

---

*Hoover's homosexuality, now part of the accepted legend, has never been established and is doubted by many biographers. The cross-dressing story, unearthed by Anthony Summers in his 1993 biography, has raised particular doubts because it contradicts evidence of Hoover's extreme discretion and self-discipline; its sourcing has been questioned by, among others, biographers Athan Theoharis and Richard Hack. If Hoover had any gay relationship, it was probably a stable, monogamous, and discreet one with long-time confidante and FBI associate director Clyde Tolson, but this too is unproven. Hoover's attraction to sex secrets and sex files, though, is well established. The possibility of his having an African-American ancestor, explored by Millie McGhee, is not unlikely given Hoover's father's family roots in Virginia and Maryland in the Antebellum South.

Throughout his life, Edgar never tired of telling the story of how Harlan Stone first asked him to take the job of director back in May 1924. He made it part of his legend. He required every young FBI recruit for the next fifty years to learn it in basic training. He insisted that every authorized FBI history feature it as an icon. No one ever questioned the story's truth.

But this, too, like most things involving J. Edgar Hoover, had a dark side. The story was based on a lie. The conception was not immaculate at all. In convincing Harlan Stone to give him the acting job that day in 1924, bright, fresh-faced, earnest young J. Edgar Hoover had cheated the older man.

Of all the abuses bothering Harlan Fiske Stone on that cool spring day in May 1924 when he decided to choose Edgar as his instrument to reform the tarnished Bureau of Investigation, none rankled him more than the anticommunist crackdowns of 1919 and 1920, already known infamously as the Palmer Raids. They were named for his predecessor, Attorney General A. Mitchell Palmer, once a leading progressive who now lived in sad obscurity in Washington, D.C. But back during his height of power in 1919 and 1920, Palmer had directed federal agents and local police to go and round up between 5,000 and 10,000 people in a three-month orgy of government bullying. Many were held for months in cramped, filthy, makeshift prisons, beaten, brutalized, railroaded, denied lawyers or access to family members, then released with no explanation, never charged with a crime.

The nation had seemed to go berserk that year, hypnotized by a Red Scare, with Palmer and his circle fanning a paranoid fever against communists, anarchists, radicals, socialists, or anyone not "100 percent American," as they called it.

Only the outspoken resistance of a handful of lawyers had turned public opinion against the crackdown and saved thousands of innocent people from being deported. Harlan Fiske Stone had been one of these dissenters. At the panic's height, he had risked his job and reputation to denounce the Red Raids. Stone had submitted public testimony to a Senate investigating committee accusing Palmer and his Justice Department of ignoring constitutional rights, conducting warrantless arrests and searches, and abusing federal power.

J. Edgar Hoover had been Palmer's special assistant when the raids began on November 7, 1919, and he had his fingerprints all over them. Palmer had assigned Edgar to run the Justice Department's Radical Division, which planned and led the operation. Edgar publicly argued its highest profile legal cases and sat at Palmer's right hand on Capitol Hill when Palmer testified about the raids to two different congressional investigating committees. In internal debates, Edgar consistently argued the most strident views: demanding more arrests, higher bail, fewer rights for detainees, and a tougher line against anyone who stood in the way. Edgar had ordered Bureau agents to compile large dossiers against many of its critics, painting them as Parlor Bolshevists and Red sympathizers, ammunition to smear them at a moment's notice. His files covered 450,000 people by 1921, a remarkable feat for the precomputer age, and they included many of Harlan Stone's closest personal friends, including lawyers, professors, and even a sitting United States Supreme Court Justice, Louis Brandeis.

None of these facts, though, seemed to reach Harlan Stone in May 1924. Instead, as the new attorney general, Stone got exactly the opposite impression: that young J. Edgar Hoover had played at most a minor role in the affair. It only made sense: Edgar had been just twenty-four years old at the time of Palmer's raids, just two years out of law school. "[H]e was just a kid, and he always insisted that he was only doing his job," claimed Ugo Carusi, Harlan Stone's executive assistant, "and I wouldn't challenge that, because I can't imagine policy being made by a fellow in his early twenties."

Edgar himself would spend a lifetime denying any major role in the raids. His FBI publicity machine would blast as a "vicious and false . . . smear" that he had led them. Edgar would tell one biographer that he "parted company" with his Justice Department bosses "in the illegal methods and the brutality sometimes employed in rounding up aliens [and was] appalled [by] agents who lacked any knowledge of the rules of evidence and who made arrests which could not stand up in court." In 1924, he would tell Roger Baldwin, head of the recently formed American Civil Liberties Union, created in response to the raids, that he played only an "unwilling part."

And Harlan Stone believed it.

To most Americans, it didn't seem to matter. The world had changed quickly since the dark days of 1919. America entered the Roaring Twenties, a happy time of Coolidge prosperity, of jazz, flappers, and speakeasies, Babe Ruth on the diamond, Jack Dempsey in the ring, Al Jolson on Broadway, live ballroom music on the radio, Mary Pickford and Lillian Gish on the silent silver screen, Post Toasties on the breakfast table, F. Scott Fitzgerald on the bookshelf, and Sigmund Freud in the bedroom. Life was good. People had little time to care about communists or other spooks.

But back in 1919, just four years earlier, it had all made perfect sense—the Red Scare, the Raids, the fear. Most thinking, informed Americans agreed: World War I had ended, but the country was still fighting, against anarchists and communists at home just as surely as it had fought the kaiser's Germany in Europe the year before. American soldiers still faced bullets on Russian soil in 1919, and Bolshevism was sweeping the world. Anarchists had exploded bombs in American streets, and people had been killed. Radicals had infiltrated labor unions and threatened to topple major industries. The country demanded safety and somebody had to act.

A. Mitchell Palmer and his team had taken responsibility. Had there been excesses? Certainly. But that didn't change the fact. The principal fact was the bombs, and the danger of more bombs, and the duty to protect Americans. Everything else took a back seat.

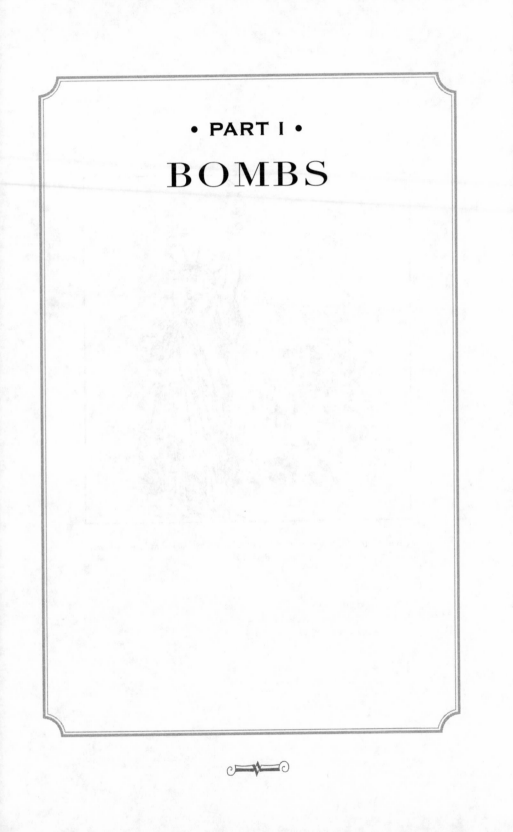

• PART I •

BOMBS

"Come Unto Me, Ye Opprest!" *Memphis Commercial Appeal* in *Literary Digest,*
July 5, 1919.

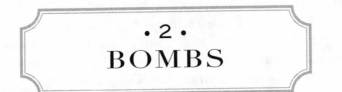

· 2 ·
BOMBS

I.   THE BLAST

Monday, June 2, 1919

PALMER HAD SPENT the night quietly at home, reading and chatting with his wife, Roberta, in the downstairs library of their home in Washington, D.C. He had waited until almost 11 o'clock before turning out the lights and going upstairs. But he couldn't sleep. Just three months into his new job as attorney general, he and Roberta had finished a whirlwind round of social calls that weekend, a flurry of dinners and receptions, a party with political friends at Washington's Shubert-Garrick Theater on Sunday, then a meeting of the Women's Liberty Loan Committee at the Willard Hotel on Monday. Now, on Monday night, instead of climbing into bed, Palmer undressed and sat in a bedroom chair, reading by a small lamp as Roberta got under the covers. He looked up occasionally to watch her dozing off to sleep. Their only child, daughter Mary, a bright teenager with blonde hair and blue eyes facing a busy school day the next morning, had gone to bed in her own room down the hall hours earlier.

The Palmers lived in a posh four-story townhouse on R Street in Washington's West End, the exclusive neighborhood between Sheridan and Dupont Circles dotted with political celebrities. Franklin Delano Roosevelt, the suave socialite assistant secretary of the navy, lived directly across the street with his wife, Eleanor, and their five children. William Howard Taft, the chubby former president with the walrus mustache, handsome Ohio U.S. Senator Warren G. Harding, and a young army lieutenant-colonel named Dwight David Eisenhower all lived within a few blocks. Their street felt like a small southern town, inbred but friendly, a narrow lane of pretty shade trees, flower beds and gardens, smells of lilac in spring and dogwood in summer.

This night, sitting in his bedroom, Palmer heard nothing from out on the street but the whirr of an occasional motorcar or the clip-clop of horse hooves on nearby cobblestones. Then, at about 11:15 P.M., his ears perked up. He began noticing sounds: a car pulling up on the street, stopping in front of the house, a door opening and closing. Then footsteps.

Outside, a man stepped out of the car carrying a suitcase. He rushed toward Palmer's front steps, but tripped in the garden a few feet from the house. He fell, and the suitcase hit the ground. Then came a blinding flash.

After that, the quiet night shattered into chaos.

"I heard a crash downstairs as if something had been thrown against the front door," Palmer said. "It was followed immediately by an explosion."

The blast was deafening. Palmer felt himself hurled from his chair and saw Roberta thrown from her bed, sprawling on the floor. With the explosion, he heard sounds of cracking walls, shattering glass, crashing furniture, and screams. Could the house be collapsing? Palmer ran to his wife. Bewildered but unharmed, he helped her to her feet, and together they rushed down the hall—the electric lights somehow still burning—and found daughter Mary in her room crying hysterically. Palmer tried to calm her. Then, gathering courage, he fumbled for his clothes, found his pants and shoes, and put them on. The house suddenly quiet again, he left his wife and daughter and picked his way downstairs, carefully avoiding broken steps, a shattered banister, piles of rubble, smoldering ash. Reaching ground level, he had no idea what to expect: fire? falling debris? intruders? gunshots?

Looking through semidarkness, he trembled at what he found. His house was in shambles. The front door had been blown in, a stuffed elk's head thrown to the floor, parquet flooring ripped to pieces, broken glass everywhere, windows crashed, cabinets knocked over. After a few minutes, he started in confusion at hearing the silence broken. A noise came from out in front of the house. It was a shout from the street. He recognized the voice of a neighbor. Relieved, Palmer let him in.

Franklin Delano Roosevelt had gone out to dinner with his wife, Eleanor, that night, and they had just returned in his new car, an open-top Stutz roadster that he prized and pampered. "I had just placed my automobile in the garage [a few blocks away from the house] when the explosion took place," Franklin would tell reporters later that night. Immediately, he and Eleanor began to run down the street.* Eleanor had to lift her skirt to avoid tripping on the hem. Reaching their home, they shuddered at the damage. The blast had blown out all their front windows. They heard their cook screaming incoherently from inside: "The world has come to an end." Franklin rushed in and dashed up the stairs to find his son James, eleven years old, standing barefoot in the hallway amid broken glass, having left his bedroom to peek outside. The other four Roosevelt children happened to be away visiting relatives in Hyde Park. Franklin grabbed James and gave him what the boy later recalled as "an embrace that almost crushed my ribs." Eleanor, more calmly, followed Franklin upstairs a moment later and ordered her son back to sleep. "Whatever are you doing out of bed at this hour, James?" she said, then, "Get yourself straight to bed!"

His family safe, Franklin went outside to investigate. R Street looked as though a tornado had struck—tree limbs knocked down, cars blown over, windows broken in every house. On his own doorway, Franklin had to step over patches of blood and fragments of a man's body, a collarbone. Blood and flesh spattered lawns and doorways all down the street; neighbors would find scraps of clothing and fragments of bone hundreds of feet away. "I went over to the attorney general's home immediately," he explained. Here, he found his neighbor Mitchell Palmer alone downstairs, picking through wreckage. Palmer appeared so shocked he could barely talk straight, and Franklin made a joke of it. "Say, I never knew before that Mitchell Palmer was a Quaker," he told Eleanor later that night. "He was 'theeing' and 'thouing' me all over the place—'thank thee, Franklin!' and all that."

Palmer regained his wits by the time detectives began to arrive. "I'm glad you are here," he told the first to reach his door. "I hope you get the man." Palmer had straightened his clothes, helped Roberta and Mary calm down and gather a few things, and began checking the damage. Soon, the street was crawling with people: neighbors, police, newspaper reporters,

---

*Franklin Roosevelt would not contract polio and lose the use of his legs until August 1921— about two years after these events—while on a vacation trip to Campobello, New Brunswick.

military officers, Justice Department agents, and curiosity seekers. The police roped off the sidewalk and set up twenty large search lights to hunt methodically for clues. They found plenty: two guns, including a blue steel revolver fully loaded, remains of a suitcase, an English-Italian dictionary, a size 15 shirt collar with a Chinese laundry mark, and a soft brown fedora with gold writing on its inside band: "De Luca Brothers, hatters, 919 South Eighth Avenue, Philadelphia." They identified lingering fumes of dynamite and nitroglycerine. They found parts of an arm, bones, flesh, a piece of scalp with long black hair, and blood scattered for hundreds of yards, including what appeared to be remains of two left legs, although they insisted only one man had died in the blast. "I believe that the man with the bomb must have stumbled over the curbing when he was on the way to Mr. Palmer's door to place the infernal machine," explained one neighbor, Virginia U.S. Senator Claude Swanson, pointing to a large hole in the ground. "The man probably fell with the bomb."

Mitchell Palmer invited a few newspapermen inside his house to photograph the damage. Of the blood and bone that littered the street, he told them simply: "I hope sincerely that these were not portions of the body of some innocent person."

A frightful picture began to emerge from reports reaching Washington, D.C., that night. Eight other bombs had exploded across America, all at about the same time, just after 11:00 P.M., each having been delivered to the home of its intended victim, men all connected with recent crackdowns against socialist radicals: Boston municipal judge Robert Hayden; Cleveland mayor Harry E. Davis; Massachusetts state representative Leland W. Powers; New York general sessions judge Charles Nott Jr.; Paterson, New Jersey, silk manufacturer Max Gold; Pittsburgh federal judge William P. Thompson, plus Philadelphia's Church of Our Lady of Victory. Two people had died: the bomber at Palmer's house and a watchman on duty outside Judge Nott's home in New York City.* Luck alone prevented dozens of more innocents from being blown to bits.

All fingers pointed to the same familiar culprit: radical anarchists. Police found a clue that seemed to cinch the case. Scattered on the ground near Palmer's house lay fifty copies of a handbill printed on pink paper in black

---

*The three judges, New York's Nott, Boston's Hayden, and Pittsburgh's Thompson, each had given out lengthy jail sentences to anarchists and socialists in recent criminal trials. Cleveland's Mayor Davis had been active in prosecuting two local anarchists there and had proposed an Ohio antisedition statute. Paterson's Max Gold had taken a hard line against strikers in his silk factory. The motive behind the targeting of the Philadelphia church was and remains a mystery.

ink. Copies were found at each of the other bomb sites that night. Palmer's skin must have crawled at reading the belligerent text. PLAIN WORDS, blared the headline. It was signed: THE ANARCHIST FIGHTERS. In between, it preached death, destruction, class warfare, and social revolution.

Mitchell Palmer grasped the essential point: "[The bomb] blew in the front of the house," he told reporters. "The door against which it was thrown leads into the library in which we had been sitting, and the part of the house blown in was in front of the library." Had he and Roberta lingered downstairs just a few minutes longer that night, they would have been killed.

The bombers had meant to murder him, and had almost killed his wife and daughter. And it was the second try in a month.

From "PLAIN WORDS":

"The time has come when the social question's solution can be delayed no longer; class war is on and cannot cease but with complete victory for the international proletariat. . . . .

"We have been dreaming of freedom, we have aspired to a better world, and you jailed us, you clubbed us, you deported us, you murdered us whenever you could. . . . The jails, the dungeons you reared to bury all protesting voices, are now replenished with languishing conscientious workers, and never satisfied, you increase their numbers every day. . . .

". . . Since the press has been suffocated, their mouths muzzled, we mean to speak for them the voice of dynamite, through the mouths of guns. . . . Do not say we are acting cowardly because we keep in hiding; do not say it is abominable; it is war, class war, and you were the first to wage it. . . ."We are . . . determined to fight to the last, till not a man remains buried in your bastilles, till not a hostage of the working class is left to the tortures of your police system, and will never rest till your fall is complete, and the laboring masses have taken possession of all that rightly belongs to them.

"There will have to be bloodshed; we will not dodge; there will have to be murder; we will kill because it is necessary; there will have to be destruction; we will destroy to rid the world of your tyrannical institutions. . . .

"Just wait and resign yourselves to your fate, since privilege and riches have turned your head.

"Long live the social revolution! Down with tyranny! THE ANARCHIST FIGHTERS."

II.   PALMER

The Armistice with Germany ended World War I on November 11, 1918, but seven months later violent upheaval swept Russia, Poland, Germany, Italy, Argentina, France, and much of central Europe. The enemy took on a new face: Bolshevism, based in Soviet Russia and pressed by a global network of armed subversives. In March 1919, socialists from thirty-seven countries, including the United States, met in Moscow to form the Third International, pledged to global revolution.

Two million American soldiers—they called them "doughboys" for the doughy flour blobs they ate in their trenches—streamed home from Europe in early 1919 having survived the trench warfare hell, this war "to make the world safe for democracy" as Woodrow Wilson had called it. They left behind sixteen million dead, including seven million civilians, a slaughter beyond comprehension. Virtually an entire generation of French, British, German, and Russian youth had vanished in the carnage, a million or more from each country. Many were butchered by machine guns, mustard gas, tanks, long-range artillery, U-boats, airplanes—a ghastly new technology of mass murder. The 116,000 American dead represented more than twice the U.S. death toll in Vietnam and more than in any other conflict except the Civil War and World War II.

What had they died for? Most Americans initially had opposed entering what they first considered Europe's own internal civil war. They reelected Woodrow Wilson as president in 1916 mainly because he had kept the country out of it since 1914. But once it jumped in and American boys faced bullets and death, the country worked itself into a hot patriotic fever with little tolerance for slackers, dissenters, or anything German. Now that it was over, a grim bravado overshadowed any pride from crushing German militarism. This didn't feel like peace, at least not the way they remembered it from before the World War.

Wilson himself, having led the country through war, had left Washington in December 1918 and been absent almost six months to lead America's delegation at peace talks in Versailles, France. There, he preached a visionary new world order, built around a League of Nations, to prevent future holocausts. But across the table, France's Georges Clemenceau and England's David Lloyd George scoffed at his naiveté and played for more tangible gains: carving up defeated empires and making Germany pay for the four-year cataclysm.

Alexander Mitchell Palmer—friends called him Mitchell—never joined the military. His Quaker beliefs forbade it. Still, he emerged from the World War as a hero. In March 1919, just four months after the armistice, Woodrow Wilson had rewarded Palmer by naming him attorney general, the newest member of his presidential cabinet. Already, friends touted Palmer as a possible candidate for president in 1920 should Wilson decide not to seek a third term.

Palmer had broad shoulders, a square jaw, friendly smile, and fleshy hands always quick with a wave or a slap on the shoulder. Just forty-seven years old, he had ridden his ambition far beyond tiny Stroudsburg, Pennsylvania, the town where his parents raised him as a devout Quaker. After graduating Swarthmore College *summa cum laude*, he returned to Stroudsburg to practice law and here he met and married Roberta Bartlett Dixon, the daughter of a small-town Maryland businessman. Over the next twenty-two years, Palmer proved himself a master politician, winning three campaigns for the United States Congress and losing a close race for the U.S. Senate—all as a Democrat—and now enjoying a tour in Washington as a cabinet member.

Palmer built his political career primarily around one key friendship: the one he had with Woodrow Wilson. They'd met long before Wilson's White House years, back when Wilson was still New Jersey's up-and-coming governor and Palmer a junior congressman from neighboring Pennsylvania. They struck up an odd rapport, Palmer the likeable, outgoing backslapper and Wilson the stiff, bookish college professor with the long face and cold demeanor. But politically, they saw eye to eye. Palmer always carried the torch for Woodrow Wilson's progressive causes, what Wilson called the New Democracy. As a congressman, Palmer introduced the bills to give women the right to vote and to bar child labor. He backed Pennsylvania coal miners and steel workers whose unions consistently backed his campaigns. When Wilson first decided to run for president in 1912, he asked Palmer to manage his campaign in Pennsylvania and help lead his forces at the Democratic convention in Baltimore.* When Wilson won, he put Palmer's name high on his initial list for a cabinet seat. He

---

*That 1912 Democratic convention in Baltimore turned into a classic, with Wilson winning the nomination on the forty-sixth ballot after trailing House Speaker Champ Clark (D-Mo.) for the first thirty. Clark received a majority, 556 delegate votes, on the tenth, but was blocked by the Democrats' two-thirds rule, the only time since 1844 that a Democrat had received a majority vote of a convention by failed to win the nomination. Democrats voted to end the two-thirds rule in 1936.

offered Palmer the post of secretary of war, but Palmer declined, insisting that his Quaker roots made him a pacifist. "I could not, without violating every tradition of my people . . . sit down in cold blood in an executive position and use such talents as I possess to the work of preparing for [war]," he wrote the president in turning down the job.

From the start, though, Palmer made his own ambitions plain. Wilson's friends noticed them even as early as the 1912 presidential nominating convention, when Wilson's fate still hung in the balance. "Palmer's first choice was himself," one of them grumbled.

During the first two years of Wilson's presidency, Mitchell Palmer stayed in Washington to serve as a congressman and shared in Wilson's progressive achievements, such as his creation of a Federal Trade Commission, a Federal Reserve monetary system, tough enforcement of antitrust laws, and a constitutionally sound income tax. In 1914, Wilson convinced Palmer to return home to Pennsylvania and run for an open seat in the United States Senate. When Palmer lost the race, Wilson thanked him for the effort by making him a judge on the U.S. Court of Claims. Then he called him back to Washington in 1917 when America entered World War I. Pacifism aside, the president needed Palmer's help in the war effort and offered him a rare opportunity. Palmer soon would make his obscure wartime title a household word: Alien Property Custodian.

Germany, through its business elite, owned almost a billion dollars in American-based assets at the start of World War I, including major corporations. "Many of the German-owned industrial concerns in the United States were spy centres," Palmer charged. As Alien Property

Mitchell Palmer with then-Governor Woodrow Wilson, circa 1912.

Custodian, it was Palmer's job to stop them from damaging American interests, and he did it with gusto. In a dazzling display of raw executive muscle, he quickly seized dozens of major German firms, thousands of patents, and millions of dollars in financial assets: the Bayer Company, where his agents found twenty-three trunks of alleged German espionage files; the railroad-industrial giant Orenstein-Arthur Koppel Company; eighteen branches of German insurance companies; the Bosch Magneto Company; the Hamburg-American shipping line; and the German-American Lumber Company, among others. He sold each of these companies to new American owners, often at bargain prices, raising charges of cronyism and fraud. He seized over four thousand German chemical patents and conveyed them to a new American company. By the war's end, he had built a staff of 300 employees spread out across four office buildings.

The campaign kept Palmer's name in the headlines throughout the war. In Berlin, they called him the "official American pickpocket." In America his nickname was the Fighting Quaker.

After the armistice, Woodrow Wilson recognized he had a popular rising star under his wing. He soon found a new mission for his friend: to restore trust in the Department of Justice. Palmer, a lawyer, jumped at the chance.

Americans had fought World War I to help protect democracy abroad, but it produced a chilling backlash against freedoms at home. Wilson's wartime Justice Department led heavy-handed crackdowns on dissenters, draft dodgers, and German nationals. It brought more than five thousand prosecutions under the wartime Espionage and Conscription Acts, sending hundreds to prison simply for giving speeches or publicly questioning the government. Typical of the excesses were the Slacker Raids against suspected draft dodgers. The largest, in New York City in September 1918, turned into a three-day frenzy as federal agents teamed up with the American Protective League (APL)—a vigilante group with 250,000 members at its peak—and together they combed saloons, pool halls, bus stops, dance halls, and street corners to detain any young man who could not produce a draft card or birth certificate to prove he was not a draft dodger. They arrested over 75,000 altogether, far too many for the city's jails. Some went without food or working toilets for days or weeks. Many were youngsters below draft age; one was a seventy-five-year-old man on crutches. In the end, less than 1 in 200 was an actual slacker.

Palmer's chance for promotion came in March 1919 when Wilson's wartime attorney general, Francis W. Gregory, announced his resignation.

The president decided that now was the time to restore moderation, and he thought of his rising star. "Palmer, our friend in 1912, has been loyal throughout," Joe Tumulty, Wilson's White House private secretary, advised him. "Palmer is young, militant, progressive and fearless. He stands well with the country, Congress, and appeals to young voters; he is effective on the stump." To Woodrow Wilson, Palmer offered the chance to put a fresh face and a loyal ally in a sensitive post.

In his first weeks as attorney general, Palmer followed the president's script. In April 1919, he recommended that 51 prisoners serving Espionage Act sentences be freed immediately by presidential pardon or commutation, and he ordered the release from parole of 5,000 enemy aliens arrested during the war plus the freeing of 2,000 prisoners still held in military internment camps, many for repatriation to Germany. He disbanded the American Protective League. He even considered proposing clemency for Eugene V. Debs, the four-time Socialist Party presidential candidate who received almost a million votes in 1912 and who was serving a prison term under the Espionage Act for speaking out against the wartime draft. But when the judges and prosecutors advised him against releasing Debs, Palmer chose not to fight them.*

Mitchell Palmer worked hard. He threw himself into the job and spent long hours at the office, but his mission drew little praise. Outside a small circle of liberal progressives, few Americans in early 1919 had any patience for moderation. World War I might have ended, but a new struggle had engaged the country. In June, it boiled over.

III.   AGITATION

The bomb attack on Mitchell Palmer's house on June 2, 1919, had not been the first. Five weeks earlier, in late April, a mail bomb delivered to the home of United States Senator Thomas Hardwick of Georgia had exploded and blown off the hands of a maid in his Atlanta home. The next day, a postal clerk in New York City named Charles Kaplan, reading

---

*Gregory insisted that few, if any, of these so-called political prisoners had been convicted for mere "expression of opinion" as opposed to "deliberate obstruction in the prosecution of the war." This was a thin distinction. Debs, for instance, was convicted for violating the Espionage Act solely for giving a speech in Canton, Ohio, in June 1918, in which he criticized the war, and the imprisonment of fellow socialists, and said, among other things: "The master class has always declared the wars; the subject class has always fought the battles. The master class has had all to gain and nothing to lose, while the subject class has had nothing to gain and all to lose—especially their lives." Gregory's prosecutors argued that Debs, by these words, had encouraged young men to resist the draft, thus obstructing the war effort. The United States Supreme Court upheld the Debs conviction in March 1919.

about the incident in a newspaper, remembered seeing sixteen packages a few days earlier that fit the description. He had pulled them aside for insufficient postage. Investigators quickly checked and found a bomb inside each one. Each was wrapped in identical brown paper with an orange tag bearing the return address of Gimbel Brothers, the well-known New York department store, and marked "Novelty—A Sample." The assassins apparently had timed them for delivery on May Day, the international workers' holiday. The intended victims of these bombs included five United States senators, four cabinet members, the commissioner of immigration, Supreme Court Justice Oliver Wendell Holmes, plus oil billionaire John D. Rockefeller and banking magnate J. P. Morgan.

Palmer had been one of those targets. An exhaustive investigation so far had failed to produce any solid leads.

Radical agitation—labor, socialist, anarchist (few bothered to notice any difference)—had been mounting all year long in 1919, matched by a growing backlash. First, in late January, a work stoppage by 35,000 Seattle dockworkers had escalated into a general strike joined by 110 other unions. They shut down the city's schools, street cars, and factories amid swirls of communist class-war rhetoric. Terrified citizens feared the worst and emptied the stores of food and guns. Politicians fanned the hysteria: REDS DIRECTING SEATTLE STRIKE—TO TEST CHANCE FOR REVOLUTION, one local newspaper headlined. "From Russia they came and to Russia they should be made to go," declared United States Senator William King, a Democrat from Utah. Strike leaders kept the city clean and well fed. They ran garbage, laundry, and milk trucks and kept food, coal, and water plentiful, and they prevented any strike-related violence. But Seattle mayor Ole Hanson still demanded federal troops to crush the uprising. The workers called it quits after three weeks.

In February, Secret Service agents announced that they had broken up a plot by a Philadelphia-based Spanish anarchist group called Pro Prenza to assassinate President Wilson.

On May 1, May Day, riots erupted worldwide, and blood flowed in a dozen American cities—much of it from reactionary violence. In Cleveland, army veterans carrying rifles with live ammunition led hecklers in attacking a socialist Red Flag parade, killing one and injuring forty. Police arrested 126 of the socialists but none of the attackers. In New York City, veterans in army uniforms stormed the Russian Peoples House, an immigrant community center on East Fifteenth Street, and forced a socialist group meeting inside, at gunpoint, to sing the "Star Spangled Banner." Later, they raided a reception at the left-leaning newspaper, the *New York*

Call, smashed furniture, drove guests into the street, and beat them so badly with fists and rifle butts that seventeen had to be hospitalized. In Boston, police and hecklers battled 1,500 flag-waving demonstrators from the socialist Lettish Workmen's Association; police there arrested 116 of the demonstrators, and local judges sentenced 16 of them to jail terms of more than a year. Three policemen and one civilian were shot in the melee. In Chicago, a crowd cheered when a sailor in uniform raised his rifle and shot a man at a victory loan pageant, wounding him for refusing to stand up and take off his hat during the national anthem.

Later that month, riots savaged Toledo, Ohio, when 13,000 striking workers at an automobile plant attacked cars carrying strikebreakers. They smashed automobile windows, dragged the scabs out of the cars, and beat them bloody. Factory guards, again recent veterans in army uniforms, fired over 100 rounds of ammunition when strikers tried to storm the plant. Bullet wounds killed two and injured two others.

These escalating violent outbreaks reflected a deeper force shaking American society that spring: an economic collapse. When World War I ended in November 1918, it left four million American soldiers and another nine million workers in war industries to be dumped chaotically on an economy short of jobs. Millions of unemployed veterans sat and stewed. At the same time, the money in people's pockets shrank in value to near nothing. The purchasing power of a 1913 dollar collapsed to barely 45 cents by 1919, with food costs jumping 84 percent and clothing up 114 percent. At the same time, salaries for workers mostly had stayed flat during World War I under government controls and patriotic restraint. Now, with peace, workers, even those *with* jobs, struggled to feed their families.

Three-quarters of American wage earners in 1919 earned their pay doing physical labor: working in factories, mining coal or copper, cutting

A breadline for unemployed men in New York City, April 1919.
American Review of Reviews, May 1919.

timber, or raising food. Often, this meant grueling twelve-hour workdays, six days a week, for pennies an hour. This was the heyday of sweat shops. These workers had no credit, no bank accounts, no old age pensions, no insurance, and no disability benefits—such items remained playthings for the lucky rich or middle class. But workers weren't powerless. They had unions, a new phenomenon that had grown explosively in the decades before World War I. The American Federation of Labor, the country's largest, had ballooned from 500,000 to almost 5 million members between 1900 and 1919. Now, with peace in Europe, workers demanded better pay. Labor leaders would call over 3,000 strikes in 1919, pulling four million men and women off the job. Barely a week went by without another big strike bringing another major industry to a halt.

This one-two-three punch of inflation, unemployment, and strikes sent shock waves through the country. Business leaders seized the chance to wrap themselves in patriotism and brand strikers as ungrateful wretches, saboteurs wrecking the nation, prone to manipulation by outside agitators. And these agitators, they claimed, came primarily from one particular, very scary place: Russia.

"Rise up and take things in your own hands," Vladimir Ilyich Lenin had decreed in a "Letter to American Workingmen" issued in August 1918. Lenin's rise to power as leader of the Bolsheviks in Russia's October 1917 revolution (which actually occurred November 7 by the Western calendar) had inspired radical leftists worldwide and terrified Western leaders. Moscow made no secret of its global ambitions. In March 1919, Lenin called together delegates from thirty-seven countries to pledge their dedication to world revolution under the *Third Communist International*. Already, American intelligence agents traced Moscow's cash and influence to hot spots around the world, including a socialist uprising in Germany called the Spartacists, a Soviet regime that had seized power in Hungary, plus the violent civil war sweeping Russia itself and its neighbor Poland. Stories of hangings, forced labor, mass murders, expropriations, and starvation flooded the cables from Eastern Europe.

Americans found it easy to transfer their wartime hatred of Kaiser Wilhelm's Germany to Vladimir Lenin's postwar Bolshevik Russia. After all, it was the kaiser's Germany that helped put Lenin in power in the first place. Lenin had been marooned in Zurich, Switzerland, at the start of World War I, and Germany sent him by sealed railroad car into turbulent postrevolutionary Russia in 1917 to make trouble. Lenin, on seizing power, quickly pulled Russia out of the war, freeing thousands of German

"The Storm Cloud in the East." *Literary Digest,*
November 15, 1919.

Vladimir Illyich Lenin.

soldiers to join the western front and kill American troops. American soldiers still fought on Russian soil in 1919 alongside White Russians who held out against Lenin's Red regime in a civil war rife with atrocities.

Native-born Americans, who comprised almost 90 percent of the country's population in 1919, saw strangers in their midst who seemed shockingly sympathetic to this Bolshevik call for treason and takeover. Of the 126 socialists arrested in Cleveland on May Day, for instance, only eight had been American citizens. The rest were all immigrants, mostly recent arrivals from Europe's poorest countries. To the eyes of many Americans, they looked like ignorant, desperate, superstitious hordes. Of the 13 million immigrants walking U.S. streets in 1920, 1.4 million had come from Russia, and another 1.6 million had come from Italy. Often, they lived cloistered together in separate neighborhoods, filthy slums in big cities where they spoke their own languages, joined mysterious clubs, and were followers of strange creeds: Jews, Catholics, Eastern Orthodox, and atheists, the official belief of communists and anarchists.

None of this seemed to bother Mitchell Palmer during his first three months as attorney general. Congress had condemned him for ignoring the threat, but Palmer held his tongue. Ole Hanson, the mayor of Seattle during the January 1919 general strike there, blasted Palmer and his Justice Department for its "weak, vacillating, and changeable" response. "I hope Washington will buck up and . . . hang or incarcerate for life all the anarchists in the country," he told crowds on his speaking tours. "The Department of Justice has accomplished nothing," complained the *Boston*

Evening Transcript, "except to attract the enmity of the anarchists to its head." It called on local police to pick up the slack. New York State had answered this call by creating a special Joint Legislative Committee to Investigate Seditious Activities under state senator Clayton R. Lusk and armed it with quasi-police powers. The Lusk Committee had seized the initiative by staging dramatic police raids against New York leftists.

Mitchell Palmer, by contrast, ordered no mass arrests after the May bomb plot or the May Day riots and called for no national crackdown. Where, critics asked, was the Fighting Quaker? Wasn't he alarmed? Wasn't he awake?

Now, the morning after the June bombing of his home, they got what they wanted. Palmer saw his wife, Roberta, still in shock and his daughter, Mary, in sporadic tears.* He invited friends to visit his destroyed house. "I stood in the middle of the wreckage of my library with Congressmen and Senators, and without a dissenting voice they called upon me in strong terms to exercise all the power that was possible to the Department of Justice to run to earth the criminals who were behind that kind of outrage," he recalled months later. "Palmer, ask for what you want and you will get it," one of them spoke up and said. "The government is behind you in whatever you do to root out this kind of revolutionary organization in this country."

Mitchell Palmer made a decision. For the rest of his time in office, he would commit his Department of Justice to the singular task of tracking down and stopping this Red Menace. It might help him politically, perhaps carry him to the White House. Or it just as easily might hurt him, even endanger his life or his family. Who could tell? "The outrages of last night indicate nothing but the lawless attempt of an anarchistic element in the population to terrorize the country and stay the hand of the government. This they have utterly failed to do," he told newspaper reporters. "These attacks by bomb throwers will only increase and extend the activities of our crime detecting force."

It was welcome news to an angry country, and brought a forceful response. "Attorney General Palmer's courage was praised on every hand," the *New York Times* reported the next morning. "Free speech has been outraged long enough," the *Washington Post* blared. "Let there be a few free treatments in the electric chair." "Every true American citizen will join

---

*It did not help Roberta Palmer settle her nerves that week to receive a letter from a friend in Brooklyn, New York, telling her: "A fitter in one of the shops here the other day had the nerve to tell me that [the bombing of her house] was but the beginning of what 'these here rich fellows is going to get' and all around you hear the threat 'you just wait till after the first of July.' One wonders where it will all end."

you in eradicating all such people from the nation," lawyer Jesse Tull wrote from Washington, D.C. The time had come to act, and Mitchell Palmer had no intention of following the mob. He planned to lead it.

IV.   THE PROBE

After spending time with friends at his ruined home on R Street that morning, Palmer rode a motorcar the mile or so through central Washington, D.C., to the Justice Department building on Vermont Avenue, just four blocks from the White House. Palmer's office had tall bright windows that looked out toward McPherson Square, with its wide green shade trees. Outside on the avenue, trolley cars glided on their rail tracks alongside automobiles—Packards and Ford Model Ts—that shared the cobblestone street with bicycles, horses, and horse-drawn coaches and carts. Men strolled by on the sidewalks in seersucker suits and straw hats. A few women wore their hair cut short in a style called The Bob, with silk dresses in bright colors, reds, pinks, and yellows, an occasional hem rising high enough to expose an ankle or high-laced boot.

Inside, Mitchell Palmer greeted a long line of dignitaries eager to see him that morning: the police chief of Washington, D.C., congressional leaders, and Justice Department officials. Newsmen crowded the hallway trying to grab a comment or take his photograph. Police had set up checkpoints all around the city, posting three hundred plainclothes detectives in front of churches and public buildings. The House and Senate sergeants-at-arms had beefed up patrols at the Capitol Building and limited access to the House and Senate galleries. Armed military and Secret Service details surrounded the White House, the Treasury building, and the War and Navy Departments. Across the country, local police departments assigned guards to shadow public figures and important buildings.

But Palmer had bigger plans that morning than simply playing defense. He intended to take the fight to the terrorists. He quickly freed up time on his schedule and sent word to two old friends to come to his office and see him. They arrived quickly and Palmer closed his office door so they could speak in confidence. His new agenda required him to install an entire new management team at the Justice Department. On the spot, he asked both of these friends to join him and spearhead his hunt for the Red Radicals.

One was John Creighton, an Illinois lawyer who had come to Washington during World War I and made his reputation by tracing enemy-controlled chemical companies as chief detective for the War Trade Intelligence

Board. Palmer offered him a post as senior special assistant in his office so he could start right away.

The other was Francis P. Garvan. Yale-educated and wealthy, Garvan had distinguished himself before the World War as a New York prosecutor winning a string of high-profile murder trials and then joined Palmer in Washington as lead investigator in his German property seizures. Garvan now sat in Palmer's old chair as Alien Property Custodian, responsible for overseeing the German properties seized during the war, a portfolio valued in the hundreds of millions of dollars. Garvan planned soon to accept a top-paying job as chairman of the Chemical Foundation, a new corporation built on confiscated German patents, and had purchased a 100-acre estate in Wheatley Hills, Long Island, where he intended to settle once in New York City. But Palmer asked him to change his plans. He appealed to Garvan with a combination of flattery and arm-twisting. He offered him the prestigious title of assistant attorney general and a mouthful of compliments. "Mr. Garvan, in my judgment, is without a superior in the business of the detection of crime," Palmer told reporters. Garvan couldn't resist.

Next, to make his plan work, Palmer needed to find the best possible chief to lead the Justice Department's Bureau of Investigation, still a relatively new office in 1919 with 300 agents operating out of 54 field offices across the country. Its agent force would spearhead any federal assault against the Reds, and the Bureau had been leaderless since April when its director resigned. Sitting in Palmer's office that day around his polished desk, the three old friends brainstormed, tossing out names of candidates. Inevitably, they kept coming back to the same one, the most famous detective in America: William J. "Big Bill" Flynn, the former chief of the U.S. Secret Service and the New York City detective force. "Flynn is an anarchist chaser," Palmer would crow in announcing the appointment. "He is the great anarchist expert in the United States. He knows all the men of that class. He can pretty nearly call them by name."

William Flynn, a wide, dapper, barrel-chested man with a tiny dark mustache, partial to derby hats and splashy midnight raids, indeed had a reputation that spanned the continent. During his years as New York City's deputy police commissioner, he led its detectives on dramatic raids against counterfeiters, gangsters, kidnappers, bank robbers, and gamblers, often going out with his coppers to share the thrill of breaking heads and making headlines. Later, as head of the U. S. Secret Service during the World War, Flynn made himself the country's premier spy chaser. He cracked a string of dramatic espionage cases, including a 1915 conspiracy by German agents to dynamite

William J. "Big Bill" Flynn.

American munitions ships in New York Harbor, then a plot to counterfeit millions of dollars in silver certificates and Treasury notes. By mid-1918, Flynn claimed to have over 15,000 German agents under surveillance. "I place a conservative estimate of [German spies] in this country at 250,000," he told an audience in California around this time, "and one of them may be working next to you, waiting on you."

As much as any single person, Flynn was responsible for bringing home-front paranoia to a boil during World War I.

Since the Armistice, Flynn, just fifty-two years old, had gone into semi-retirement, living comfortably in New York City with his family, running the Federal Railway Administration police, and indulging his passion for writing crime novels. "Mr. Flynn looks you in the eye and immediately you begin to take a mental invoice of your past life," one newsman wrote of him. "Yet when he laughs, his face lights up and you readily see the humor of Irish parentage in his eyes."

Palmer didn't mind if Flynn was a publicity hound. He picked up his office telephone, called New York, and got Flynn on the line at once. Without much ado, he offered him the top job at the Bureau of Investigation. Flynn hesitated, but Palmer pushed him by offering a salary of $7,500, almost twice the normal level of $4,000, and promised to get the money from Congress. "[A]s he told me, he has half a dozen little Flynns, and he has been working for the Government so long that he has not laid anything by," Palmer explained to a Congressional committee that month, justifying the pay raise. Palmer also promised him an absolute free hand in running down radicals.

In less than twenty-four hours, Palmer had assembled his new team and proudly announced it to the press. Historian Stanley Coban would later characterize this group—Palmer, Flynn, Garvan, and Creighton—as "extraordinarily susceptible to the fear and extravagant patriotism so prevalent in 1919." Still, Palmer beamed at the reaction in the newspapers; "perfectly splendid," he called it.

They got to work immediately. This would be a new and different kind of investigation. Justice Department agents tracked the physical evidence of the June bombings, but this only scratched the surface. Palmer planned nothing less than to break the back of radicalism in America. "I am really quite as much interested in the prevention of those crimes, if not more so, than the punishment of the perpetrators after they have been committed," he told a jam-packed congressional hearing a few days after the bombing of his house. Flynn went further and described the probe to the *Brooklyn Citizen* as "a sifting process in which the career of every noted Anarchist in the country is being scrutinized and analyzed, in one of the greatest man hunts the country has ever known."

Within days of the June bombings, the lawmen struck in a dozen cities, including Boston, Philadelphia, Pittsburgh, Cleveland, New York, and Paterson, New Jersey, making sixty-one arrests in the first twenty-four hours. They had no evidence yet to connect any of these suspects to the crime; Flynn himself called the arrests "precautionary measures."* Justice Department agents had been tracking radicals for years, particularly during the World War, and had compiled long lists of suspects. Now, they used them. In Cleveland, where Mayor Harry Davis's house had been bombed, federal agents raided a Russian meeting hall and arrested twenty-eight men attending a class in automobile repair. The agents jailed them all and turned them over to immigration officials, who held eleven for possible deportation. Agents in Philadelphia arrested two men they found carrying 125 steel-jacketed dum-dum cartridges, maps, and street guides of Philadelphia, Camden, Cleveland, and Pittsburgh—cities where bombs had exploded—and two vials of what they called a "suspicious liquid."

In making these arrests, Flynn's men wasted no time on legal niceties. They simply grabbed their suspects off the street and locked them up—no warrants, no explanations. Jackson Ralston, a lawyer in Washington, D.C., heard five separate stories that week of suspects being held *incommunicado*, beaten, searched, questioned, then released a few days later. In one case, he filed a *habeas corpus* petition in a local court trying to get one

---

*The idea of "preventive detention," used here, is alien to American law except in narrow circumstances involving material witnesses, immigration, or wartime. Arrest requires "probable cause" that a person has broken the law, not that the person *might* break a law in the future. Even recent proposals to expand preventive detention in national security cases—raised with greater force since September 11, 2001—presume senior-level oversight and a showing of "actionable intelligence" of a pending threat. Whether Flynn could have argued such a case here is doubtful. But in 1919, this was common. In February, for instance, Chicago police arrested twenty-nine "idlers," simply, in their words, "to see who they were and why they were not working."

man released, but police only shrugged and said they were "holding him under the directions of the Department of Justice." The judge ordered the police to free the suspect, but this came only after he had spent eight days behind bars, his head bloodied and bruised. In another case, Ralston demanded a hearing and asked a Justice Department agent what right he had to conduct a warrantless search of a man's apartment, and the agent answered simply: "By my own right. I did not have to have any."

Flynn himself rushed between New York, Philadelphia, and Washington, talking with newspapermen along the way. The country grew fascinated with the probe, and Flynn always stopped to share a few quotable pearls or pose for photographs. He had "more than 100 leads," Flynn told one reporter in mid-June. "We know the source from which the bomb operators came," he told another, "and I feel safe in predicting that all those responsible will ultimately be apprehended." As the days went by, though, the newsmen grew impatient, and Flynn increasingly frustrated. Hadn't he cracked the case yet? Didn't he have any suspects? After a while, Flynn began to walk away.

In fact, behind the scenes, his investigation had stalled. One by one, his agents were studying the clues, following their trails, and meeting one dead end after another. For the shirt collar with the Chinese laundry tag found on Palmer's lawn, they visited every Chinese laundry shop in each of the eight cities where bombs had exploded, ultimately tracing it to one on Lawrence Street in Brooklyn, New York. But a house-to-house canvass of the neighborhood failed to produce a suspect. A necktie fragment found at the bomb scene led them to the Silver Rose clothing shop in New York City where a salesman named Rosen recalled selling one like it to a man he described as a Slovak or an Italian, possibly connected to an Italian theatrical company. They analyzed the Italian-English dictionary found at Palmer's house and found it to be a 1913 edition of which ten thousand copies were sold. They visited an Italian bookstore in Philadelphia, but the clerk could not remember any purchasers well enough to describe them. They traced another clue, the brown fedora hat with the name of the Philadelphia shop printed on the inside band. They visited the shop, but the owner claimed that he had sold or repaired dozens like it and could not remember any particular customer. They traced a fragment of shoe to a cobbler on Avenue B on New York's Lower East Side who recalled repairing it for someone he described as a "foreigner" whom the agents later identified as a Polish man, but who was a loyal citizen.

On the "Plain Words" leaflet, they visited print and stationery shops across the country comparing paper stock and ink types, but they found no matches. The body parts, too, had failed to produce a suspect. After weeks of hard work, Flynn had no leads on the identity of the dead bomber or the people with whom he may have been connected.

But while they had nothing on the crime itself, Flynn's men had found something else: strands of vaguely connected evidence that easily wove themselves into a grand conspiracy. In Pittsburgh, his agents questioned one secret informant, a Russian-born anarchist, who recognized the design of the June bomb planted in that city as being like one he'd made himself back in Russia before the 1917 revolution. It was "either made by a Russian or made by someone else who had been taught the manufacturing by Russians," he insisted. He identified "maccedonic powder," a salt compound used in Russian bombs, as the chemical agent found on a fragment of the Pittsburgh device, and he pointed to the Union of Russian Workers, a far-left immigrant labor group, as the likely bombers.

A Boston-based special agent looking into the bombing there of local judge Albert Hayden found what he considered clear links to the local socialist underground. Judge Hayden had presided at the trials of May Day rioters and given out stiff jail sentences to several of them. The agent analyzed the "Plain Words" leaflet and claimed to recognize it as the handiwork of a well-known local socialist named Louis Fraina, editor of the left-wing magazine *The Revolutionary Age*, who had been convicted in 1918 of violating the Conscription Act by his antiwar speeches. "I am convinced that the pink circular entitled 'Plain Words' . . . has been written by Louis C. Fraina and I base my opinion on the fact that I have taken this man's speeches for the last two years in short-hand at the Dudley Street Opera House in Roxbury, as well as at the Grand Opera House in Boston, on innumerable occasions." He added: "It should be noted that Fraina is the sweetheart of Martha H. Foley, the leader of the May Day rioters who has been heavily sentenced by Judge Hayden."

This Boston-based agent listed thirty-seven radical groups operating there which he considered capable of violence, but he saved his strongest warning for a circle of Jewish communists who met at Shapiro Hall on Leveritt Street and reportedly received money from overseas delivered by traveling Bolsheviks. "[T]he Jews had a six day meeting of representatives from all over the United States and the two factions, the Bolsheviks and Mensheviks got into a row with the result that the majority went to another hall," he reported, citing secret sources. "The fight was about whether they should start a revolution in the United States at once, or only at a more opportune time later on."*

Jews, radicals, socialists, Russians, communists, bombers—the images mixed together. America faced danger. A conspiracy was afoot, with the bomb at Palmer's house the opening attack. Though Flynn could connect no names to these bombers, he assumed he knew who they were. "The theory that [the attacker] was an Italian has been discarded," one Justice Department source told the *Washington Post* that month, despite their finding an Italian-English dictionary at the crime scene. "That he was a foreigner is practically certain and that he was a Russian is thought to be extremely probable." These Russian Reds were evil, dangerous men and women, and somebody had to stop them.

V.   THE PLAN

On June 17, 1919, two weeks after the bombing of his home, A. Mitchell Palmer called together his new staff: Flynn, Garvan, Creighton, and a few others. They took over a conference room in the Justice Department building, brought in coffee, food, and cigarettes, and closed the door so they could talk undisturbed. Their purpose was to confront the core question: how to protect America.

Palmer explained his concern to the men sitting around the table. As he saw it, two distinct threats were facing them: First, in the short term, radicals could attack again at any time. Justice Department agents were now monitoring hundreds of radical newspapers and magazines from across the country, including dozens in foreign languages like Russian, German, and Yiddish, and they saw what looked to them like repeated references to upcoming actions, though always vague, as if in code: "There is a great deal of talk to that effect," Garvan would tell a congressional committee. The July Fourth holiday, just two weeks away, provided a fat target. Palmer himself had received a confidential tip that one radical group planned to explode a bomb in the House of

---

*This charge of a Jewish-led conspiracy matched reports then emanating from the War Department's Military Intelligence Division about Jews, alleging that they dominated the Russian and Hungarian soviet power grabs, and pointing to revelations in a recently discovered Russian document racing through intelligence circles called *The Protocols of the Elders of Zion*, which detailed a worldwide Jewish conspiracy. American Military Intelligence officers continued to use the *Protocols* as a reference well into the 1920s, long after it had been proved to be a fake. Within Woodrow Wilson's circle, Secretary of State Robert Lansing echoed these anti-Jewish attitudes. "A vigorous propaganda in favor of that pernicious doctrine [Bolshevism] is being conducted," he wrote in his confidential notebook that summer. "It seems to be largely in the hands of Jews."

Representatives on June 26 and assassinate Alabama Congressman William Bankhead—the father of future actress Tallulah Bankhead. Separately, Cleveland mayor Harry Davis, himself a target of one of the June bombs, reported hearing threats of an armed parade being organized for July 4 "as part of plans to overthrow law and order in Cleveland," he claimed.

Second, over the long term, Palmer saw the horde of alien radicals living on American soil and spouting Bolshevik, anarchist rhetoric as posing a continuing danger. How serious was the threat? In Russia, Lenin's Bolshevik Party was said to have numbered barely 10,000 when it seized power in Russia in 1917. Yet estimates of hardcore radicals in America in 1919 ran as high as 60,000. Even if they could never topple the government itself, they could still cause a lot of violence—bombs, riots, crippling strikes, attacks on officials.

In New York City, the Lusk Committee already had made headlines by staging dozens of dramatic raids on radical offices, including one on the official site of the new Russian Bolskevik Mission to the United States. This Mission acted as Moscow's only functioning embassy in the United States, though the American government had not granted Lenin's regime official recognition. Lusk's detectives had smashed in the front door, seized private papers, and dragged Ludwig A. Martens, the mission's chief, down to its office at City Hall and forced him to testify in a closed-door executive session and spill secrets of Russian aid to American leftists. Lusk's detectives treated Martens, a diplomat, like a criminal. But rather than drawing criticism, Lusk won himself loud applause in the press and nods of approval from Washington.

Palmer and his team haggled for hours that day over what to do. The more they learned, the more they grew alarmed. They studied the best intelligence available—from Flynn's investigation, from Military Intelligence, from local police, the State Department, and any other sources they could find—and it convinced them all that the country was at risk. More attacks would come; the only question was when. Palmer saw little difference between socialists, Bolsheviks, anarchists, communists, radical labor leaders, and the rest. To him, they all appeared as one interconnected mass of potential violent treason. "We have received so many notices and gotten so much information that it has almost come to be accepted as a fact that on a certain day in the future, that we have been advised of, there will be another serious and probably much larger effort . . . [a] revolution, a proposition to rise up and destroy the government in one fell swoop," Palmer had told Congress earlier that week. His words echoed around the country. Who could doubt him? He was the attorney general.

Even more startling to Palmer was the fact that, until now, the federal government repeatedly had ignored this threat—and he, Palmer, himself had been one of the worst offenders. Even more so had been the Labor Department, which was responsible for implementing the immigration and deportation laws. Justice Department agents had known for years about radical groups and tried to shut them down. But each time, they claimed, Washington bureaucrats got in the way. Boston agents had arrested fifty anarchists in 1918, and local immigration officials had ordered them all deported, but their superiors in the Labor Department's Washington headquarters had released the suspects on bond, "thus giving them an opportunity to plan these outrages," a local Boston agent complained. These same Labor Department higher-ups had freed another half-dozen aliens held for deportation in Pittsburgh despite the aliens' membership in the Union of Russian Workers, a known anarchist group.

Now, Palmer had an idea, which he laid out for Flynn, Garvan, Creighton, and the others—a way to solve this problem once and for all.

During World War I, Congress had passed laws making it a crime for anyone to advocate the violent overthrow of the United States government, but these statutes, particularly Section 3 of the Espionage Act, expired with the end of hostilities.* As a result, no federal law remained on the books allowing Federal prosecutors to jail a communist rabble-rouser unless he committed a separate crime. Only the states, thirty-seven of them including Illinois and New York, had peacetime antisedition laws in effect.

But Palmer had found another way to skin this cat, by using the immigration laws. Congress had strengthened the Immigration Act in 1918 to allow the government to deport any alien, that is, any immigrant who had not yet become a citizen, who was an anarchist or who belonged to any group that advocated the violent overthrow of the United States government. This cut a far wider swath that any state or federal antisedition law, peacetime or wartime, and it applied to *any* immigrant no matter how long he or she had lived in the country. They could be

---

*The Federal Espionage Act of May 16, 1918 (section 3), provided that "Whoever, when the United States is at war, shall . . . willfully utter, print, write, or publish any disloyal, profane, scurrilous, or abusive language about the form of government of the United States . . . or the flag . . . or any language intended to bring the form of government of the United States . . . into contempt, scorn, contumely, or disrepute . . . shall be punished by a fine of not more than $10,000 or imprisonment of not more than twenty years, or both." Other sections of the Act applying in peacetime dealt more specifically with military information.

deported immediately once the secretary of labor made the proper legal finding.*

To Palmer, this opened a door. "[T]he deportation statute ought to be used liberally against these alien anarchists, these alien trouble makers, and that is one thing we propose to do," he had told Congress earlier that month. Now, he expanded on the idea.

Why not get rid of these alien radicals all at once, as many as possible? Round up all the members of all the radical groups and send them packing. All the government needed to show was that the group preached violence against the government—an easy case with regard to anarchists or communists—and that the alien was a member. Nothing more. Then they could simply put them on a ship and send them back to Russia, Italy, or wherever else they came from. Palmer proposed a two-pronged operation: federal agents would round up and detain all the aliens who held memberships in violent groups and have them deported. Then the Justice Department would press the state governments to prosecute those radicals who happened to be American citizens. Palmer's Justice Department would help the state prosecutors by providing evidence, experts, or whatever else they needed.

Word leaked out across Washington, D.C., that day that Palmer and his team were meeting behind closed doors to work out a plan to crush the radicals, and by late afternoon about fifty newspaper reporters jammed the hallway outside his office in the Justice Department building. Palmer decided to reward them by sending Bill Flynn, John Creighton, and Frank Garvan to meet them and announce the decision: "A drastic policy of deporting all alien radicals of the dangerous type and the imprisonment of others" had been agreed to, the *Washington Post* reported. The Justice Department would wipe out anarchy in a single blow. "If we can . . . round up those men and upon proper proof rush them back to Europe, you will find this agitation subside very rapidly," Garvan added.

Palmer himself explained the idea the next day in a commencement speech to the graduating class at Georgetown University. "There is no room, and there is no need, in this country for those who resort to violence to impress their ultra-radical views upon the people or the Government,"

---

*The Immigration Act, as revised on October 16, 1918, provided: "That aliens who are anarchists; aliens who believe in or advocate the overthrow by force or violence of the Government of the United States; aliens who disbelieve in or are opposed to all organized government; aliens who advocate or teach the assassination of public officials; aliens who advocate or teach the unlawful destruction of property; *aliens who are members of or affiliated with any organization that entertains a belief in, teaches, or advocates the overthrow by force or violence of the Government of the United States or of all forms of law* . . . shall be excluded from entry into the United States.*" (Emphasis added.)

he told them. "The Government proposes to protect itself [and malcontents] should go back to the countries from which they came."

In making his decision, Mitchell Palmer never bothered to consult with his old friend Woodrow Wilson, the president of the United States. President Wilson was far away in Europe, across the ocean, at the Versailles peace conference redrawing the maps of Europe and the Middle East, and had little time to bother with domestic problems. That was why he had cabinet members. Wilson had been gone from Washington almost continually for six months, with one brief visit home in late February 1919, and he might not return again for weeks or months until he had won agreement for his precious League of Nations. In all the diplomatic excitement, Wilson had only found time to send Palmer a single two-line telegram on learning about the bomb explosion at his house. It read simply: "For Attorney General: My heartfelt congratulations on your escape. I am deeply thankful that the miscreants failed in all their attempts. Woodrow Wilson."

Mitchell Palmer refused to wait. He would brief the president later.

The decision made, they all got down to work. Within the week, Palmer and Garvan traveled up to Capitol Hill and asked Congress to give them a special appropriation of $500,000 to finance their Red-hunting campaign, bringing the Justice Department's total crime-fighting budget to $2 million. "[W]e have every reason to believe that the Russian bolsheviki are pouring money in here at that rate a month," Garvan told senators in justifying the amount. Congress ultimately agreed. Who could argue these days with Mitchell Palmer? The bombing of his house had made him a national hero.

To implement their aggressive plan, Palmer and his team decided they needed to do one more thing, to create a new office in the Justice Department devoted exclusively to hunting Reds: tracking them, compiling their names and addresses, building the legal cases against them, coordinating the investigations, collecting literature, and leading the overall effort. They would place this new Radical Division inside Flynn's Bureau of Investigation so it could tap into the Bureau's network of agents and field offices. But its chief would report directly to Palmer as a special assistant. Whoever led this new office would play a crucial role in the operation. He had to be the right person, someone uniquely talented and dedicated, with legal training and organizational skill.

They quickly decided on a name. How about that eager, hardworking young fellow who made such a mark during the World War years? He has studied these issues and made himself the Department's leading expert on radicals. He was always looking for new assignments, and he always handled them well.

This seemed a good spot for him. They all agreed. How about that young man, J. Edgar Hoover?

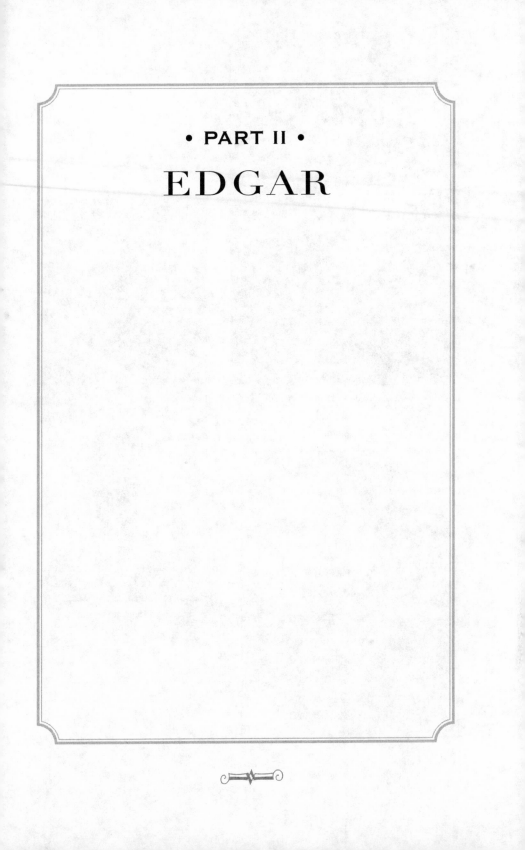

• PART II •

EDGAR

Edgar with his childhood bicycle, circa 1905.

Edgar as a cadet at Central High School, circa 1913.

Edgar as a child with his parents, Dickerson Naylor and Annie Marie Scheitlin Hoover.

EDGAR

J OHN EDGAR HOOVER kept his desk clean, its glass-covered mahogany surface polished, and he gave everything he touched a sense of order. He sorted his papers into neat piles or put them out of sight in cabinets. He kept a map of the United States hanging on his office wall where he could see it clearly from his leather desk chair, a telephone in easy reach of his hand. During the day, sunlight flooded into the room from a window facing Vermont Avenue, along with sounds of traffic from the street below. Anyone who came inside saw it as a place fit to entertain top officials, to confer on the most important issues, make decisions, and do business

Edgar knew all about the band of Red Hunters being formed in the Department of Justice in June 1919. His prim, clean, well-ordered office gave him one of the best seats in town from which to watch it, just a few doors down the hall in the Justice Department from the large sunny corner suite of the great man himself, A. Mitchell Palmer.

Palmer had hired Edgar onto his office staff just a few weeks earlier, and

Edgar had met the attorney general a handful of times, at his job interview and at staff meetings, but he still hardly knew him well. Edgar was still so new that he hadn't even figured out the office mail system yet. An irritated clerk nagged him that month for sending out letters without the required initials, addressed to the wrong room, and in the wrong form. Still, even as a green newcomer, Edgar could see something big was afoot. He read the newspapers and heard the gossip. The June bombings had electrified the country, sparking waves of patriotism not seen since the World War, and Palmer's Red Hunt promised to be the most exciting, high-profile case in years. Edgar ached to be part of it. He saw the key players come and go around the office each day, Palmer, Flynn, lawyers Frank Garvan and John Creighton, always in a rush and followed by reporters. Edgar never missed a chance to stop one of them in the hallway, ask how things were going, and offer to help.

They ignored him at first, but Edgar kept pushing. Within days of the bombing, he began taking the initiative to sniff out leads and pass them along to John Creighton in formal notes that he always signed "Respectfully, J. E. Hoover." He jumped on one lead contained in a note sent to the office by North Carolina U.S. Senator Lee Overman about a conversation that a friend of his overheard between two suspicious-looking Italians on a train, and another that came from a man in Dayton, Ohio, who claimed he heard a man in a movie theater saying there would be another bomb explosion on July 4. Both these leads proved groundless, but Creighton and Palmer noticed Edgar's hustle. They liked this hardworking young man who always looked sharp in his dark suits and crisp white shirts, and always had something to say. They began inviting him to meetings and giving him odd jobs, like assigning field agents to chase down leads or briefing the War Department on the latest twists in the probe.

Edgar loved this work, the excitement. Agents combed the country looking for the bombing criminals, and nobody knew which clue might break the case and win the glory. He probably even stuck his face into Palmer's day-long conclave in mid-June where Palmer laid out his plan to deport thousands of radical aliens. If so, Edgar would have used the chance to speak up and impress the boss yet again with his poise and crisp command of facts.

By August 1, when Palmer called the newspaper reporters into his office to announce his decision to create a new Justice Department Radical Division dedicated to rooting out the Red Menace, Edgar had made his impression. Few of the reporters covering the story bothered to mention his name in their accounts. Edgar was still a nobody in America back in August 1919. But it still raised a question. Why him? On paper, he barely seemed qualified for the job. He was just a kid, twenty-four years old, two years out of school, a bachelor living at home with his parents who used a family connection to win his first job at the Justice Department. Why trust this crucial assignment to an unproven youngster? But to Mitchell Palmer and his brain trust, the choice seemed obvious. Edgar had impressed them all. He was the rising star.

This young man was a local boy. A few boyhood friends called him "Speed," his cousins called him "J. E.," and around the office he was "Mr. Hoover," but most people still just called him Edgar. The J. Edgar would come later. He came from Washington, D.C., which his family had called its home for generations. His father had spent his entire working life as a federal clerk, rising to the position of Supervising Map Printer at the Coast and Geodetic Survey.* His mother came from a line of Swiss diplomats who settled in the capital before the Civil War. "I think that early in his career, J. E. decided that he was going to achieve something big, and I don't think he let himself be distracted from that," Edgar's niece Margaret Fennel, who grew up in the house next door, recalled of those early days. Edgar was born on New Year's Day, 1895, the same year as future baseball slugger Babe Ruth, future football legend George Halas, and future Hollywood film stars Bud Abbott and Buster Keaton. Queen Victoria still ruled Britannia in 1895, a czar ruled in Russia, as did kings in Italy, Spain, Greece, and Serbia, a sultan in Turkey, and emperors in Germany and Japan. In America, Wild West outlaws like John Wesley Harding, Butch Cassidy, and the Dalton Gang still roamed the range, and inventor George Selden won the first American patent that year for what most people still considered a hair-brained new contraption, a horseless, gasoline-powered automobile, particularly useless since no paved roads existed yet to drive it on. The Wright brothers would not fly their first airplane for another eight years, and network radio would not exist for another three decades.

Edgar grew up in a house just seven blocks from the United States Capitol, at 413 Seward Square. Back then they called it Pipetown, a bustling neighborhood of government clerks, shop owners, and craftsmen and their families, including a growing mix of African-Americans,

---

*This agency long ago merged into today's National Oceanic and Atmospheric Administration, or NOAA.

unusual for the segregated South. "They were nice houses, two stories, with three bedrooms upstairs; downstairs there was a dining room, kitchen, and front and back parlors that were separated by an invisible line—you simply didn't go in the front parlor," Margaret recalled. She remembered it as a bright, friendly place. "There was a big back yard that was really nice. Nanny [Edgar's mother] loved flowers and she was always gardening. There was a grape arbor, there were roses, bleeding hearts, lilies-of-the-valley."

Edgar, the youngest, thrived as a boy. His two older siblings, brother Dickerson Jr. and sister Lillian, both moved out of the house when he was small, leaving him to live alone with his parents. Dick, fifteen years older than Edgar, purchased the house next door, so he, his wife, and his daughters Margaret and Anna remained part of the family. Lillian, thirteen years older, had married in 1908 and moved away with her husband to far-off rural Lanham, Maryland. Another sister, Sadie Marguerite, died of childhood diphtheria in 1893. Edgar's mother had barely gotten past the grief from Sadie's death when she became pregnant with him.* Maybe that's why she always made him her favorite.

Little Edgar found plenty of hobbies and projects, be it at school, at church, or frolicking in the neighborhood. He kept a diary, took odd jobs, carried groceries for local ladies, and started a one-penny family newspaper, all before he turned twelve years old. A family photograph shows him playing with a bicycle, flashing a big boyish grin. Always ambitious, he insisted his parents send him to Washington, D.C.'s Central High School, a daily three-mile walk from home but then considered the city's premier academy for talented teenagers.** Edgar tried to make the school's football team, but the coach rejected him for being too small. So, instead, he excelled at track and debate. His favorite activity was the school's cadet corps, a junior ROTC program. Cadets drilled twice a week and joined in a citywide competition each spring, a major event that drew thousands of spectators to Washington's American League Baseball Park, later renamed Griffith Stadium. Edgar loved posing in his blue military

---

*There is a theory that Edgar was born to an African-American mother and adopted by the Hoovers, based on discrepancies in certain birth and census records. But this has not been substantiated, and the genealogist who investigated the claim believes it to be false.

**Central High School no longer exists. In 1913, when Edgar attended, it was located on Seventh Street NW between O and P Streets in what is now Washington, D.C.'s Shaw neighborhood. It moved in 1916 to Thirteenth and Clifton streets, NW, and its building is today home to Washington's Cardozo High School, named for Washington, D.C., educator Francis Cardozo.

cadet uniform with its white gloves, stiff collar, shoulder stripes and baton, standing at attention with ramrod-straight posture. He wore it to school on practice days and to church on Sundays as well.

Edgar had a winning way with schoolmates. His cadet comrades chose him as their company captain, and his classmates elected him their class valedictorian, even though his grades ranked him only fourth. They described him in the school yearbook as "a gentleman of dauntless courage and stainless honor: 'Speed' is one of the best Captains. . . . He is some debater too. . . ." He could be funny and high-spirited. "He was one of the world's worst teases," his niece Margaret remembered. "Oh, the sleepless nights I used to spend when he'd tell me that if I swallowed an orange seed a tree would grow out of my belly button."

"Is that noise a lion coming roaring down the street or is it an approaching thunderstorm?" the Central High newspaper asked, tongue in cheek in a 1911 edition. "O, no, sir; it's just Hoover counting cadence for Company B."

Edgar savored these friendships. "The saddest moment of the year was when I realized that I must part with a group of fellows who had become a part of my life," he wrote in a school column at graduation in 1913. "I want every man of Company A of 1912–13 to look upon me as their friend and helper wherever we might go after this year."

After graduating in 1913, he turned down a scholarship from the University of Virginia and enrolled instead at George Washington University, a local school that allowed him to live with his parents while taking law school classes at night. During the day, he took a $30-a-month clerk's job at the Library of Congress, a five-block walk from his house, to earn extra money. He put in grueling twelve-hour workdays with little sleep. At George Washington, he made the extra effort to earn two degrees, a Bachelor's and a Master's of Law, before graduating. But it was at the Library of Congress that inspiration struck him. Edgar's job there involved cataloguing new books, and the Library had recently adopted a groundbreaking new system to keep tabs on its bulging collection of over a million volumes plus hundreds of thousands of journals, manuscripts, and newspapers. Similar to the Dewey Decimal System, developed separately about the same time, it assigned each item an index card with a unique code indicating its topic, title, author, and location.

Sitting at the Library of Congress cataloguing books, Edgar marveled at this new system and the power it gave him to locate any single item instantly in the Library's voluminous stacks. He imagined how, with a few tweaks, he could use it to track anything he liked, even people. He could use it to find anyone, even in a vast country of 105 million souls spanning an entire continent. He could use it to hide things, too, just by manipulating the code. By the time he left the Library, Edgar had so mastered the system and impressed his bosses that they doubled his salary. "I'm sure he would be the chief librarian if he'd stayed with us," a co-worker remarked a few years later.

After finishing law school in 1917, Edgar needed a new job. America had just entered World War I in April, and Congress had authorized conscription for healthy young men. But that same month, April 1917, Edgar's father left his federal government job with no pension. Financially, that made it impossible for Edgar to join the army. He had to stay home and support his parents, or at least that's what they said. It was William Hitz, Edgar's mother's uncle, who put in the good word with friends at the Justice Department to get him a draft-exempt position there. Once in the door, though, Edgar stood on his own. "From the day he entered the Department, certain things marked Hoover apart from scores of other young law clerks," Jack Alexander, a friendly journalist, wrote in 1937. "He dressed better than most, and a bit on the dandyish style. He had an exceptional capacity for detail work, and he handled small chores with enthusiasm. He constantly sought new responsibilities to shoulder and welcomed chances to work overtime. When he was in conference with an official of the department, his manner was that of a young man who confidently expected to rise."

Edgar had the good luck in 1917 to be hired by John Lord O'Brian, a prominent lawyer from Buffalo, New York, who had been recruited to come to Washington and take charge of the Justice Department's new War Emergency Division. O'Brian's office soon mushroomed into a staff of more than seventy-five lawyers and clerks fielding every imaginable war-related crisis, from enforcing the Conscription Act, to prosecuting spies and profiteers, to cracking down on sedition and dissenters, to stamping out scare stories like the rumor sweeping the East Coast in 1918 that German spies had sabotaged American food by putting ground glass in wheat and flour.

O'Brian quickly promoted Edgar to Special Agent and assigned him to the Alien Enemy Bureau, a special unit he created to handle legal questions relating to treatment of Germans on American soil. With almost a million German noncitizens in the country at the start of the war, mostly recent immigrants, a dazzling range of issues crossed Edgar's desk, from arrests of potential saboteurs, to detentions of German seamen marooned in American ports, to the policing of restricted zones around harbors and military bases. By 1918, the United States government held over 6,200 Germans in army-run detention camps, and it required another 450,000 of them to register and carry government-issued identity cards. John Lord O'Brian ultimately put Edgar in charge of the entire Alien Enemy office, the largest unit in his wartime bureau. "I discovered he worked Sundays and nights," O'Brian explained years later. "I promoted him several times, simply on merits."

By the time World War I ended, Edgar decided he liked the Justice Department and wanted to stay there. He went to O'Brian and asked him for help. O'Brian had already announced his intention to leave Washington and return to his private law practice in Buffalo, but he agreed. "At the end of the war, at the time of the Armistice, he told me he would like to continue in the permanent side of the Department of Justice," O'Brian reminisced years later. "I took that up personally with the new Attorney General, A. Mitchell Palmer."

Palmer agreed as well. In March 1919, soon after he settled into the Justice Department as attorney general, he brought Edgar over, installed him down the hall as a special assistant, and assigned him a mix of routine work: answering letters from grouchy congressmen, fielding telephone calls, occasionally checking a legal issue. And whenever a question came up about Germans, aliens, radicals, or spies, Edgar was the one he asked.

Already on July 1, a full month before Palmer installed him as head of the new Radical Division, Palmer awarded his young assistant a fat pay raise, from $2,000 to $3,000 per year. It was Edgar's fifth promotion since joining the Justice Department in 1917, more than tripling his original salary. At age twenty-four, he was earning more money per year than his father had earned upon retirement from the federal government after forty-two years of service.

Then came the offer to head the new Radical Division and help lead the Department's drive against the Reds. For Edgar, it was the chance of a lifetime. He was ready to seize it and run.

If good fortune seemed to shine on young J. Edgar Hoover at his office in the Justice Department in mid-1919, he faced a very different situation, however, when he came home each night to the small house where he still lived with his parents. A gloomy crisis hung over the Hoover household that year: his father's mental illness.

Edgar's father, Dickerson Naylor Hoover, was a slender, good-natured man with a thin face, mustache, and small eyes. In 1913, after months of worsening symptoms—withdrawal, long silences, erratic fears—his wife, Annie, had called in a doctor who diagnosed Dickerson with "melancholia" and committed him for treatment to the sanitarium in Laurel, Maryland. Most of the details of this episode are lost. The relatively primitive science of medical psychiatry in 1913 cast a fearful veil over mental conditions like depression, hysteria, or psychosis. Families treated their ill members as a source of shame, notwithstanding the stylish new theories of Vienna's Dr. Sigmund Freud. They kept Dickerson's disease a secret even from close relatives. "I knew he had a nervous breakdown there at one time," Edgar's niece Margaret recalled years later. "He was up at Laurel at the sanitarium. Why, I really don't know."

How long did Dickerson Hoover stay at the Laurel hospital? Did they commit him again a second or third time? It's all unclear. Also unknown is the exact treatment they administered to him there, though typical would have been shock therapy—electric or cold water—drugs, or perhaps physical restraints. When he came out, Dickerson had gotten worse.

What did Dickerson Hoover really suffer from? This, too, is a mystery. Looking back today at scant medical records, it is impossible to know. He could have had the same clinical depression that afflicts large numbers of adults, especially older men, only aggravated by the brutal shock treatment. Or he could have experienced a serious psychotic episode, perhaps misdiagnosed or poorly described by contemporary doctors. Whatever the truth, Dickerson Hoover went back to his government job after leaving the Laurel Sanitarium, but his weakened mental condition prevented him from functioning normally. So, in April 1917, the Coast and Geodetic Survey forced his retirement and sent him home, with a one-sentence letter that failed even to say "thank you," and no pension.*

Edgar never spoke of his father's illness outside the family, but he faced it every day during this period. Beside the financial strain, it cast a pall over a once-cheerful household. When Edgar returned each night after

---

*It read: "Sir: The Department is in receipt of your resignation, dated April 5, 1917, as plate printer at $2,000 per annum in the Coast and Geodetic Survey, and has accepted the same, upon recommendation of the Superintendent, to take effect at the close of business on April 11, 1917. By direction of the Secretary: Respectfully, Clifford Hastings, Chief of Appointment Division, Department of Commerce." J. Edgar Hoover held onto this cold bureaucratic letter to his father and kept it in his files for the rest of his life. The modern Civil Service Retirement System providing pensions for federal employees would not be created until 1920.

work, he saw his father, a gaunt, gray-haired, broken-down man, silently brooding on the front porch in his wicker chair, or hiding inside, lashing out at family members or else chasing his mental ghosts in the darkened basement, growing weaker and skinnier by the month.

In happier days, Edgar shared a deep bond with his father, and the father clearly loved his son. Dickerson wrote Edgar dozens of letters from the road whenever he was away, gushing with affection, signing them Pops or Papa. "Yesterday I saw a lot of little boys like you at the fair," he wrote home to him

Edgar's father, Dickerson Naylor Hoover, on his porch chair.

from a business trip to the Midwest in 1904. "I dug up a pretty wild flower which I have mailed to you—you can plant it and watch it grow. . . . Give Mama a hug and kiss for me and I will pay you when I come back." Then in another a few days later, "Love to all with a kiss for yourself. I have a big favor to ask you. [I]t is give Mama a hug and a long sweet kiss. Good bye. Papa." Dickerson took his family on annual vacations, weeks by the ocean at Cape May, New Jersey, or with relatives in Virginia.

The Hoover home at 413 Seward Square in Washington, D.C.

But if Edgar loved his father, he never quite respected him, even before the disease. Instead, for his role model, he always looked to his mother, Annie Marie Scheitlin Hoover, a stout, outgoing, and opinionated woman. She came from highbrow stock. Her grandfather, John Hitz, came to Washington to represent the

Swiss government back in the 1850s as its first consul-general in America. Here he became a local celebrity during the Civil War by caring for wounded soldiers, and later he established himself as a prominent figure in Washington society through the late 1800s. A banker and philanthropist, he joined inventor Alexander Graham Bell in founding the Volta Bureau for the deaf. Edgar remembered his funeral in 1908, when Edgar was just thirteen years old. Edgar marked it in his diary and evidently found it a stunning affair. It drew over a hundred well-wishers including celebrities like inventor Bell, Helen Keller, Red Cross founder Clara Barton, and E. M. Gallaudet, founder and president of Washington's Gallaudet College for the deaf. Dr. Leo Vogel, the Swiss minister to the United States, delivered a eulogy in German.

Others of Annie's relatives were among the capital's most accomplished citizens. William Hitz, Annie's uncle, sat as a justice on the District of Columbia Supreme Court. Another cousin, Harold Hitz Burton, would become mayor of Cleveland, Ohio, and a United States senator.

Annie demanded her children follow in these footsteps, especially Edgar, her precious little favorite. Dickerson would tell his son, "Don't study too hard" or "Enjoy yourself and have a good time" or "Don't let Mama work too hard." But not Annie. "So glad to hear you were perfect in your spelling and arithmetic," she wrote home to him one time from a vacation trip in 1905. "Study hard both your lessons and your music and try to be a very good boy." Edgar decided early on which of these voices he wanted to follow. "Mrs. Hoover . . . kept alive the disciplinary tradition in her home, rewarding obedience and punishing disobedience with military impartiality," journalist Jack Alexander wrote in 1937 after hearing Edgar talk about it. "Her domestic justice set up in [Hoover] a pattern of scrupulous regard for law and zeal for punishing wrong-doing. . . ."

With his older brother, Dick, jealousies got in the way. Dick, too, had won a promotion in 1919 to a high-profile new job, deputy inspector general of the Steamboat Inspection Service. Still, he chided Edgar, stopping him on the sidewalk to ask, "How is the attorney tonight?" and noting how his "General" outranked Edgar's "Major." Even years later, as a middle-aged adult, Dick still carped about how their mother played favorites, giving little Edgar special treatment, even making Dick as a teenager babysit for him. "I have wheeled Edgar a thousand times around Capitol Hill in one of the old-fashioned, high-wheeled baby buggies that mother bought for him," Dick told a reporter in 1934, trying to make a joke of it; "it was a daily chore. . . . I'd tuck his bottle under the pillows of the baby carriage and sometimes we would be gone for hours."

By mid-1919, Edgar increasingly tried to flee his crowded home. He joined clubs to be around other young men, like the Masonic Lodge and the Kappa Alpha and Sigma Delta fraternities. He took long walks with his niece Margaret, Dick's daughter, sometimes three nights a week during summer, to points as far away as Columbia Road in northwest Washington, then taking a streetcar home. Edgar didn't mind that Margaret was thirteen years younger than he was. They went out to see movies together and laughed and talked. She remembered him once taking her to the Fox Theatre on F Street to see *The Perils of Pauline*. "I cried and cried and he took me home and wouldn't take me again."

Edgar apparently tried to escape the family altogether in 1918, just after World War I, by asking a woman named Alice to marry him. He had met her at the Justice Department where she worked as a typist, and they had gone out on a few dates. He sent her a note just after the Armistice to meet him one night at the Lafayette Hotel en route to a friend's party where he planned to pop the question. But Alice never came; she ran off to marry someone else.

If Edgar felt hurt or humiliated by the incident, he didn't let it distract him. He shook it off and went back to work. As a young adult, this was Edgar's favorite place, his neat, clean, well-organized Justice Department office where he spent long hours at his desk, from early morning to well past dark, six or seven days a week. This was his refuge. At work, he controlled his own fate. Here, he rubbed elbows with famous people and joined in the most exciting events of the day. Here he excelled. This was his future.

· 4 ·
BUREAUCRATS

Secretary of Labor William Bauchop Wilson—no relation to President Woodrow Wilson—had no desire to pick a fight with Mitchell Palmer over the Reds in June 1919. A child of poor Welsh immigrant parents, Wilson had gone to work in the Pennsylvania coal mines as an eleven-year-old back in 1873, joined the United Mine Workers of America, rose to become its international secretary-treasurer, and served three terms in the United States Congress before President Wilson had tapped him for the cabinet seat in 1913.* Now, almost sixty years old, tired and distracted, Secretary Wilson had taken month-long absences from his post all through 1919 to care for his wife, Agnes, who had suffered a paralyzing stroke. In twenty-two years of marriage, Agnes had borne and raised ten children with Secretary Wilson, but the children

---

*In Congress, Wilson had authored the 1912 bill to create a separate Department of Labor. President Wilson, by naming him secretary in 1913, awarded him the distinction of becoming its first secretary.

mostly lived far away in central Pennsylvania. As Agnes's health took a bad turn, Wilson's own health suffered from the strain. He could barely think about work.

But some fights he could not avoid. Wilson had seen the reports of Palmer's plans to launch a deportation drive against hundreds of radicals and anarchists as a way to crush the Red Menace. Palmer had crossed a line. His goal of restoring law and order might be laudable, but he was going about it in a way that threatened to ride roughshod over the law and over Wilson's agency. Wilson decided he had to speak up.

As secretary of labor, William B. Wilson in 1919 presided over an agency with 2,000 employees scattered around the country and was responsible for employment policy, worker safety, and immigration. World War I had stretched the agency to its limit. Secretary Wilson and his staff had overseen the transfer of six million men and women from civilian jobs into military production while avoiding strikes in railroads, coal, steel, and other vital industries—an effort that involved constant mediation between business and labor under military urgency.

William Bauchop Wilson, Secretary of Labor, seen here circa 1900 as a young official of the United Mine Workers Union.

The effort left him exhausted. A year after the Armistice, with his wife stricken, Secretary Wilson virtually disappeared from official Washington. He rarely showed his face either at the Labor Department's headquarters building on G Street or even at Cabinet meetings with the president.

But now, based on the advice of his top aides, Secretary Wilson signed his name to a letter they prepared for him and sent it flying across town to Attorney General A. Mitchell Palmer. "I have observed from several recent newspaper reports that apparently it is the intention of the Department of Justice to undertake considerable special work in connection with . . . members of the anarchistic and similar classes," it said. "I assume [you] have in mind the possibility of referring [these cases] to this Department," he went on, since, "of course, the enforcement of the only laws which authorize deportation . . . is vested in this Department."

Wilson's point was clear and direct: Palmer had invaded his territory. Federal immigration law gave Palmer's Justice Department no power to deport anyone. Instead, it assigned this authority *solely* to the Secretary of Labor. "[A]ny alien [found to be unqualified] shall upon warrant of the Secretary of Labor be taken into custody and deported," the 1917 statute read. And it gave the power to detain and question aliens for deportation purposes exclusively to Labor Department immigration inspectors, not to Justice Department agents.* If Palmer went ahead and launched his deportation drive without clearing the whole operation with Wilson's Labor Department first, it would certainly fail, leaving Wilson's agency to take the blame. His plan had all the signs of a bureaucratic power grab.

But fighting it would be treacherous, particularly with Secretary Wilson spending so much time away from the office caring for his wife. To handle things during his long absences, Wilson had worked out an arrangement to divide his official duties between his two top deputies: Solicitor John Abercrombie and Assistant Secretary Louis F. Post. To Abercrombie he assigned responsibility for all the immigration issues. To Louis Post he assigned most of the rest—employment, labor statistics, and worker safety. John Abercrombie, a gray-haired, soft-spoken man who wore wire glasses that punctuated a round, fleshy face, had spent ten years as president of the University of Alabama before coming to Washington as a congressman in 1913 and joining the Labor Department during World War I. Abercrombie hated the immigration portfolio. "The work was extremely disturbing to him," Louis Post recalled, "and several times he assured me of his wish to resign, but I urged him to wait." John Abercrombie had nothing special against immigrants and no squeamishness about deciding deportation cases. Instead, what Abercrombie hated so much about the immigration duties was the backroom politics.

Immigration had been a supreme headache in American government for decades, and a turf war had been raging inside the Labor Department

---

*And that wasn't all. The Justice Department's own appropriations law, controlling its use of funds, allowed it to spend its crime-fighting budget *only* on fighting crime, that is, on detecting and prosecuting lawbreakers, *not* on preparing deportation cases.

over it ever since the Department first opened its doors in 1913. Congress had initially created a separate, Federal Immigration Bureau in the 1890s to enforce legal barriers designed to keep select undesirables from entering the country: polygamists, criminals, indigents, mental incompetents, people carrying contagious diseases, and Chinese laborers under the Chinese Exclusion Act.* But by 1919, the Immigration Bureau had grown so enormous that it threatened to swamp the rest of the Labor Department by its sheer size, claiming 70 percent of the Department's budget and 80 percent of its staff.** To Louis Post, this situation defeated the entire point of having a separate cabinet agency dedicated to helping workers, turning the entire Labor Department, as he saw it, into nothing more than "a government agency for keeping aliens out."

The Immigration Bureau's flagship station at New York's Ellis Island had processed over 600,000 newcomers entering the country each year from 1903 to 1914, but World War I cut these numbers drastically. Since 1917, Ellis Island had been used mostly as a prison, a place to detain wartime Germans, postwar radicals, and stranded souls denied entry into the United States but blocked by the World War from crossing back over the ocean to return home.

The current immigration chief, officially titled the commissioner general, only aggravated the problem. Anthony Caminetti, a vain, strong-willed California political boss, considered the Immigration Bureau his personal fiefdom. Woodrow Wilson had picked Caminetti for the post in 1913 partly because Caminetti claimed immigrant roots—his father had come from Italy during the 1850s—but mostly to pay a political debt. Caminetti had led Wilson's presidential campaign in California and helped deliver important voting blocs at the 1912 nominating convention in Baltimore. Caminetti had long dominated the California legislature and chaired the state Democratic Party in Sacramento, backed by powerful mining and agriculture interests. Even after coming to Washington to head the Immigration Bureau, Caminetti continued to insist

---

*The Naturalization Act of 1870 started closing the door on Asians by limiting immigration to only "white persons and persons of African descent." The Chinese Exclusion Act of 1882 went further and prevented Chinese without family already in the United States from entering the country except for certain diplomats, merchants, and students, and it barred Chinese Americans from applying for naturalization. It was repealed in 1943.

**The immigration control function was moved from the Department of Labor to the Department of Justice in 1940, and then was absorbed into the new Department of Homeland Security upon its creation in 2003.

that President Wilson's White House get his blessing before filling patronage jobs in California.

In addition, Caminetti's philosophy placed him directly at odds with the rest of the Labor Department's top leaders. Rather than helping workers to gain better pay and conditions, Caminetti saw his job as fighting communists and troublemakers. In the 1890s, he used his political muscle in California's state legislature to help crush labor unions trying to organize against grape growers in the Central Valley. In Washington, D.C., as immigration chief, he shocked insiders with his naked xenophobia, insisting that Congress address what he called the "Asiatic menace" by enacting strong laws to exclude Hindus, Chinese, Japanese, and Malays. In February 1919, he called for expelling over 6,000 alien anarchists—long before Palmer ever got the idea—and he led a campaign to deport fifty-four members of the socialist-leaning Industrial Workers of the World arrested on the West Coast.

When the anarchists who tried to send sixteen bombs through the New York City post office in May 1919 included him as one of their targets, Caminetti took it as a compliment. "His table was piled mountains high with undespatched business," Frederick Howe, then-commissioner at Ellis Island, once complained. "He argued by pounding the table, swinging his arms, and evading the issue."

John Abercrombie, whom Secretary Wilson had made responsible for supervising the Immigration Bureau, complained endlessly about Caminetti and the headaches he caused. But instead of confronting Caminetti, Abercrombie usually just let him have his way, often rubber-stamping Caminetti's decisions in deportation cases without even looking at the file. Abercrombie welcomed the chances he found to leave Washington and wash his hands of the whole mess by turning over his immigration portfolio to Louis Post, who backstopped him in his absence.

But Louis Post, too, had his own history of run-ins with Caminetti. Post, seventy-one years old, with a scruffy beard and political roots stretching back to Civil War–era New York City, was a big city progressive intellectual, the kind that Caminetti despised. Post had lived in Chicago for fifteen years before joining the Labor Department in 1913 and produced a magazine there called *The Public* that promoted leftist causes and featured cartoons on its back cover showing fat businessmen smoking big cigars and wearing suits covered with dollar signs. The few times he clashed with Caminetti over deportation cases, it was usually to stop them. For instance, when Caminetti in 1917 tried to deport the famous anarchist Emma Goldman, who had just been imprisoned under the Espionage Act for opposing the wartime draft, it was Louis Post who refused to sign the paperwork, claiming Caminetti had failed to provide enough evidence. He knew that Caminetti had hated him for it ever since.

Now, though, they had to put their bickering aside. Mitchell Palmer, an outsider, had threatened their turf, and all three of them—Abercrombie, Caminetti, and Louis Post—had to stick together to face him. John Abercrombie waited until Secretary Wilson himself came into the office, on one of his rare visits, to raise the issue with him personally. They all agreed on what to do. Neither Secretary Wilson nor his top staff had any quarrel with Mitchell Palmer personally, but they knew enough not to be suckered. So instead, in his letter to Palmer, Wilson suggested that their two staffs sit down face-to-face, privately, and talk things out. That's what bureaucrats did.

It took only a few days to arrange a meeting. On June 19, barely a week after Wilson's letter, the Labor Department's top brass came marching across downtown Washington to the Justice Department building on Vermont Avenue, stepped inside, and made their way to the attorney general's suite. Here, Mitchell Palmer put on his best smiling face and backslapping charm to greet them. He invited them inside, closed the door, gave them places, and within a few minutes the two groups of business-suited men sat facing each other like rival gangs across a table: Palmer and his Red hunters on one side, the Labor Department chiefs on the other. Secretary Wilson himself did not attend; he had gone back home to be with his sick wife. But he sent his top two players, Abercrombie and Caminetti, along with a seasoned Labor Department lawyer named A. Warner Parker who had litigated dozens of deportation cases in federal court.

Palmer got right down to business. Palmer could be persuasive in close quarters, using his physical size, his big hands and loud voice, a hard slap on the shoulder, a wink or a pointed question, to prod anyone who disagreed. Sitting in his office, eyeball-to-eyeball with Abercrombie and Caminetti, Palmer spoke for himself. Wilson's letter had thrown a monkey wrench into his plans, he told the others. He, Palmer, had pledged himself to smash the Reds who staged the June bomb attacks, and he had no desire to see his plan fouled up over legal nit-picking. The two departments, Labor and Justice, had to work together. Yes, Labor had the legal power to issue deportation orders, but Palmer's Justice Department had resources—money and a network of agents around the country—that he could use to "assist" them in the job. How? His Justice Department agents could compile lists of the names of all the aliens they considered dangerous and wanted deported. Then Palmer could transmit the names over to the Labor Department, which could go ahead and use its legal power to issue the needed warrants. It was that simple.

John Abercrombie and Caminetti must have squirmed in their leather seats on hearing these demands. Certainly, they wanted to help Palmer, and just as certainly they wanted to avoid having Palmer tag them as obstructionists. They knew the political pressures driving Palmer in his insistence. Just that week on Capitol Hill, a Louisiana congressman named James Aswell had grabbed headlines by proposing a bill that made it a federal death-penalty offence for any alien Red to throw a bomb or plant explosives. And Senator Miles Poindexter, a Republican from Washington State, was preparing a resolution accusing Palmer of foot-dragging, requiring him to report to Congress on whether he had clamped down yet on the radicals "and if not, why not, and if so, to what extent." Meanwhile, in New York City, the Lusk Committee continued to grab attention with its dramatic raids, sending its squads of club-swinging police barging into, most recently, the left-leaning Rand School, New Jersey's Ferrer Colony, and the lower Manhattan offices of the Socialist "Left Wing Section" and the left-leaning newspaper, the *New York Call*.

But for all their sympathy, Caminetti and Abercrombie both recognized that Mitchell Palmer was swimming in treacherous legal waters, and they were amazed that the attorney general, the country's top lawyer, seemed not to understand it. So they let their own lawyer, A. Warner Parker, do the talking.

Parker spoke up. "What about evidence?"

"When the Attorney General gives orders for warrants of arrest," Palmer explained, "the warrants must issue upon the certificate that there is sufficient cause. He will possess the proof but must not be required to produce it."

"But that cannot be done," Parker interrupted.

Mitchell Palmer stopped and glared for a moment. "Do you mean to tell me that there is no law under which you can issue a warrant for the arrest of an alien when I certify that he is subject to deportation?"

"Mr. Attorney General, not only is there no such law, but no such law would be Constitutional if there were one." Parker tried to hide his condescension as he explained to the attorney general how each individual warrant for each individual alien required a showing of "probable cause," the Constitutional test. The government could not simply arrest people at whim. The Immigration Bureau had published a set of detailed procedures—Rule 22—to cover this point directly, he explained. That way, they were sure to comply with the legal requirement for due process of law.*

Due process of law? Palmer slapped the table. What about the threat to the country?

The meeting ended abruptly after a few more minutes, and the Labor officials walked out shaking their heads. Back across town in their own building, A. Warner Parker described the whole scene to Louis Post, who had not attended the meeting. Post marveled at the attorney general's high-handed, oddly naive manner, though he chalked it up to nerves. "The bomb explosion in front of his residence, supplemented with the detective stories that were thrust upon him [by Flynn and Garvan], would sufficiently account for his remarkable attitude," he wrote later.

But while John Abercrombie, Parker, and Louis Post sat in their Labor Department offices and griped about Palmer's *faux pas*, Caminetti, the headstrong immigration chief, had his own ideas. Away from the others, he decided to take matters into his own hands. Without telling them, he scribbled a note to Palmer's deputy, Frank Garvan, suggesting they try again. Only this time, the Justice Department officials should first take the trouble to read the law. "[I]t might be useful . . . for you and Mr. Creighton to have in your possession copies of the pamphlet of this Bureau containing the Immigration laws and rules and I am accordingly sending you by messenger two copies," he wrote.

But that wasn't all. Caminetti had another thought. He had no problem with Mitchell Palmer's goal of trying to stage mass deportations of radical foreigners. In fact, personally, he applauded the idea. The problem to Caminetti was that Palmer's plan needed discretion. There were too many noses in this tent. The next time they met, he told Garvan, they should limit themselves to a smaller group. To Caminetti, this meant excluding not only Palmer but also his own Labor Department superiors. They didn't need John Abercrombie in the room, and certainly not Louis Post.

---

*There was some room for confusion on this point. Federal courts in 1919 held that alien noncitizens, once inside the country, enjoyed Fourth and Fifth amendment guarantees of due process of law, but they placed deportation proceedings themselves in a gray area, classifying them as "administrative," where basic liberties were not at stake, and thus not triggering full Constitutional protections. And without a Constitutional requirement, Labor Department regulations could be changed.

Caminetti's Immigration Bureau could work this plan out on its own. Then, after it was finished, he and Palmer could present it to Abercrombie and Secretary Wilson as a done deal. That way, Caminetti could run the show by himself, without interference, the way he liked it best.

Edgar missed the meeting in Palmer's office that day. He had not started yet in his new job as head of the Radical Division and probably had not been invited. Edgar, too, would have walked away shaking his head. He understood the legal issues and would have stopped Palmer from making a fool of himself.

Edgar's first assignment at the War Emergency Division in 1917 had been to handle "the important work to be done in connection with the Department of Labor," according to employment records. At the time, this "important work" mostly involved legal issues relating to German sailors marooned in American ports at the start of World War I or spies slotted for deportation. But soon, spending time with the Immigration staff in Washington and at Ellis Island, Edgar got to learn their names and faces, the rules they worked under, and to hear their gossip.

Edgar knew, for instance, that Caminetti, the gruff immigration chief, could be their best ally, the toughest anticommunist in Washington after Palmer himself. But Caminetti needed special handling. Edgar knew that, beyond his brittle personality, Caminetti had a personal score against the Department of Justice. Six years earlier, in 1913, shortly after Caminetti left California and came to Washington to head the Immigration Bureau, Justice Department agents had arrested his oldest son, Frank Drew Caminetti, a rambunctious twenty-two-year-old, and charged him with white slavery, claiming that he had abandoned his wife in Sacramento and eloped to Nevada with an underage woman. The salacious scandal had humiliated Caminetti and his wife. Things got worse when a federal prosecutor in California quit his job claiming that Washington higher-ups had ordered him to go slow on the case, sparking charges that Caminetti had used his political muscle to get special treatment for his son. Caminetti almost lost his job altogether, as several congressmen demanded he be fired. He was saved only when Labor Secretary William Wilson stepped forward to protect him, claiming that he, Secretary Wilson, not Caminetti, had requested the delay in order to allow Caminetti to stay at his desk in the Immigration Bureau a few more months before having to travel home to California to attend his son's trial.

Ultimately, a jury convicted Caminetti's son Drew on one count of violating the Mann Act, illegally taking an unmarried woman across a state line for immoral purposes, and a judge sentenced him to eighteen months behind bars at San Quentin, plus a $1,500 fine.

Edgar knew all about the Caminetti scandal. Still, he respected the old man, his strong ego and solid resolve, and he had an idea how to win him over. The next time these issues came up, Edgar would handle things himself. He would get the job done.

· 5 ·
RACE RIOTS

J UST AS HE was getting ready to start his new job as chief of Mitchell Palmer's Radical Division that summer of 1919, Edgar watched his city edge closer to the brink of a collective nervous breakdown. On top of all the Red Bolshevik hysteria, it burst into its worst race riots since the Civil War, a violent spasm that touched everyone in reach.

For weeks, local Washington newspapers had featured lurid headlines about the rape of a white navy man's wife, allegedly by a "negro fiend." Then, on one steamy Saturday night in July, as white army and navy veterans mingled and drank at local saloons and pool halls, a rumor began to spread. A black man arrested by police as the suspected rapist had been released. The veterans decided to take matters into their own hands. A hundred or so gathered in the street, many wearing their military uniforms. They stormed into a black neighborhood in nearby southwest Washington and began a four-day orgy of beatings, shootings, and terror. Police refused to intervene as the mob spread into other parts of town and it soon was punching, kicking, and clubbing black passersby in front of the White House and the nearby Central Market.

Washington, D.C., had ballooned by 1919 into a city of more than
400,000, 75 percent of them white, but it contained a black community
larger and more prosperous than any other in America. The city held
scores of high-paid African-Americans: teachers, ministers, lawyers, and
businessmen, as well as scores of black army veterans. Seeing the police
fail to protect them, black Washingtonians decided to arm themselves
and fight back, collecting guns, knives, and brass knuckles. Casualties
mounted on both sides. At least five blacks and ten whites died in the
melees, including two white District of Columbia police officers, and
another 150 people were reported clubbed, beaten, or shot. City leaders
closed the saloons and theaters and brought in 2,000 armed troops to
restore order, but ultimately only a well-timed summer rain drove the
hotheads back inside and quelled the violence.

Police never solved the original rape that sparked the riot.

A wave of antiblack violence swept the country that summer, the ugly
mood of anti-Red, antilabor backlash spilling over. Twenty cities reported
riots, and white mobs lynched twenty-eight black men in the first half of
the year, including seven black army veterans still wearing their World
War I uniforms. In Chicago, the killing of a black teenager who accidentally swam into the white section of a city beach set off thirteen days of
street-fighting that killed 23 blacks and 15 whites, injured an estimated
537, and left 1,000 black families homeless. In Philips County, Arkansas,
whites launched a killing spree that netted twenty-five black men officially dead and another hundred claimed as missing, their bodies
allegedly thrown into the Mississippi River.

Edgar could not hide from the outburst even if he didn't participate
himself. The Washington riot came within a few blocks of his Capitol
Hill home, close enough for Edgar to hear the screams and sniff the gunfire. Each morning going to work at his Justice Department office, he
walked or rode the streetcar down Pennsylvania Avenue past scenes of
the worst fighting. African-Americans lived all around Edgar, though he
barely knew them. His city was a Southern town that practiced segrega-
tion by race and class. His Central High School had no black students;
his church had no black parishioners; his office at the Justice Department
had no black employees other than low-level clerks or cleaning women.
President Woodrow Wilson, champion of the New Democracy, had
turned the clock backward during his first term by resegregating the Post
Office and Treasury departments and firing almost all black political
appointees. The only African-Americans Edgar saw in his house were the

maids his mother hired to help cook and clean, and she treated them no better than any other Southern matron of the era. When a kitchen maid named Belle once complained about the work, Edgar's mother quickly put her in her place. "[Y]ou should have heard her impudence," she wrote to him about the incident. "I told her after she was through with her work she could quit as I was not paying her for her impudence. . . . I think she has been with us a little too long."

Edgar reacted to the riots much like his Southern neighbors. He saw blacks at least partly to blame for bringing the violence on themselves, and he saw those demanding equal rights as just one more radical group—like the anarchists, the labor militants, or the immigrant communists. A few weeks later, in his new job as Radical Division chief, he would open a broad investigation on "negro activities" and keep particular tabs on Marcus Garvey, a rising New York–based agitator whose newspaper, Negro World, seemed to Edgar to preach Bolshevism. In one of his first weekly reports to Mitchell Palmer, he would dismiss the Washington riot as an affair prompted by "numerous assaults committed by Negroes upon white women." He would find reason to blame the victims for the Arkansas killings too, tracing them to "certain local agitation in a Negro lodge." And behind it all, he saw Reds. "[A] secondary cause of the trouble was due to propaganda of a radical nature," he noted, pointing to rabble-rousing black-owned magazines like New York's The Messenger, which in turn, he said, was being fed propaganda by socialists.

The problem always came back to the same source: radicals. The world was heading out of control in 1919, and Edgar saw it in his own backyard. It was with this background that he now got set to report for work in his new role: Radical Division chief.

· 6 ·
RADICAL
DIVISION

EDGAR WOULD INSIST years later that he never wasted his time reading dime-store detective novels while growing up as a youngster. "I never cared for them," he told an interviewer once after he became head of the FBI. "The average detective story is usually so absurd and fantastic that it is ridiculous." But that didn't mean that crime didn't fascinate him.

As a teenager, he spent one summer visiting an aunt in Roanoke, Virginia, just as the trial was starting on one of the most gruesome murders ever to hit nearby Carroll County. A few months earlier, twenty men on horseback had ridden up to the courthouse in tiny Hillsville, the county seat, where Floyd Allen, a backwoods moonshiner and local landowner, was being tried for kidnapping. The men, Allen's kin, dismounted, barged inside, raised their shotguns, and, in a hail of fire, murdered the judge, the prosecutor, and the sheriff and wounded several jurors, all before whisking Allen off into the woods. Police captured them all after a few weeks. Day after day that summer, Edgar would slip away from his aunt's house and elbow his way into the courtroom to watch the spectacle as six members of

Allen's gang stood trial for murder. At least three ultimately were sentenced to hang. To Edgar, this was the best entertainment in town.

Now, as an adult in 1919, he had his own new detective force to set up and unleash upon the world, but it was no silly dime-store novel, and his target was no backwoods moonshiner. He was chief of the Radical Division of the United States Department of Justice.

Edgar came to work on August 1, his first day on the job, with a grand vision for his new enterprise. "[I]t was the original intention [for the Radical Division] to specialize entirely upon the deportation cases," he would tell Palmer in his first quarterly report. But this didn't last long. He decided his mission to defeat the Red Menace demanded a new approach and quickly expanded his mandate to something bigger. A friendly biographer would put it this way: "Young Hoover was instructed to make a study of subversive activities in the United States to determine their scope and what action could be taken in the field of prosecution."

To Edgar, this "study" meant nothing less than building a system to keep tabs on every single identifiable radical person in the country—tens or hundreds of thousands of them if need be. Edgar decided he needed to know everything about them: who they were, where they lived, what they said, whom they spoke to, and what groups they belonged to. He needed this information in order to decide what to do with them: whether to deport them, prosecute them, or leave them alone. It didn't matter to Edgar if not a single one of them ever committed a crime. They were, after all, radicals. Who could know what they would do tomorrow?

Edgar knew this was a sharp departure that flew in the face of earlier practice. When Attorney General Charles Bonaparte had first tried to create a permanent detective force in the Justice Department in 1907, Congress blocked him twice, fearing that it might turn into a spy system or central police force similar to the Pinkerton strikebreakers hired by private companies, goons who used violence and underhanded tricks to destroy unions. But Bonaparte refused to be denied. He waited until Congress had closed its doors and left town for a recess in 1908, then secretly reassigned thirty-four agents to the new unit, and presented it as a *fait accompli*. Thus was born what would later become the FBI.

Now, a decade later in 1919, Edgar decided to throw away restraint, and his bosses Flynn and Palmer happily agreed. With the country facing attack from Bolskevik-inspired radicals, Edgar saw an effective secret police force under his control as an obvious necessity.

He set up shop with his usual meticulous eye for detail. He started by

assembling a staff, a tight circle of trusted aides to act as his personal van-
guard. As his private secretary, he hired Helen Gandy, a slim twenty-two-
year-old with dark hair, pretty eyes, and a narrow face. Gandy had left her
home in New Jersey and come to Washington alone in 1918 to find a job.
She took a few classes at the Corcoran Art School and Strayer Business
College, then landed a typing position at the Justice Department. Here,
she met Edgar, and office gossip had it that she and Edgar had gone out
on a few dates during the war. "They had a good time, but they weren't
attracted in that way," an aide later confided. "It cooled off, but later—
when he needed a secretary—he called her." Edgar first interviewed
Gandy for a position in March 1918 while he was still at the War Emergency Bureau. He asked her about her personal life, and Gandy told him
she had no immediate plans to marry. Edgar liked that answer, and he
hired her immediately. Around the office, he called her "Miss Gandy,"
and she called him "Mr. Hoover." Critics would later paint her as a
"wraith-like, grim-faced spinster," but with Edgar she had a pleasant voice
and gentle manner, capable, polite, and loyal.

Along with Helen Gandy, Edgar also brought in two classmates of his
from law school at George Washington University. One, Frank
Baughman, was an outgoing, shoulder-slapping sort whom Edgar's niece
Margaret remembered dropping by the Hoover home on Seward Square
to pal around. "It was about this time that J. E. became quite a sharp
dresser," she recalled. "I remember [he] and Frank used to wear white
linen suits." The other, George F. Ruch, was more studious and intellectual; Edgar assigned him to help him draft legal briefs and reports.

But his bureaucratic empire extended far beyond this inner clique. As
chief of the Radical Division, Edgar had access to the Bureau of Investigation's network of field agents spanning the country. During the World
War, this staff had ballooned from 122 agents in 1914 to over 300 in
1919. Now, flush with money from Congress to fight the Red Scare, it
launched a new hiring spree and by 1920 would almost double in size
again, to 579 agents.

To Edgar's sharp eye, though, these new-hire agents, and plenty of the
older ones, spelled trouble. Many were shockingly unqualified, unedu-
cated bruisers and incompetents cast off from local police departments or
private detective agencies. "[M]any of the special agents had little or no
knowledge of the requirements of the immigration law," Edgar complained privately, citing their sloppy reports and lazy work habits. And
the headquarters staff was little better, often losing or misfiling papers.

Edgar found this chaos appalling. He received a staggering number of regular reports from the field, between 600 and 900 in a typical week, and needed a first-rate system to manage them. In addition, he insisted that each major bureau provide him a weekly summary of all the radical activities in its area, and send him copies of radical literature they seized in raids and arrests. He also set up information-sharing arrangements with key government offices like the War Department's Military Intelligence unit, the State Department's foreign desks, the British Embassy, the Lusk Committee in New York State, and even the Royal Canadian Northwest Mounted Police. And this was on top of the over-200 radical magazines and newspapers his office received weekly from around the country.

To organize this galaxy of information, Edgar almost immediately directed his staff to create what would be his boldest innovation of all. At first he called it the Editorial File System. At its core was a card index modeled on the one that he had found so fascinating at the Library of Congress. For each person whose name appeared in any of the hundreds of reports he received from across the country, his office typed up a separate index card that included their name plus any groups or organizations they belonged to, any periodicals they wrote for, and where they lived, along with a separate index card on every club, society, organization, or periodical they came across. Each of these cards, in turn, they cross-referenced to link it with every document in the Bureau's massive files that mentioned the person or group.

Within two months, Edgar's system contained over 50,000 cards, and five thousand more were added each week. Within a year, the total would top 100,000. With it, Edgar could respond to any telegram he received from anyplace in the country asking about radicals in any particular city, or the activities of any given person or group, simply by pulling a card and going straight to the file with the right information, all in less than two minutes, a process that previously would have taken hours or days.

Edgar bragged about his innovation. But, already the deft bureaucrat, he insisted that his bosses take credit for it. It would be Big Bill Flynn, the detective chief, who crowed in his 1919 annual report that *his* new Radical Division "has probably accumulated a greater mass of data upon [radicalism] than is anywhere else available." Edgar made certain that any important letter intended to go outside the office contained a blank signature line so it could be signed by one of his superiors, Palmer, Flynn, or Frank Burke, a deputy brought in by Flynn to help him manage the office.* But a telltale "JEH" in the top corner usually gave away the true author.

At the same time, Edgar demanded respect. He refused to allow anyone in the Bureau to pull rank or question his authority, no matter how much older or more senior. When he heard that the Cleveland office had launched a raid in September without first getting his permission, he complained directly to Mitchell Palmer. He demanded that the Cleveland bureau chief submit a full report, and he refused to accept the bureau chief's excuse that a telegram from Washington with contrary orders had accidentally sat unopened for days in an office mailbox. Similarly, when Edgar learned that an internal letter from the Bureau's Philadelphia office had leaked into the hands of a suspicious Brooklyn man, Edgar hit the ceiling. He complained this time to Flynn's assistant Frank Burke and demanded that heads roll in Philadelphia. Nobody trifled with Edgar, and he would slam anyone who tried.

With his growing power base, Edgar still had no time to rest. He had to turn his mental energy to the assignment itself, cracking down on the Reds. And if the first rule of war was to know your enemy, then Edgar started in a hole.

Who were these dangerous radicals with the odd foreign names that flooded his file cabinets and his boxes of index cards? Aside from his wartime job tracking Germans, his own life experience told him almost nothing. Edgar rarely had the chance to meet immigrants or leftists while growing up in the narrow world he came from: Capitol Hill, Central High School, his local church, or his Masonic lodge. Edgar and his family took their vacations in Cape May, New Jersey, or Roanoke, Virginia, not in Boston, New York, or other big cities where immigrants congregated and, as his kind saw it, fouled the air with their incomprehensible languages and strange ideas. Washington, D.C., had a few small immigrant enclaves, but not in Edgar's neighborhood. He never studied history in college and spoke no foreign languages beyond high school French. He never joined a labor union, went on strike, or joined a protest.

So, instead, he read books. He borrowed dozens of reference works from the Library of Congress on Bolshevism, socialists, and Russia. He studied

---

*Frank Burke had cut his teeth chasing opium dealers as police chief of Tampa, Florida. Flynn hired him to join the Secret Service and help catch German spies during World War I, and Burke personally broke a major espionage case by shadowing a German agent on New York's Sixth Avenue elevated train, grabbing his briefcase, and escaping on a passing trolley. Flynn then promoted him to run the Secret Service's New York office and the Police Section of the United States Railroad Administration.

the Communist Manifesto, the Third International, the platforms of the radical parties, hundreds of articles from radical magazines, and all the reports from his field agents. But it was always as an outsider, taking in all their words at face value, the hot air, boasting, and bluster along with the rest.

Over time, he learned some turbulent history. Radical socialism had been brewing in America for decades, born in the bloody clashes that stained every step of the early labor movement. Starting with the Molly Maguires, the secret Irish immigrant society that first organized eastern Pennsylvania coal mining regions in the 1870s, workers had used violence to win demands, and employers had used violence to stop them. The Reading Railroad had hired Pinkerton detectives to infiltrate the Molly Maguires, and ultimately collected or concocted enough evidence to convince local courts to convict over a dozen Mollies for murder and hang them. When private detectives or local police and militias failed to keep agitators under control, Washington stepped in. President Rutherford Hayes called out federal troops to break the first intercity railroad strike in 1877, resulting in more than seventy people dead in violent clashes. A few years later, in 1892, when steelworkers shut down Andrew Carnegie's factories in Homestead, Pennsylvania, his manager, Henry Clay Frick, sent 300 armed Pinkertons to seize them back. Seven workers and three strikebreakers died in the shootout before National Guard troops restored order.

Edgar, like most better-off Americans, found it easy to blame the workers for the escalating shrillness. Anarchism, a doctrine steeped from the beginning in hot violent rhetoric, bared its teeth as early as 1886 with the Haymarket killings in Chicago. These occurred when police tried to disperse a late-night street rally called to protest the shootings by police the day before of six unarmed strikers at Chicago's McCormick reaper factory. Someone threw a bomb, killing seven policemen and wounding fifty others, mostly police as well. The incident set off shock waves as Americans recoiled at the image of Russian-style bomb-throwing radicals infecting the New World. A Chicago jury convicted eight self-described Anarchist leaders for the Haymarket deaths, though five of them had not even been present on the street when the bomb was thrown. They hanged four of the Haymarket defendants, and a fifth killed himself in jail by swallowing a dynamite blasting cap. Illinois governor John Peter Altgeld later pardoned the rest, and police never identified the actual bomber.

Anarchism found its clearest voice in Emma Goldman, a dynamic Russian who reached America in 1885 and soon emerged as the country's leading radical orator. Spellbinding on the stump, she caused a riot in New

York City in 1894 by urging striking garment workers to break into the homes of wealthy people on Fifth Avenue and seize the bread off their tables. She spent a year in prison on New York's Blackwell's Island as a result. A few years later, Leon Czolgosz, the self-proclaimed Anarchist who assassinated President William McKinley in 1901, claimed that Emma Goldman had inspired him when he attended one of her speeches before he committed the crime. "Anarchism stands for direct action, the open defiance of, and resistance to, all laws and restrictions, economic, social, and moral," she declared in one of her essays. "Everything illegal necessitates integrity, self reliance, and courage. . . . No real social change has ever come about without a revolution."

Emma Goldman struck a chord with the immigrant poor. Beyond her radical politics, she became a symbol of free love in the 1890s when she divorced her husband and moved in with Alexander Berkman, a fellow radical who would be sentenced to fourteen years in prison for trying to murder Henry Frick during the Homestead steel strike. Her magazine, *Mother Earth*, reached over 10,000 subscribers, and her books *Anarchism and Other Essays* and *Prison Memoirs of an Anarchist* each sold thousands of copies. A trained nurse, she spoke not only about politics but also about then-indelicate topics like "Celibacy or Sex Expression," "Walt Whitman, the Liberator of Sex," and argued for birth control. By the time Edgar began to study her in 1919, Emma Goldman sat once again behind bars in a state penitentiary, she, too, convicted under the Espionage Act for urging young men to resist the draft during World War I.

Trade unions like the American Federation of Labor grew like wildfire during the Progressive Era, but they mostly closed their doors to unskilled industrial workers like coal and copper miners, steel mill workers, and timber cutters. To fill this gap, a more radical strain emerged—the Industrial Workers of the World, the I.W.W., or "Wobblies." Formed in 1905 by William D. "Big Bill" Haywood, it called on these unskilled workers to create One Big Union to confront the capitalist beast, an openly socialist concept. Haywood didn't blanch at matching company strong-arm tactics with his own violence and sabotage, and his reputation soon won him an indictment for murder in the death of Idaho governor Frank Steunenberg, whose house was dynamited in 1905 after a mining strike. Haywood hired Clarence Darrow, the country's most celebrated court-room tactician, to defend him, and Darrow won Haywood an acquittal from a jury.* A few years later, in 1911, two other labor activists pled guilty to bombing the *Los Angeles Times* building in California in a union dispute, killing twenty people. Even Darrow as their defense lawyer could not get them off; he felt lucky to save them from the electric chair. Darrow came within an inch of prison himself in that case on jury tampering charges. He escaped Los Angeles after two trials and a hung jury.

During World War I, the Justice Department cracked down on agitators. In 1918, it indicted over four hundred I.W.W. leaders under the Espionage Act and convicted all but a handful in mass trials in Chicago and Sacramento. It jailed virtually the entire national committee of the Socialist Party by the end of 1918. "I feel guilty to be at large," Eugene Debs, its leader and a presidential candidate, joked ruefully just weeks before he too was prosecuted.

In was only since the Armistice with Germany that the tide had turned. Communists had triumphed in Russia in 1917, and ever since the World War similar uprisings had erupted all across Europe. Edgar read piles of reports on how radicals in America in 1919 were taking the offensive as one union after another went on strike. They flaunted their strength in loud public rallies like the May Day Red Flag parades and countless smaller meetings. Some 6,000 Reds had jammed New York's Madison Square Garden just a few weeks earlier in June 1919 to denounce the Lusk Committee and its raids. They waved red flags, a crime in New York State, and cheered for five full minutes when Ludwig Martens, the Bolshevik emissary to the United States, appeared on stage. The speakers included a Who's Who of recently jailed socialists openly preaching revolution. "Here in America we can sweep this Government out of existence," roared one, Charles Ruthenberg, who himself had organized the 1919 May Day parade in Cleveland, defying the undercover police and federal agents who stalked the affair.

Edgar studied all of this. He absorbed it and analyzed it and distilled it. In late August 1919, he sent one of his best Chicago-based agents to cover a convention there where, word had it, Red leaders planned to settle an internal clash that would reshape American communism for years to come. Edgar gathered all the information he could find and, soon, a plan began to form in his mind. He would make them pay.

---

*No direct evidence connected Haywood to the crime. The case against him was based primarily on the testimony of a man named Harry Orchard, who had acted as bodyguard for a union official. Orchard, after being closeted in prison for several days with a Pinkerton detective, confessed to the murder, but also charged that Haywood and others had instigated it. Darrow's successful attack on Orchard's credibility, plus his emotional summary to the jury—an eleven–hour oration that brought tears to many eyes—won the case.

· 7 ·
REDS

A NEW SOUL, A new life is coming into the world," wrote William Bross Lloyd in praise of his creation, "the life and soul of the real revolutionary proletariat movement in America, and its first cry strikes terror to the heart of our ruling class." So was born the American Communist Labor Party, and with it the American Communist Party, both springing to life in Chicago during a heady five-day period in late summer 1919.

"The American Communist Party, we decided, had to be an American party led by Americans, in the same way that the Bolshevik Party was a Russian party led by Russians," echoed Benjamin Gitlow.

As revolutionary leaders go, Benjamin Gitlow and William Bross Lloyd made strange bedfellows. Lloyd was about the last person anyone would expect to find manning the communist barricades. Thin, elegant, pampered, Harvard-educated, and very rich, Lloyd was the son of Chicago muckraking journalist Henry Demearest Lloyd, who in 1894 had authored the best-selling book *Wealth Against Commonwealth*. William gave his reformist father shivers by marrying a granddaughter of Cyrus McCormick, inventor of the McCormick reaper and heiress to his

William Bross Lloyd.

fortune. William, as a result, now owned a mansion in suburban Winnetka, an office in the Tribune Building, and employed a chauffeur, a private secretary, and a full-time financial advisor. Chicago newspapers dubbed him "The Millionaire Socialist." Lloyd used his money to pay bail for I.W.W. president Big Bill Haywood during his murder trial in Idaho and foot legal fees for Eugene Debs, but he also relished the street fighting hard knocks of far-left politics. Lloyd had defied police in early 1919 by driving his car down Chicago's State Street and waving from it a large Communist red flag, a crime in Illinois. He refused to take it down even after a chanting crowd and a squad of police surrounded him and demanded it, and he smiled for the cameras as they dragged him off to jail for disorderly conduct. "[T]he red flag was his most valued flag, and if he could not fly the red flag [in Chicago] he would go to Russia," he told the judge, according to one witness.

Lloyd enjoyed making incendiary speeches calling on workers to arm themselves with guns and dynamite. "Lloyd, in my opinion, possesses the ability of carrying the audience with him during his ultra-revolutionary outbursts [and] is such a menace to the country that he rightly should be put in a penitentiary or an institution for the insane," a federal agent reported after hearing one of Lloyd's performances in Detroit.

Benjamin Gitlow.

Benjamin Gitlow, by contrast, was raised in poverty by Jewish Russian parents who fled the czar and settled on Manhattan's crowded Lower East Side.* He attended public schools, but he got his real education from street protests, secret political meetings, and free seminars at New York's Cooper Union. He remembered as a child getting to see Mother Jones, the legendary union organizer, address a rally of leftists in Manhattan: "A tall, strong-featured elderly woman took the platform amid the outburst of applause, her voice was clear, powerful. It rang out condemnation of the injustice meted out to the miners." Benjamin Gitlow had found his calling. He took a job as a retail sales clerk, joined the union and soon became its president. He won a seat in the state assembly in 1917, running on the Socialist Party ticket, one of ten Socialists sent to Albany that year. After World War I, inspired by the Russian Revolution, he joined the march toward radicalism.

Though worlds apart, Gitlow and William Bross Lloyd shared one thing in common. They were both native-born American citizens. Nobody could deport them from their own country. Now, in 1919, they stood together at the forefront of American communism.

It was Eugene Victor Debs, a forceful, articulate lawyer from Terre Haute, Indiana, who first formed the American Socialist Party back in 1901. Debs had already gained national prominence at the time by organizing the American Railway Union, leading it in its epic 1894 strike against the Pullman Palace Car company, and spending six months in jail for his role in the contest. Over the next twenty years, Debs built the Socialist Party into a vital mainstream force. He ran for president five times as a Socialist and drew over 900,000 votes in 1912. Socialist Party candidates won hundreds of elections during this period as state legislators, mayors, city councilmen, and two even served in the United States Congress, Wisconsin's Victor Berger and New York's Meyer London. The Party's magazine, *Appeal to Reason*, reached 760,000 subscribers at its peak, and the party still boasted 104,000 dues-paying members in January 1919, ranging from highbrow reformers to low-brow manual laborers, moderates to radicals to Bolsheviks.

But in mid-1918, federal prosecutors charged Debs with violating the Espionage Act for giving a speech against the wartime draft. Convicted,

---

*Gitlow grew up on Cherry Street next to the East River, the same street where New York's Tammany Hall Boss William M. Tweed spent his boyhood in the 1830s. In Tweed's time, it was a working-class native-born neighborhood, in Gitlow's time a Jewish-Italian immigrant slum.

Eugene Debs speaking to workmen, circa 1913.

he began serving a ten-year prison sentence that year in the federal penitentiary in Atlanta, Georgia. By mid-1919, without Debs to keep order, his Socialist Party was tearing itself apart. Over 90 percent of Socialist Party members in 1919 were immigrants, and 70,000 of them belonged to foreign-language federations, primarily Russians. Jealousies between Russian- and English-speaking factions broke out routinely, each side claiming to be the more zealous."These Russian Federationists openly regard themselves as the only simon-pure 'Bolskeviks' in the world—not even excluding Russia," Lloyd himself grumbled.

By Spring 1919, the Socialist Party's moderate leaders recognized that radical extremists dominated the membership, and they decided to clean house. Starting in May, they began a state-by-state purge, ultimately expelling over 20,000 members. In response, the radicals declared war. A group that included Gitlow, Lloyd, journalist John Reed*—all native Americans—plus Boston's Louis Fraina and several leading Russians met in New York City to plot revenge. These insurgents called themselves the Left Wing Section, opened an office in Manhattan on West Twenty-ninth Street, and took over publication of

---

*Reed, author of *Ten Days that Shook the World*, chronicling Lenin's Bolshevik takeover, was played by actor Warren Beatty in the 1981 movie *Reds*, which Beatty cowrote and directed. Maureen Stapleton played Emma Goldman in the film; Paul Sorvino played Louis Fraina.

The Revolutionary Age, a magazine founded by Fraina in Boston, as their official voice.

This new group needed a platform, and for this they turned to Gitlow. Working feverishly that summer, Gitlow produced a stunning document called "The Left Wing Manifesto," a call to arms for America's militant working class. In it, Gitlow made the case for Revolutionary Socialism to demolish and replace the American government. "[I]t is necessary to destroy the parliamentary state [and] deprive the bourgeoisie of political power, and function as a revolutionary dictatorship," he proclaimed. He mapped out a strategy for radical socialists to seize power by building on labor walkouts like the Seattle General Strike. "The revolution starts with strikes of protest, developing them into mass political strikes, and then into revolutionary mass action for the conquest of the power of the state," he explained. "Revolutionary Socialism does not propose to 'capture' the bourgeois parliamentary state, but to conquer and destroy it . . . by annihilating the political power of the bourgeoisie." Once in power, the new Dictatorship of the Proletariat would seize key industries, nationalize banks and corporations, repudiate public debt, and crush anyone who stood in its way.

Louis Fraina was so pleased with Gitlow's "Manifesto" that he decided to publish it in *The Revolutionary Age* as a feature for its July 5, 1919, edition, with a record print run of 16,000 copies. William Bross Lloyd backed the effort from Chicago by sending Fraina a $650 open-ended contribution and agreed to pay the salary of one of Fraina's office workers until the magazine became solvent, if ever.

The breaking point came on August 31, 1919, when the Socialist Party convened an emergency convention in Chicago to settle its internal split. It met at Machinists Hall on South Ashland Boulevard in a second-floor ballroom lined with American flags and dotted with undercover detectives. Both sides came ready to fight. Barely had the meeting started when John Reed led a group of unregistered left-wingers into the hall to claim seats. "John Reed had about 50 husky Russians and Finns lined up to 'start something . . . supplied with bricks and knuckles,'" wrote one of the federal agents spying on the event, a Military Intelligence* man, "every one of [them] had blood in his eyes. One of them even borrowed my pocket knife."

*The War Department's Military Intelligence Division regularly conducted surveillance on American citizens inside the United States at this time, and had offices in most major American cities. A clear division leaving domestic surveillance to the FBI and limiting Military Intelligence to work outside the country would not be established until World War II.

The convention leaders moved to expel Reed and his insurgents. "If you do not sit down and be quiet I will call the police," announced the chairman, Adolph Cermer. When Reed's group refused, Cermer signaled for a squad of about thirty Chicago police to come marching into the hall and clear them out. Fistfights and clubbings erupted everywhere. Reed punched one of the platform speakers in the face before police could drag him from the room. "You are Right Wing enemies of the revolution!" another left-winger screamed. "Go ahead with your dirty work! Expel us from the party!! We will soon meet you in bloody battles on the barricades!"

William Bross Lloyd rushed into the building at about this time and threw himself into the brawl, incensed that any self-respecting Socialist would hide behind capitalist-lackey police. "One cannot help wondering," he wrote afterwards, whether these were the same police "who shortly before beat up the striking I.W.W. restaurant workers."

Outside on the sidewalk, having been forcibly ejected, the dissidents quickly reassembled. They licked their wounds and walked a few blocks down Ashland Boulevard to a building they quickly dubbed the "Smolny," after the Smolny Institute in Petrograd where the Russian Bolsheviks first set up their own headquarters. Here, many of the dissidents had already convened under the leadership of Louis Fraina and the Russian-language federations and announced the creation of their own new organization, the Communist Party of America. Emotions overflowed. "Delegates and visitors rose spontaneously. Our singing of the *Internationale* fairly shook the building and ended with thunderous applause for Revolutionary Socialism and Communism," Gitlow recalled. They adopted a charter taken largely from Gitlow's "Left Wing Manifesto," and vowed loyalty to Moscow and the Third International. They voted to require every member to sign a pledge of fealty to the Party and its core principle: the conquest by the proletariat of the power of the state.

Once they finished singing songs and got down to business, though, infighting broke out immediately. Russians controlled the party's power structure, and Americans found themselves locked out. Reed, Gitlow, and Lloyd each tried to address the group in English, but it ignored them. Lloyd found the spectacle disgusting, "the whole crowd [being] petty political intriguers without principle, seeking simply power and the control of organization expenditure." Gitlow grew particularly annoyed at Louis Fraina; "his whole demeanor gave to many the impression that he considered himself the Lenin of America," he wrote.

The next morning, on Monday, September 1, the Americans staged their own walkout. Lloyd, Gitlow, John Reed and about fifty others, including a handful of undercover federal agents and police, all marched together back to Machinists Hall where the Socialists were still meeting on the second floor, and they reassembled instead on the first floor in a small billiard room. Here, they announced formation of their own new entity, the Communist Labor Party. They voted William Bross Lloyd their sergeant at arms and Benjamin Gitlow a national committeeman. Their platform differed hardly at all from that of the Russia-dominated group they had just left, but the Communist Labor Party demanded no loyalty pledges from its members and avoided direct appeals to violence. Still, it preached "overthrow of capitalist rule," "conquest of political power," and "capture of state power."

Over the next four days, they appointed a platform committee, a committee on international relations, one on socialist publicity, another on ways and means. They installed a mimeograph machine and littered the hall with copies of their reports, haggling over each word in them. They called each other "comrade," adopted the hammer and sickle emblem, and chose the name "communist" to mark themselves as revolutionary. They sang a song to open each session, either "The Red Flag" or "The Internationale," and at the end of each they gave the Bolskevik Yell, its words written on a blackboard at the front of the room:

Bolshevik, bolshevik, Bolshevik, bang!
We are members of the 'Gene Debs gang.
Are we rebels? I would smile.
We are with the soviets all the while.

Ultimately, they moved into a larger room at the I.W.W. Hall on Throop Street, and they held a mass meeting at the Old Style Inn on Division Street that drew over eight hundred supporters. William Bross Lloyd was so pleased that, when the convention ended, he reached into his deep pocket again and floated $380 to buy railway tickets for all the delegates to get home, this on top of the many dinners and lunches and rounds of schnapps, whiskey, and vodka he financed along the way.

Over the next few months, the new Communist and Communist Labor Parties worked tirelessly to convert old Socialist Party members to their rosters. Between them, they sent out tens of thousands of membership cards, circulated sign-up sheets at local clubs and union halls, and absorbed entire branches wholesale, often without even telling the individual members they had switched parties. When the dust settled, the old Socialist Party of Eugene Debs saw its membership depleted, down from over 100,000 to barely 25,000. Two new Communist parties took its place, one mostly Russian, the other led by Americans, estimating their combined support at about 60,000. But size didn't matter for now. There would be time to grow, and, meanwhile, they had work to do. For now, Benjamin Gitlow and William Bross Lloyd stood on stage together and joined the cheers.

But perhaps the busiest man of all at the meeting in Machinists Hall, as he had been at all the meetings that week—Socialist, Communist, and Communist Labor—was a nondescript fellow who kept to himself and hardly spoke to anyone. George F.R. Cummerow worked for the United States Department of Justice. He was a special agent in the Chicago office of the Bureau of Investigation. He had been assigned to attend all the meetings that week, sit quietly, and take notes. He did his job well. During the conventions, Cummerow recorded each resolution, each speaker, each song, each committee chosen, each officer nominated and elected, each address of each meeting room, every vote, and most important, all the names—or as many as he could scribble down—of all the people who came to join the party. Nobody thought to ask him who he was or why he'd come. He was just another comrade.

Cummerow, a lawyer by trade before joining the Justice Department, would report back to the new office in Washington he worked for, the one that was headed by that bright young fellow named Hoover. Cummerow worked for the Radical Division, and they kept him very busy.

⊙━◆━⊙

Edgar read all the reports coming out of Chicago from the communist conventions, though his own Chicago man, George Cummerow, gave the best account. Edgar must have laughed at the stories of walkouts and counter-walkouts by competing communists. He saw no difference at all between them: Communist, Communist Labor, or whatever. He dismissed their dramatic split as petty infighting, "minor disagreements over the administration," as he put it, "though the ultimate aim of both parties is the same." Edgar saw the bigger picture. Both of these new parties, Communists and Communist Laborites alike, shared the same program of advocating the violent overthrow of the United States government. Neither tried to hide the fact. On the contrary, they announced it proudly in their charters.

Edgar saw the implication. This was his hook to make Mitchell Palmer's vision a reality. Under the 1918 Immigration Act, any alien affiliated with either of these parties could be deported immediately.*

Edgar by now recognized several of the names of the leading Reds in Chicago. Louis Fraina, for instance, he knew as the man from Boston whom his Boston-based special agent had fingered months ago as the likely author of the leaflet "Plain Words" that was found outside Palmer's house the night of the June bombing, a fact that created a possible link between these communists and that crime. He recognized Benjamin Gitlow as author of the "Left Wing Manifesto," and he recognized John Reed as author of *Ten Days that Shook the World* and as editor of the *New York Communist*.

William Bross Lloyd's name also jumped off the page. Edgar already had seen the thick file that his agents had compiled on Chicago's Millionaire Socialist. It included reports on several of Lloyd's fiery speeches, including one he gave to a cheering crowd of Socialists in Detroit in March 1919. "[Lloyd] stated that the Department of Justice is committing burglaries [and] the War Department is committing numerous murders by forcing into military service conscientious objectors and conflicting [*sic*] atrocities and tortures on them," wrote the agent who attended it, "[and he said] the workers must have a big stock of dynamite and men trained to use it so they can open the doors of the arsenals and furnish the workers with arms. [Lloyd] stated further that he believed in force and that the workers should freely use it."

Edgar found Lloyd's speech so disturbing that he immediately flagged it for Palmer's assistant, John Creighton, to see. "I am attaching hereto a speech made by William Bross Lloyd," he wrote to Creighton in July 1919. "I am calling this to your attention in order that you may see the type of speeches that are being made by American citizens."

By early September, Edgar had studied the reams of papers, books, reports, and index cards crossing his desk and found a pattern. Mitchell

---

*Documents released from the Russian State Archives since the fall of the Soviet Union include a mid-1919 directive from the Communist International in Moscow, signed N. Bukharin, instructing American sympathizers to form a Communist Party in the United States, affiliated with Moscow and uniting disaffected elements of the Socialist Party with the I.W.W., dedicated to promoting proletarian dictatorship through "revolutionary mass action (strikes and insurrections)" and destruction of conservative labor unions like the American Federation of Labor. But the split of the American movement into two competing groups—Communist and Communist Labor—was a serious deviation from the plan.

Palmer wanted to deport as many radical immigrants as possible, based on their ties to violent radical groups. Edgar had now identified six such groups at the cutting edge of the radical movement:

1. the *El Ariete Society*, centered in Buffalo, New York, with about 12 members
2. the *Communist Party of America* with about 40,000
3. the *Communist Labor Party* with about 10,000
4. the *Union of Russian Workers* with 4,000
5. the *I.W.W.* estimated at 300,000
6. the *L'Era Nuova Group*, centered in Paterson, New Jersey, estimated at 25

Edgar put the I.W.W. at the bottom of his list for now, despite its being the largest and oldest. The I.W.W. had been careful to avoid any direct call to overthrow the United States government, making it a bad fit under the immigration statute. Similarly, Buffalo's El Ariete Society and Paterson's L'Era Nuova Group remained small and mysterious; nobody knew yet exactly how to find them. That left three big targets, the Communists, Communist Labor, and the Union of Russian Workers, each with thousands of members and baldly-stated programs of violent, Bolshevik-style socialism.

Edgar knew his next step. He reported to Palmer: "It is my intention to endeavor to obtain a decision from the Commissioner General of Immigration to the effect that the sentiments expressed in the manifesto of the [Communist and Communist Labor] Parties are in violation of the Immigration Laws relating to deportation." This would set the stage for a first round of mass arrests and deportations. Once the Labor Department had agreed, he could submit to them a full list of member names along with the evidence needed to qualify for deportation warrants. After that, all he had to do was to round them up.

This was only part of the job, though. "If such a decision can be reached, it will result in the elimination of certain undesirable aliens, but it of course will not affect citizens connected with the party," Edgar continued. Leaders like Benjamin Gitlow, William Bross Lloyd, and John Reed were American citizens and outside the reach of the immigration laws, but Edgar had no intention of letting them get off. To his mind, these dangerous men deserved to be in prison. He would use his friends at the Lusk Committee and local prosecutors in Chicago to sweep them into his net.

The time had come to act, and Edgar had a plan. To make it work, everything now depended on his winning the cooperation of one person: Anthony Caminetti, the commissioner general of immigration. With Caminetti's help, Edgar could make these deportations go smooth as silk. Without it, they'd never get off the ground. To win over Caminetti, Edgar had to earn the man's trust by giving him something he wanted, and here, too, he had done his homework. Edgar would offer Caminetti the biggest fish in the radical sea: Emma Goldman.

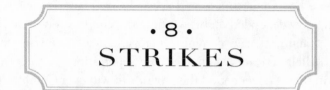

· 8 ·
STRIKES

I F ANY TRUE American still doubted that the country sat on a powder keg of revolution in September 1919, the events that month settled the issue, at least as far as J. Edgar Hoover and his boss A. Mitchell Palmer were concerned. That month, the radicals laid three new cards down on the table that followed Benjamin Gitlow's "Left Wing Manifesto" to a tee.

Chicago steel workers announcing the walkout, September 1919.

First, in Boston, the large bulk of the city's police force, 1,117 out of its 1,544 officers, walked off the job and went on strike. No such thing had ever happened before in a major American city. Pandemonium resulted. For four nights, criminals ran free, looting shops, smashing windows, and starting fires. Governor Calvin Coolidge, a terse, flinty-eyed lawyer originally from rural Vermont, belatedly sent National Guard troops to restore order, but they were late and outgunned. They had to recruit hundreds of volunteers to help as temporary policemen, including army veterans, college students, and local businessmen. Tensions peaked one night when nervous guardsmen fired their rifles on a South Boston mob, killing two people. Boston's Central Labor Union, an umbrella group representing all the organized workers in the city, called for a general strike, threatening to surrender Boston to the revolutionists.

The threat struck fear among Americans already shaken by months of Red Scare agitation and a summer of race riots. Samuel Gompers, president of the American Federation of Labor, appealed to Governor Coolidge to mediate a compromise and allow the striking policemen back to work. Coolidge refused. "There is no right to strike against the public safety by anybody, anywhere, any time," he answered bluntly. The policemen had broken the law, and Coolidge refused to allow a single one back to his old job, even if it meant hiring and training an entire new force from scratch.

The outburst made Calvin Coolidge an overnight sensation. The country saw him as a steady-handed leader bringing clarity to chaos. Calm returned; no general strike materialized. Federal troops and volunteer police ultimately restored order to Boston and would continue to patrol the city for two more months until it hired and deployed its new police force.

Two weeks later, a bigger shoe dropped as 365,000 steel workers in fifty cities walked off the job demanding better pay and union recognition, one of the largest strikes yet in American history. Steelworkers typically worked twelve-hour days in hellish factories for $1,466 a year or less,

"Striking Back." *New York Evening World,* in *Literary Digest,* September 27, 1919.

but company leaders cried Bolshevism and demanded state and federal troops to keep order. Judge Elbert H. Gary, chairman of the United States Steel Company, refused to recognize the strikers and launched a relentless campaign against them of propaganda and quasi-military violence. He ordered local sheriffs, police departments, and militias near Pittsburgh to place 25,000 men under arms as riots broke out in city after city. Indiana sent eleven companies of its state militia to Gary, and federal troops followed.

Twenty strikers would die in violent clashes, and soldiers, police, and company detectives would arrest hundreds more as the strike dragged on for three months. Ultimately, beyond the deaths, workers would lose $112 million in wages before the strike collapsed, gaining nothing.

Then, in late September, as the steel strike sizzled, the United Mine Workers voted to stage a coordinated walkout by all coal miners in the country, targeted for November 1, 1919. The coal miners demanded a nationwide contract, a 60 percent pay raise, a six-hour workday, and a five-day workweek. Coal was America's principal fuel in 1919; it ran railroads, heated peoples' homes, and powered factories and ships. Wartime laws had declared coal an essential military commodity and barred strikes. A strike-created coal shortage, particularly in winter, could cripple the economy and cause widespread hardship, exactly the conditions to spark a Red revolution. And with a half million workers walking off the job, it would be the biggest strike yet.

Edgar, sitting at his nerve center in the Justice Department, saw hundreds of reports cross his desk in September and October on the police, coal, and steel strikes. His agents had infiltrated each of these unions, and to his eyes they had Red spattered all over them. A Newark special agent reported in September that the I.W.W. had sent agitators to Boston to aggravate the police walkout, and Edgar immediately alerted his bureaus all over the Northeast to track their movements. He instructed his Boston agents "to ascertain whether or not the radicals are in any way responsible for the condition."

So, too, with steel. Here, suspicion centered on the strike's principal leader, William Z. Foster. This tall, wiry, articulate man may have been "the most energetic and intelligent of the strike organizers," as the contemporary historian Frederick Lewis Allen called him, but he also had a long trail of socialist ties. Foster had been an I.W.W. organizer before World War I and a special correspondent to the I.W.W.'s magazine, *Solidarity*, and also wrote a pamphlet promoting syndicalism, a European brand of revolutionary socialism that called on militant unions to seize control of key industries. Soon, excerpts from Foster's radical speeches began to appear in newspapers under headlines like LENINE RED RUNS STEEL STRIKE and STRIKE IS PART OF REVOLUTIONARY MOVEMENT. Samuel Harden Church, president of the Carnegie Institute in Pittsburgh, summarized Foster's philosophy as "the seizure of all property, the destruction of the United States government, and the adoption of race suicide as national policy."

Even A.F.L. President Samuel Gompers, who originally had hired Foster to organize the steelworkers for his union, found Foster's rhetoric downright scary. "Foster had been so insistent that the strikes should take place upon the day set that I began to doubt his sincerity," Gompers confided later in his memoirs, claiming he feared that Foster might try to sabotage the A.F.L. and turn it into a Russian-style socialist front.* Edgar himself learned from Military Intelligence that month that I.W.W. president Bill Haywood had sent agitators to steel plants in Youngstown, Ohio, and Pittsburgh and South Bethlehem, Pennsylvania, to stir the pot, and socialists bragged about it. The *Cleveland Socialist News,* one of the left-wing newspapers Edgar collected, headlined: HALF MILLION WORKERS IN OPEN CLASS WAR, and the *Chicago New Solidarity,* an I.W.W. mouthpiece, branded the steel strikers' mission as being to "crush the capitalists."

Sitting in the office, Edgar sent Mitchell Palmer a barrage of reports that month painting an alarming picture. These strikes—police, steel, and coal—reeked of revolution. Radical communists and anarchists might comprise only a tiny fraction of the American public, but these striking unions gave them a disciplined army numbering together close to a million, and strategically deployed to cripple vital American industries. "Radicals are taking advantage of every opportunity to instill Bolshevism and Soviet principles into the steel workers," Palmer told newspaper reporters, citing Edgar's work. Free speech had gone too far in America. "I want the advocacy of sedition made a crime," Palmer insisted. "These radicals preach this sort of thing to ignorant persons who can't understand English and who are readily led to all sorts of radical ideas, and under our laws we must stand idly by with our hands tied."

---

*Gompers was so concerned about communist meddling in the steel strike that he sent a back-channel message to I.W.W. president Bill Haywood telling him "to keep his hands off the steel workers' affairs or go back to jail," as one Military Intelligence agent reported. The agent went on: "Haywood is not anxious to return to jail, so he recalled about 50 agitators he had sent to Gary and other steel centers."

As the weeks passed, Edgar began to see his anti-Red mission as more than a job. It was fast becoming his life's crusade. He refused to let anything distract him, either at home or at work. A delegation from the United Mine Workers came to see him that month to complain about the murder of two union officials during a strike in Breckinridge, Pennsylvania, allegedly by the same local police who were now refusing to investigate the killings. Edgar only shrugged. "[I]t appears that there is no federal question involved as it is purely a matter for the local authorities," he told them. Similarly, when asked to investigate a riot that broke out that month in Omaha, Nebraska, he lost interest as soon as he found that no Reds were behind it. It had been just another lynching of another African-American man, "merely a purely local matter involving a Negro who assailed a white girl," he wrote. According to reports from his Omaha office, a mob had stormed the Omaha jailhouse, burned it, pulled the black man from his cell, and hung him with a rope. Federal troops had entered the city to prevent a bloodbath in black neighborhoods. "[A]s soon as the Negro had been lynched the mob spirit subsided, showing that there was but one purpose in it—namely, the lynching of the negro," Edgar concluded. "No property was destroyed other than the opening of hardware and pawn shops to procure firearms."*

Edgar had bigger concerns on his mind than mere murder of union officers or lynchings of black men. As he saw it, that wasn't his job. He saw his country at war with radicals, a pernicious enemy capable of unspeakable evil. He refused to take his eye off the ball. Local police could handle the rest.

---

*Newspaper reports described the carnage as far worse. After storming and seizing the city jail, the mob had seized the mayor and tied him to a street pole to punish him for his audacity in failing to turn over the black man in the first place. After they hanged the black man, they dragged his body through the streets and then burned it. When water was turned on the mob to protect the jail at one point, they responded by throwing bricks and breaking over fifty windows. The police reportedly rounded up forty black Omaha citizens after the lynching, locked them in the mail car of a train to Wyoming, and told them not to come back. The two thousand federal troops set up eighteen machine guns around Twenty-fourth and Lake streets to protect the nearby African-American neighborhood. Two men were reported killed in the affair, including the lynched prisoner.

· 9 ·
PARTNERS

B Y MID-SEPTEMBER 1919, they came to terms, old Caminetti and young Hoover. Caminetti had a bald head fringed with gray hair, small dark eyes, and a big white bushy mustache. Though shorter than Edgar by a few inches, Caminetti at sixty-five years old still looked down on him from the vantage point of more than forty years' seniority. Caminetti literally had gown up, gotten married, raised a family, become California state party boss, and served two terms in the United States Congress all before Edgar was even out of diapers. And he insisted on having his own way, whether in running his California ranch, the California Democratic Party, or his domain as commissioner general of immigration.

Now, they were bosom pals.

Edgar left nothing to chance in his wooing of Caminetti. Starting in early August, he began finding time several days each week to leave his office, walk the dozen or so blocks across downtown Washington, past the White House, and over to G Street where the Labor Department had its

Anthony Caminetti (right),
Commissioner General of Immigration.

headquarters. Here he went inside, found Caminetti's office, and knocked politely. Sometimes, if Caminetti was busy, he would step down the hall to see John Abercrombie, the solicitor and acting secretary. He always brought some news or gossip they wanted to hear, some new tidbit about Palmer or Flynn, or the latest reports from the field. But at first, Edgar mostly just came in, sat down, and listened. He gave them the chance to talk, especially Caminetti. He asked the commissioner general for his advice. What was the best way to handle deportation cases? What case rulings should he read? What problems should he look out for? Then he sat back and let Caminetti tell his stories, spout his opinions, and voice his complaints. Through it all, Edgar deferred. On days he found it impossible to leave his desk, he called Caminetti on the telephone or sent him letters. One time that month, when he wanted to circulate written instructions to his own staff detailing the rules of evidence in immigration cases, Edgar made a point to show the paper to Caminetti first and let him make suggestions.

"[C]onferences were immediately held with the Commissioner General of Immigration and amicable relations established," Edgar reported to Palmer in September 1919. The seduction went well.

For his part, Caminetti probably dismissed Edgar at first as a mere messenger boy sent by the Justice Department's top brass to waste his time. But Caminetti had a keen sense about people from his years in politics. In Edgar, he sensed someone who might be useful, someone he could do business with. He saw good pragmatic sense in allowing this young man to court him.

All the ingredients were there for a good match. All it needed was a spark.

Then one of them mentioned the name Emma Goldman. Most likely it was Caminetti first, using her as an example for his favorite complaint: why he hated interference from his superiors in the Labor Department. Caminetti had been trying to deport Emma Goldman for at least two years, since 1917. He had started proceedings against her back then, immediately after Goldman had been convicted under the Espionage Act for opposing the wartime draft. Caminetti based his action on the grounds that she was an admitted anarchist, which was an automatic basis for deportation so long as she was not an American citizen. He prepared a warrant for her arrest and sent it up the chain of command, where it landed on the desk of Louis F. Post, the assistant secretary of labor who was filling in for the absent Secretary Wilson. Post returned the warrant to Caminetti unsigned. His cover note explained that he saw "no evidence in the accompanying record to show prima facie that [Goldman was] an alien."

To Caminetti, this excuse was preposterous. By 1917, Emma Goldman had lived in the United States for thirty-two years, and she had never taken out citizenship papers. Instead, she claimed her citizenship on two grounds: her 1894 marriage to a man named Jacob Kersner whom she divorced a year later, and the citizenship of her father, who became naturalized in 1894 long after Emma had left his household. To Caminetti, both these grounds reeked of fraud, and he could prove it.

To Caminetti, the problem was not the evidence. The problem was Louis F. Post. To Caminetti, Post was a Parlor Bolshevik of the worst sort, a liberal progressive who hobnobbed with big city intellectuals and socialists. And worse, during the time Louis Post lived in Chicago and published his liberal magazine, *The Public*, Post had actually defended Emma Goldman as an innocent victim when police arrested her briefly after the assassination of President McKinley in 1901. He had even invited her as a dinner guest to his home.

Edgar listened to Caminetti, and it hardly surprised him to hear the old man ranting this way about the problem, his face turning beet red. Edgar had heard plenty of similar talk about disloyalty at the top of the Labor Department. Just recently, Edgar's friends at Military Intelligence had issued a secret warning that Bolsheviks in Chicago and New York were "operating wide open, directly under the eyes of the authorities" and laid the blame at the feet of these same bureaucrats: "Unfortunately they enjoy the protection of Secretary of Labor Wilson and his entire outfit and are using this patronage to foster their tricky, destructive propaganda."

Caminetti was itching to take another run at Emma Goldman. Goldman had been serving her espionage prison sentence at the state penitentiary in Jefferson City, Missouri, but it was due to end in just a few weeks, on September 27, 1919. After that, she would be released a free woman, and the thought of Emma Goldman running around the country, preaching her radical anarchism at a time of national crisis, exploding bombs and crippling strikes, seemed inconceivable to Caminetti. Somebody had to stop her.

Edgar agreed. He probably thought up the idea himself, and just waited for the chance of Caminetti's mentioning it so he could pounce. Deporting Emma Goldman could carry big dividends. High-profile female criminals were still a rarity in America in 1919, but Goldman presented a compelling choice as a celebrity villain to headline the anti-Red campaign. She appealed to every popular prejudice: she was Jewish, Russian, a free-loving divorcee, an admitted anarchist with a criminal record, and was tied to violent men who had committed murder and attempted murder. Millions loved her, but tens of millions hated her. If Edgar and Caminetti could succeed in deporting Emma Goldman, the most famous anarchist in America, it would be a major victory and send a chilling message to the Reds.

Caminetti had already ordered his Immigration Bureau lawyers in April 1919 to conduct a fresh review of Emma Goldman's citizenship and sent an inspector to question her in her jail cell. They had already assembled more than enough evidence, they thought, to undermine her claims. Goldman's 1894 marriage to Jacob Kersner had never been properly recorded, and Kersner's own citizenship had been cancelled in 1909 based on allegations of fraud. Records also confirmed that Goldman had been twenty-five years old at the time her father became a citizen, placing her outside his authority. "According to the records there would appear to be no legal objection to the deportation of Emma Goldman under the anarchy act of October 16, 1918," Caminetti's lawyers concluded. The question was simply one of "policy," that is, whether Washington had the backbone to do it.

Caminetti had sent a copy of this new legal report to Secretary Wilson and asked for a quick meeting to agree on moving forward. Instead, after five months, he had not received even the courtesy of an answer.

Caminetti had no doubt about the reason. Those closet Bolsheviks who ran the Labor Department were blocking him again: Wilson, Abercrombie, and particularly Louis Post.

Maybe Caminetti had planned this entire discussion as a test for this sharp young Mr. Hoover from the Justice Department to see just what kind of clout he could deliver. Could Edgar help break the logjam? He jumped at the chance.

"Emma Goldman and Alexander Berkman are, beyond doubt, two of the most dangerous anarchists in this country and if permitted to return to the community will result in undue harm," Edgar reported back to John Creighton immediately after meeting with Caminetti. He quickly conceived a plan to break the impasse—a clever bureaucratic game of shadows. First, Edgar had Creighton send Caminetti a formal note inquiring on behalf of the Justice Department about the status of the Goldman and Berkman cases, throwing the full weight of Mitchell Palmer behind the question. Then, Caminetti used Creighton's note as an excuse to prod his own Labor Department superiors for an answer. "As these cases are of importance, I would appreciate receiving such instructions as you have to offer," Caminetti wrote to Secretary Wilson a few days later, attaching Creighton's request along with his own written inquiry. Wilson, by then fully aware of Palmer's zeal on anything to do with Reds, quickly folded his cards. He scribbled his answer on the bottom of the page: "Issue warrants. WBW."

If a test it had been, Edgar passed it with flying colors. He had taken less than a week to break a five-month logjam. "Mr. Caminetti immediately took steps for the sending out of these warrants," Edgar reported back to Palmer and Creighton. A United States Marshal would serve the warrant on Emma Goldman in her prison cell on September 12, two weeks before her expected release, setting bond at $15,000. After waiting two years for a breath of freedom, Emma Goldman would suddenly find herself facing a whole new round of legal tangles with the federal government.

But even more important to Edgar, he had won Caminetti's confidence. Now was the time to raise the bigger issue: the notion of a mass deportation of radical immigrants, Mitchell Palmer's grand vision. Edgar mentioned it to Caminetti one day at about this time and found an eager listener. Caminetti had relished the idea ever since first hearing Palmer explain it in his office a few weeks earlier. He took little prodding to come on board now that he had found someone in the Justice Department he could trust, his new friend Edgar.

Edgar suggested, as a dress rehearsal, that they start with the Union of Russian Workers. He explained to Caminetti how the Union of Russian Workers made a better target than the recently-formed Communist or Communist Labor parties because it was a more established group, founded in New York in 1907 by William Szatow, a Russian émigré who, since the 1917 revolution, had returned home to become chief of police in Petrograd under the Bolsheviks. Since then, the Union had grown tentacles in a dozen American cities and claimed over 4,000 members, all Russians, its socialist-communist rhetoric straight from Moscow. To Edgar, the Union's clear ties to known Bolsheviks made it a clean legal target under the Immigration Act, and his agents recently had tracked several of its members traveling to West Virginia and Pennsylvania coal towns to stir up labor trouble. Edgar envisioned a *coup de grâce*, "a simultaneous raid made throughout the country," as he put it, "taking into custody all these persons."

It didn't take long for them to finalize the details. "The plan that comes to my mind is that this office should submit to you the individual cases of each of these persons," Edgar told Caminetti in a letter in late October 1919, "and if the evidence of the same satisfies you as to their undesirability, warrants could then be issued upon the entire lot and at a specified time." With warrants in hand, Edgar's agents could round them all up, turn them over to Caminetti's immigration inspectors, and off they'd go back to Russia. What could be more simple?

But secrecy would be essential. "It is needless to say that this matter is to be treated in a strictly confidential manner," Edgar stressed in his note. This operation would push government powers to the limit, invade the lives of hundreds of people, including citizens as well as immigrants, and Edgar wanted no risk of any federal judge blowing the whistle on them prematurely. Within days, he sent out instructions for his field agents to compile lists of names. With a green light from Palmer, Edgar rolled up the sleeves of his starchy white shirt and prepared to deliver his first big coup, a vicious one-two punch: a national raid against the Russian Reds, and the deportation of Emma Goldman.

• PART III •

THE FIRST RAID

"The Patriotic American." *Chicago Tribune*, in *Literary Digest*, June 28, 1919.

· 10 ·
THROMBOSIS

P RESIDENT WOODROW WILSON came home from Paris to a hero's welcome in July 1919, having grasped the crowning achievement of his presidency, an agreement to end the Great European War to End All Wars, seven months after the Armistice. Reaching Washington, Wilson recognized that most of this Treaty of Versailles consisted of sour compromises aimed at settling Old World grievances. It forced Germany to admit guilt for the war, give up the disputed province of Alsace-Lorraine, and pay $15 billion in reparations, assuring economic pain for years to come. With mandatory limits on its future military power, it left Germans to feel victimized by an arbitrary peace, a bitterness that zealots like young Adolph Hitler would fan into a seething rage and another round of global bloodletting just twenty years later.

But Woodrow Wilson considered himself victorious. In speech after speech, he touted the one key point in the treaty that he had insisted on and considered essential: a League of Nations. This League had become Wilson's life's mission, his justification for spilling American blood in the cataclysm—a mechanism to prevent future wars. The country greeted his idea with wide applause. Even Henry Cabot Lodge, the Republican chairman of the Senate Foreign Relations Committee, paid it lip service initially, though he insisted that the Senate should first qualify the treaty by adding reservations to protect American sovereignty. But Woodrow Wilson refused to compromise. Instead of negotiating with Lodge, he insisted the Senate ratify the treaty in its pure state. And when they refused, he decided to rally the country and force the Senate's hand. He would use the strongest weapon in his arsenal, his eloquence.

Woodrow Wilson excelled as a speaker, able to command soaring language, elegant metaphors beautifully delivered. He could use words to stir listeners to emotional peaks, and he made a sensation in 1913, his first year as president, by breaking tradition and coming to Capitol Hill to deliver his State of the Union address in person, the first president to do so. In an age before radio* or television, though, Wilson had only one way to reach the American people with his own voice. He had to get on a train, crisscross the country, and stop to speak in every major city where he could find an audience. And so that's what he decided to do. Still exhausted from his European negotiations and the strain of World War I, Wilson rejected his doctors' advice and left Washington on September 3, 1919, just two months after coming home. He boarded a special railroad car called the "Mayflower" and set off for Columbus, Ohio, the first stop on a planned thirty-speech, ten-thousand-mile odyssey to sell the League of Nations. "Never have I seen the president look so weary as on the night we left Washington for our swing into the West," Joe Tumulty, the president's private secretary, recalled.

Attorney General A. Mitchell Palmer had made a point to see his old friend Woodrow Wilson shortly after Wilson's return from Paris in July. The president granted Palmer at least two formal private appointments that summer, one in mid-July and another in late August, and doubtless they shared many other private moments as well. What exactly Palmer told the president face to face about his ambitious plan to round up and deport thousands of immigrant Reds is unclear. Certainly, it had to come up in conversation. It is hard to conceive that Palmer

---

*Radio would not become widespread in America until the mid-1920s. Only four broadcasting stations operated in 1920; that number would explode to over 500 by the end of 1922. By 1933, President Franklin D. Roosevelt would be able to reach the country instantly with radio fireside chats broadcast coast-to-coast and heard by millions.

A healthy Woodrow Wilson in 1916, throwing out the first ball of the baseball season.

would have hid it from the president, or that the president would fail to ask. Woodrow Wilson studied newspapers as sharply as anyone, and they were all full of Red Menace talk that summer, with Palmer's own bluster making up a good part of it.

Besides, other cabinet members were also speaking that summer with the president about the problem. Robert Lansing, his secretary of state who had just returned with Wilson from Paris, was sounding alarms just as loud as Palmer's. Lansing, too, saw an imminent threat of communists rising up in America; "revolution in the air—it may even be a bloody revolution," he wrote in his journal. Lansing worried not about Palmer's zealousness but, on the contrary, Woodrow Wilson's lack of it: "The peril seems to me very great. On the other hand the president has as much as said that he is not afraid of this growing tendency [toward radical communism] but on the contrary he feels that it springs from the awakening consciousness of a right which is essentially just." To Lansing, this attitude defied reality and spelled disaster: "We will be faced with the greatest labor strikes that this country has ever seen. I do not doubt that there will be serious disorders, violence and blood-shed, because the demands of labor will be beyond reason."

Lansing, Postmaster General Albert Burleson, and Joe Tumulty, the president's private secretary, all backed Palmer in his anti-Red stance.

And what did Woodrow Wilson really think? Nobody quite knew, because the president never quite said. Whatever he felt privately about Palmer's plan, whether he supported it, opposed it, or simply didn't care enough to argue over it, the result was the same: He never gave Palmer any clear signal to slow down. Most likely, the president's mind was elsewhere. Wilson had devoted his first term almost exclusively to domestic reforms, his progressive agenda of helping workers and consumers, and trying to avoid foreign entanglements. "It would be the irony of fate if my administration had to deal chiefly with foreign affairs," he had confided to friends at the time. However, all this took a back seat once America had entered the World War. And in its aftermath, the president had now set his focus on achieving his singular life's mission of ending war altogether. With the Red Scare raging, he set off across the country to sell his League of Nations.

Three weeks later, disaster struck. Late on the night of September 25, 1919, after a speech in Pueblo, Colorado, Woodrow Wilson fell gravely ill. He complained of headaches and fatigue, and his doctors ordered him to return promptly to Washington. He needed rest, they insisted. Back at the White House a few days later, Wilson collapsed unconscious on a bathroom floor. He had suffered a thrombosis, similar to a catastrophic stroke, in his brain. For almost a month, his wife Edith kept him hidden in his bedroom. She allowed virtually nobody to see him except herself, the doctors, and occasionally Joe Tumulty. She excluded everyone else— cabinet members, senators, reporters, even old friends. Edith became his gatekeeper, and the White House issued a stream of bland public statements saying the president was resting and getting better. "I am not interested in the president of the United States. I am interested in my husband and his health," she insisted. When decisions emerged from the White House during these weeks, it was impossible to figure out who had made them: the president, his wife, or Joe Tumulty.*

This arrangement soon became impossible to keep up. By the end of

---

*Secretary of State Lansing approached Tumulty around this point and suggested having the vice president assume Wilson's powers, citing the Constitution's provision for a president's "inability to discharge" his duties. But Tumulty grew indignant. "Mr. Lansing, you may rest assured that while Woodrow Wilson is lying in the White House on the broad of his back I will not be a party to ousting him. . . . And I am sure that Dr. Grayson will never certify to his disability." The vice president himself, former Indiana governor Thomas R. Marshall, was never close to Woodrow Wilson's inner circle, rarely attended cabinet meetings, and was best known for observing during a Senate debate in 1917 that "what this country needs is a really good five-cent cigar."

October, Edith and the doctors decided that the president was well enough to see at least one of his cabinet members, the one with the most urgent business, the one whom the president most trusted. It was Mitchell Palmer.

Wilson's illness left a vacuum at the center of American government just as a series of domestic crises struck, and Palmer seemed to be the one drawn in to fill the void. He came as close as anyone in October 1919 to being an authoritative voice from Washington. It fell on Palmer to announce plans to get tough on corporate profiteers as American consumers faced sky-high prices for food, clothing, and fuel. Palmer took the roles of federal food and fuel administrators, wartime posts resurrected to address these economic storms. And, most pressing of all, it was Palmer who seized the moment publicly to address the looming coal strike.

By late October, the United Mine Workers had all its pieces in place to launch a nationwide walkout on November 1. Palmer had decided on a daring preemptive action, but first he wanted the president's blessing for his plan. He asked for an appointment, though he had little hope of getting one. Palmer had been shut away from Woodrow Wilson for weeks, just like all the other cabinet secretaries. When a reporter asked him about Wilson's health after a Columbus Day speech he gave that month, Palmer had snapped back: "You read the papers, don't you?" When the reporter followed up by asking, "Does any cabinet member know any more about it than what he reads in the paper?" Palmer simply shrugged and said, "No."

But on October 30, the call came from the White House that the president would see him. So for the first time in over a month, Mitchell Palmer came to the White House and walked up the staircase to the president's bedroom. Here, they allowed him twenty minutes. Other than Admiral Cary Grayson, Wilson's doctor, who never left the room, they would be alone. Palmer must have gasped at seeing his old friend. Instead of the handsome, dynamic Woodrow Wilson he had known for twenty years—dashing, brilliant, and articulate—he saw lying in bed before him a crippled man, unable to hold himself upright, his left side paralyzed, his hands white and clammy, his face contorted and covered with white whiskers, eyes distant. What exactly they said remains a mystery. Whether the president actually agreed to Palmer's plan on the coal strike, or whether he could even follow the conversation, no one knew except Wilson, Palmer, and Grayson.

Afterward, Palmer put the best public face on the president's health. "Alarming rumors concerning the president's condition quite unfounded," he wrote to Roland Sletor Morris, the U.S. Ambassador to Japan that week. "Physically weak, but in every other respect in splendid shape." On the coal strike, he claimed a mandate. "I went over the whole situation with the president," Palmer told newspaper reporters the next day, "and the president gave his approval to what had been done. He also made certain suggestions of his own which I cannot discuss at this time."

This was enough of a mandate for Palmer to launch his attack. The day before the planned coal strike, he sent his Justice Department lawyers into Federal District Court in Indiana to seek an injunction against it, citing the Lever Act, the wartime price-fixing statute: "The strike is a violation of law and there can be no compromise with those who violate the law," he announced. Woodrow Wilson's White House issued a statement as well, calling the strike "not only unjustified but unlawful," though, according to historian Gene Smith, "No one believed the president wrote it. (He did not. Tumulty did.)"

"The proposed strike, if carried to its logical conclusion, will paralyze transportation and industry," Palmer went on. "[It] will put cities in darkness, and if continued only for a few days, will bring cold and hunger to millions of our people; if continued for a month, it will leave death and starvation in its wake. It would be a more deadly attack upon the life of the Nation than an invading army."

Within the day, Federal District Judge Albert B. Anderson issued an order declaring the strike illegal and forbidding any leader of the United Mine Workers from participating in it. John L. Lewis, the union's recently elected new president, acted coyly. He ordered his union leaders to comply with Judge Anderson's order, at least technically. Then they sat on their hands as 400,000 miners walked off the job, which led to a blistering round of Red-bashing newspaper headlines: COAL STRIKE IS A COMMUNIST PLAN, screamed the Los Angeles Times; and APATHY OF MEMBERS, IT IS SAID, ALLOWS REDS TO CONTROL LABOR UNIONS, echoed the Pittsburgh Post.

"The people want a showdown," Ole Hanson, the mayor of Seattle during its January 1919 general strike, told a crowd at New York's Waldorf-Astoria hotel that week, demanding Washington crack down on strikers. "They want no more compromises and un-American surrenders. Toleration of anarchy had brought its usual rewards. . . . If the Reds were where they ought to be, they would need no coal for heat."

Palmer, too, toughened his rhetoric. "There are men in this country who have no sympathy for our form of government," he told officials in

Harrisburg, Pennsylvania, the heart of steel strike country, pointing to strike leaders William Z. Foster and John L. Lewis. "They would transplant the chaos of Russia to American soil. They have gained influence in the councils of organized labor . . . as blatant advocates of ultraradical doctrine seeking to force the hands of sane and patriotic leaders in their organizations."

Mitchell Palmer took the public lead, and the White House signaled no complaint. Somebody had to deal with the grimy, violent issues twisting the mind and soul of the nation that winter. Why not him? Palmer and that young man of his, John Edgar Hoover. They seemed more than willing to get their hands dirty.

EDGAR COULD BE excused for thinking New York City a strange, exotic place. One time when he was just ten years old, his parents went by themselves on a two-week holiday to New York and Boston. One day during the trip Edgar received a letter from his mother written on fancy stationery from a place called the Hotel Empire on a fancy street called Broadway. "My dear little Edgar," he read, "while Mama is writing you this letter, the steam cars are flying past my window. The elevated road passes right by the window, the street cars in front of the door—New York is a very busy place—Yesterday afternoon we took a ride on the sight seeing Automobile all through Central Park, along River side Park and Fifth Avenue, such beautiful houses, it seemed like Fairy Land to see such lovely places, hope some day when you are older you may be able to see all the wonderful sights of New York. . . . Yours lovingly, Mama."

Fourteen years later, Edgar still regarded New York City as alien territory. He had visited New York a few times during World War I on business for the Enemy Alien Bureau. In New York, he saw Germans,

Russians, and Jews living in packed, filthy neighborhoods where no one spoke English and the streets smelled from garbage and were jammed with pushcarts. It was in places like New York that the traitors lived, the German alien enemies and the disloyal seditionists his agency held for deportation on Ellis Island.

After the Armistice, Military Intelligence considered New York so infected with dangerous Reds that it developed a plan to defend the city against an imminent Bolshevik uprising. The plan called for ten thousand soldiers to defend Manhattan, another five thousand for Brooklyn, and mobile machine gun nests to patrol neighborhoods where Russian Jews lived. Already, the military had sent six thousand Springfield rifles to New York to bolster local National Guard units. The War Department expanded this plan during 1919 to be able to defend against simultaneous uprisings in other immigrant enclaves like Detroit, Chicago, and Boston.

In early October 1919, Edgar again came up to New York City, this time to study the evidence in the Emma Goldman case. It was his first visit since becoming chief of the Radical Division, and his staff of local agents there decided to show him a good time. As a student at George Washington Law School, Edgar had joined a fraternity called Kappa Alpha and he enjoyed palling around with the other young men, but his priggish morals sometimes got in the way. "[He] took a dim view of such antics as crap games, poker, and drinking bouts," one member remarked a few years later. Now, Edgar's agents in New York City had something better to offer him than booze or vice. They would show him some real-life action.

Edgar's men worked out of a large office on the fourteenth floor of the building at 14 Park Row, just below City Hall in lower Manhattan. One of the agents had recently infiltrated the local chapter of the Union of Russian Workers and caught wind that a group of Russian radicals planned to stage a protest that day against America's postwar military presence on Russian soil. They had no parade permit, though, and the agent had tipped off the New York City Police Department, which decided to stop it.

This would be a fine show for the visiting VIP from Washington. Edgar's agents picked a good vantage point to catch the fireworks. These protestors would all be members of the Union of Russian Workers, the very group that Edgar had chosen as the target for his first big deportation raid. Now, as the agents planned it, their boss would see these people close up, their dirty clothes and long-nosed faces, hear their shrill voices and catch their foul smells.

The parade started peacefully that afternoon as the Russian protestors, numbering about five thousand, pressed their way up Fifth Avenue under a gray sky until reaching Eighth Street. Here, they suddenly found their way blocked by three hundred club-wielding New York City police officers, including about a hundred on horseback. Without warning, the police charged, galloping up on their horses, swinging their clubs, smashing heads, driving the horses to kick up their steel-shod hooves. A few of the Russians resisted, but the police quickly arrested them. Then, as if on cue, a crowd of soldiers, sailors, and other local toughs happened to appear on the sidewalk and happily rushed into the street to join the police in kicking and punching the Russians.

The battle ended after about twenty minutes with eight protesters arrested, all charged with "criminal anarchy," the state's antisedition law. "[T]here had been a clash between the police of New York and a parade of Russians at Washington Square," Edgar scribbled in his notes later that day. He added, "It resulted disastrously for the Russians." This violence hardly seemed out of place in October 1919. Martial law and domestic strife governed half a dozen American cities that month for different reasons, be it the steel strike, the police strike, or race riots, including Pittsburgh, Gary, Omaha, and Boston.

Edgar's agents weren't finished with him, though. For a nightcap, after dinner, they took Edgar uptown to the Central Opera House, the large sports stadium and music hall on East Sixty-seventh Street. No basketball game, boxing match, or concert was scheduled for tonight, though.

Mounted police in 1919, here breaking up a protest in Philadelphia.

Instead, local socialists had rented the hall to stage yet another protest rally, this one to demand freedom for Tom Mooney, a San Francisco I.W.W. organizer who sat on death row in California convicted of throwing a bomb at a Preparedness Day parade in 1916. Leftists widely believed that Mooney had been framed by prosecutors. Similar protests on Mooney's behalf had been blocked that day by city officials in Portland, San Francisco, and Seattle.

Edgar marveled at the 3,000 cheering people who packed the hall, waving red banners and shouting radical slogans, primarily Russians, Jews, Finns, Poles, Italians—all jabbering away in broken English or foreign tongues. The speakers onstage included leading Parlor Bolsheviks like liberal lawyer Dudley Field Malone, recently jailed cartoonist Robert Minor, and socialist New York City alderman Algernon Lee. Many in the crowd wore fresh bandages or sported black eyes from their fight with city policemen that afternoon, and the speakers mostly ignored Tom Mooney to aim their verbal fire instead against police brutality and suppression of free speech.

Sitting in the crowd, Edgar found the whole affair laughable. Rally organizers announced from the podium that they had collected $300 in contributions "for the burial of babies killed on the afternoon of the parade," Edgar jotted in his notes. "As a matter of fact, however, no one had been killed, but the audience readily believed the violent statements." It alarmed Edgar not only that these radical speakers could spread such blatant untruths, but that they were allowed to talk in public at all. Free speech? To Edgar, it seemed ridiculous. Here he sat surrounded by the socialist-communist-anarchist rabble, the enemy within, rallying its troops right under his nose, hiding behind legal niceties. "None of the speakers over-stepped the line prescribed by law, though some of the persons in the audience who became over-enthusiastic did make remarks that were violations of law," Edgar noted, eyeing the hall like a one-man grand jury. "It is quite obvious that a law should be passed whereby the subjects advocating such methods as they did could be reached at the present time." If only he could get out of his chair and arrest some of these people.

The next morning, he got down to work. With the Emma Goldman deportation case coming up soon, Edgar spent a full day reviewing boxes of files being compiled at the New York bureau and on Ellis Island. He had promised Caminetti to build a legal case against Goldman so strong it would hold up in any court, and he meant to keep his word. He took the train back to Washington, D.C., that night and spent another full day behind closed

doors in Caminetti's office going over the case with A. P. Schell, the immigration inspector whom Caminetti had handpicked to conduct Goldman's
deportation hearing on Ellis Island. Together, they pawed over the evidence
Edgar had laid out in a seventy-page memorandum he wrote containing
forty exhibits, mostly speeches and articles from Goldman's thirty-year
career. "This office has given its entire attention for the last week to the
preparation of evidence in the Emma Goldman case and the same is now in
final form," he reported to Palmer on October 18.

Edgar planned to hang Emma Goldman on her own words. "I am a
'revolutionist' by nature and temperament and as such I claim the right
for myself and [my followers] to rebel and resist invasion by all means,
force included, consequently a destructionist," she had written. He
quoted her directly. He laid out the evidence linking her to President
McKinley's assassin, and documented how she had spent thirty-two years
on American soil since emigrating from Russia but never held a steady
job except for eighteen months—not counting her years of writing and
speaking—and she had never applied directly for citizenship.

On the biggest legal hurdle, proving that she was not an American citizen, Edgar had found records from a 1909 Justice Department legal
review that seemed like icing on the cake. Emma Goldman based her
claim of citizenship primarily on her 1887 marriage to Jacob Kersner, but
these records showed that the marriage ceremony had been performed by
a rabbi never properly ordained and who therefore had no right to do so
under New York State law. On the other hand, her divorce from Kersner
a year later had been fully lawful, performed by the chief rabbi of Baltimore. After that, the review said, "she fell in love with Alexander
Berkman" and lived with him out of wedlock.

To seal the case, Edgar produced documents demonstrating that Kersner's citizenship had been cancelled in 1909. "His naturalization seems to
have been secured by politicians," he argued. Kersner had never protested
to keep his citizenship; he may have been dead at the time it was taken
away from him, and Emma Goldman was not named in the suit.

Edgar arranged with Caminetti for a top-ranking Immigration Bureau
lawyer to attend the Ellis Island hearing in case anything unexpected
came up, and he planned to come himself. He was starting to like New
York City, this place where he could face the enemy eye to eye. Soon,
he'd be making the trip all the time. This might be a place where traitors
lived, but it was also a place where he planned to beat them.

· 12 ·
EMMA

"MISS GOLDMAN, DO you swear to tell the truth, the whole truth, and nothing but the truth, so help you God?"

"I affirm to tell the truth," she answered, carefully avoiding any reference to a Supreme Being.

Inspector A. P. Schell convened the hearing on the morning of October 27, 1919, on Ellis Island, that small spit of land in New York Harbor on which stood the Immigration Bureau's huge processing center. Schell sat at a wooden dais in the front of a formal examination room just off the side from Ellis Island's cavernous main hall. Emma Goldman spoke from a wooden chair next to him. She had cut her dark hair short and wore a pretty dress, but could not help looking like the tired, stout, fifty-year-old woman she had become, the decades of stress worn into her face, her lips hardened into a stern expression, part defiant, part fearful, her eyes glaring out from behind rimless glasses.

Edgar sat directly in front of her at the table for government lawyers, close enough to study her as she spoke, to see the lines in her face, the gray strands in her hair, the sagging flesh in her arms. He must have felt as though he knew her on some level, having spent so many hours studying her life. Did he go up to her, introduce himself, make small talk, maybe shake her hand? In 1909, as a fourteen-year-old boy, Edgar had ridden a streetcar all the way from downtown Washington across the river to Alexandria, Virginia, to watch Orville Wright make one of the first demonstration fights in his new flying machine, then afterwards he pushed his way forward through the crowd to shake the inventor's hand. If he shook Emma Goldman's hand that day, did he value the moment, as he had with Orville Wright?

"What is your full name?" Inspector Schell asked.

"Emma Goldman Kersner."

"What is your name today?"

"Emma Goldman."

Edgar followed Schell's questioning of Emma Goldman from the script they had developed beforehand, ready to jump in at any time to help clarify a point or supply a document. Flanking him at the government

Emma Goldman in 1917.

table were senior Labor Department lawyer A. Warner Parker, local federal prosecutor David Cahill, and John Creighton from his own Justice Department office in Washington who had taken the train up that day to see the performance. Edgar and Caminetti had spent a full month trying to arrange this hearing. Emma Goldman's lawyer, Harry Weinberger, had raised one delay after another. Caminetti origi-nally had set it for September 27 in Missouri at the state prison, the same day as her release, but Weinberger had insisted on moving it to New York City, causing a weeks-long hiatus.

As a result, Emma Goldman was able to pay her $15,000 bond in September and walk out of prison, whereupon she enjoyed a hero's reception. "In St. Louis we were almost mobbed by friends, reporters, and camera-men who came to meet us at the station," she wrote. "I could not bear to see so many people and I was eager to be left alone." Traveling east, she stopped in Chicago and then in Rochester, New York, where her sisters and her eighty-one-year-old mother still lived. Emma's mother, an

A younger Emma Goldman in 1911.

activist in her own right, could not help but brag about her famous daughter. When the chairman of a local group tried to cut off a long-winded speech she was giving one time, she happily crowed: "The whole United States Government could not stop my daughter Emma Goldman from speaking, and fine chance you have to make her mother shut up!"

Back in New York City, Emma Goldman found her life in shambles after her years behind bars. The government had seized her papers and banned her books and magazines. Her money had gone to pay lawyers, and she dared not write or speak, despite receiving plenty of invitations from left-wing groups. "I did not want to be trapped by spies and informants, who are always found in radical organizations," she told Mollie Steimer, a recently arrested Russian activist. Instead, she settled quietly into a small apartment with her sister to await her next meeting with the law.

Now, after just four weeks of freedom, Emma Goldman found herself testifying on Ellis Island. She listened closely as Inspector Schell began showing her each of the forty-four speeches and articles Edgar had identified to prove she was an anarchist, and having her confirm that, yes, in fact, she had written them. "I found the inquisitors sitting at a desk piled high with my dossier," Goldman wrote in her memoirs. "The documents, classified, tabulated, and numbered, were passed on to me for inspection. They consisted of anarchist publications in different languages, most of them long out of print, and of reports of speeches I had delivered a decade previously. No objection had been made to them at the time by the police or the federal authorities. Now they were being offered as proof of my criminal past and as justification for banishing me from the country. It was a farce I could not participate in, and I consequently refused to answer any questions. I remained silent throughout the 'hearing.'"

After a break of several days, which Goldman's lawyer requested, Inspector Schell reconvened the testimony and asked her next about her radical views:

"Miss Goldman, are you an anarchist?"

"I decline to answer," she said.

"Do you deny that you are an anarchist?"

"I decline to answer."

"Do you believe in the overthrow by force or violence of the Government of the United States?"

"I refuse to answer."

"Do you advocate the assassination of public officials?"

"I refuse to answer."

Inspector Schell found nineteen different ways to ask the same question, and Emma Goldman's response never varied. At the end, he announced his finding: "This alien has refused to answer any question pertaining to the charges contained in the warrant, notwithstanding the fact that every opportunity was afforded her. The record which contains her speeches and writings shows conclusively that the charges in the warrant have been sustained. I RECOMMEND DEPORTATION."

But Emma Goldman had one more trick up her sleeve that day. Before the hearing even started, she had decided it would be a sham and wrote a statement that her lawyer, Harry Weinberger, handed out to newspaper reporters. She hoped it would land on front pages across the country. In it, she protested what she called "these star chamber proceedings, whose very spirit is nothing less than a revival of the ancient days of the Spanish Inquisition or the more recently defunct Third Degree system of Czarist Russia."

> If the present proceedings are for the purpose of proving some alleged offense committed by me, some evil or antisocial act, then I protest the secrecy and third-degree methods of this so-called "trial."
>
> If—as I have reason to believe—this is purely an inquiry into my social and political opinions, then I protest still more vigorously against these proceedings, as utterly tyrannical and diametrically opposed to the fundamental guarantees of a true democracy.

*Every human being is entitled to hold any opinion that appeals to her
or him without making herself or himself liable to prosecution. . . .
The free expression of hopes and aspirations of a people is the
greatest and only safety in a sane society.*

That night, after the hearing ended, Emma Goldman's friends held a
dinner for her at the Brevoort Hotel. They sold tickets for the affair at
$3.00 apiece and beer for another $2.75. Over two hundred people
jammed the ballroom, plus the usual coterie of spies and undercover
agents: at least one from the Lusk Committee, two from the Justice
Department, and one from Military Intelligence. One of the Justice
Department agents described the crowd as "distinctive personalities,
ranging from bobbed hair and tailored suits to French headdresses and
evening gowns." To Margaret Scully, the Lusk Committee spy, "the
majority were Russian Jews and looked it."

"We had opposed the plan for an exclusive affair," Goldman herself
wrote. "We preferred Carnegie Hall or some large theater where a popular
admission price would allow large numbers to attend."

Emma Goldman, given her turn at the podium, spoke mostly that
night about prison. "In the isolation and loneliness of the cell one finds
the courage to face the nakedness of one's soul," she had confided earlier.
"Emma brought greetings from all the prisoners, who said they never
wanted to be released until all the prisoners were released," the Justice
Department agent reported. "Prisons do not curb the fighting instinct,
they are smoldering always within the walls."

She ended with this: "To the Dep't of Justice men present I wish to say
for their benefit that I am going to continue preaching revolution, as long
as I am in the U.S. and out of jail."

Edgar read the reports on Emma Goldman's speech at the Brevoort
Hotel that night. He had no intention of letting her stay free to preach
revolution, especially after her smearing the deportation hearing as a star
chamber proceeding and getting her invective published. "Her statement
was handed out to newspaper men for publication before the hearing had
been completed," he complained later, "thus showing the fact that she
was determined to circulate propaganda against the government." When
he heard that she was planning to launch a speaking tour while her legal
appeals were pending, he put his foot down. "In view of information
which I have received from New York, I believe it would be advisable to
endeavor to have the case against Emma Goldman closed and forwarded

to you for disposition at the earliest possible moment," he urged Caminetti, the immigration chief, who agreed. "[T]his bureau will leave no stone unturned in this direction," he wrote back.

Emma's days were numbered. Edgar would see to it.

By now, though, he had bigger fish to fry. Plans were well under way for his next big strike, a raid against the Union of Russian Workers. Edgar, through Frank Burke, had already in late October sent Caminetti a first list of radicals for deportation. Caminetti, on receiving it, had scribbled a note in the corner: "Full information regarding these aliens transmitted to Mr. Hoover/Dept. of Justice by phone today. A.M.C." Edgar gave his own agents until November 3, 1919, to assemble their final target lists along with proper evidence: "affidavits setting forth the names of the secretaries, delegates and organizers of each local [proving that] the person is a member of the Union of Russian Workers and is actively engaged in propaganda work for this organization." Punctilious to the last, precisely on November 3, Edgar sent a near-final list naming eight radicals from the Newark territory, twenty from New York, and six from Baltimore, along with a formal request: "It is the desire of the Bureau of Investigation to shortly have taken into custody the leaders of each of the locals of the Union of Russian Workers," he wrote. "In order that actual results may be accomplished in purging the communities of these undesirable elements, this department requests the cooperation of the immigration inspectors at the time when the round-up of these persons will be made."

Caminetti saluted. "The [Immigration] Bureau is prepared to join you in the work suggested and would be pleased to meet you on the subject at your convenience," he wrote, and handed the note to a special messenger to race across town to Edgar. Caminetti already had conferred with John Abercrombie, his superior in the Labor Department, who had to sign off on each of the deportation warrants, and Abercrombie offered no objection. To his immigration inspectors, Caminetti gave a final all clear signal. "Proceed at once," he told them.

By early November, Edgar's tie to Caminetti had grown so close that Caminetti's own staff on Ellis Island installed a direct telephone wire to Edgar's desk in Washington, "in the belief," they reported, "that Mr. Hoover could secure your views upon this matter and transmit them to this office much more quickly than if we resorted to the ordinary telephone (including the expense thereof) or the telegraph."

Time was nigh. The pieces were in place. The raids were on.

· 13 ·
THE FIRST RAID

The long expected master stroke of the United States against Anarchy in America has come.
—*New York World, November 8, 1919*

The raids were made at the direction of A. Mitchell Palmer, Attorney General.
—*Department of Justice statement, November 8, 1919*

T HEY CHOSE TO send a message with the date: Friday, November 7, the second anniversary of Russia's Bolshevik takeover, the day, according to Mitchell Palmer, that he began fighting back. Palmer's agents struck in fifteen cities simultaneously, from Boston to Detroit, Cleveland to Chicago, Newark to San Francisco. They waited until 9:00 P.M. in each time zone, just after dinner, when people came out to visit friends, enjoy theater shows, or attend meetings. They came armed with clubs, police backup, and over two hundred Labor Department deportation warrants naming leaders of the Union of Russian Workers, tonight's target. The warrants had been mailed or telegraphed to the selected cities, timed carefully to arrive just hours in advance of the raid to avoid tipping off possible spies. Palmer's men had alerted the State and War departments to seal off the borders with Canada and Mexico to prevent any suspects from trying to escape.

Edgar carefully kept his name out of all the press releases and news accounts of that day; Palmer wanted the headlines for himself. But no one could deny this was Edgar's job from start to finish.

New York City yielded the biggest haul. There, Justice Department agents, joined by local bomb squad detectives, converged on the Russian Peoples House, a community center on East Fifteenth Street near Union Square. The Union of Russian Workers had its office on the top floor of the building and Palmer's undercover men expected dozens of members to show up that night for a meeting. The rest of the four-story building housed classrooms, lecture halls, game rooms, a basement cafeteria, and lobbies.

Shortly before 9:00 P.M., squads of federal agents and local detectives drove up in long black motor sedans and parked all around the building. They placed guards at every door to cut off escape routes as the raiding party formed outside on the street. It consisted of about thirty men including both federal agents in white shirts, ties, and winter coats and police wearing blue uniforms, copper badges, and carrying long wooden batons. The Justice Department's top detective, Big Bill Flynn, came up from Washington, D.C., to oversee the operation and, at his signal, the raiders pushed their way inside through the front door. Once in the building, their leader, Agent Frank Francisco, showed his badge to the handful of young Russians who happened to be in the lobby. Jeers, taunts, and hisses greeted him. "When . . . our backs were turned, several pop bottles were thrown at us," Agent Francisco reported.

Francisco, by his own later account, gave a small speech at this point to the growing crowd: "[I] informed these men that there was to be no violence or resistance, that we were there to make an investigation, and we wanted their cooperation; that we did not want to apprehend anybody that was innocent." But the catcalls kept coming. "I heard several voices in the rear call the Department of Justice and police 'sons of b___' and other vile names," he recalled. He ordered the police immediately to grab the disturbers, drag them outside, and arrest them.

Francisco and his men now began scouring the building from top to bottom. This was how a "roundup" worked. They would detain everyone they found, haul them into the cars waiting outside, drive them downtown to headquarters, search and question each one, and then figure out whom to hold and whom to release. This would prevent any guilty party from slipping away unnoticed. As a result, they felt free to treat any person they found in this four-story, big-city public building as a suspect, and handle them like any other potential bomb-throwing Red.

And like any other dragnet, part of the goal was to teach these Reds and Russians a lesson they would not soon forget.

After securing the lobby, Agent Francisco and his men climbed the stairs to the third floor where they found two night-school classes in session, each with about twenty-five students. He sent his detectives barging first into one, a Russian-English language class, demanding attention. "Out in the hall, everybody," the lead detective shouted, according to witnesses. "Line up there, and don't make any noise!" When one student, a young Russian woman, objected, he yelled: "Shut up, there, you, if you know what's good for you." The students obeyed. They stood up from their desks, took their books, filed out into the hallway, and followed the detective's orders to walk downstairs. But here, things got messy. The stairway was steep, dark, and narrow. As the students began filing down, a few policemen started pushing them, making them fall atop each other, plummeting down the stairs, banging heads and faces on the hard wooden floor, tumbling one over the other in an avalanche of bodies. One Justice Department agent, Edward Anderson, later claimed that it was a student who started the melee. He insisted he had been leading the group down and "upon reaching the head of the stairs [I] was violently pushed and thrown down the entire flight, causing bruises on [my] arm and leg." Most likely, he was simply caught in the scuffle.

Another student remembered it this way: "a few detectives came in, searched everybody, including me, after which I was struck on the head with a blackjack, and thrown downstairs." Another described how, when he stepped into the hallway, "I was struck on my head . . . by one detective, who knocked me down again, sat on my back, pressing me down to the floor with his knee and bending my body until blood flowed out of my mouth and nose. I was then taken to a sink to wash my face" he went on. "After this, I was thrown down stairs where I fell with my face down to the ground floor, after which I was arrested."

Meanwhile, back on the third floor, Agent Francisco now sent his detectives into the other room, this one an algebra class. The teacher inside, startled to see an agent entering his class waving a gun, tried to ask a question but the agent stopped him, grabbed his glasses, then "struck me on the head and simultaneously struck two others and beat me brutally," the teacher recalled later. Then the agent ordered all the students into the hallway. "After I was beaten and without strength to stand on my feet, I was thrown down stairs and while I rolled down, other men, I presume also agents of the Department of Justice, beat me with pieces of wood which I later found out were obtained by breaking the banisters," the teacher explained.

That done, Francisco and his men fanned out to cover the entire fourth floor, hit the Russian Union offices, the back lobbies, and every place in between, snaring and beating anyone they found. All the major newspapers sent reporters to cover the action; Palmer's agents had tipped them off in advance. They all caught the violence. "A number of those in the building were badly beaten by the police," the *New York Times* reporter wrote, "their heads wrapped in bandages testifying to the rough manner in which they had been handled." Asked about bloodstains all around the building, a Russian man told the *New York World* how the police used "a twelve-inch steel jimmy and a stair banister on the heads of the members." A janitor described how every one of the Russians taken outside had "a cut scalp at least." "Every man caught in that house was beaten up by the police," attorney Isaac Schorr later complained. "Not one of them offered resistance, but they were terribly beaten and many kicked downstairs."

The thrill of the fighting fed on itself. It wasn't enough just to bust heads. Palmer's agents came with orders to search and, in their zeal, they left no stone unturned. After they'd finished, the building looked "as if a bomb had exploded in each room," the *New York World* reported. "Desks were broken open, doors smashed, furniture overturned and broken, books and literature scattered, the glass doors of a cabinet broken, typewriters had apparently been thrown on the floor and stamped on. . . . In the back parlor of the first floor were bloodstains over floor papers, literature &c., and the washbowl was half full of bloody water." Many months later, Palmer and his men would deny having ransacked the building that night. They would swear that vandals had come in during the night after they left. But at the time, in November 1919, they made no denials, either for the damage or the beatings. If anything, they gloried in it.

By the time they

Destruction inside the Russian Peoples House after the November 1919 raid.

finished, Palmer's agents rounded up 211 suspects from the Russian Peoples House and took them all downtown to the Justice Department's bureau office on Park Row near City Hall. Here, they began to sift out the Reds. As the night wore on, they systematically questioned, fingerprinted, and photographed each one, conducting interviews in every spare corner of the suite. They brought in translators since many of the prisoners spoke no English, just Russian or Yiddish. Following orders from Washington, they promptly released anyone who could show he was an American citizen. After all, none of these suspects had been accused of committing any crime, so they had no grounds to hold them. The agents spent hours that night trying to identify actual members of the Union of Russian Workers and match Labor Department warrants to names and faces. They searched all the men's pockets and wallets and bags, and detained anyone they found carrying a Russian Union membership card, anyone whose name had appeared on a Russian Union membership list, and anyone whose face had been spotted by an undercover agent at a Russian Union meeting. If they didn't have a warrant for him already, they wired the man's name to Washington along with an affidavit to get one.

This process lasted until 4:30 A.M. During the whole time, they barred any lawyer, friend, or family member from seeing the prisoners. Orders from Washington directed that they hold the suspects *incommunicado*. To the outside world, it was as if they had dropped off the earth. Any friend who dared to come and ask about a detainee faced the risk of being arrested himself or brutally harassed. In Bridgeport, Connecticut, where similar postraid interrogations were going on that night, a man came to the local jail to ask about a detained friend and quickly found himself surrounded by six guards who peppered him with questions about local Russians. "[The lead agent] brought a rope and tied it around my neck, stating that he will hang me immediately if I do not tell him who conducts the meetings and who are the main workers in the organization," he later charged.

By daybreak in New York City, the Justice Department agents had freed all but 38 of the original 211 prisoners captured the night before at the Russian Peoples House. They now took these last 38, the actual documented Reds, ordered them to march downstairs and outside into the street, and led them the dozen or so blocks through the narrow alleys of lower Manhattan to Battery Park where they boarded the ferry to Ellis Island. A *Chicago Daily Tribune* reporter who witnessed the scene noted how most had "bandaged heads and black eyes." One prisoner shouted, "We're going back to Russia—that's a free country." At Ellis Island, these prisoners joined some 30 other Russians brought over from New Jersey, making a total of 65 prisoners whom the agents handed over to immigration officials for deportation. By Monday, with more arrivals from distant places, the number would top eighty.

Palmer's raids in other cities had been no less sweeping. In Detroit, his agents converged on Turner Hall, a large theatre where 1,500 people had gathered that night to enjoy a Russian-language play. The agents ringed the building, blocked the exits, then sent a Russian-speaking deputy inside who mounted the stage, interrupted the performance, and told the audience to stay calm: "Ladies and gentlemen: Government and police authorities are here to conduct an investigation," he announced in Russian. "The building is surrounded by policemen, and there are many others scattered through this audience. Any attempt to escape will be useless." He ordered the men to line up on the left side of the hall, told the ladies to leave, and told anyone with a Canadian passport they would be taken to the border and escorted out of the country. All the rest, several hundred, they detained for questions. By daybreak the next morning, after releasing the American citizens and those unconnected with the Russian Union, they had whittled the prisoners down to forty.

So it went in a dozen other cities. Near Pittsburgh, Justice agents and local police raided a pool hall and arrested twenty Russians, all fingered by steel company detectives as having been leaders during the recent strike. In Bridgeport, Connecticut, they rounded up sixty men, mostly from boarding houses on the city's east side. In each case—New York, Detroit, Bridgeport, Newark, Cleveland, and the rest—only a small fraction of those detained actually turned out to be members of the Union of Russian Workers. In no case did the federal agents carry criminal arrest warrants, and they carried no search warrants of any kind. They had no need. They were only "assisting" the Department of Labor in its deportation work. They had no legal authority themselves to be arresting any of these people.

And of the Red prisoners themselves, how many of them were actually violent revolutionaries? For Palmer's purposes, it didn't matter. When his agents that night asked the secretary of the Union of Russian Workers about it, he admitted that his group routinely gave a membership card to anyone who paid his dues, even if he came by just for a sip of schnapps or a game of pool, never actually read the Union's principles or manifestos, didn't know what they said, never asked, and never cared.

Friday night wasn't the end of it. On Saturday night, they struck again.

This time, it was the New York Lusk Committee that led the operation. They sent an army of about five hundred New York City policemen, thirty-five state troopers, and dozens of Bomb Squad detectives fanning out across Manhattan, Brooklyn, and the Bronx. Rather than the Union of Russian Workers, the Lusk raiders targeted two other groups: the Communist Party and the Socialist Left Wing Section. They hit seventy-one locations. "[T]hose found were hustled into patrol wagons and taken to Police headquarters, hurried to the gymnasium on the top floor and there questioned at length, their statements being taken by stenographers," explained a *New York World* reporter who went along for the ride. They followed a process similar to Palmer's the night before, though the Lusk raids saw far less violence. Lusk's men reported hauling in almost a thousand prisoners, but, after the all-night questioning and searching, they found grounds to hold only thirty-seven. They had to release all the rest for lack of evidence. "Oh, many of them tore up their membership cards or attempted to" while being taken into custody, Senator Lusk himself explained sheepishly the next day, trying to explain the small yield.

Between the two raids on Friday and Saturday nights, November 7 and 8, federal agents and local police had taken prisoner over twelve hundred men and women in New York City alone, detained them, interrogated them, and scared them out of their wits. Of these, barely seventy-five actually had belonged to any of the targeted radical groups, let alone knew what they stood for. And out of all those held, only two had been charged with any violation of American law, in this case the New York State criminal anarchy statute. One was James Larkin, a well-known Irish Sinn Fein activist who had led a strike against British shipping in 1914. The other was Benjamin Gitlow, author of the "Left Wing Manifesto."

Edgar had spent the entire day Friday in Washington, D.C., in his Justice Department office, glued to his desk and telephone, sweating every detail of the operation. He fretted over loose ends, working till the last minute to make sure each raider was armed with warrants, instructions, and information. He had spent hours at Caminetti's office the night before and fumed over what he saw as sloppy preparation. Caminetti had not mailed out the first batch of warrants to Chicago until Wednesday afternoon, just forty-eight hours before the operation, and had failed to post similar packages of warrants to Pittsburgh, Boston, New York, Baltimore, and Buffalo until Thursday, though these he sent under a Special Delivery stamp.

Edgar dreaded mistakes. He had never run anything this big before in his life, where anything fouled up would reflect squarely on him. He fretted that the warrants would fail to reach his agents in time. First thing Friday morning, he picked up his telephone and called each of the eleven of his field bureaus involved in the operation and found the agents furious. Immigration inspectors had failed to keep appointments with them, claiming they had received no instructions from Washington. Edgar fired off an angry note to Caminetti: "I have repeatedly requested that the officers of your service located at the towns where these persons are residing be instructed by telegram to confer and cooperate with the local offices of the Bureau of Investigation," he wrote. "I have this morning . . . been advised that immigration inspectors *have not* apparently received any warrants or instructions *from you* dealing with the [raids] and the responsibility for failure in this matter *can not* be assumed by this Department [of Justice] if your officers have not been advised." Edgar insisted that Caminetti "take personal charge of the matter," as he put it, and fix it.

Edgar had known Caminetti for just a few weeks at this point, but already he thought nothing of browbeating the old man. He handed the note to a messenger and sent him scrambling through Washington's morning rush hour traffic to place it directly in Caminetti's hand at the Immigration Bureau, and then sent Caminetti a full, final list of all the names targeted for warrants. "I am sending this merely for your use in checking over your lists," he explained. He probably also picked up the telephone and barked directly into Caminetti's ear.

Caminetti, for his part, stayed calm. He seemed to tolerate Edgar the same way a parent might indulge a pushy, petulant child. Like Edgar, he too spent the day in Washington at his desk, glued to his telephone, working his staff of clerks and messengers. After getting Edgar's finger-pointing note that morning, Caminetti dictated a terse response and sent a messenger to run it back across town to Edgar: "The [Immigration] Bureau is checking up and will attend to this matter by wire and long distance telephone and will notify you later as to results."

In the end, things went smoothly. As the night wore on, Edgar's office became a nerve center as messages poured in from around the country. His desktop became a clearinghouse for data on the numbers of Reds caught, literature seized, and legal questions to untangle. When his agents in Chicago and Newark reported that they had captured thirty-four Reds beyond those whose names had appeared in their original lists and needed Labor Department warrants to hold them, Edgar took care if it promptly, sending the names and supporting affidavits to Caminetti under plans they worked out beforehand. "I would appreciate it if you would arrange to have warrants in these cases telegraphed to the respective offices as these persons are being held awaiting the arrival of the same," he wrote. Before the weekend was out, almost four hundred additional warrants would be issued, bringing the total to about six hundred.

Edgar also received news about what his agents were finding in their adventures. Some of it was electrifying. In Newark, New Jersey, they reported discovering a counterfeiting plant complete with plates, presses, and a large stash of banknotes ready for circulation, plus five pistols: three revolvers and two automatics. In Trenton, New Jersey, they unearthed what appeared to be a bomb factory at the home of one Russian Union official, complete with gunpowder, copper and brass wire, electric batteries, and wax paper. "Red flags, guns, revolvers, and thousands of pieces of literature were also taken by the Department of Justice agents," he reported.

Working long into the predawn hours that Friday night, Edgar quickly launched himself into the next phase of the assault: winning the propaganda war. By dawn, he and his staff had used the flood of incoming reports to prepare press statements, raw meat to feed the newspapers. The Russian Reds had PLANNED TO BOMB FIFTH AVE. STORES, screamed one headline, PLOT TO KILL HIGH OFFICIALS, TAKE PROPERTY, END RELIGION, howled another. "Proof that Lenin himself had dictated the Bolshevist operations in this city was said yesterday to be in the hands of agents," reported a third. As icing on the cake, Edgar prepared for release what his office described as a secret "Manifesto" seized from the Russian Union's Baltimore office. Translated from the original Russian-language text, it laid out an elaborate scheme to take power in America—"the most dangerous piece of propaganda ever disseminated by any radical organization in the United States," Palmer's assistant attorney general Frank Garvan announced in a statement Edgar's office prepared. Several newspapers printed long excerpts of it on their front pages:

> What should be our means of carrying on the fight? . . . We must consciously hasten the elementary movement of the struggle of the working class; we must convert small strikes into general ones; and convert the latter into an armed revolt of the laboring masses against capital and State.

At the time of this revolt we must at the first available opportunity proceed to an immediate seizure of all means of production . . . and make the working class the masters in fact of all general wealth. At the same time we must mercilessly destroy all remains of governmental authority and class domination, liberating the prisoners, demolish prisons and police offices, destroy all legal papers pertaining to private ownership of property, all field fences and boundaries, and burn all certificates of indebtedness . . . to blow up barracks, gendarme and police administration, shoot the most prominent military and police officers, must be the important concern of the revolting working people.

In the work of destruction we must be merciless, for the slightest weakness on our part may afterward cost the working class a whole sea of needless blood.

The country bubbled with excitement. Finally, people said, someone in Washington had stiffened his spine and hit back against these Reds. Mitchell Palmer could not have been more pleased. By Monday, under Edgar's direction, his agents had delivered more than three hundred alien radicals to immigration officials across the country for deportation, including over eighty to Ellis Island alone. Most were being held on bail of $10,000, far more than they could afford to pay. Newspaper reporters jammed into Palmer's Washington office to capture any pearls of wisdom from the famous Red fighter. Palmer promised "no let-up" in the raids, declaring, "This is the first big step to rid the country of these foreign trouble makers." He read the newspaper headlines and was delighted to see how almost without exception they painted him a hero. "It is gratifying to the public to know that the Department of Justice has what appears to be a complete grasp of the situation regarding the Bolshevik operations in America," the *Washington Herald* commented in a typical piece.

In fact, Palmer's stroke against the Reds was yielding him quick dividends all across the landscape. Problems seemed to disappear. On November 8, the day after the raid, the bitter national coal strike collapsed. Federal District Judge Albert Anderson in Indiana issued a new court order demanding that United Mine Workers Union President John L. Lewis affirmatively end the work stoppage. This time, Lewis decided not to play games. He did not mention Palmer's heavy-handed raid as his reason, but his timing made the connection clear. "I am just as good an American now as I ever was," Lewis insisted as he sent letters to each of his union locals telling them to return to work. Most of his half-million members obeyed and dropped the strike, though about a hundred thousand diehards continued regardless. Even these last holdouts would call it quits in mid-December in exchange for a flat 14 percent pay raise, a pittance compared to their original demands.

Mitchell Palmer's stock rose even as that of his president, Woodrow Wilson, continued to sink. The same week as the raid, the United States Senate voted to adopt a series of crippling reservations to the Treaty of Versailles that effectively destroyed any chance of American participation in Wilson's League of Nations. Many of Wilson's own Democrats abandoned him on the key votes. On November 19, about a week later, they rejected the entire treaty, thirty-eight in favor, fifty-three against. Democratic Party leaders took notice. A presidential election loomed ahead in 1920, and if Woodrow Wilson could no longer lead his party, then the party would find someone else. "Mr. Wilson's political leadership is even now passing on to Attorney General A. Mitchell Palmer, who is industriously reshaping Democratic policy," noted a *Washington Herald* political columnist that week. A *Providence Journal* reporter who spoke to several Democratic insiders studying the next presidential election found that a "considerable number are known personally to favor Mr. Palmer." Edgar's mentor was looking like a shoo-in as the next resident of the White House.

Palmer didn't waste the opening. By mid-December, he sent organizers to set up campaign offices in Illinois, South Dakota, and Pennsylvania. Already, the political handicappers saw a two-man race taking shape for the Democratic presidential nomination in 1920, pitting Palmer against William Gibbs McAdoo, the popular former secretary of the treasury and the president's son-in-law. McAdoo had led the Liberty Bond drives during World War I and, as director general of railroads, had made himself a favorite with the railroad and other unions. By leaving the cabinet soon after the Armistice to make money on Wall Street, McAdoo would avoid being tainted by any connection to the Red Scare or the League of Nations failure. He would be tough to beat, but, between them, insiders still gave the edge to Palmer. Palmer had delivered results. He had shown courage and energy facing down the radicals. His November Red Raid had been a sensation, and it had been only a dress rehearsal. The next raid, the big one, would be a blockbuster.

· 14 ·
CENTRALIA

I F ANYONE IN the country still needed one more incitement in late 1919 to push them into a fit of rage against Red radicals, they found it on November 11, Armistice Day. It came in news from a small logging town of 10,000 people nestled in the dense old-wood forests of Washington State.

The I.W.W., the radical Industrial Workers of the World who called for One Big Union, had long been strong around Centralia. Logging in 1919 was a dangerous job, working with saws, hatchets, and falling trees, and loggers were among the worst paid and most brutally treated of all employees. Timber owners controlled the towns, and police in lumber areas refused to tolerate strikes or unions. Tensions in Centralia had bubbled for half a decade. Two years earlier, a crowd had stormed the town's I.W.W. Hall during a Red Cross parade, claiming that a local Wobbly had started trouble by giving an antiwar speech. They had smashed the doors and windows, taken out all the furniture, and burned it in the street. More recently, local citizens had formed a Protective League and hatched plans to corral all the local Wobblies at gunpoint and force them out of town. Murders of I.W.W. leaders by company detectives were common in these parts, especially during strikes. In August 1917, an I.W.W. organizer working with striking copper miners in Butte, Montana, named Frank Little was taken from his hotel room at gunpoint and hanged from a railroad bridge. Earlier, strikebreakers in Everett, Washington, had murdered five I.W.W. organizers who were trying to organize lumber workers there. Wobblies routinely carried guns to protect themselves.

Still, most people in Centralia expected Armistice Day 1919 to be a happy affair. It was the first anniversary of the ceasefire with Germany. Flag-waving women and children lined the streets for an American Legion parade with a brass band, a Boy Scout troop, and, as its grand finale, the Legionnaires themselves, including soldiers wearing freshly starched military uniforms, army khakis and navy blues, many of the men just back from long tours of duty overseas in Europe, Mexico, Russia, and other hot spots. But at one point the parade route passed right in front of the I.W.W. Hall, a small building up a hill from Tower Avenue, the town's main street. The I.W.W. men suspected a trick, that the Legionnaires might use the parade to launch an attack, just as they had during the Red Cross parade two years earlier. They brought pistols and waited inside the building and on a nearby rooftop. "The I.W.W. expected trouble here yesterday, and they were prepared for it," a local prosecutor would explain the next day. "When the parade was almost over without trouble appearing, they decided to start it themselves."

What exactly happened at first when the parade finally did pass the I.W.W. Hall is not clear. There was confusion. Marchers passed by, then stopped, backed up. Some broke ranks. There were shouts and threats, and a few soldier-paraders moved toward the I.W.W. Hall. And, as they did, inside the building a nervous trigger-finger flinched. A shot rang out, then another. Soon, bullets came zipping down from the rooftop onto the parade. One soldier fell dead and a dozen others dropped on the pavement in pools of blood.

Seeing where the shots came from, dozens of servicemen broke from the parade and stormed the I.W.W. Hall. They busted in through the door and scoured the building looking for the assailants. They found sixteen men inside and beat them to a bloody pulp before taking them into custody, dragging them through the street to the town's jail, locking them inside, and posting guards out front to prevent a mob from hanging them on the spot. A few soldiers spotted a man running off, gun in hand. They chased him and finally cornered him on the banks of the Skookumchuck River, a nearby stream, as he was trying to ford his way across. Before they could grab him, the man, an I.W.W. officer named Wesley Everest, raised his gun, a revolver, and fired half a dozen shots at his pursuers. He hit one man and killed him. The soldiers grabbed Everest, punched him, kicked him, knocked out some of his teeth with a rifle butt, beat him some more, and took him off to jail.

Four soldiers died in the gunfire. One of them, Lieutenant Warren Grimm, had served almost a year in Siberia in the American Expeditionary Force, was a former University of Washington football star, and was a leader of the local Protective League. Another, Arthur McElfresh, had recently returned from sixteen months of foreign duty in Europe and Mexico.

Fury swept the Northwest and the country. Newspapers headlined the story as simple murder: RED SNIPERS KILL ARMISTICE PARADERS, led the *Atlanta Constitution*; NORTHWEST ROUSED AGAINST REDS; RADICALS PLOTTED CENTRALIA ATTACK, echoed the *New York Times*. Within twenty-four hours, police arrested 127 Wobblies in raids in four cities, including Seattle and Tacoma. Soldiers surrounded a nearby pool hall popular with logging men, forced more than a hundred of them to line up inside against a wall, searched their pockets, and arrested sixteen who carried I.W.W. cards. Armed vigilantes scoured timber camps throughout the region looking for radicals and seized any they could find.

But the most brutal backlash came in Centralia itself: At about 7:30 P.M. on the night after the attack, the electric lights in Centralia all flickered off at once, leaving the town dark. At precisely that moment, six darkened cars drove up and parked in front of the jail. A group of men got out, their faces covered, and overpowered a lone watchman. Inside they found Wesley Everest, the Wobbly who had shot a soldier while trying to escape. They took Everest from his cell, shoved him into one of the cars, and drove him to a bridge over the Chehalis River at the edge of town, cutting him with a knife along the way. There, they tied a rope around his neck, tied the rope's other end to the bridge, and threw him over the side. When he didn't die right away, they pulled him up, fitted his neck with a longer rope, and hanged him again. Somehow he still lived, so they hanged him a third time, though not before beating him savagely, breaking his bones until he screamed. Finally, after the third hanging, his body still twitching in the noose, they riddled him with bullets.

The whole country seemed caught up in the passions. Demands flooded Washington: "We must smash every un-American and anti-American organization in the land. We must put to death the leaders of this gigantic conspiracy of murder, pillage, and revolution," cried a full-page advertisement printed in several Northwest newspapers including the *Tacoma Ledger* and the Seattle *Post Intelligencer* and *Business Chronicle*. The ad listed as its villains "the I.W.W., the Non Partisan League, the so-called Triple Alliance [a local farmers' group], the pro-German socialists, the closed shop unions, the agitators, the malcontents, anarchists, syndicalists, seditionists, traitors, the whole motley crew, Bolshevists and near-Bolshevists." American Legionnaires blamed the Centralia killings on "the failure of the Federal government to prosecute or deport men preaching sedition." Two days later, federal agents responded by raiding the offices of the *Seattle Union Record*, a pro-union newspaper that dared to suggest that the Centralia killings were "the result of a long series of illegal acts" by antilabor zealots. The raiders seized the newspaper's plant, arrested its editor and top employees, and charged them with violating the Espionage Act.

Labor leaders feared even worse violence. "A dangerous state of public excitement has been lashed into being that menaces the peace of this community," one complained in a telegram to Palmer. "Feeling is running high over the murder at Centralia, and is growing bitter among the workers as a result of this cowardly attempt to fasten the guilt on their innocent shoulders."

In Washington, D.C., the flood of anger reached the highest levels of government, going beyond even Mitchell Palmer's Justice Department. Secretary of State Robert Lansing virtually shook with rage at the news, calling the shootings "an act of cold-blooded, ruthless barbarity, without excuse and without defense." To Lansing, it made the threat crystal clear. "[T]he American people now are awake to the reality of the peril," he wrote in his private notebook. "Too long have we [allowed] these fanatics to enjoy the liberty which they now seek to destroy."

Edgar himself, sitting back at the Justice Department, jumped on the chance to learn every last detail of the massacre. "If you can obtain for me all the facts surrounding the Centralia matter [then] I will be very glad to answer these communications if you so desire," he wrote to one Justice Department colleague, though he avoided taking any direct responsibility for the investigation itself. Edgar had his own full plate that month, and he meant to keep his eye on his mission: striking the final blow against radicals in America. He would avenge the Centralia victims in his own way through his final knockout punch: the Big Raid.

· 15 ·
CRIMINAL
COURT

BENJAMIN GITLOW FOLLOWED the two policemen as they led him
into the courtroom. He sat down alongside eighteen other prisoners
snatched by Lusk Committee raiders in their Saturday-night sweep,
looking tired and bedraggled after three nights in jail. Chief City Magistrate William McAdoo—no relation to presidential hopeful William
Gibbs McAdoo—presided on the bench. McAdoo was the same judge
who had issued the original arrest warrants for the raids three days earlier and now he would hear the prisoners' pleas for bail. Gitlow faced a
battery of celebrity prosecutors in the cramped courtroom that
morning, starting with Charles Newton, the attorney general of New
York State, who came down from Albany to grab his share of the lime-
light. At Newton's side sat Lusk Committee chief counsel Archibald
Stevenson and a gaggle of aides. Newton had decided to single out
Gitlow and throw the book at him. He had charged him with criminal

anarchy,* advocating the overthrow of the government by force or violence, through the publication of his magazine, *The Revolutionary Age*, and its fiery call to arms, "The Left Wing Manifesto." For this, Benjamin Gitlow faced twenty years in prison.

Gitlow knew all along that this could happen. He had seen scores of socialists and radicals jailed during and since World War I, from Eugene Debs to Emma Goldman to I.W.W. president Bill Haywood and over a hundred of his members. Federal prosecutors had won more than five hundred Espionage Act convictions during the World War. Gitlow himself had barely escaped being arrested once already in an earlier Lusk Committee sweep. He knew the police watched him constantly, and that plenty of the people who came around his party offices smoking cigarettes or making small talk were undercover police spies. "The Communist Labor Party has a kitchenette on the 3d floor of 43 west 29th St.," one had reported just a few weeks earlier after poking his head in to buy a copy of *The Voice of Labor*, Gitlow's latest publication. "Several young men were preparing food there this evening. This evening young men were shooting pool there. There were young men and women going in and out of the place."

The Lusk raiders had made their latest raid the costliest yet for the Communist Labor Party. Party leaders made up most of the detained prisoners. John Reed had been one of the few lucky ones to escape, having left the country a few days earlier on a trip to Russia. Otherwise he, too, would have been caught.

To represent him before Judge McAdoo that day, Benjamin Gitlow had retained the services of Charles Recht, the Socialist Party's regular lawyer whose clients these days seemed to include virtually every communist in New York City. Recht was a tireless thirty-two-year-old who had spent his boyhood in czarist Russia before coming to America and working his way through New York University Law School. Already he had won freedom that week for eleven of the Lusk prisoners by filing *habeas corpus* petitions, arguing successfully that the prisoners had not been charged with any

---

*The New York State Criminal Anarchy statute (Penal Code Article XIV, section 160 et seq.) in 1919 provided that: "Any person who: 1. By word of mouth or writing advocates, advises or teaches the duty, necessity or propriety of overthrowing or overturning organized government by force or violence, or by assassination of the executive head or of any of the executive officers of government, or by any unlawful means . . . [i]s guilty of a felony and punishable by imprisonment of not more than five years, or by a fine of not more than five thousand dollars, or both." The statute also made it a felony to publish or print any such advocacy, or organize or assemble any group of anarchists, or leave the state with the intent to advocate anarchy elsewhere.

crimes. But Recht worked under a handicap. Not only was he swamped with work defending dozens of communist clients, but he also had irritated Judge McAdoo by publicly maligning the raids as "Cossack methods . . . worthy of the palmiest days of Czarist Russia [and] an outrage to public decency." Gitlow now saw for himself how Judge McAdoo had gotten his dander up. When Recht early in the day tried to convince the judge to reduce the $15,000 bail he imposed on each of the prisoners, McAdoo found every excuse to slap him down.

"These men are poor and cannot raise the money," Recht had pleaded, "and they have been maltreated as prisoners, left without food for hours and not permitted their rights under due process of the law." But Samuel Berger, the New York State deputy attorney general, flatly denied the charge. "The prisoners were not maltreated," he insisted. "In view of the seriousness of this crime I say that the bail is quite lenient."

Judge McAdoo, sitting at his high wooden desk, settled the issue by quoting from his favorite new source document, the *Communist International*, adopted in Moscow and endorsed by the Communist Laborites at their Chicago convention. It called for global revolution and proletarian dictatorship. "I hold that the Communist Party has declared a state of war against the United States and the Government of the State of New York," he ruled from the bench, and he charged each individual prisoner, as a party member, with responsibility for every word of the *International*, whether he had read it or not. "I will not reduce the bail one dollar."

But that wasn't all. "Our Government is at war with Russia," McAdoo went on, referring to the American soldiers still serving in Siberia. When Recht interrupted to point out that, technically, no state of war actually existed between Russia and the United States, McAdoo pounced on him. "Who killed 111 American soldiers whose bodies are being brought back from Russia?" he demanded. "It was the Soviet Guards of Russia. Now let's get back to the law."*

Gitlow spent another night in jail, his fourth, before Judge McAdoo finally heard his case the next morning. He called on Charles Recht to take the floor again. Gitlow's "Left Wing Manifesto," Recht argued, was simply a restatement of old ideas penned by Karl Marx sixty years ago and

---

*America's intervention in Russia began in 1918 as part of an allied effort to bring Russia back into the World War. Initially, about 8,000 Americans joined some 70,000 Japanese troops in Siberia around Vladivostok, with French and British troops joining after the Armistice with Germany in November 1918. American forces had largely completed their withdrawal from Russia by June 1919, except for a small contingent that remained through the end of the year. Overall, 416 American soldiers died in the Russian campaign and another 359 were wounded.

long accepted by the Socialist Party of Eugene Debs, a legitimate, lawful organization in America. He described it as "peaceful writings containing abstract reasoning," claimed the government was trying "to make a crime of socialism," and argued that the charges against Gitlow be dismissed.

But once again, Recht found no sympathy in the courtroom. "We are quite familiar with the working of the proletariat dictatorship, as established in other lands," answered Alexander Rorke, the district attorney, brushing aside the point. "This manifesto means the conquest of the Government by bullets rather than ballots."

Judge McAdoo listened until the lawyers finished. Then he adjourned the court, sent the prisoners back to their cells, and retired to his chambers. It took him just a few hours that afternoon to produce a fifteen-page legal decision covering both Gitlow and James Larkin, the Irish radical charged on similar grounds. He called everyone back to present it from the bench. "These two defendants, Gitlow and Larkin, are beyond doubt two of the prominent leaders in this revolutionary scheme," he announced. "They are men of intelligence, with considerable experience in public affairs, and all this either from honest fanaticism or muddled thought they have perverted into the most dangerous channels. As they stand today, as against the organized government specified in the statute, they are dangerous men."

McAdoo pronounced them "clearly guilty," and ordered that they be held for the grand jury.

Benjamin Gitlow's friends at the Communist Labor Party took a collection to pay $15,000 in bail so he could go home and sleep in his own bed that night. But afterward, Gitlow and his lawyer, Charles Recht, sat down and had a serious talk. Gitlow's trial, when it came, would involve more than just the fate of one single man. It could provide a national platform to defend the radical cause. Charles Recht recognized his own limitations; he was exhausted and overworked from defending dozens of other communists tangled in the Red Scare, and he saw no relief on the horizon. Gitlow would need someone else to handle his defense, a different lawyer, one with a spotless reputation for patriotism, national prestige, and experience in arguing labor's viewpoint in high-profile contests, someone who would not be intimidated by local tyrants like Judge McAdoo and who would not run scared from taking the case.

Not many lawyers in America fit that profile in 1919. But one did. A few days later, after getting permission from the Party's executive committee to pay his hefty retainer, they sent a telegram to Chicago addressed to Clarence Darrow.

• PART IV •

"PARLOR BOLSHEVIKS"

In addition to the revolutionary organizations we have had a great many . . ."parlor Bolsheviks," the Philistines of our social period, who, enveloped in cigarette smoke and airs of superiority, have lost the touch of just proportion in their measurements of "the good and the bad in modernism," and lent themselves to writing and talk and financial contributions—these people seldom take the risk of doing anything—toward paddling along the revolutionary flood.

A. Mitchell Palmer, June 1, 1920

As a matter of fact, don't you think these high-brow anarchists, these college professors, these Harvard and Yale anarchists . . . who write articles about anarchy—these fellows who weep in articles about the laboring class but never labored a day in their lives, who prate about the poor and their rights, are more dangerous than the poor ignorant fellow who is willing to take his hatchet and go out and break up the Government or any of its representatives he can reach—don't you think that the high brow, the high-brow philosophical anarchist, is the more dangerous of the two?

Congressman Philip Campbell (D-KS),
Chairman of the House Rules Committee, April 28, 1920

HARVARD

F AR UP NORTH in Boston, Massachusetts, Felix Frankfurter stood at the podium of Faneuil Hall and called for order. His voice barely carried over the thousands of cheering people, mostly families of Russian immigrants. For Armistice Day 1919, some prominent local blue bloods with names like Ripley, Chafee, and Brooks had organized a rally to urge that Woodrow Wilson's administration recognize Soviet Russia. They chose Faneuil Hall because of its rich history of political protest. Samuel Adams had demanded American independence here in the 1770s and William Lloyd Garrison had called here for an end to slavery in the 1850s. The atmosphere in 1919 was no less chilling. That very morning, Boston newspapers reported new raids and arrests in Cambridge against radical leaders, on top of the prior week's attacks by Mitchell Palmer and the Lusk Committee.

Felix Frankfurter had refused to lead this gathering when the organizers first approached him about it. Frankfurter knew he would be a special target of critics. Just four months earlier, Frankfurter had almost lost his job as professor at Harvard University Law School over smears that he was too Red. "I told [the organizers] that they ought to get a good respectable Beacon Hill Yankee to preside," he recalled later. But after a few days, they came back to Frankfurter and told him that everyone else on the list had refused the job as well, afraid of being attacked in newspapers, perhaps losing their jobs, being ostracized by friends, or even arrested by Palmer's agents. Finally, Frankfurter agreed: "I said, 'I'll be damned if I'm going to be as timid and cowardly as all the rest,'" he wrote later, adding a touch of bravado. "If nobody else will do it, you'll simply have to take the loss of having me preside."

Felix Frankfurter was a foreigner, born in 1882 in Vienna, Austria, who

Felix Frankfurter teaching class at Harvard Law School in the 1930s.

came to New York City as a child, grew up on its Lower East Side, and attended City College. There he worked hard and won admission into the highest bastion of American learning: Harvard Law School. Gifted and outgoing, Frankfurter had a buoyant charm that melted away social class barriers that blocked most of the promising immigrant men his age: "Felix had two hundred best friends," his wife Marion said of him. Short, round-faced with blue-gray eyes peering out from behind thick wire-framed glasses, he never seemed to stop talking. At Harvard, Frankfurter caught the eye of one of his professors, a rising Yankee Republican lawyer named Henry Stimson, who asked Frankfurter to join him as an assistant when President Theodore Roosevelt appointed Stimson to be the United States attorney for New York City in 1906, and then in 1911 when President William Howard Taft named Stimson his secretary of war.[*] Frankfurter's exposure to Washington's top figures during this period changed his life. After Stimson left Washington at the end of Taft's presidency, Frankfurter returned to Cambridge to teach at Harvard Law School, and there he built a reputation in administrative law, authoring two textbooks in the

---

[*]Stimson would return as secretary of war a second time, called back in 1941 by President Franklin D. Roosevelt when America entered World War II. Stimson would serve through that conflict, retiring in September 1945 at seventy-eight years of age.

field. But the country's entry into World War I brought him back to government. This time, it was Woodrow Wilson's secretary of war, Newton Baker, who summoned him to Washington. He stayed for the duration, working in the War Department and then the Labor Department, first as a dispute mediator and then as chair of the War Labor Policies Board, a joint government-industry panel that tried to balance production demands with fairness to employees.

When Frankfurter returned to Harvard Law School after the war in 1919, though, he found himself the target of a whispering campaign, a flood of innuendoes implying that this Jewish, foreign-born professor might be too Red to trust with the education of Boston's elite young men. Word of the problem reached one of Frankfurter's Washington friends, Supreme Court justice Oliver Wendell Holmes, and Holmes asked another of their mutual friends, instructor Harold Laski, about it: "Every once in a while, faintly and vaguely as to you, a little more distinctly as to Frankfurter, I hear that you are dangerous men. . . . What does this mean?" Laski reported back that there was "a real effort in Boston to make Frankfurter's position here untenable." The Harvard Corporation already had vetoed the appointment of one of Frankfurter's students, Gary Henderson, to a teaching position for making allegedly pro-Bolshevik remarks. Law school dean Roscoe Pound had threatened to resign over the interference.

Felix Frankfurter had given his enemies plenty of ammunition. For one thing, serving during World War I as a Labor Department mediator, he had involved himself in two sensitive cases involving alleged radicals, and each time he sided publicly with the Reds. One of these became an international *cause célèbre*. It involved Tom Mooney, a San Francisco I.W.W. organizer convicted of bombing a Preparedness Day parade in 1916, killing ten people and wounding another forty. Mooney and his co-defendant Warren Billings sat on death row as anarchists staged huge rallies on their behalf in cities from Chicago to Moscow to New York. Felix Frankfurter investigated Mooney's trial on behalf of the Labor Department and found it riddled with bias and mistakes. "The utilities sought 'to get' Mooney," he wrote, citing how prosecutors had relied on company-hired private detectives to build their case. Frankfurter urged that Mooney be pardoned and given a new trial on lesser charges, but local officials angrily rejected the idea and denied any unfairness.

The other case made an even bigger splash. It involved an ugly incident in Bisbee, Arizona, where, in July 1917, armed vigilantes from the town had roused a group of two thousand striking copper miners from their beds one morning at the crack of dawn, marched them at gunpoint to the town's train station, loaded them into cattle cars, rode them out into the desert, and abandoned them without food or water and threatened to kill any who returned. One of the Bisbee vigilantes, Jack Greenway, happened to be an original Rough Rider during the Spanish-American War who had joined Theodore Roosevelt in his famous charge up San Juan Hill in Cuba. Greenway complained to his blustery old commander about Felix Frankfurter's critical report on the expulsion and Roosevelt jumped to defend his Rough Rider friend by blasting the attack: "[Y]ou have taken, and are taking, on behalf of the administration an attitude which seems to me to be fundamentally that of Trotsky and the other Bolsheviki leaders in Russia; an attitude which may be fraught with mischief to this country," he wrote to Frankfurter in a letter that found its way into newspapers. "No human being in his senses doubts that the men deported from Bisbee were bent on destruction and murder."

And if siding with Reds and picking fights with former presidents wasn't bad enough, Felix Frankfurter had also committed the sin of being unapologetically Jewish. Beyond the social snubs he encountered routinely—Eleanor Roosevelt on meeting Frankfurter called him "An interesting little man but very jew"—Frankfurter took a leading national role in the recently formed Zionist movement that aimed to build a Jewish national home in Palestine. After World War I, in 1919, Frankfurter had joined another top Zionist leader, Supreme Court Justice Louis Brandeis, on a mission to promote the cause, including a tour of Palestine plus a side trip to Poland to investigate the plight of Jews being starved and persecuted there in violent pogroms.

When the Versailles peace talks reached a critical stage, Brandeis asked Frankfurter to travel to France and represent the Zionist cause there. Frankfurter met personally with Woodrow Wilson at least two times to seek his support for the British government's recently issued Balfour Declaration supporting a Jewish homeland in Palestine, as well as reporting on conditions in Poland. Frankfurter's persistence won him no friends in Woodrow Wilson's circle. The War Department's Military Intelligence office at that moment was painting a starkly negative picture of Zionism for American leaders, depicting it as part of an international Jewish conspiracy. American military intelligence director Marlborough Churchill, citing Polish sources, blamed the problem in Poland in 1919 on what he claimed was a plot by Jews to seize large portions of that country: "The only explanation considered possible is that the design [by Jews] is to make Poland the commercial Judea from which as a basis European trade will be controlled, especially the great coming market of Russia," he reported. "Already the world's press is said to be controlled to a considerable extent in favor of printing news of pogroms here, which I am informed in every quarter do not exist." Military Intelligence reports routinely portrayed Bolshevism as a Jewish movement gone awry and Jews as being at the center of American Red agitation.*

By the time he returned to America and reported to Cambridge to take up his teaching job, Frankfurter's reputation had preceded him. Anonymous tongues wagged that this Felix Frankfurter was a troublemaking Red sympathizer. Roscoe Pound, the Law School's new dean, worried about the situation and came to Washington, D.C., to discuss it privately with Justice Brandeis. Brandeis could not believe what he was hearing. "What are you worried about?" he asked. "Hasn't Frankfurter got tenure?"

"Oh, yes, but they'll want to take away his courses in public law by which he might corrupt the young and their outlook on American law," Pound answered.

"Oh, don't worry about that. It doesn't matter what he teaches. If he were to teach Bills and Notes, he'd be teaching himself." To his wife, Brandeis wrote: "They are gunning hard for Felix."

Frankfurter finally won over the Boston skeptics in his usual way, by confronting them face to face and reassuring them with his outgoing nature. Soon, the commotion died down. "People meet him, and the adjective 'dangerous' melts as the snow before the sun," Harold Laski reported back to Holmes that fall.

But now, just as the original uproar had barely subsided, this new one came up. On agreeing to chair the pro-Soviet Armistice Day meeting at Faneuil Hall, Felix Frankfurter knew he would draw critics all over again. He crafted his speech to be "three hundred percent kosher," as he put it, ripe with quotations from American Founding Fathers and British Tories.

---

*In fact, Military Intelligence officers went further that year and shadowed Brandeis, a sitting Supreme Court justice, on his trip back from Europe in September 1919. They filed a report with top officials based on unnamed informants questioning Brandeis's loyalty, claiming that "there are some thirty members of [Justice Brandeis's] party and [the source] understood that all favored the Soviet form of Government and were on there [sic] way to this country as active propagandists." Military Intelligence had been tracking Brandeis's Zionist activities since at least February 1919.

He delivered it with his usual tongue in cheek. "I dare say I shall be called a 'Bolshevik' . . . in fact I am sure of it," he told the capacity crowd, winning a few nervous chuckles. "I have no patience for the Bolshevik form of government. . . . But I know as little or even less of what is supposed to replace it." Then he turned over the podium to other speakers such as U.S. Army colonel Raymond Robins, who had served as the Red Cross's commissioner in Russia after the revolution and had seen the atrocities with his own eyes. "The last two years have been a period of stupid blundering, starvation, and misery, of stupid and criminal blockade and intervention. Our policy has stamped Bolshevism in, instead of stamping it out," Robins told the room to repeated applause. "I don't believe American institutions are endangered when a few foreigners gather on a street corner."

The storm came quickly. Any rational debate over American recognition of Russia's new government became lost in catcalls. Newspapers blasted Frankfurter and Robins for their "Praise [of the] Bolsheviki" as calls and telegrams flooded the Harvard Law School dean's office from angry alumni. Within days, Frankfurter received a phone call from Thomas Nelson Perkins, a blue-blood lawyer who served as counsel to the Harvard Corporation. "What's this Communist meeting you presided over?" Perkins demanded before Frankfurter could even say "good morning." He demanded that Frankfurter meet him for lunch and then lectured him on his bad judgment. He was a "very unreasonable man," Perkins told him. But Frankfurter held his ground. "Sanity and goodwill do not just happen in this world," he told Perkins. "They must be fought for and won."

In the end, they chose not to fire him. Once again, Felix Frankfurter quieted the waters. People liked him. "Wherever Frankfurter is, there is no boredom," muckraking historian Matthew Josephson would write of him in 1940. "As soon as he bounces in—he never walks, he bounces— the talk and laughter begin, and they never let up. He brings with him the sweep of national affairs and the human interest of personal gossip." Frankfurter knew he was safe at Harvard for now. He had friends in Washington like Justice Brandeis and Oliver Wendell Holmes. But for how long? And at what cost? "Of course it won't be comfortable for a time," he told Dean Roscoe Pound around this time, "but there is no illusion about American affairs in my mind and why should anyone right now expect 'comfort.'" The world was changing, and not in a good way.

· 17 ·
POST

LOUIS F. POST, the assistant secretary of labor, had demanded this meeting. He sat at the table and tried not to look down at the pile of papers that sat in front of him on the tabletop. They comprised the deportation orders for Emma Goldman, and the question for Post was straightforward: Should he sign them? He found the idea sickening, but he saw no logical way out. Post had originally blocked Emma Goldman's deportation back in 1917 for lack of evidence. Now, the case had come back to him with a thick new file, a long hearing transcript, and a finding by Inspector A. P. Schell that all the legal tests had been met. Still, Emma Goldman's lawyer, Harry Weinberger, had requested a chance to come in person and make his plea. Louis Post had agreed, hoping perhaps Weinberger might come up with a good argument for his much-despised client.

The law demanded that each deportation case be decided by the secretary of labor or his designee, and, normally, Secretary Wilson left these decisions to his Labor Department solicitor, John Abercrombie. But since

Louis F. Post in an earlier, undated photograph.

it was Post's own earlier ruling on Emma Goldman that was being reopened, Abercrombie had insisted that Post decide it again. So now, all four of them sat uncomfortably around the table in Post's office at the Labor Department in Washington, D.C.: Post, Caminetti, Abercrombie, and Weinberger.

Post asked Harry Weinberger to speak first, and Weinberger made a simple case. He needed time, he said. With it, he argued, he could still find evidence to prove that Emma Goldman was a United States citizen, making the deportation invalid. The United States government had spent years compiling its case against her; why not give him a few more weeks? Harry Weinberger was "a bright boy," as one undercover Lusk Committee agent described him, "shrewd, careful in his statements, forceful and mighty alert and keen." Still, when he finished, Louis Post could only shake his head. As far as he was concerned, Weinberger had failed to make his case. He left too many questions unanswered. For instance, if Weinberger had leads on evidence to prove Emma Goldman's citizenship, why hadn't he raised them earlier, back at Ellis Island before Inspector Schell had issued his ruling? Why would an extra two or three weeks make any difference now when Weinberger had failed to produce anything new over the past two months? Weinberger had no good response.

Louis Post understood the implication. The 1917 Immigration Act required that any noncitizen anarchist be deported. Emma Goldman, over a thirty-year career, had distinguished herself as the most outspoken anarchist in America. Once the evidence established that she was not a citizen, she had no remaining defense. "Whether or not I liked the law did not enter into it," Post would explain years later. "This law was mandatory. I had no choice but to measure it by the facts presented in the record of hearing."

How had it come to be that expressing an opinion—anarchism, socialism, or any other -ism—was now a crime in America during war and a deportable offense afterward? And if it was, how could any honest person draw a logical line to separate viewpoints that were truly dangerous from those that were simply new or controversial, or that criticized the government?

Louis Post cringed at the idiocy of the Immigration Act, the way it treated all anarchists the same. It defied reality as he knew it. Some anarchists were what he called "philosophical," even pacifists like the writer Leo Tolstoy. "There are various kinds," he wrote. "At one extreme are malignant conspirators and destructive revolutionists; at the other are apostles of peace, preachers of the principle of non-resistance, of 'turning the other cheek,' persons supremely harmless except to those perverted imaginations which anticipate violent revolutions as consequences of non-resistant propaganda." How could anyone confuse the two? Had they forgotten how to think?

Louis Post had a scraggly dark beard and wore wire glasses that made him look vaguely like Leon Trotsky, the fiery Bolshevik war minister. But at seventy-one years old, Post had gray streaks in his beard, and his eyes sagged with fatigue. Louis Post's career had spanned the frontiers of the Progressive Age. Raised in New Jersey in the 1850s, he had been too young to join the Union Army and fight in the Civil War, but he went South during Reconstruction as a court stenographer and worked with a military prosecutor in Charleston, South Carolina, to build cases against the Ku Klux Klan at the height of the Klan's postwar reign of terror. Back home in New York City, he gravitated toward politics and joined the Republican club of "Gentleman Boss" Chester Alan Arthur, the future president. He bolted Arthur's machine after an argument and found a job writing editorials for a small newspaper called the New York Truth, linked to Tammany Hall.*

---

*Post's New York Truth earned him a brief flash of national fame during the 1880 presidential campaign between Republican James Garfield and Democrat Winfield Scott Hancock by publishing the "Morey letter," which purported to show Garfield's indifference to Chinese immigration, a lightning-rod issue that year on the West Coast. Garfield proved the letter to be a forgery, and Post had to spend several days in court defending the newspaper against charges of fraud. Garfield lost California in the election by fewer than 150 votes out of over 160,000 cast, though he won the presidency in a historically tight race.

But Louis Post found his spiritual light in the 1880s in Henry George, the San Francisco writer-economist whose hugely popular book *Progress and Poverty* launched a national movement for the Single Tax. This peculiar brand of social ideology urged that society should reshape itself by basing all government taxation on the sole basis of land holdings (rather than excise taxes, import tariffs, or taxes on income), placing the burden on the wealthy. "I fairly devoured the book," Post wrote years later. He described George's idea as a "moral principle [that] the earth is common property, and that the best way to make it so in fact is to take over its annual values for public use by means of taxation [levied solely on] land owners."

The Single Tax crusade reshaped his life. Post became friends with Henry George and edited George's two newspapers, the *New York Standard* and *The Leader*. When Henry George in 1886 took the unlikely step of running for mayor of New York City, Louis Post became his campaign manager. Together, they waged an exciting contest in which George ran a close second to a Tammany Hall Democrat named Abram Hewitt and easily outpolled the Republican, young Theodore Roosevelt. Had it not been for the usual Tammany Hall vote stealing and ballot–box stuffing, they might have won.

Louis Post left New York City in 1896, lived briefly in Cleveland, then settled in Chicago to become part of the Chicago *intelligentsia*. Here, he wrote almost a dozen books, including a history of the 1886 mayoral contest, two essay collections titled *Ethics of Democracy* and *Social Service*, a homage to Henry George titled *The Prophet of San Francisco*, and a study of family relations called *Ethical Principles of Marriage and Divorce*. He won national acclaim, though, through *The Public*, a monthly magazine he coedited for fifteen years with his wife, Alice Thatcher Post. They described it as "A Journal of Fundamental Democracy" and its circulation reached 16,500 by December 1912, large enough to carry heavy influence in progressive circles, a must read for top politicians, labor leaders, journalists, lawyers, and academics.

By the time Woodrow Wilson won the presidency in 1912, Louis Post had built such a large following that friends launched a petition drive to win him a spot in the new administration, a drive spearheaded by no less than William Jennings Bryan, Wilson's incoming secretary of state. Post came to Washington in 1913 as the new assistant secretary of labor, and here he fit well into Woodrow Wilson's first-term milieu, with its focus on domestic causes like empowering unions, ending child labor, busting trusts, and reforming business—all liberal ideas he had championed back home. But 1917 changed everything. "From the moment that our country plunged into the World War, great and grasping financial interests boldly rushed toward the financial top, and greedily reached out and up and down to utilize governmental machinery for private profit," Post wrote in looking back on the era. Old-line progressives found themselves frozen out. Post used his Labor Department position to push back against these "grasping" powers, fighting to stop them from breaking labor unions under the pretext of military urgency. Now, with peace restored, he saw the antilabor, antiprogressive tilt growing worse under a new pretext, the Red Scare. And the deportation cases stank worst of all.

In one run-in back in 1917, Louis Post had tried to fight this tide with help from his Chicago friend Clarence Darrow, whose articles he often ran in *The Public*. Post arranged for Darrow to intervene in a deportation case involving a young Chicagoan named Schulim Melamed who worked at a Sears-Roebuck factory. Melamed seemed to pose no threat to anyone despite his calling himself an "anarchist." Post got permission for Darrow to question the man in Chicago, and Darrow used the opportunity to demonstrate that Schulim Melamed's brand of anarchism amounted to reading books by Tolstoy, Thomas Payne, and Walt Whitman. Melamed belonged to no radical groups, owned no guns, and admitted that it was impossible to get along without having a government. He gave no speeches, urged no violence, and didn't push his political views on friends or co-workers. Asked what it meant to be an anarchist, he said: "I believe in individual freedom, freedom of press, thought and act, without interfering with somebody else's private life."

Darrow argued that to deport Melamed was nonsense, and even the then-attorney general, Thomas Gregory, agreed. But Labor Secretary Wilson felt the statute gave him no choice, and his immigration chief, Caminetti, backed him up. Wilson ordered Melamed deported. Later that year, Congress, aware of the argument, removed any doubt by making the immigration statute even tougher, expanding the list of deportable offences to include a wider definition of "anarchism" plus membership in radical groups.

And so now he came full circle. Louis Post sat facing Emma Goldman's deportation case with no fig leaf to hide behind. He marveled at the firestorm the Justice Department had whipped up against her since the November raids. Post had known Emma Goldman over the years. They

hung around the same Chicago social circles. He recognized that she
earned her popularity by more than her radical politics. He respected her
work as a nurse, her role articulating the hopes of the immigrant poor, her
outspoken support for labor. He didn't care much for her anarchism, but
he never considered it dangerous compared to the violent revolutionary
types who bombed peoples' houses. "[S]he is one of those disbelievers in
violence who anticipate forcible resistance to peaceable developments of
anarchistic policies," he wrote, "and therefore in support of those policies
justify the use of force as a defense against force."

After Harry Weinberger finished his argument and answered a few
questions, Louis Post reached the end of the line. He picked up a pen and
scratched a note across the bottom of Weinberger's most recent letter:
"After conference pending final decision, as requested above, the application for further time is denied. The case is closed and the alien is
ordered deported. Alien allowed to be wired of final decision as above."
He passed the page across the table to John Abercrombie, who signed it
as well with a matching date.

Then he turned to Harry Weinberger sitting next to him and said, "If
Tolstoy himself were in this country, he would be deported under the
present anarchist law."

"Why not substitute the name Jesus Christ instead of Tolstoy, because you
would also deport him for his views under this law," Weinberger shot back.

Post said nothing. He didn't argue the point. "No question of sympathy
on the one hand nor of antipathy on the other was involved," he wrote
later in trying to explain his decision. The law had spoken. How could
the law have been so ridiculous? Only two weeks earlier, three days after
the November raid, the United States Supreme Court had issued its
latest opinion upholding the Espionage Act, under which hundreds of
wartime dissenters had been jailed for nothing more than speaking their
minds. The Court's earlier decisions on this issue had been unanimous. The
only hope that Louis Post and people like him saw in the situation was that,
this time, in this case called *Abrams v. United States*, two of the nine justices
dissented. One of them, Louis Brandeis, was a Jew and could be painted as a
Red sympathizer. But the other had no such taint. He was the oldest member
of the Supreme Court, a Boston Brahmin and Civil War veteran whose
dissents often carried more weight in legal circles than a dozen majority
opinions. No one yet had ever doubted the patriotism of Oliver Wendell
Holmes.

· 18 ·
FREE SPEECH

FELIX FRANKFURTER READ the dissent at his home near Harvard Law School the morning after his pro-Soviet speech at Faneuil Hall. He scribbled out a letter to his friend and mentor: "Dear Justice Holmes, And now I may tell you the gratitude and, may I say it, the pride I have in your dissent. You speak there as you have always spoken of course. But 'this time we need education in the obvious' and you lift the voice of the noble human spirit."

For six months, Frankfurter had been leading a quiet campaign to persuade Holmes to change his view on the Espionage Act. Now, finally, it had happened.

Felix Frankfurter had known Oliver Wendell Holmes for almost a decade since Frankfurter first came to Washington in 1911 as a young War Department lawyer. His Harvard professor John Gray had introduced them and they sparked a quick friendship, despite obvious differences in background and the fact that Holmes was the elder by forty-one years. From the minute he met Oliver Wendell Holmes, Felix Frankfurter worshipped the famous justice. He called Holmes "one of the most impressive personalities of the day." Holmes in 1919 was seventy-eight years old at a time when the average life expectancy for American men at birth was just 47.1 years. Holmes had served in the Civil War and arguably saved the life of President Abraham Lincoln one time in July 1864 when Lincoln came to Fort Stevens to see the action as Confederate general Jubal Early attacked Washington, D.C., from the north. Holmes, then a twenty-three-year-old infantryman, saw the president standing exposed and shouted: "Get down, you damn fool, before you get shot."

After the Civil War, Holmes taught at Harvard Law School and served as Massachusetts chief justice before President Theodore Roosevelt appointed him to the Supreme Court in 1902. Here, Holmes showed his independence. He broke from the Court's 1905 decision in *Lochner v. New York* that struck down a law limiting work hours for bakers, for instance, famously declaring that "the constitution is not intended to embody a particular economic theory." He recognized a right of workers to form unions and took a pragmatic approach where the law touched on burning social issues.

Justice Holmes, for his part, found young Felix Frankfurter a refreshing companion, "a very vivid, articulate youngster." Holmes had no children; he and his wife Fanny lived alone in their Washington, D.C., home and, during the summer, at Beverly Farms, their retreat in Massachusetts. He came to appreciate the time he spent with the lively circle of friends that Felix Frankfurter drew together: future socialist Harold Laski, rising journalist Walter Lippman, among others. They shared long talks about politics, the law, the Constitution, the World War. Holmes liked to

Justice Oliver Wendell Holmes.

take walks, and passersby around Washington sometimes got to have a good laugh at seeing short, young Felix Frankfurter struggling to keep up with tall, lanky Oliver Wendell Holmes, with his long arms, long legs, and unmistakable gray mustache. One night, Holmes pulled Frankfurter aside and told him, "My son, it was a good piece of luck that I fell in with you." They grew to be such close friends that on Holmes's seventy-fifth birthday in 1916, his wife Fanny, concerned about her husband's advancing age, singled out Felix Frankfurter to ask a deeply personal favor: "I want you to promise me that when you see the slightest drop in the quality of [his] opinions that you will let me know," she asked him. "That day he will get off the bench."

Holmes had followed the attempts that summer by Boston busybodies to pressure Harvard Law School into dropping Frankfurter from its faculty, and he found it alarming. What had come over the country these days to make people panic at the sight of an innovative thinker like his young friend Felix Frankfurter, labeling him a dangerous Red sympathizer? Holmes had put his foot down over the issue. He wrote a letter to Harvard University president A. Lawrence Lowell expressing his disbelief that the Law School would even consider throwing Frankfurter or Roscoe Pound to the wolves. He cited his "very strong feeling that Pound and in his place Frankfurter have and impart the ferment which is more valuable than an endowment, and makes a Law School a focus of life."

This ferment and the country's vicious reaction to it gave Oliver Wendell Holmes sleepless nights that year. Early in 1919, Holmes had authored three Supreme Court decisions upholding the Espionage Act against attacks that it violated the Constitution's First Amendment guarantee of free speech. Now, he regretted them. The most important was *United States v. Schenck*, in which two Socialist Party leaders had been jailed for printing 15,000 leaflets and mailing them to army draftees urging them to oppose conscription, though not by refusing to serve. Prosecutors had painted this action as obstructing the war effort: Espionage. The issue hit a raw nerve. Holmes remembered his own generation's brush with wartime treason, the bloody 1863 Civil War draft riots that killed over a hundred people in New York City and exploded while he was serving in the Union Army. Holmes also remembered the mob suppression of abolitionists in Boston in the 1850s, and he himself had once urged students to read "books of an agitating tendency."

"The most stringent protection of free speech would not protect a man in falsely shouting fire in a theatre and causing a panic," Holmes had written in *Schenck*, grasping for some point of logic to divide acceptable free speech from what would be deemed criminal sedition. "When a nation is at war many things that might be said in time of peace . . . will not be endured so long as men fight." He had laid down a measuring stick for the future: "The question in every case is whether the words used are used in such circumstances and are of such a nature as to create a clear and present danger that they will bring about substantive evils." The same day in a separate case, Holmes had applied this "clear and present danger" test to uphold sending Eugene V. Debs to prison for giving a speech against conscription.*

But instead of calming the waters, Holmes found that his *Schenck* ruling only raised a hornet's nest of bitterness. Longtime friends like New York federal appeals judge Learned Hand, University of Chicago law professor Ernst Freund, and Harvard's Zechariah Chafee all wrote long, pointed critiques. Chafee mocked Holmes's fire-in-a-theatre metaphor in a *Harvard Law Review* piece by turning it on its head: "How about the man who gets up in a theatre between the acts and informs the audience honestly but perhaps mistakenly that the fire exits are too few or locked? He is a much closer parallel to Schenck or Debs." Chafee went further. He asked Harold Laski to arrange a tea with Justice Holmes and, sitting privately with the Justice, he took the opportunity to vent at length over the issue. Holmes listened politely but held his tongue. "[Holmes] is inclined to allow a very wide latitude to Congressional discretion in the carrying on of the war," Chafee told friends in reporting on the meeting, but he added his impression that had Holmes been on the Debs jury, "he would have voted for acquittal."

Just as startling for Oliver Wendell Homes, when anarchists in May 1919 sent sixteen bombs for delivery through the New York City post office, all luckily stopped for insufficient postage, one of them had been addressed to him, putting Holmes on the same death list as Anthony Caminetti and A. Mitchell Palmer.

Then, just a few months later, events gave him a fresh chance to look at

---

*Case precedents at the time supported Holmes's view. In fact, the argument against Debs echoed the justification offered six decades earlier by President Abraham Lincoln in 1863 for jailing and banishing a former Ohio congressman, Clement Vallandigham, during the Civil War. Vallandigham had given a speech criticizing Lincoln, the war effort, and Emancipation, thereby violating a martial law edict then in effect. Lincoln argued that Vallandigham, through his words, was "laboring, with some effect, to prevent the raising of troops [and] to encourage desertions from the army. . . . Must I shoot a simple minded soldier boy who deserts, while I must not touch a hair of a wily agitator who induces him to desert?"

the issue again, this time as the Supreme Court heard the case of *Abrams v. United States*. The facts here were no less compelling than those in *Schenck*: A judge had sentenced five Russian immigrants, including an eighteen-year-old girl, to twenty years in prison for circulating two leaflets—including one written in Yiddish—to workers at a munitions plant, calling on them to strike in protest against American intervention in Russia. None of the workers actually had stopped working, and few had evidently even read the leaflets. Still, this was enough to convince a jury and seven Supreme Court justices that they were guilty of espionage.

This time, Oliver Wendell Holmes refused to go along. After the weeks of prodding from legal friends, the angst of seeing Felix Frankfurter threatened with expulsion from Harvard Law School, and the maturing of his own conscience, he saw the issue differently. He refused to abandon his "clear and present danger" test for applying the First Amendment's guarantee of free speech, but he argued instead that the Court had misused it:

> Congress certainly cannot forbid all effort to change the mind of the country. Now nobody can suppose that the surreptitious publishing of a silly leaflet by an unknown man, without more, would present any immediate danger that its opinions would hinder the success of government arms or have any appreciable tendency to do so.

That said, however, Holmes took another step and reframed the entire issue in terms of how America needed to breathe fresh ideas to grow and mature. Free speech was not just something to tolerate; it was the nation's life's blood:

> [W]hen men have realized that time has upset many fighting faiths, they may come to believe . . . that the ultimate good desired is better reached by free trade in ideas—that the best test of truth is the power of the thought to get itself accepted in the competition of the market, and that truth is the only ground upon which their wishes safely can be carried out. That at any rate is the theory of our Constitution. It is an experiment. As all life is an experiment. Every year if not every day we wager our salvation upon some prophecy based upon imperfect knowledge.
> While the experiment is part of our system I think that we should be eternally vigilant against attempts to check the expression of

*opinions that we loathe and believe to be fraught with death, unless
they so imminently threaten immediate interference with the lawful
and pressing purposes of the law that an immediate check is required
to save the country.*

A few days later, after his opinion came out, Holmes heard the explosion over the speech that his friend Felix Frankfurter had given to the pro-Soviet rally at Faneuil Hall, and he decided to send him some advice. "The time for going into a fight each must judge for himself," he warned. "I think you are too level-headed to be looking for martyrdom. Martyrs I generally suspect are damn fools."

Felix Frankfurter was happy to listen to Holmes and put politics aside that Christmas season. He had happier things on his mind. On December 20, 1919, he married Marion Denman, the daughter of a Congregational minister from Longmeadow, Massachusetts. Typically for him, Frankfurter arranged to have the wedding performed among his favorite judges and lawyers. Benjamin Cardozo, the chief justice of the New York State Court of Appeals, conducted the ceremony in the chambers of federal appeals court justice Learned Hand.* His mother, Emma, refused to attend the wedding, upset that her son was marrying a gentile. His father had died five years earlier. "Felix is safe. It couldn't have been better if I had deliberately arranged it. She's wise and grown-up and good to look upon—a real companion," Laski reported back to Holmes in Washington on his protégé. "The Boy is very happy. The girl is still rather reticent and shy . . . but she makes him sing an unceasing song."

The next morning, as Felix and Marion prepared to drive off and enjoy their honeymoon at Southern Pines in North Carolina, Frankfurter picked up the newspaper and read about the latest turning of the screws by A. Mitchell Palmer and his Red Scare legions. It was peculiar. The headlines all talked about the sailing of an old ship from New York Harbor carrying the first load of detained immigrant radicals across the ocean back to where they came from: back to Russia. Nobody was laughing about the *Buford.*

---

*In 1932, Cardozo would be nominated to the Supreme Court to take the place left by Holmes and, in 1939, Frankfurter would be nominated to take the place left by Cardozo.

• PART V •

THE BIG RAID

"One National Strike He Didn't Plan." *New York Times Magazine*, in *Literary Digest*, February 14, 1920.

EDGAR TOOK THE train to New York City on Saturday, December 20, 1919, to savor the climax of all his work. He dressed warmly that night to join Caminetti, some agents from his New York bureau, and a circle of dignitaries including congressmen and newspaper reporters, as they all rode together down to Battery Park and boarded a ferry for the short trip across the harbor. It was almost midnight as they neared Ellis Island. There, in the puddles of light from electric lamps under a cold, clear sky, they saw a large tugboat-barge, its gangplank down, waiting to take on passengers. This night, before dawn, Edgar would witness 249 Reds being deported, expelled from America and sent back to Russia, including Emma Goldman herself. It was one of the proudest moments of his twenty-four-year life.

In the six weeks since the November raid against the Union of Russian Workers, Edgar had tackled one hurdle after another to produce this triumph: an inmate silence strike, a hunger strike, legal appeals by Emma Goldman's lawyer, interference by Labor Department higher-ups, and the logistical nightmare of finding a way to send a large group of undesirables

across the ocean and across battle-scarred frontiers into war-torn Bolshevik Russia. The effort taxed every ounce of Edgar's single-minded
stubbornness.

The silence strike came first. Edgar had learned about it soon after the
November raid had sent eighty prisoners to Ellis Island. Under the Labor
Department's Rule 22, these prisoners had been told immediately they
had the right to hire lawyers, and all but a handful chose the same one,
attorney Isaac Schorr of the National Civil Liberties Bureau. Schorr
insisted that 98 percent of his clients, and perhaps all of them, wanted to
go back to Russia, even if they had to pay their own way and the expenses
of their families. The only thing they insisted on was a guarantee that
they would reach Soviet-controlled territory, where they expected to
receive a warm welcome. Otherwise, they refused to budge.

Soon, they started refusing to speak, not even answering to their
names, making it impossible for Ellis Island officials to identify them, let
alone conduct their deportation hearings. Edgar found a quick solution;
he provided the immigration inspectors with photographs that his agents
had taken of each Red when they were first questioned at Park Row.
Once they identified the prisoner from his picture, they could go ahead
and deport him whether he chose to defend himself or not. "Expedite
fullest possible extent hearings of Russian Workers cases," he pushed
Caminetti to telegraph his staff.

Edgar beat the hunger strike by letting the prisoners go hungry; some
went without food and water for two, three, and four days before giving it
up. At another point, he heard that a visitor had sneaked a small camera
into the Ellis Island compound and given it to a prisoner. "[T]he next
time they would probably arrange to smuggle in a revolver," he warned
Caminetti, and they tightened security all around.

By early December, Edgar had lost patience with nitpicks and delays.
He met face to face with the entire Ellis Island inspector corps, and
together they hammered out a plan to wrap up all the cases quickly. The
Immigration Bureau promised to throw every available resource into the
effort, reassigning stenographers and lawyers from other cases. On any
close one, they agreed to hold the file open "for a conference with Mr.
Hoover," and Edgar promised to spend one full hour each day at the
Immigration Bureau to keep things moving.

Then came a final wrinkle. Some of the Red prisoners started complaining that they had families in America, including young children
born on American soil, which made the children citizens. It would be

inhumane to separate them, they argued. Their wives and children would become destitute without breadwinners. Edgar's patience snapped, especially when he heard that Labor Secretary William Wilson actually had agreed and ordered to delay indefinitely the deportation of any alien who had a family that wanted to join him. Edgar stormed into Caminetti's office and insisted he register a protest. "I was informed by Mr. Hoover . . . that he wanted it understood that the Department of Justice did not agree with the ruling," Caminetti telegraphed Washington. To Edgar, these were sob stories, and this was no time for them. These immigrant communists had threatened the country and must be made to leave. In the end, he and Caminetti found an easy way to get around Wilson's order. They just ignored it.

Finally, there was the ocean crossing. Russia in 1919 remained a country at war, with Reds fighting Whites, Poles invading from the west, and Japanese and American troops encamped in Siberia. Allies blockaded its ports, its European frontier was impassable, and Lenin and Trotsky froze any contact with the outside world. To thread this needle, Edgar arranged with the War Department to borrow an aging 5,000-ton troop transport ship called the *Buford*, built in Belfast in 1890 and purchased by the United States Navy to carry soldiers to Cuba during the Spanish-American War. The *Buford* had seen glory days. She had once steamed from Manila Bay in the Philippines through the Suez Canal to New York City in just 81 days, a very respectable speed at the time. But sailors called her a "sea roller" for the way she pitched and bounced in foul weather. Tonight, the *Buford* waited in New York's lower harbor under tight security. Her captain carried sealed orders, and, to guard her dangerous cargo, she carried an escort of four army lieutenants and fifty-eight soldiers, all armed. The ship would carry the prisoners to Finland. From there, Finnish and American troops would escort them across the icy frontier to Russia and transfer them to the Red Army. Edgar insisted that the *Buford* wait in port in Finland until the prisoners had joined their Soviet brethren. "This latter arrangement would eliminate any accusation of bad faith upon the part of the United States," he explained. After that, they were on their own, and good riddance, he felt.

With plans in place, he finally felt confident enough that week to joke about it. Edgar wrote to a friend at Military Intelligence and asked him to send maps of Russia, Finland, Estonia, and Latvia so he could study "the proposed vacation which a few of our anarchist friends will shortly take to Northern Russia."

Meanwhile, as Edgar and his distinguished guests approached in the darkness, the guards on Ellis Island were hustling through the large prison-like Dormitory and Baggage Building, banging on doors to wake the 249 selected inmates, telling them to get up, gather their things, and move quickly. Nobody had mentioned to them beforehand that this was the night of their departure. Most had simply gone to bed.

Emma Goldman had surrendered herself to Ellis Island on December 5 after exhausting all her legal appeals. Her lawyer, Harry Weinberger, had taken her case all the way to the United States Supreme Court and been rejected at each step. On Ellis Island, Goldman shared a cramped room with two other women in the Dormitory and Baggage Building, which, despite its sterile look and massive size, still had a bright, sunny cafeteria and a rooftop promenade where she could stretch her legs and enjoy a panoramic view of lower Manhattan just across the harbor. She was lucky. Most of the inmates lived packed into dormitory halls holding up to three hundred people, men separated from women, sleeping on metal-frame bunk beds arranged in tight rows. Emma Goldman had suffered a neuralgia attack shortly after arriving and been treated by a local dentist, but he could not stop the pain. She had resigned herself by now to leaving America, her home for more than thirty years. Russia, after all, was the new frontier, the great experiment. One day during the recreation period she walked around the promenade with Alexander Berkman, her lover of twenty years, and they talked it over. "I decided that if Sasha [her pet name for Berkman] was to be driven out of the country, I would go with him," she wrote, "it was unthinkable that he should join the Revolution [in Russia] and I remain behind."

Emma Goldman had refused to leave quietly, though. In November, after the deportation hearing but while her legal appeals were still pending, she insisted on making one last speaking tour. "It seemed preposterous," she wrote of it later, with Red Scare fever sweeping the country, "yet I could not refuse." Overflow crowds came to see her in New York, Chicago, Detroit, and stops in between. Two thousand people jammed her speech at Detroit's Auto Workers Hall, six thousand at Chicago's Carmen Hall, and fifteen hundred more at Chicago's West Side Auditorium. "No ordinary assemblies, these," she remembered. "Monster demonstrations they were, a tempest of vehement indignation against government absolutism and of homage to ourselves." At each stop, Emma Goldman appealed to her friends to unite and resist what she saw as the government's wave of tyranny. "Labor should make an organized demand for [jailed socialist] Kate Richards O'Hare, and other prisoners," she told a New York audience. "We must all stick together, and our enemies be damned." In Chicago, she mocked the way American men put women on a pedestal but thought nothing of locking them in prison for speaking their minds. "Would I had the power and means to take those men and bring them to the Missouri state penitentiary and show him what is being done with his consent to women in the United States; not foreigners— in Illinois NOT Russia. . . ."

Now, on Ellis Island, she saw the end coming. "Get up now! Get your things ready!" she heard the guards shouting at her door. "Hurry, there! Hurry!" The guards took Goldman and the other prisoners down a long, dark corridor made chilly by drafts of freezing winter air rushing against the tile floors and walls. They stood and shivered. As they waited, messenger boys came to collect last-minute telegrams they scribbled on scraps of paper to send to wives, lawyers, and friends they'd never see again. Then an officer told them to march. Deep snow blanketed the ground outside as guards led them from the dormitory building into the icy air and to the gangplank that led to the tugboat-barge at the water's edge. This, in turn, would deliver them to the *Buford*.

Edgar had assigned undercover agents to cover every stop of Emma Goldman's speaking tour and send him back detailed accounts, including descriptions of the crowds and the names of anyone who appeared with her on stage. He and his Military Intelligence allies pressured several sponsors to cancel her bookings, such as one at Chicago's Continental Hotel. Finally, though, the tour ran its course. Now, Edgar and his dignitaries stood alongside the dock watching the prisoners file past them between two rows of guards. Colorado U.S. congressman William Vaile, one of Edgar's party, described Edgar that night as a "slender bundle of high-charged electric wire." The two groups—the prisoners and Edgar's dignitaries—stood close enough to see each other, to make out faces and strike up odd, brief conversations. Congressman Vaile spoke for a moment with a young Russian man who explained that he hadn't been given time to cash a paycheck from the silk mill where he worked. He complained he'd lived in America twenty years, had a mother and sisters here, and didn't know anyone in Russia. The Congressman gave him a pack of cigarettes. Another man asked Edgar if he could cash a $3,000 check for him, since he hadn't been able to visit a bank since his arrest. Edgar offered to send the check to the man's friends and have them cash it. "I wouldn't trust you people to give it to my friends," he said. "All right," Edgar replied, "take it to Russia and trust the Bolsheviki."

One prisoner, Peter Bianky, the president of the Union of Russian Workers before the raid, spotted House Immigration chairman Albert Johnson* among the dignitaries, confronted him, and told him that, in the future, he and his radicals would stop blowing up buildings and instead break heads. "Meaning my head, I suppose," Johnson said with a laugh. "Yes, your head and others like it." Alexander Berkman, seeing Big Bill Flynn in the crowd, shook his fist and shouted, "We'll come back. And when we do, we'll get you ____."

Emma Goldman appeared wrapped in a long gray and black fur coat. Someone yelled "Merry Christmas, Emma," to which she responded with a thumb to her nose.

After the prisoners had all boarded the tugboat, Edgar and the dignitaries followed to join them on the first leg of their trip. Edgar and Congressman Vaile together made their way forward to the boat's kitchen and found Emma Goldman sitting there, having taken off her coat and unbuttoned her sweater in the hot, stuffy room. Goldman recognized Edgar immediately on seeing him, the bright young man from the Justice Department who had engineered her deportation. "She was quite bitter against Mr. Hoover because he had not given notice to her counsel, Mr. Weinberger, of the time of the departure," Congressman Vaile recalled. They, too, struck up a conversation. "Haven't I given you a square deal, Miss Goldman?" Edgar asked.

"Oh, I suppose you've given me as square a deal as you could," she answered. "We shouldn't expect from any person something beyond his capacity."**

"I confess that her pale intellectual face, with her black hair falling in great gulfs over her ears, inspired me with sympathy for her sorrow," Congressman Vaile wrote of the encounter. "This was the beginning of the

---

*Johnson had made himself a regular on Ellis Island in November 1919 chairing an investigation into charges that Frederick Howe, the Ellis Island ex-commissioner who had resigned in October, had been too soft on Red prisoners. Only 60 out of the 679 detained during Howe's tenure had been deported, and he had allowed Ellis Island to become "a gambling house, a bawdy house and a forum of Bolshevism," as Johnson charged. Howe had tried to humanize Ellis Island by building playgrounds, organizing orchestras and choral clubs, running schools for children of detained families, allowing inmates to stroll the grounds, decorating the dormitory halls with paintings, and sponsoring work-release programs for women charged with "moral turpitude." He also brought charges against food and baggage contractors for defrauding immigrants. Johnson never allowed Howe to testify at the hearings to defend himself.

**Edgar would transform this statement for later writers of authorized biographies, having Emma Goldman say, "At least, Hoover was fair."

end of the United States," he recalled Emma Goldman telling them. "Time was when this country had professed to welcome the downtrodden of other lands. . . . As the old Russia had fallen so the new United States would fall, and for the same reasons."

After a few minutes, they reached the *Buford*, and here the two groups separated. Emma Goldman and the 248 other prisoners were led aboard the larger ship. Edgar, Congressman Vaile, and the dignitaries stayed behind on the tugboat, which waited until 4:20 A.M., long enough to watch the *Buford* lurch forward and steam off into the predawn blackness, carrying in her belly 51 anarchists, 184 members of the Union of Russian Workers, 3 aliens convicted of crimes of moral turpitude, 9 found likely to become public charges, 1 procurer, and 1 man who had entered the country surreptitiously—the largest single deportation in memory.

The newspapermen quickly dubbed the ship with a new name: The Soviet Ark.

In the days before her exile, though, Emma Goldman had focused whatever rage she still had left not against Edgar, Caminetti, or even A. Mitchell Palmer, but rather against someone she had once considered a friend. "To my amazement I learned that the official who had signed the order for my deportation was Louis F. Post," she wrote in her memoirs. "It seemed incredible. Louis F. Post, ardent single-taxer, champion of free speech and press, former editor of *The Public*, a fearless liberal weekly, the man who had flayed the authorities for their brutal methods during the McKinley panic, who had defended me, and who had insisted that even [McKinley assassin] Leon Czolgosz should be safeguarded in his constitutional rights—he now a champion of deportation? . . . I had been a guest at his home and entertained by him and Mrs. Post. We had discussed anarchism and he had admitted its idealistic values. . . . And he, Louis Post, had now signed the first order for deporting radicals."

Friends tried to calm her, telling her that Post had no choice. He had to do his duty as a government official. "If he were a man of integrity, Louis F. Post should have remained true to himself and should have resigned," she insisted.

Harry Weinberger, her lawyer, certainly heard this outburst. How much of it he carried back to Post himself is unknown. But Louis Post—reading the newspaper accounts the next morning in his Washington office about the brusque manner in which his order had been carried out, that Secretary Wilson's direct instruction not to deport aliens with families had been ignored, and how the taste of blood had

The *Buford*, or Soviet Ark.

only whetted the appetites of the self-anointed Red Scare avengers—
would have understood her anger better than virtually anyone else in
Washington.

Edgar himself saved all the newspapers from the next morning and cut
out all the headlines and articles he found proclaiming his achievement.
He saved these clippings in his official scrapbook, early samples of trophies he would collect all his life on important milestones. Already,
Edgar was preparing the next step. His agents were compiling names and
affidavits for the next strike, the biggest yet, aimed at the next two radical groups on his list: the Communist Party and the Communist Labor
Party. But instead of a mere 220 warrants as he had sought originally

Newspaper photo of "Leading Personages on the *Buford's* Passenger List":
Goldman, Ethel Bernstein, Peter Bianki, and Alexander Berkman.

Emma Goldman photographed at Ellis Island shortly
before embarking for Russia.

against the Union of Russian Workers, or even the 600 eventually issued, this time Edgar would start the bidding by requesting more than three thousand. And given the math in November when agents had detained hundreds of suspects to sift out mere dozens of actual party members, the next raid easily could capture ten thousand or more.

Edgar slept well that night. He was certain he had made the country safer.

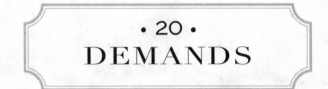

· 20 ·
DEMANDS

AFTER SIGNING EMMA Goldman's deportation order a month earlier, Louis F. Post hoped he would never see another such case again. Word traveled fast through his circle of liberal friends in Chicago and New York. By now, they all knew the truth: that it had been he, Post, who had sent Emma Goldman into exile, and that Goldman herself considered him a shameful coward for it. He had to wonder: Is this why he had given up the life he loved in Chicago, his magazine *The Public*, his progressive friends, his books and lecture tours—all to come to Washington, D.C., and shame himself over these deportations? To be part of this anti-Red hysteria? Coming to work each morning that month, he hid from the crisis by burying himself in other Labor Department work, like helping coal miners after their recent failed strike, or trying to mediate a threatened new railroad walkout, or tracking the impact on workers of soaring food prices. But now he found himself on Christmas Eve, sitting in his office, when a message came to him at his desk. Secretary Wilson needed to see him immediately. Louis Post got up and made his way down the corridor. Reaching the secretary's office, he opened the door and stepped inside to find three men sitting around the table, in the middle of an argument.

Louis Post had a keen eye for faces. He enjoyed the chance occasionally to pick up a pencil and sketch a portrait on the blank page of a scrapbook. He always made a person's eyes their sharpest feature. One sketch he had drawn years before and kept was of a young girl in a shawl and bonnet, carrying a wicker basket. She was looking back over her shoulder and Post made her face achingly pretty. Perhaps he based it on the memory he had of his first wife, Anna Johnson Post, whom he had watched die of consumption almost thirty years earlier in 1891, wasting away as he and doctors sat by helplessly. Anna had given Post his only child, a son, Charles, who now lived with his family in New York City. Louis Post had met his current wife, Alice Thatcher, the next year and married her in 1892. Alice became his intellectual soul mate for the next three decades, sharing his politics and coediting his magazine and books.

Now, on Christmas Eve 1919, Louis Post sat down at the table in Secretary Wilson's office and studied the faces of the three men glaring back at him: Caminetti with his bushy white mustache, narrow eyes, and cheeks red from shouting; John Abercrombie gray and slouching in his chair; and Secretary Wilson, his small eyes muddled and indecisive, his face tired and distracted. Post looked down at the tabletop and saw lying there a pile of neatly typed pages. These were what the argument was over, the latest demands from Palmer's Justice

Sketch of a young girl in Louis Post's personal scrapbook.

Department. He picked them up and glanced them over as Abercrombie explained the situation. That week, Caminetti had received two packages from Palmer's assistant, Mr. Hoover. Together, they asked that the Labor Department issue 2,718 deportation warrants, designed for yet another spectacular dragnet raid. Three other letters on the way would raise this total to almost 3,300, fifteen times more than the number issued prior to the November raids. The targets this time were the Communist Party of America and the Communist Labor Party, the two largest radical groups in the country after the I.W.W.

Where would they put so many people, one of them asked? There weren't enough spare jail cells in the country to hold them, and the letters insisted on setting bail in each case at $10,000 apiece, an impossible sum at a time when most workmen earned less than $2,000 per year, had no savings, and no access to credit. But Caminetti had a quick answer: They'd send them all back to Russia on a whole new fleet of Soviet Arks. That was the whole point. They were communists, for God's sake.

To make things worse, Palmer, through his Mr. Hoover, had given them a deadline: "All warrants for arrests in these cases should be prepared and issued not later than Saturday, December 27, due to the urgency of the matter." Since this was Christmas Eve, meeting this deadline meant assigning clerks to work through the holiday.

Caminetti had presented these demands to Abercrombie earlier that day and insisted he sign the 3,300 new warrants immediately. After all, he argued, they were no different from the six hundred warrants Abercrombie had signed for the November raids. Palmer, again through his Mr. Hoover, already had demonstrated that the Communist Party advocated the violent overthrow of the United States government, which qualified it as a radical organization under the 1918 Immigration Act. And the Communist Labor Party, he had shown, was "exactly similar" to the Communist Party, "both being pledged to the principles and tactics of the 3d International; the difference, as pointed out, exists only in leadership."

But this time, John Abercrombie refused. He insisted on first talking it over with Secretary Wilson, and Wilson, in turn, insisted on bringing in Louis Post. Abercrombie explained that he was concerned not only with the sheer number of warrants, but also with what he saw as the poor quality of the cases. The Justice Department had sent over stacks of sworn affidavits to support these warrants, but almost every single one of them was based either on hearsay or on some undisclosed secret. A typical affidavit from a Boston field agent named Daniel O'Connell said simply this:

1. I am a SPECIAL AGENT of the DEPARTMENT OF JUS-TICE, attached to the investigative forces of the Bureau of Investigations of said Department in the District of Massachusetts:

2. That in the course of my personal investigations, I am informed and verily believe the following facts to be true:
   (a) That BORIS BELADA is an alien, subject of RUSSIA;
   (b) That he is an active member of the COMMUNIST PARTY;
   (c) That the COMMUNIST PARTY is an organization which advocates the overthrow by force or violence the government of the United States.

Signed and notarized, December 27, 1919.

Abercrombie had seen hundreds of affidavits exactly like it, word-for-word duplicates with bare, unsupported statements of "information" and "belief." He found them "so flimsy that he refused to sign the warrants . . . without first scrutinizing the proof in each case, and the proof had not been made available to him," Post recalled him saying.

Of course, Abercrombie had approved exactly this same type of evidence for the warrants he signed back in November, as Caminetti doubtless pointed out. But this time, with so many more, and seeing just how cavalierly the Justice Department had run its November operation, he was having second thoughts.

Louis Post sat and listened to Caminetti and Abercrombie, the fiery Italian and the smug Southern academic, as they argued back and forth. Even Caminetti had to admit that such a massive raid might create a logistical nightmare. If Palmer's agents went out and rounded up three thousand Reds and dumped them on his Immigration Bureau, they had no facility big enough to hold them and not nearly enough inspectors and translators to conduct hearings. The process could take months, maybe years to finish. Meanwhile, innocent bystanders—which had been the large majority of those jailed in November—would rot behind bars along with the guilty. Processing just the 249 Reds deported on the *Buford* in December had stretched their system to the breaking point. Even now, seven weeks after the November raids, scores of prisoners still sat in jail cells waiting for decisions in their cases, unable to pay the $10,000 bail. And even in those cases where the immigration inspectors had finished their hearings and found no evidence to back up the Justice Department's claims, they still could not release the prisoners because Palmer and his Mr. Hoover had insisted their agents be given another chance to beef up their cases.

It had become a mess, with Palmer grabbing the headlines and then dumping all the knotty details in their laps. When Palmer received pleas from wives of the Reds deported on the *Buford* to join their husbands in Russia or be given charity to help feed their children, Palmer washed his hands of it. "As the deportation of alien anarchists does not fall within the province of the Department of Justice," he told them through his Mr. Hoover, "I am therefore transmitting [the complaints] to you for appropriate action."

But what could they do? Louis Post hated to admit it, but neither he, Wilson, nor Abercrombie could think of a single justification for denying the warrants short of declaring public war against Mitchell Palmer and his crusade, which would open them up to charges of coddling Red criminals. Politically, Louis Post knew they would lose that fight. Palmer would steamroll them easily, both in the newspapers and at Woodrow Wilson's cabinet table, even if the president could raise himself from his sick bed to actually take charge of something for the first time in months. So they talked and argued that Christmas Eve, shouting and snarling and grumbling, and in the end they decided to surrender. "The country was wild on the subject of the suppression of anarchy; every newspaper was full of it," Abercrombie would testify months later, trying to justify his actions that day. "The department [of Labor] was greatly embarrassed by its inability to function adequately on account of lack of funds."

They all agreed on a letter for Secretary Wilson to sign responding to the Justice Department demands, a cold porridge of mealymouthed evasions: "Although the Department of Labor is in doubt as to whether affidavits based on information that cannot be revealed at the hearings establish the constitutional requirement of 'probable cause' for arrest," it said, "it will issue the warrants requested and will proceed to consider the cases developed by the arrests as rapidly as its meager facilities will permit." The die was cast. The caveats and warnings meant nothing. In fact, only one possible answer from the Labor Department that Christmas Eve could have stopped Palmer from marching forward: a clear, firm No. But William Bauchop Wilson had no more stomach to fight. Caminetti beamed at the outcome. He had finally put his superiors in a box and now he enjoyed watching them squirm.

For the record, Secretary Wilson's letter to Palmer explained his concerns. "I feel . . . that it is due to you to say that the limitations of the Immigration Service make it impossible to immediately dispose of all these cases," it said, and it did take a stand on one point: "We cannot . . . assume the responsibility of injury to innocent parties which would probably result from a hasty and imperfect examination of these cases. . . . I have therefore directed that bail be fixed at $1,000 each, except in unusual and extraordinary cases."

Mitchell Palmer received Secretary Wilson's letter that weekend and did not even bother to answer it until after the operation had started. He gave it to Edgar, and Edgar cranked out a response in a few days. In it, he defended the simultaneous nationwide raids as a police tactic and then ridiculed Wilson's logic for reducing bail as a pointless exercise in revolving-door justice: "permitting these persons to be released upon bail of $1,000 will be merely taking [them] into custody . . . and immediately releasing of the same . . . which fails to accomplish any material result."

Louis Post spent Christmas Day, 1919, in Washington, D.C., with his wife, Alice, and his son, Charles, who came to visit from New York City. At Christmas dinner, he probably tried to avoid dwelling on what he had done in the office the night before, soiling his reputation once more. But even Louis Post could not conceive of the rage and reaction that would soon be unleashed by their decision to grant Mitchell Palmer his 3,000 warrants. In effect, he and his Labor Department colleagues had given Palmer exactly what he had asked for: just enough rope to hang himself.

Edgar spent the Christmas of 1919 at home with his parents in Washington, D.C., in the small house on Capitol Hill where they all still lived together. Papa's mental sickness aside, Edgar's family had much to celebrate that year. Both he and his brother, Dick, enjoyed exciting new jobs, his nieces Margaret and Anna were growing into vivacious teenagers, and Mother Hoover still ruled the roost. Edgar earned enough money that year to help buy a fine Christmas dinner for the family, and Dick and his wife and daughters joined them from next door. Edgar ordinarily would have relished the table talk, the laughter and noise and palling around. His brother could tease all he wanted, but Edgar had a firm leg up as the family's star since his name had appeared in the newspapers regarding the Emma Goldman case. Edgar could answer Dick's teasing questions about his work with Mitchell Palmer with a condescending brush-off about how secret it all was. Annie Marie Scheitlin Hoover could be proud of her favorite son.

But the pressure showed on him as well. Edgar worked hard and seemed to carry a huge burden; sometimes he turned the strain on his family, snapping at them impatiently. It was around this time that a doctor told Edgar he needed to start smoking cigarettes to relax his nerves. Edgar tried, but he disliked smoking alone, so he convinced his niece Margaret to join him and keep him company. Perhaps he thought he was doing her a favor—that she would benefit too from the healthy effect of the cigarettes.

Whatever few hours Edgar managed to spare to be with his family that Christmas, his office demanded the rest. All that month, Edgar consumed himself in planning the Big Raid. He worked his staff ragged sending detailed orders to the field, compiling long lists of target names to ship over to Caminetti at the Labor Department for new warrants. Edgar insisted on bringing dozens of bureau chiefs into Washington—an expensive, time-consuming trip from faraway places like Chicago, Boston, or Detroit—to brief them on the operation, while demanding meticulous planning at every level. In New England, his Boston-based agents worked with local police, businessmen, and private detective agencies to identify suspects, and they also planted dictaphone listening devices in meeting halls used by local communist groups. In Manchester, New Hampshire, for instance, they bugged the local Cigar Makers Union, the Polish, Lithuanian, and Ukrainian Clubs, and broke into the local Tolstoi and Polish Clubs five times, searching for evidence and names.

Edgar also asked Military Intelligence to poll its West Coast offices for names of I.W.W. members they were tracking to beef up his target lists.

Edgar took barely a single day off during this period. Beyond the raids themselves, his job as chief of the Radical Division required him to worry over any possible threat of a new anarchist terror attack in the meantime. In early December, he went into a panic when a Philadelphia-based agent reported hearing that radicals were planning to launch a Christmas "reign of terror"—a mail bomb spree similar to the one that failed in May when anarchists tried to send sixteen bombs through the New York City Post Office. Edgar immediately assigned dozens of agents in different cities to trace the story. But after a few days, the original Philadelphia agent admitted that his source had gotten his information solely from a girl he had met at a dance party who was apparently trying to seduce him. "[I]t was apparent that the informant did not have any real knowledge of the radical situation," he confessed, though not until after giving Edgar and his staff several sleepless nights.

That month, Edgar also finished putting together a legal brief

demanding the deportation of Ludwig Martens, Bolshevik Russia's emissary in New York City—essentially Lenin's ambassador to America. Since
Martens belonged to no American radical groups and he avoided making
any controversial public statements, Edgar had to stretch hard to find any
legal pretext for deporting him under the 1918 Immigration Act. In the
end, he decided to try indicting the entire Russian-based Bolshevik Party
of Lenin and Trotsky. Since the Russian Bolsheviks had urged world revolution through their Third International, arguably their whole government could be seen as urging the violent overthrow of the United States
Government, making any of its members or officials subject to deportation, including Ludwig Martens.

The argument was full of holes. Moscow had never declared war on
Washington, and for the American government to let a deportation
statute dictate its foreign policy toward Soviet Russia stood normal diplo-
macy on its head. Still, Edgar put his theory forward. He submitted the
brief to Caminetti, who sent it up to Abercrombie who, in turn, checked
with Secretary of State Robert Lansing about the protocol of deporting a
sitting diplomat for a foreign government, albeit one the United States
had never formally recognized. Nobody blinked. "Abercrombie called to
ask if there was any diplomatic reason why Martens (Bolshevik representative) should not be deported," Lansing wrote in his calendar that
month. "I said there was no reason and to 'go ahead.'"

Mitchell Palmer appreciated the point more than anyone. As the *New
York Call* put it: "America's foreign relations will be governed by the
attorney general instead of by the Secretary of State." Palmer had one
more bureaucratic scalp to hang from his belt.

Edgar tracked hundreds of reports crossing his desk that month
showing how his assaults already had thrown the American communist
movement into disarray. He may have laughed out loud at seeing one
item about Louis Fraina, the radical ideologue from Boston who published *The Revolutionary Age*, had led the new Communist Party of
America at its founding convention in Chicago, and was a rumored
author of the "Plain Words" leaflet found at the June 2 bombing sites.
Fraina had escaped arrest during the November raids in New York and
Boston, but his escape only raised suspicions among his own comrades.
Someone inside Communist Party circles accused Fraina of being a
traitor, a Justice Department spy working secretly for Mitchell Palmer.
The idea was laughable on its face, showing just how paranoid the com-
munists had become. Fraina, a self-taught Italian immigrant, had

authored three books on revolutionary socialism, went to jail for sedition during World War I, and coauthored the Communist Party platform. He was as true a Bolshevik as anyone alive in America. Edgar knew the charge against Fraina was a fraud. He quickly tracked down its source, a Justice Department agent who was playing both sides of the fence. Edgar promptly fired the agent.*

Still, Ludwig Martens, the Soviet envoy, had convened a secret trial in Brooklyn in front of half a dozen Communist elders to hear the charges. Louis Fraina denied them and cleared his name, but he felt so spooked by the whole affair that he decided to flee the country within the month and plead his case in Moscow.

But of all the loose ends gnawing at his mind that December 1919 leading up to the Big Raid, none seemed to get under Edgar's skin worse than the lawyers. He still fumed over Isaac Schorr, the attorney from the National Civil Liberties Bureau who had popped up at Ellis Island after the November raids to represent the prisoners there. It was Schorr who coached them to launch their silence strike, and it was Schorr who went to the liberal New York Call and accused Palmer and his men of brutality in the assault on the Russian Peoples House in New York City. "His practice has been, in my opinion, far from ethical," Edgar complained to John Creighton privately that month. But he didn't stop there. He seemed fixated with Isaac Schorr, and he allowed his irritation to fester all through the Christmas season. He grabbed Caminetti and asked him about having Schorr banned from practicing law before the Immigration Bureau, and had one of his local Special Agents file a written complaint about Schorr with Ellis Island Commissioner Byron Uhl.

Edgar began to track Isaac Schorr, to collect facts about him that appeared in reports from his agents, starting with his own complaint letters but soon adding other things: the fact that Schorr once signed a retainer contract with the Union of Russian Workers; that he once

---

*The agent was named Ferdinand Peterson, and Edgar had hired him in October 1919 to spy on Ludwig Martens. Peterson infiltrated Martens's office, and then, apparently trying to ingratiate himself, he offered Martens proof that Fraina, a rival, was an undercover agent for the Justice Department, which would explain Fraina's suspicious escape in the November raid. Petersen claimed that he had seen Fraina at least three times at the Justice Department's office on Park Row and had seen cancelled checks signed by Flynn with Fraina's name on them, all flatly untrue. It is temping to think that Edgar was behind this plan; the idea of destroying Fraina this way seems far too clever for Peterson. But there is no evidence to support the theory. It seems Petersen was lying to everyone. He apparently allowed Martens's deputy, Santeri Nuorteva, to review his reports to Edgar, disclosing names of undercover agents, forcing Edgar to fire him.

offered a job to a lawyer who had represented a New Jersey anarchist; that
Schorr's name appeared on a list of people who had contributed money to
a defense fund for Russian deportees; that Schorr was involved in a sale
of machinery to a Russian company attached to the Bolsheviks. None of
these facts taken alone meant anything, but together they could create a
potent innuendo to smear or blackmail him should the need ever arise.

Edgar kept all these items about Isaac Schorr in a file, which he incorporated into his Radical Division's general information bank on suspected Reds. He had his staff type up an index card for Isaac Schorr and
gave it a reference code: Old German 377465. Edgar used this designation for all his Red files—Old German or OG—to fit alongside earlier
Department files created during the World War.* The next time Isaac
Schorr stuck his nose into Edgar's business, Edgar would be armed and
ready to punch back.

But he didn't stop even there. For the upcoming Big Raid, Edgar
wanted to make absolutely sure that no left-leaning lawyer could foul
things up the way Isaac Schorr had done on Ellis Island. He decided to
get to the root of the problem: the Labor Department's Rule 22 that
required immigration inspectors to tell each prisoner of his right to
counsel as soon as he was detained. To Edgar, this rule defied logic. It was
a recipe for lawless radicals to beat the system. He badgered Caminetti
over it, sending him letters to remind him of the problems in November.
His stiff bureaucratic prose barely masked his urgency: "I would appreciate an early reply to my letter of the nineteenth," he told Caminetti, "in
order that the same condition may not arise when future arrests are made
of undesirable aliens."

Caminetti needed no convincing. He, too, like Edgar, had no scruples
about fixing things to slam the door against future embarrassments by
lawyers like Isaac Schorr. Caminetti waited until New Year's Eve, *after* Secretary Wilson had left town for the holiday, to launch his sneak attack.
This way, he would be sure to find John Abercrombie—who would have to

---

*These files, including the one on Schorr—the first case of Edgar creating a secret file on a
person primarily a political enemy—were microfilmed by the FBI in 1951–1952 along with the
index card catalogue, and the originals were destroyed. The National Archives' official description of the OG or Old German series reads as follows: "Investigative Records relating to
German aliens ('Old German Files'), 1915–1920. These records are arranged numerically, 1
through 391,901. They constitute file 8000, the original 'Miscellaneous Files' designation for
investigations of German aliens; however, the 8000 File was later separated because of its size.
The records include reports, memorandums, and other documents relating to investigation of
German aliens, who were politically suspect at the time."

approve or deny the last-minute rule change—in the office alone. Caminetti first sent Abercrombie a formal memorandum on the issue and then went to confront him personally the same day. With the doors closed, he told Abercrombie that the government had to stop lawyers like Isaac Schorr from gumming up the works, or things could get out of control. He showed Abercrombie a copy of a December article in a magazine called *The Communist World* that advised radicals arrested in the future to keep their mouths shut. Caminetti proposed a simple fix: Change Rule 22 so that immigration inspectors, instead of being forced to tell prisoners of their right to counsel "at the beginning" of a hearing, could wait until later, "as soon as such hearing had proceeded sufficiently in the development of the facts to protect the Government's interest." This way, he argued, aliens in the future would testify "telling the truth in most instances as [they] saw it, without being hampered by the advice of counsel."

John Abercrombie had no energy left to argue. He yielded on the spot. "I approved [the rule change] on the 31st day of December, with the understanding that when Secretary Wilson returned to Washington it would be brought to his attention," he insisted later. Abercrombie knew, of course, that Secretary Wilson was not scheduled to return to Washington until almost January 20. The Big Raid was set for January 2.*

Edgar celebrated his twenty-fifth birthday on New Year's Day 1920, and now he could do it with one less worry. He had worked his heart out getting ready for the Big Raid, and he used what little spare time he found during the holidays to dig deeper into what he saw as the communist mind, reading polemics such as *The Red Dawn* by Harrison George and *Proletariat and Petit-Bourgeois* by Austin Lewis, and I.W.W. president Bill Haywood's *I.W.W.: The Greatest Thing on Earth*. He never seemed to turn his eye from the issue and covered every conceivable detail of the raid personally. Still, he felt he was on pins and needles. His jittery nerves anticipated a concept that bureaucrats in the 1940s would start to call Murphy's Law: "Anything that can go wrong will go wrong." For instance, on the very eve of the vast national operation, who could imagine that some showboat of a local prosecutor would try to foul things up in Chicago? And that even Mitchell Palmer would not be able to stop him.

---

*The Federal Administrative Procedures Act, which generally requires public notice and comment before Federal agencies can issue or amend regulations like Rule 22, would not be enacted until 1946.

· 22 ·
CHICAGO

MACLAY HOYNE HAD his own idea about how to deal with Reds and no special love for Mitchell Palmer. Palmer and his Justice Department might run things in Washington, D.C., but not in Chicago. Here, as the Illinois state's attorney for Cook County, Maclay Hoyne ruled the law enforcement establishment as its top prosecutor. Hoyne had watched the Lusk Committee in New York City win headlines by going its own way and launching its own dramatic raids against the Reds. Hoyne decided to do the same thing in Cook County. That autumn, he announced his own late conversion to the crusade: "The Reds in this country, and particularly in Chicago, are a real menace and peril," he told the gaggle of newspaper reporters who always trailed him around City Hall, eager for good copy, "a gigantic conspiracy [has] been formed throughout the United States to overthrow the United States government."

Mitchell Palmer might be trying to use his Red Raids to make himself president of the United States, but Maclay Hoyne had his own ambition: to become mayor of the city of Chicago.

Maclay Hoyne had politics in his genes. Both his father and grandfather had been ranking Chicago Democrats and candidates for mayor at different times. His grandfather, Thomas Hoyne, actually won an election for the office in 1874, but a judge had voided the outcome over charges of vote fraud. Hoyne himself had won election as Cook County state's attorney in 1912 and, since then, he and his staff had won almost five thousand convictions against big-time gangsters and small-time crooks. In 1918, he indicted the Chicago chief of police and, more recently, had sent detectives to raid both the mayor's office and the Chicago school board looking for corruption. Just weeks earlier, his raiders had hit the offices of the Sherman Service, Inc., private detective firm, notorious for vicious union-busting tactics during the recent steel strike—including arson, head-beating with steel blackjacks, and vandalism designed to frame strike leaders. Hoyne had convened a special grand jury after the city's summer race riots and won indictments against more than a hundred, largely black, defendants.

His raids and prosecutions won him big headlines, and Hoyne knew how to use them. Earlier in 1919, Hoyne had thrown himself into the biggest local carnival of all, the race for mayor of Chicago. He ran as an independent, breaking from the Democratic Party and accusing both his opponents of corruption and of being too cozy with crooked local gas and streetcar companies. The *Chicago Tribune* endorsed him for his reform platform: "Hoyne is nobody's man but his own," it pronounced. "His Americanism is clear. He has nothing to explain." Hoyne ran a strong third and had kept his name in the headlines ever since, positioning himself smartly for another try. With a fine ear for scandal, he had recently sent his detectives sniffing around the city's American League baseball team, the Chicago White Sox, which had lost the World Series in October to Cincinnati amid rumors of a possible fix in cahoots with East Coast gamblers.

Critics called him a grandstander. Physically imposing, Hoyne had played football at Williams College as a halfback, and he reputedly had answered one letter from a political enemy by saying: "My dear sir—Yours of the eighteenth instant received and in reply I say you lie and you know you lie and [you] know I know you lie. Yours truly __."

Now, at the end of 1919, Maclay Hoyne saw opportunity knocking at the door again, this time in the form of the anti-Red crusade. He traveled to Washington, D.C., and met with Mitchell Palmer to make plans. Hoyne wanted to launch his own separate raid against local Chicago

Reds, striking on the same day as Palmer's Feds and using a coordinated target list. To do it right, he brought together a circle of local businessmen who put up $40,000 of their own money for an investigation. They hired a private detective firm and worked with the local Military Intelligence office to compile a list of suspects. Palmer, for his part, agreed to back Hoyne's operation with dozens of federal agents.

But somehow, in late December, the plans got mixed up. According to Hoyne, Palmer had told him originally that he intended to launch his Big Raid on New Year's Day 1920, so Hoyne slated his own operation for the same day. But when the Justice Department sent out its final orders in late December, they changed the date to January 2, one day later. Hoyne spotted the discrepancy, but instead of changing his own plans to match Palmer's, he decided to leave them be. He would go ahead on January 1 and win a full day of headlines for himself.

When Mitchell Palmer found out about it, he blew his stack. By going first on January 1, Hoyne risked blowing the whistle on Palmer's entire national effort, possibly giving Reds across the country a full day's warning to run and hide. Palmer immediately sent his special assistant, John Creighton, racing across the country by train to Chicago hand-carrying a written plea for Hoyne to delay his raid by at least one day, until January 2. But Maclay Hoyne met with Creighton and read Palmer's letter, and it only made him angry. He refused to budge. When Creighton then reported back to Washington that Hoyne still intended to strike on January 1, Palmer ordered Creighton to withdraw all federal support from Hoyne's operation. Maclay Hoyne, hearing this final decision, decided to go ahead anyway.

And off he went. On New Year's Day, 1920, at 4:00 P.M., armed with two hundred warrants from a local judge, each made out simply to "John Doe," Maclay Hoyne's detectives and squads of Chicago police set out across the city in a fleet of taxis and sedans. By nightfall they had rounded up more than two hundred suspects. They hit the Communist Labor Party's office at the Clarion Book Store on North Clark Street. They took thirty-nine prisoners at the I.W.W. Hall on Throop Street, and grabbed twenty more at the Communist Party office on the South Side, among dozens of other arrests. All the while, Palmer's men stood aside. They closed the door to Chicago's Federal Building at 5:00 P.M. "We are not cooperating in any way," local agent P. J. Brennan told reporters. "And I can say absolutely nothing concerning our plans."

At the end of the day, Maclay Hoyne pulled a crowd of newspapermen into his office and told them clearly and precisely how the attorney general in Washington, D.C., had lied and cheated and turned his back on the City of Chicago. "Yesterday morning I received a letter from Attorney General Palmer . . . requesting that I should not proceed with the raids," he told them. "I told [Palmer] I could not comply with the request, as my plans were made. . . . Apparently Attorney General Palmer or some of his friends are playing petty politics with the situation and are pursuing a pussyfoot policy. . . . I do not believe Nero or any other fiddler can be elected President of the United States."

As a final insult, Hoyne directed his staff to leak rumors that Palmer's men tried to sabotage his operation. "[W]ithout any doubt," one told a reporter, "[the Reds were] tipped off by some employe or attaché of the department of justice."

Back in Washington, D.C., Mitchell Palmer tracked these New Year's Day events by long-distance telephone. At the end of the day, he called his own gaggle of newspaper reporters into his office and told them that 1920 would be a year of "open season" on Reds, of "unflinching, persistent, and aggressive warfare." As for Hoyne, he didn't say a word—as if the Chicago state's attorney never even existed. Palmer was not going to let some two-bit grandstander like Maclay Hoyne rain on his parade.

As for Edgar, January 2 promised to be the biggest day of his career so far, bigger even than the Soviet Ark and the Emma Goldman case. Besides, he had a better idea to deal with Maclay Hoyne. When a friend in Chicago sent Palmer a copy of a satirical political flyer poking fun at Hoyne, calling him a "fake reformer" and worse, Palmer gave it to Edgar, and Edgar made it the first entry in a new file he opened up on Hoyne. As with lawyer Isaac Schorr, Edgar made Hoyne's file part of his data bank on suspicious Reds and gave it its own index card and reference number: Old German 383427. Some day it might come in handy, in case they ever had another run-in with Maclay Hoyne and needed to keep him under control.

I T CAME OFF beautifully. On Friday, January 2, 1920, Mitchell Palmer's men struck in thirty-three cities and dozens of small towns coast to coast, from Portland, Oregon, to Portland, Maine. By midnight, they reported making over 2,500 arrests; by the end of the weekend, estimates of the total detained would reach 5,000. Whatever the actual number—there is no reliable official count—it would be the largest single-day police roundup in American history.

Palmer's fear that Maclay Hoyne's premature raid on New Year's Day might tip off radicals and allow them to escape the dragnet never materialized. They were sitting ducks.

New Year's Eve 1920 had been a gloomy one in most of the country. Fear, want, and violence had cast a pall over late 1919. The playful, happy Roaring Twenties of flappers, speakeasies, and jazz was a far way off. Prohibition, slated to begin nationwide on January 16 and already in effect through dry laws covering most areas, chilled many celebrations.

New York City abandoned its traditional Times Square jubilee. The city had been spooked all that week by stories of poisonous homemade wood alcohol corrupting local liquor stocks and killing several people in nearby Connecticut. These were dangerous times. It was dangerous to drink, dangerous to talk, dangerous to join a union or go on strike, dangerous to stick out the wrong way in a crowd. Harvard defeated Stanford in the Rose Bowl by a score of 7 to 6 that New Year's Day, but few people knew or cared. No radio or television existed yet to carry the game, and college sports seemed distant and irrelevant to the millions looking for jobs or the factory workers struggling to keep pace with soaring prices.

Still, it was the holidays and people made merry as best they could that weekend, going to dances and parties and looking for fun. On Friday night, many got more excitement than they bargained for.

As in November, Palmer's men struck simultaneously at 9:00 P.M. in each time zone across the country. Swarms of agents, police, and volunteer deputies swooped down on meeting halls, pool rooms, dance halls, political meetings, night classrooms, and hundreds of individual homes to round up suspects. They hit twenty-seven towns in New England alone, bagging seven hundred prisoners, including fifty-seven in Boston and 161 in tiny Nashua, New Hampshire. They seized three hundred suspects in Detroit and more than five hundred in New York City. It had all been neatly planned. Palmer's undercover agents had infiltrated almost every communist group and used their influence to call meetings that night so members would come together in groups, making them easy to arrest.

In Lincoln, New Hampshire, agents burst into the home of a man named Fred Chaika at 11:00 P.M., after he had gone to sleep. They pushed into his bedroom, grabbed him from bed, arrested him, refused to show him a warrant, handcuffed him despite his having a broken wrist, threw him into the back of a car, and took him to a local clubroom where they locked him up with fourteen other suspects. In Nashua, they raided the St. Baptiste Hall where the local Lithuanian Club was having a New Year's dance. Agents came in, stopped the music, searched and handcuffed all the men, loaded them in cars and wagons and drove them to a local police station along with thirteen women, one of whom was a mother of three children. Then, at the police station, the agents confronted one of the women with a suitcase filled with communist newspapers and two family prayer books they said they'd seized from her house and demanded she confess to being a Red. When she refused, they sent her home.

In Boston, raiding parties hit eighteen separate branches of the local Communist Party. In Chelsea, Massachusetts, they raided a dance. In nearby Lynn, Massachusetts, they hit a meeting hall on Market Street where a group of Jewish men were talking about setting up a cooperative bakery. In each case, they arrested everyone in sight. In Brockton, Massachusetts, they rounded up ten men from their beds at home. In Detroit, they raided a New Year's party being held at Shore Hall, which had a restaurant on the street-level floor that was popular with Socialist Party members. They arrested the dancers, the musicians, the waiters, the cooks, and all the patrons eating dinner, including a handful of ex-servicemen. In none of these places did they meet any resistance. As in November, Palmer asked the State and War departments to patrol the borders to prevent radicals from escaping to Canada or Mexico. One suspect from Detroit was captured a few days later in Laredo, Texas, trying to reach Mexico.

In New York City, police needed twenty-three wagons to carry all the suspects they captured that night to the Justice Department office on Park Row and then to Ellis Island by ferry. They hit the Communist Party office on Tenth Street where some fifty men were holding a meeting; they rushed in with pistols in the air, shouted "Hands up!" and took them all downtown. The New York agents made a special point to shut down the local radical newspapers. They raided the office of the Communist *Elore Hungarian Daily* in Greenwich Village, ransacked its files, posted guards in the pressroom, and banned any further printing. They arrested its editor, Eugene Neuwald, handcuffed him, drove him to a local police station, held him there for several days, then transferred him to Ellis Island, where they held him for nine additional days before releasing him without a hearing, all while barring him from seeing his lawyer or his wife.

Many prisoners complained that agents beat them with blackjacks or revolvers while arresting them; the veracity of these accounts is impossible to know decades later. "In my case, when I was arrested, four men came into the room in the evening, when I was partly undressed, and was doing exercises in arithmetic, and asked my name and told me to go along with them. They showed me a badge but did not tell me the reason for my arrest," one New York Russian man testified at his hearing. On the way to Park Row, "they were beating me in the sides with their handcuffs." In Buffalo, Palmer's men had assembled an army of 230 local police and a fleet of two hundred motorcars driven by volunteer chauffeurs. At 9:00 P.M., they fanned out and rounded up over 250 suspects within half an hour. In that case, the secretary of the local Buffalo Communist Party was himself a Justice Department undercover agent who had arranged the meetings that night and supplied copies of membership cards and address lists to the police.

In Chicago, agents rounded up over a hundred radicals—anyone left on the streets after Maclay Hoyne's raid the day before. Their biggest haul came from hitting a school on North Robey Street funded by Ludwig Martens' Soviet Mission in New York. The school had been created that year to teach job skills to Russian immigrants thinking of returning home. Jane Addams, the writer-reformer who created the Hull House settlement to help Chicago's poor and who knew many of these Russians from her work, described how an automobile repair class was being held at the school that night when the police came and arrested the teacher plus all sixty-four pupils and seized all the textbooks. They made a special point to take the math books, she said, "because the algebraic formulas appeared so incriminating." By Sunday night, between the federal and local operations around Chicago, they had collared 357 radicals there. "We are going to get them all—every one of them—if it takes a month or six months," John Creighton told reporters at the end of the weekend. "At least we can promise one certain development. Chicago aliens will have a bright soviet ark all to themselves on this journey."

Maclay Hoyne, who temporarily put aside his feud with Mitchell Palmer to join the action, added a special touch. While the federal agents were sending most of the Reds they captured in Chicago to nearby Bridewell Prison, Hoyne decided to take several dozen from his own raid and house them in a Cook County jail alongside regular Chicago gangsters. Not surprisingly, a fight broke out. Jail guards looked the other way as local toughs decided to punish the Reds, cornering them in a cell and kicking and punching them with abandon. A local reporter who witnessed the scene described several of the Red suspects afterward as having "black eyes, cut lips, bruised faces, and other indications of battle."

By midnight on Friday, Palmer's Justice Department reported that it had detained almost 2,600 suspects so far and it gave a detailed list to the newspapers:

Arrests as of midnight, January 2, 1920

Ansonia, Ct.	12	Hartford	2	St. Paul	9
Baltimore	35	Kansas City	12	St. Louis	25
Berlin, N.H.	40	Lawrence	19	Springfield, Mass.	65
Boston	37	Lowell	46	Toledo	8
Buffalo area	135	Lynn	47	Youngstown	16
Bridgeport	15	Los Angeles	1	Wellesley, Mass.	2
Cambridge	1	Louisville	21	Waterbury, Cn.	7
Cleveland	100	Manchester, N.H.	65	Worcester	86
Chelsea	24	Meriden, Ct.	3	Wilkesbarre, Pa.	70
Chicopee, Ma.	16	Milwaukee	50	Connecticut	
Detroit	400	Nashua, N.H.	161	towns	11
Denver	6	New York City	700	Rhode Island	
Erie, Pa.	2	Oakland, Cal.	18	cities	30
Grand Rapids	6	Portland, Ore.	20		
Holyoke	20	Philadelphia	200	Total	2585
Haverhill	21	Pittsburgh	21		

On the surface, it looked like another triumph, a crisp, clean, efficient operation taking violent Reds off the street and making America a safer country. One nameless Department official, probably Edgar himself, explained that they had what he called "perfect cases" against 2,720 of the aliens jailed so far, meaning they could demonstrate (a) that the person was a noncitizen and (b) he belonged to the Communist or the Communist Labor Party, the basic grounds for deportation.

On Monday, Mitchell Palmer claimed victory: "[T]he backbone of the Communist movement in the United States has been broken in the raids and the movement can be prevented from again becoming a menace," he crowed. Journalists sang his praises. "His principles are not in the marketplace. . . . He is no poser . . . he is an idealist who does not talk about ideals. His public work, however, is itself eloquent upon the subject of the loftiest patriotism," one of them, William T. Ellis, wrote in a typical fawning profile in that month's *American Review of Reviews*. "The placid face of Palmer should not divert the eye from that fighting jaw. He is not bellicose; but he is brave with the courage of a people who for centuries have dared all for conscience's sake. . . . There is something almost brutal as well as noble about the 'yea is yea' and 'nay is nay' of the Quaker's candor."

Palmer's crusade resonated all through January 1920. Beyond the raids themselves, the New York State legislature in Albany voted on January 7 to expel all five of its assemblymen who had won election as Socialist Party candidates and the United States Congress on January 10 voted to expel its lone Socialist member, Representative Victor Berger of Wisconsin. Even Palmer considered these last steps to be excessive; the Socialist Party had never preached violence, and he had never included it as a target in his raids. Palmer, already pressing his campaign for the

"The Quicker and Harder, the Better." St. Louis Republic,
in American Review of Reviews, January, 1920.

White House, seized on the chance to be gracious. "The Socialists are loyal and patriotic men, though radical," he told one audience in criticizing the Albany decision, even as he chose that same month to endorse a new bill in Congress to drastically limit free speech. The bill, introduced by Ohio congressman Martin Davey, would make it a crime in peacetime not only to commit sedition but also to "promote" sedition—a term so vague that it could be used against just about anyone who criticized the government—and it set penalties as high as ten years in prison for native-born American citizens and for immigrants denaturalization and deportation.

Mitchell Palmer could ask Congress for almost any power he wanted that month and expect them to deliver it. Had the presidential election of 1920 occurred in January, he would have captured the White House in a landslide.

But this appearance was deceiving; the applause was premature. The sheer size of Palmer's Raids had made them a national sensation, but had also sown the seeds for a backlash. An avalanche of problems was beginning to form, and the burden of addressing it would fall not on Palmer himself, who was far too busy accepting the country's applause. It would fall instead on his bright young assistant getting an abrupt education in American government at the highest level, J. Edgar Hoover.

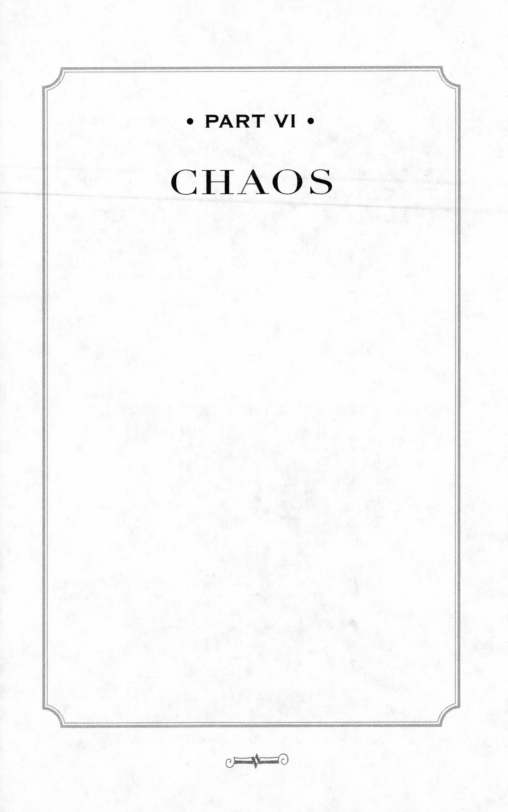

• PART VI •

CHAOS

Arrested "Reds' held in the reception room at Ellis Island, January 1920.

An unidentified prisoner in his cell at Boston's Deer Island.

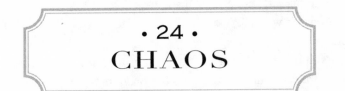

· 24 ·
CHAOS

A S IN NOVEMBER, Edgar spent the day of the Big Raid, Friday, January 2, 1920, in his office at the Justice Department. A special telephone line connected his desk to his field bureaus across the country, and he used it constantly that night, to get updates, check rumors, and keep score. Edgar made a practice of marking the large map on his wall with color-coded pins and paper flags to watch his operations unfold neatly before him. In this case, the flags showed a clean wave from east to west. A typical instruction to the Boston bureau that week directed: "On the evening of the arrests, this office will be open the entire night and I desire that you communicate by long distance to Mr. Hoover." Edgar was a veteran now of these late-night vigils, having earned his battle scars in November and December. This time, he stayed calm all day while waiting for 9:00 P.M., when the action started. He raised only a few small points with Caminetti, his senior partner at the Immigration Bureau a few blocks away. Edgar contacted him once during the afternoon to complain about an immigration inspector who failed to show up at a rendezvous point with an agent, though Edgar's agent claimed it was because the particular inspector was a "dope fiend"—cause for a local investigation, not a national crisis.

The first indication Edgar saw that something had gone wrong came in the postmidnight hours as thousands of prisoners began pouring into local jails and police stations around the country. Telegrams flooded into Edgar's office containing long lists of names of suspects never mentioned on any of the prior target lists. In each case, the agents demanded warrants. Edgar had anticipated getting some requests like these; he had worked with Caminetti to obtain almost four hundred postarrest warrants after the raids in November. Without them, his agents had no legal basis to hold the prisoners and the immigration officials had no authority to take them off their hands, so it was essential to get them issued, signed, and wired back to the field as fast as possible. But back in November, Edgar's agents had limited the problem to a manageable size. They had been able to search and question almost every one of the hundreds of prisoners within a few hours of capture, sifting out the American citizens and nonradicals and releasing almost all of them before dawn the next morning, leaving only a relatively small number to turn over to the Immigration Bureau for deportation. But this time, in January, it was different. This time, they had thousands. The system was choking.

All night long, the lists kept coming, along with piles of massproduced affidavits to support the needed warrants; 163 from New York City, 66 from Boston, 41 from Philadelphia, 16 from Grand Rapids, and 17 from St. Paul, just in the first few hours. Edgar warned Caminetti early Saturday morning that things were getting out of hand. "I desire to bring to your immediate attention what appears to be the absolute necessity of reverting to the old arrangement for the obtaining of telegraphic warrants," he told him. But Caminetti could do little more than crank out the warrants as fast as he could.

This chaos in Washington, though, was nothing as compared to what was happening out around the country as thousands of suspects that night found themselves being herded into jails, police stations, and makeshift centers—many of which quickly deteriorated into terrifying hellholes.

The worst problems developed in Boston and Detroit. In Boston, local immigration commissioner Henry J. Skeffington had arranged to take over

Deer Island, a small spit of land in Boston Harbor where the city had recently finished building a new prison.* Boston officials agreed to provide food, light, heat, and other services as prisoners streamed in from all over New England on Saturday and Sunday and were loaded onto a ferry to reach the island penitentiary. Soon, more than six hundred people found themselves crammed into the Deer Island prison, overwhelming its three hundred bunks and handful of working toilets. Despite subfreezing January temperatures, the cells remained unheated for three days. Food grew scarce, and tempers flared as guards kept jamming more prisoners into the over-crowded cell blocks and turned deaf ears to prisoners' pleas to contact their lawyers, friends, and families. One inmate committed suicide by throwing himself out a fourth-story window as others stood nearby and watched; two contracted pneumonia. Boston Penal Commissioner Thomas O'Brien warned of possible riots after learning that there were only twelve immigration guards to keep order. "I fear that their imprisonment for a long period of time without the possibility of occupying their minds and hands with some tasks, may result in an outbreak," he wrote to Skeffington as he demanded federal soldiers. Skeffington instead arranged with the local American Legion for armed military veterans to come and keep watch.

As stories of the squalor on Deer Island reached the mainland and alarmed local Boston citizens, Skeffington warned them against paying attention to what he called "sob stories" from jailed Reds. "Remember the bombs, those nefarious engines of death sent through the mail," he told one group. "These men would not hesitate to kill you."

In one incident, Boston police and federal agents greeted a group of prisoners arriving at the train station from Manchester, New Hampshire, en route to Deer Island. They took these prisoners, about a hundred and forty men and women, lined them up in pairs, shackled their wrists in handcuffs and chained their ankles together with leg irons, and then marched them the long way through the freezing streets of Boston's slums, inviting crowds of people to come and spit insults and throw garbage at them from the sidewalk as newspaper photographers snapped their pic-tures. The prisoners reacted by singing songs and shouting Bolshevik slo-gans until they reached the ferry station. "Chains and handcuffs . . .

---

*Deer Island today is the site of a wastewater treatment plant. It has been connected to the mainland since 1938.

seemed to have only slight depressing effect upon [them]," wrote a *Boston Herald* reporter who witnessed the scene. Meanwhile, at the Justice Department office on Water Street, hundreds of wives and mothers, many crying hysterically, elbowed their way inside to ask what had become of missing friends, fathers, sons, and husbands. "Some of the young women were leading young children who, clinging to their mothers' skirts, looked [on] with frightened eyes," a *Boston Globe* reporter wrote in describing the scene.

Photograph of Boston prisoners in chains. *American Review of Reviews*, February 1920.

Even worse was the situation in Detroit. Here, to handle the flood of prisoners, agents and local police had commandeered the top floor of Detroit's old Federal Building/Post Office, which had a long corridor and rotunda. Within two days, the population of this makeshift prison swelled to eight hundred men and women—all locked inside the single hallway with no windows, no ventilation, and no place to sleep except on the bare stone floor. Prisoners waited for hours to drink from a single water fountain or use the single bathroom; most went without food for twenty hours. At night, they huddled under newspapers and overcoats as the stench grew unbearable. They remained jailed there for up to six days without access to lawyers or family until Detroit Mayor James Couzens finally insisted they be moved, claiming they posed a sanitation threat to the city.

At this point, the Detroit agents decided to farm out the prisoners to local police precincts, but this barely improved the conditions. In one local station, police jammed about 130 prisoners into a single "bull pen," a small, one-window cellar that had only wooden benches and a stone floor, designed to hold petty criminals. They gave them no food beyond the contributions they received from the few family members lucky enough to track them down and pass baskets through a grate in the door.

The Detroit crisis, like the Boston crisis and those in other cities, all landed on Edgar's desk. As time stretched into hours, days, and weeks, he handled one flare-up after another, barking out orders, crafting telegrams and letters, talking on the telephone, asking questions and demanding answers. On January 7, five full days after the raids, Edgar's Detroit agents first told him that they needed warrants for 145 named prisoners—it had taken them that long just to make a list—and Edgar pushed Caminetti to have them "expedited as much as possible to relieve congestion at that point." Two days later, he received another list from Detroit, this one requesting 101 more warrants. It would take until January 19, almost three weeks after the raid, before he could push the Detroit agents to finish sifting out and release the American citizens and clear noncommunists, bringing their total number of prisoners by then down to about three hundred, mostly moved to a nearby army fort.

In some cities, Justice Department agents tried their best to treat the prisoners humanely. In Philadelphia, for instance, agents rounded up more than a hundred suspects and jailed them in Moyamensing Prison. There, they worked around the clock to weed out American citizens and nonradicals, conduct initial hearings, and set bail. They released most of the inmates within forty-eight hours and arranged for about a dozen families to be supported by private charities while husbands waited for final decisions in their cases.

But this was the exception. More typical was the scene at New York's Ellis Island where agents brought over five hundred prisoners from raids all over the region. "It was midwinter and the authorities on the Island were not prepared," lawyer Charles Recht recalled. "There were not enough cots and bedding. . . . Among the captors, the rule of the fist prevailed." They packed them in, three hundred to a room, on rows of three-level steel bunks without mattresses and "cleaned as frequently as inadequate janitor's force will permit," as one immigration inspector conceded, and "if dirty at any time due to their own uncleanly [sic] habits." Fevers swept the dormitories and at least two prisoners—possibly eight—died there of pulmonary pneumonia. One of these, an illiterate Russian immigrant named Mike Marzinik, who was seized from his home in Passaic, New Jersey, had served during World War I as a doughboy in France and been honorably discharged.

Ellis Island Commissioner Byron Uhl complained that he had warrants to cover only about 150 of the 500 inmates. He was holding all the rest illegally. But still he announced that he would refuse to accept bail for any inmate until all the preliminary hearings had been completed, promising to keep the whole bunch locked up for weeks or maybe months. City leaders in New York that week insisted on going further and building what they called a "concentration camp" to hold these Reds. When lawyer Charles Recht, hired by both the Communist and Communist Labor parties in New York and New Jersey to represent their members on Ellis Island, sent two assistants there to interview inmates, the Ellis Island staff turned them away. "Some five hundred men have been held incommunicado for the last ten days, and I would like to inquiry [sic] how long it will be before we will be permitted to see our clients," he complained to Secretary Wilson in mid-January. He got no answer.

Recht did manage to smuggle one snippet of legal advice onto the Island through a friendly charity worker. "The problem of how to communicate this advice to the prisoners in separate pens on the Island was solved by the dusty window panes," Recht explained. "With their fingers they wrote my instructions in a Russian phrase which became an echo of the deportation proceedings of the six hundred: 'Nie otvetchaytie na vopros!' (Decline to answer)."

Even after bail had been set for many of the inmates, Ellis Island officials blocked him again. Recht sent a man carrying Liberty Bonds to post the bail only to have him barred from even stepping onto the ferry.

The fact was, Edgar had no sympathy for what he considered bellyaching from these detained Reds over their tough jail conditions, and his staff, up the line and down, all felt the same. Edgar insisted on holding every last prisoner as long as possible. To release even a single possible communist would defeat the whole point of the enterprise. Edgar complained to Caminetti that "[m]any of the subjects taken are scattered in local police stations and offices . . . resulting in unsanitary conditions and much congestion." But what bothered him more was exactly the opposite problem: figuring out how to keep these prisoners locked up until all the warrants could be issued, all the hearings held, and a fleet of ships assembled to take them back to Russia, Poland, Lithuania, Italy, or wherever else they had come from.

Each day for two weeks after the raid, Edgar sent between twenty and thirty or more letters and telegrams to Caminetti to nail down these details, and he called him on the telephone repeatedly. He grew frantic at how long it took Caminetti to issue warrants, and he accused him of jeopardizing the whole operation over it. "I am informed that the attorneys for the alien communists held at Ellis Island are planning to sue out writs of habeas corpus in all cases of alien communists . . . upon whom warrants have not yet been issued by you," he wrote Caminetti in early January, and he raised the same point a few days later after receiving urgent wires from Baltimore, Detroit, and Jacksonville, where lawyers likewise threatened to file legal protests.

Their arguments over bail grew especially vehement. Edgar scoffed at the Labor Department directive setting bail for all the prisoners at $1,000. This was equivalent to a full year's wages for many factory workers at the time, but Edgar barraged Caminetti with demands that this paltry sum be increased. In one case, he insisted that a group of nineteen prisoners in Newark consisted of nothing but "young men and single [who] have admitted membership in the Communist Party and unless bond is fixed at $10,000, these persons will disappear." In another, Edgar protested the imminent freeing on $1,000 bond of a man arrested in Connecticut named Alfred Skerron, whom Edgar considered particularly dangerous because, after the November raids, he had become active in "organizing and collecting funds" to help hire defense lawyers for jailed radicals. Edgar insisted his bail be raised to $5,000 to keep him behind bars.

Caminetti happily joined with Edgar in finding some ways to tighten the screws. He instructed his immigration inspectors to refuse to accept any bail in cash. Instead, he insisted that they demand bonds and, at the same time, he made these bonds almost impossible to find. When lawyer Charles Recht visited both the National Surety Company and the Maryland Casualty Surety Company, two of the largest bond dealers in the region, trying to purchase bail bonds for some of the New York–area communists, they slammed their doors in his face. Both companies refused to do business with him for what they called "patriotic reasons," he told the *New York Call*. Someone from Washington had warned them to back off. In another case, Recht took the train to Washington, D.C., and met with John Abercrombie at the Labor Department to plead on humanitarian grounds that he lower the bail for eleven particular men being held in Hartford, Connecticut. Abercrombie agreed, but when Recht arrived in Hartford the next week with bonds in hand to free the men, the local inspectors refused to accept them. The local immigration staff apparently had taken Abercrombe's decision and simply tossed it away.

Ironically, Edgar's strict line on bail did not stop the top communist leaders from buying their way out. The Communist Labor Party boasted in February 1920 that it had bailed out every single one of its leaders on Ellis Island and Deer Island within the month, using party coffers and fund raising. Instead, it was the rank and file workingmen who found themselves hopelessly unable to raise the funds.

It took weeks for things finally to fall into place. Eventually, though, they did. With warrants finally secured and bail set high as possible, Edgar first had the chance to focus on the next step in the process, the deportation hearings. Before being deported, each prisoner had the right to appear before an immigration inspector, hear the evidence against him, answer questions, and respond to the charges, with a court stenographer keeping a full verbatim record, and a lawyer present. The transcripts of these hearings would be the legal basis for any final decision in his case. Ultimately, the secretary of labor himself or his designee had to decide each case based on this record. Failure to present proof at this stage meant the prisoner should go free. The immigration inspectors all worked under the supervision of Caminetti, but mostly they took their jobs seriously and tried to be fair.

Edgar insisted on controlling this process. One day in early January, about a week after the raids, he walked over to the Labor Department and sat down with Caminetti to talk it over. It was probably the first time the two had seen each other since the big night, and what tired, haggard faces they would have shown. The bond that these two hard-edged men had formed by this point was a strange one indeed, young Edgar freely pestering and badgering away at gray old Caminetti, who seemed to take it with a shrug, happy to indulge his bulldog protégé. They didn't seem close in any personal way. There is no hint that Caminetti ever invited Edgar to his home, introduced him to his wife, took him out to dinner, or shared a few drinks or laughs. Instead, it was always business, all the time, pragmatic, focused, and impatient. They decided that day on a handful of steps to speed up the hearings: Edgar would supply Caminetti with a hundred photostat copies of the exhibits from the briefs he wrote to use against the Communist and Communist Labor parties. Caminetti, for his part, would issue orders to expedite the proceedings: "Care should be exercised not to overburden the record with unnecessary testimony after it has been shown that the alien's case is within the purview of the [immigration statute]," he told his staff. Caminetti agreed to allow one of Edgar's agents to attend each hearing and present evidence. "The Department of Justice man would sit at the opposite side of the table from me, and he would have his voice in the hearing to the same extent that I would," recalled one of the lawyers who participated in some ninety of these proceedings in Chicago. "He would act as though he were attorney for the government in the case."

And then, when they finished, Edgar walked back over to his office and went back to work, just as he always did. And the country, he assumed, would applaud them for it. Or so it seemed in January 1920.

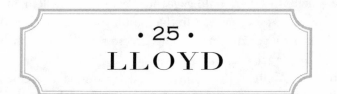

WILLIAM BROSS LLOYD loved a good dustup with police, but he missed the Red Raids in Chicago that weekend, missed his chance to get arrested again, maybe throw a punch at a detective, and pose for the photographers before paying bail and riding off in his chauffeured limousine. Instead, Lloyd spent New Year's weekend, 1920, quietly with his family at his home in Winnetka, Illinois, an hour's train ride north of the city. Lloyd lived in a large white mansion with wide green lawns, a long driveway, pretty flower gardens, and breathtaking views of Lake Michigan. It sat just across the road from a vacant lot that the town flooded with water each winter to create an ice rink where Lloyd loved to take his sons Bill and Jesse and his daughters Mary and Georgia skating. Theirs was a busy household brimming with talk and fun and politics. His wife, Lola Maverick Lloyd, not only led Winnetka's Women's Club but also its local Socialist Party, and she used their home to hold secret meetings of the I.W.W. She became almost as big a celebrity as he the prior summer when she traveled to Geneva, Switzerland, as a founding member of the Women's International League for Peace and Freedom. When her husband ran for the Illinois seat in the United States Senate in 1918 as a Socialist, Lola Maverick Lloyd stumped across the state with him and often drew the larger, friendlier crowds.

But this day, William Bross Lloyd was disappointed. It seemed almost an insult that no detectives either from Maclay Hoyne's office or the federal Justice Department had raided his house yet to arrest him or even ransack his papers. As a founding member of the Communist Labor Party, he felt he had just as much right as Benjamin Gitlow or any other radical in America to be in the thick of things. So Lloyd was pleased to hear a knock at the door at about 8:00 P.M. that Sunday night, just after dinner. He answered it himself; his butler apparently had the night off. Opening it, Lloyd saw standing outside in the snow not the Chicago police but, instead, a nicely dressed young man carrying in his hand a small notebook. He introduced himself as William Sadler, a reporter for the *Chicago Herald and Examiner*. He came all the way from Chicago, he said, because his editors wanted to know if Mr. Lloyd, the Millionaire Socialist, had any comment on the recent raids. Could he come in?

William Bross Lloyd took Sadler's coat and led him into the sitting room where a fire was crackling on the hearth. He doubtless offered the reporter something to drink, maybe a slug of brandy to warm his body or some whiskey to loosen his tongue. As Sadler settled into a plush sofa, Lloyd came and joined him. What an opportunity this presented! Lloyd had missed his chance to be arrested in the Big Raid, but here was something perhaps just as good: a platform. He decided to trust this young man. He sat with him alone as his wife and family gabbed away in another room. Then Lloyd opened with a shocker. "Mr. Lloyd told me . . . that the United States was facing, in his opinion, the most terrible revolution which had ever occurred in the world," Sadler recalled, "a revolution which would be far more bloody than either the French Revolution, and would even eclipse the great world war in the number of people killed."

If William Bross Lloyd had ever considered moderating his tone or lying low while the Palmer-Hoyne crackdowns ravaged Illinois, he quickly abandoned the idea, launching into a full-bore attack as Sadler scribbled furiously in his notebook to capture the outburst. What about the government's plan to deport thousands of Reds? "[F]or every person deported from the United States . . . there [will] be at least 100 people to take their place," Lloyd snapped. "The revolution [will] come suddenly. If it breaks so suddenly, there [will] be no chance to stop its progress. It [will] spread all over the country like wildfire," he argued. Nothing short of Russian-style Soviet socialism could work in America, he said. "Russia is built on a firm foundation of liberty and equality for every one, and this country now occupies the same position as Russia did under the administration of the czar." What about violence? "Violence is the only way," Lloyd went on. "They have used violence on us, and in using violence they have stirred the people so . . . to return it," he said. "Those who take up the sword shall perish by the sword."

Sadler asked question after question, and Lloyd continued his rant—the fire crackling, the drinks flowing. Only one question from the young reporter seemed to throw Lloyd off stride. "There is a warrant out for the arrest of Mr. [I.W.W. president Big Bill] Haywood, who is a member of the Communists, and why is there none for you?" Sadler asked. Lloyd paused. Why indeed? He wondered. What was wrong with Hoyne and Palmer? Did they not understand that he, William Bross Lloyd, was just as much a communist as Haywood, and probably a more important one? Certainly, it was just a matter of time, he told Sadler. He was "reddest of the Reds," he insisted. He tried to shrug it off. "But that doesn't matter. After all, the main thing is not the isolated case of an individual here and there. The big thing is the revolution."

They spoke for about an hour that night in the sitting room, and Sadler managed to get it all down in his notebook: Lloyd's incendiary rhetoric, his musings about being arrested, his embrace of violence, his hostility toward the government, as well as the cozy ambiance of his Winnetka estate. When the *Chicago Herald and Examiner* ran his story the next day, Lloyd had no reason to complain on reading it—other than its paying too much attention to Bill Haywood and not enough to him. In fact, Lloyd was forming an idea in his mind, and the more he considered it, the more he liked it. Here was a good use for his money. If he was arrested, he could hire the best lawyers in America, take his case to the United States Supreme Court, and perhaps have these Red Raids declared unconstitutional. Lloyd was no immigrant. He was a native-born citizen. He had rights. "I would do this on my own initiative, as an American citizen, and as a member of the Communist Labor Party," he told a *Chicago Tribune* reporter on Monday, January 5, the day Sadler's piece had run. "The state's attorney [Maclay Hoyne] is a capitalistic official representing a capitalistic state and dealing capitalistic justice. The idea that he is an impartial prosecutor is all bunk."

William Bross Lloyd would soon get exactly what he wished for. On

January 20, Maclay Hoyne would announce that his Chicago grand jury had brought forth an indictment naming Lloyd and thirty-four other founding members of the Communist Labor Party, charging them all with violating the Illinois "overthrow" act by threatening the violent toppling of the United States government. Lloyd would need the best lawyer in America, not to win a test case in the United States Supreme Court but just to keep him from spending the next twenty years in Joliet prison. Lloyd himself might be too pure in his revolutionary orthodoxy to hire the likes of Clarence Darrow, who was an unabashed capitalist, but Lloyd raised no objection when all the other defendants in his case insisted as a group on drafting Darrow to lead their defense team.

Maclay Hoyne would arrange for twenty of them to be tried together as a group. With perfect political pitch, Hoyne had cast the show trial of the age.

· 26 ·
HEARINGS

ITH THE GROUND rules set, Caminetti's inspectors in early January began conducting hearings in detention centers across the country for the thousands of prisoners nabbed in the January raids. It was a laborious process even under the best conditions, but after a few days a new and troubling pattern began to emerge. On studying the evidence, Caminetti's inspectors were finding that many of these prisoners actually seemed innocent of anything even approaching radicalism. Once put to the proof, the cases collapsed.

In cities like New York, Boston, and Chicago, Edgar's field agents repeatedly found themselves unable to prove that the suspects were even members of the Communist or Communist Labor parties, the foundation for the entire operation. In many cases, Edgar's men refused to talk at all, claiming they had secret sources to protect. Benjamin Bachrach, a lawyer hired by local communists in Chicago to represent prisoners arrested there, recalled sitting through at least six hearings where the inspector asked the Justice Department agent at the end if he had any more evidence to present and the agent simply declined, saying, as Bachrach described it, that he "thought that it was in a confidential way, and he could not produce it—was not at liberty to produce it. That would be all."

Even where the agents did speak freely and could easily prove the prisoner's membership in the Communist Party, many of the cases were laughable. In Chicago, for instance, lawyer Bachrach recalled how virtually none of the Red suspects he represented had any concept that the Communist Party concerned itself with anything but Russia. "[T]hey each and all of them had an idea that by joining this organization [it] might influence President Wilson to withhold the troops from Russia, so that their brothers and relatives might not be killed," he explained. Bachrach, a Republican lawyer who had never dealt with Russian immigrants before, claimed to be as surprised as anyone to learn that "until the interpreter . . . read certain excerpts from the different manifestoes . . . they had no idea what the principles of the Communist Party were—not one of them," as he put it. Most of these men had joined the Socialist Party of Eugene Debs, not the Communists, and had gotten dragged into this mess only because their Socialist Party chapters had been transferred automatically into the new breakaway Communist organizations after the Chicago conventions the prior August. They had received substitute membership cards in the mail, but nobody told them what the difference meant.

Bachrach represented one group of Italians arrested on Chicago's West Side who claimed that the only reason they joined the Communists was to learn to play music and read English. Federal agents laughed at this excuse until one of the Italians insisted on translating a set of actual minutes from one of the Party's meetings to prove they were telling the truth, that the Communist leaders, in fact, had convinced them to join on that basis. This fact came out, though, only after the Italian men had been sitting behind bars for several weeks at Bridewell Prison.

A church organization sponsored a survey of the prisoners snatched in the January raid that confirmed this pattern.* It showed that a large majority of them, 74 percent, were Russians, and another 14 percent were Poles and Lithuanians. Some 80 percent had lived in the United States for six years or longer. Most were married, about a third had applied for American citizenship, and many of the rest had tried to apply for naturalization

---

*In this survey, published in May 1920 by the Federal Council of the Churches of Christ in America, the author, Constantine M. Panunzio, visited the prisons and detention centers at Hartford, Connecticut, Pittsburgh, Pennsylvania, Youngstown, Ohio, and Detroit, and interviewed 168 prisoners there. In addition, he examined the official Labor Department files of two hundred cases selected from around the country.

but got lost in the bureaucratic maze. Their reasons for joining the Communist Party varied widely. When asked about it, most pointed to education. The Party sponsored classes in subjects ranging from arithmetic to language to history to auto repair and cooking. It gave them the chance to join a choir or an orchestra, to learn about politics, or to keep up with Russian current events. Others said they joined it to be around friends and countrymen. The communist headquarters often had pool rooms and lounges to read newspapers or share gossip. They sponsored dinners and dances and games of cards and chess. "The [Party chief] told me they have music and singing, and that I could pass a pleasant evening," one prisoner explained during his hearing. "I want to belong for the purposes of enlightenment and discussion," another testified.

Asked what communists stood for, the prisoners here, too, gave a kaleidoscope of answers: "You see, we recognize in communism to not have in our country kings," one Russian explained. "We were just used as animals," another said, pointing to abuses under the Russian czar. "I wanted to be naturalized so I could vote, but they would not take me," another said. And so it went: "brotherhood, equality, and truth," or "an organization for teaching culture and education," or "a union for the purpose of teaching illiterate people by blackboards." But the most common answers came back to simple friendship: "to enjoy the evenings because there was no other place to go," as one put it. With few exceptions, the survey found these prisoners to be "the common run of work folk: storekeepers, shop-workers, shoemakers, carpenters, mechanics, unskilled laborers, and the like [and] only a small number of these aliens could be classed as dangerous radicals."

But technically, the law drew no line over *why* a person joined the communists or whether he or she was really dangerous. These men and women as party members stood convicted as charged, ripe for deportation.*

Still, information began seeping out from the dungeons of Boston's Deer Island, Chicago's Bridewell Prison, New York's Ellis Island, Detroit's Federal Building, and dozens of other detention centers. The news began to register on the public mind. Descriptions of the mass arrests, the squalid prisons, and now questions about the weak cases—all appeared in the

---

*Note that virtually none of these suspects were "illegal" or "undocumented" immigrants in the modern sense that they had slipped into the country unseen outside the formal system. Since generally they had come by ship from Europe, virtually all had passed through an immigration station such as Ellis Island on landing in America, even if they had not yet become citizens.

press. What had Mitchell Palmer done? At first, only the most predictably liberal voices complained about his Raids, like the *New Republic,* the *Nation,* or the left-leaning *New York Call,* whose front-page headline on January 3 had read: PALMER'S BID FOR PRESIDENCY SEEN IN FRESH ARRESTS.

But this began to change. On January 12, 1920, Francis Fisher Kane, the United States attorney in Philadelphia who had overseen both the November and the January raids in that city, quit his job in protest. "I am obliged to take this step because I feel out of sympathy with the antirad- ical policies of Mr. Palmer and his methods of carrying them out," he wrote to President Woodrow Wilson in a public letter. "I am strongly opposed to the wholesale raiding of aliens that is being carried on throughout the country." A few days later, Dartmouth College president Ernest Hopkins told the *New York Times* that "the present activity against alien radicals in this country is purely political byplay to enhance the political aspirations of the attorney general [who has] interfered with freedom of thought and speech, such as the constitution of the United States expressly guarantees."

Even some staff members inside Caminetti's own Immigration Bureau grew increasingly bitter over what they saw as unprofessional conduct by Palmer's men. In Seattle, they filed an angry protest after a mid-January operation: "The police, acting upon instructions from the Department of Justice, went into the restaurants, pool rooms, lodging houses, cigar stores, and the different places down town, and rounded up everyone in those different places, regardless of whether a man was eating his dinner or not," Seattle immigration commissioner Henry M. White wrote to Caminetti on behalf of his entire office. "I appreciate that the manner of making these arrests was spectacular, and made a good newspaper story, but I want to voice my protest. Some of the men brought in were loyal American citizens, as far as we know—some were returned service men. . . . We have never gone on the assumption that we had the authority to throw a blanket around an entire community and subject American citi- zens and all others to an arrest in order to secure one or two accused."

Even competing papers like Chicago's two largest circulating dailies, the *Tribune* and the *Daily News,* voiced the same squeamishness over the operations there:

> There are elements in every large city who want to bring
> about a revolution, or who think they do. Some of them are
> witless and some dishonest. Some are mistaken humanitarians
> and idealists. Some are covetous and grasping. Some are

potentially murderous. Some are intellectuals who have
thought much and not enough. Some are visionaries, outraged
by the sight of man's injustice to man. Whatever they are,
they are supposed to have certain rights, and we treat the sup-
position lightly—and do it without many apologies. . . . We
are not for the legal lynching of any man.

Chicago Daily Tribune, January 3, 1920.

Yet there is danger in the dragnet methods of rounding up
alleged revolutionists and anarchists. . . . Not every radical is
a "red" and not every "red" is a criminal anarchist, bomb
manufacturer, or advocate of physical force.

Chicago Daily News, January 6, 1920.

Back in Washington, Edgar tracked this criticism, and on January 13
he saw the most serious challenge yet appear on the horizon. Word
reached him that day that a group of lawyers in Boston had decided to
intervene using the biggest legal stick at their command. "*Habeas Corpus*
petition filed this morning for one hundred and twelve aliens held at
Deer Island under deportation warrants," Edgar read in a telegram to
Palmer from Boston's United States Attorney Thomas J. Boynton. "Basis
of petition is that warrants are defective in that they do not specify any
acts of aliens. Hearing on petition set for Thursday at ten o'clock."

The Latin words *habeas corpus* mean "produce the body," and the
responsible government official had to do just that, to present the prisoner physically in court and establish the government's right to keep him.
In effect, it empowered a judge to cut through any tangled legal knot and
determine directly if a person was being held properly. For the first time,
this would allow a federal judge to examine the underlying logic of the
Palmer raids, the use of the 1918 Immigration Act to make membership
in the Communist and Communist Labor parties a basis for mass arrests,
detentions, and deportations.*

---

*The Constitution does provide that the *habeas corpus* privilege can be suspended in "Cases of
Rebellion or Invasion [where] the public Safety may require it," and President Abraham Lincoln used this authority to lift it during the Civil War. More recently, President George W.
Bush convinced Congress to suspend habeas corpus rights for aliens determined to be "unlawful
enemy combatants" against the United States, or awaiting this determination, through the
Military Commission Act of 2006. This followed earlier attempts by Bush to suspend the writ
unilaterally by military order in 2001. See Hamdi v. Rumsfeld, 542 U.S. 507 (2004).There is
no indication, however, that Edgar or Mitchell Palmer considered proposing to suspend it in
1919 or 1920 to support their crusade against the Reds.

Worse still for Edgar and Palmer, the judge hearing this case was no friend of the Justice Department. George Weston Anderson, a former Boston federal prosecutor and a United States district judge since 1918, had recently given a speech to the Harvard Liberal Club in which he vilified Palmer and his Red Raids as "hysterical" and "appalling." "There are Reds, probably there are dangerous Reds," Anderson had said. "But they are not half as dangerous as the prating pseudo patriots who under the guise of Americanism, are practicing murder [and] shooting at sunrise. . . . Patriotism and Americanism are being disgraced by those using them for personal and political notoriety." And that wasn't all. Judge Anderson, a lifelong Boston native, happened to know the local volunteer lawyers representing the Deer Island inmates and knew that they were in over their heads in handling this case. But Anderson also knew where to find help for them. He had plenty of friends among the crowd at the Harvard Liberal Club, including several members of the Harvard Law School faculty who would be happy to step in. For instance, one of the professors who heard Anderson give his speech that night was that foreign-born Jew who already had risked his job twice that year by siding with Reds and Zionists, the one with the name that sounded like a German sausage: Frankfurter.

Palmer sent a wire back to his United States Attorney in Boston on receiving news of the *habeas* petition. In it, he showed exactly whom he trusted to handle the case: "Forward at once by special delivery [the court's preliminary ruling] attention Mr. Hoover." This, in the end, would be Edgar's job.

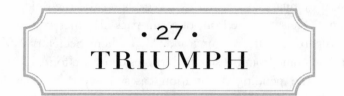

· 27 ·
TRIUMPH

BEFORE THIS DAY, Edgar rarely got the chance to stand up in public and argue a legal case for the Department of Justice. Even at the Emma Goldman deportation, he had sat quietly off to the side as an immigration inspector conducted the questioning. Edgar loved the thrill of standing on his own feet and debating in front of an audience, using his words as weapons to make people laugh or cheer while leaving his opponent looking look small, stupid, or just wrong. As a teenager he had led his debate team at Central High School, winning twelve victories in twelve contests during his senior year. He once even wrote a column about it for his school newspaper. "[Debate] teaches one to control his temper and free himself from sarcasm; it gives self-possession and mental control," he said, "it brings before the debater vividly the importance of clean play, for . . . slugging in the form of false arguments and statements proves of little use; and lastly, it gives . . . a practical and beneficial example of life, which is nothing more or less than the matching of one man's wit against another."

Now, on January 21, 1920, three weeks after the Big Raid, Edgar had his chance. He sat at the front of a jam-packed conference room in the Labor Department in Washington, D.C., where Secretary William B. Wilson had come from his sick bed to preside over a formal legal debate central to the pending deportation cases. Lawyers representing four Chicago communists had requested the chance to appear and argue that membership in the Communist Party should not, in itself, be grounds for deportation under the 1918 Immigration Act. Their case boiled down to one essential point: that the Communist Party did not actually advocate the violent overthrow of the government. To Edgar, this point was absurd, and he came prepared to knock it down.

Edgar faced four lawyers across a wide table representing the communists, each much older than he and with a prominent national reputation. They included Swinburne Hale of New York, Benjamin Bachrach of Chicago, and Morris Katzoff of Boston—all representing communist suspects in pending deportation hearings or *habeas corpus* suits—plus Isaac Ferguson, the Chicago-based general counsel of the Communist Party itself. These lawyers had chosen to bring a test case this morning, that of Englebert Preis, an immigrant from Austria arrested in Chicago on January 2 who admitted to being a Communist Party member. Preis's situation presented the issue squarely. He raised no question of proof or evidence, only the single point of law. If Secretary Wilson agreed that membership in the Communist Party was a sufficient reason to deport Englebert Preis under the 1918 Immigration Law, then all the hundreds of other deportation cases could go forward. If not, then they would all be dropped. The entire January raid would have been for nothing.

Secretary Wilson had already decided this issue once before in approving the original three thousand warrants for the raid in late December, but now he had agreed to reconsider the matter. With the stakes so high, Mitchell Palmer decided to send his best advocate to argue his position. He trusted young John Edgar Hoover to do the job right.

Since the January raids, Palmer had increasingly pushed his protégé into the spotlight. Early that month, the Justice Department released copies of the briefs Edgar wrote documenting the evil faces of the Communist and Communist Labor parties. Newspapers mentioned him by name as the author. Edgar became the person who spoke to congressmen and senators about the issue. He even traded letters with *Baltimore Sun* columnist H. L. Mencken, who wrote to ask for a copy of one of Edgar's papers on communism. "There is enough first-class detective work going on under Palmer's direction at this moment to supply grist to the mills of a score of mystery-fictionists," William T. Ellis wrote of Hoover in the *American Review of Reviews.* Edgar showed himself astute at building his nascent public image. He contacted opinion leaders like Lyman Abbott, editor of *The Outlook,* and sent them background material on the communist threat. He supplied newspapers across the country with prepackaged stories and cartoons to spice up their coverage, "furnished to you without charge, carriage prepaid, by the Department of Justice," his cover letter said, all slanted his way and signed by A. Mitchell Palmer. One of these circulars, for instance, included photographs of four sinister-looking arrested agitators under the headline "Men Like This Would Rule You."

Secretary Wilson asked Edgar to speak first that day at the Labor Department. Edgar exhibited no shyness standing before the roomful of lawyers, newspapermen, and politicos. He looked sharp in a crisp suit, white shirt, gold tie clasp, and black shoes, his dark wavy hair combed back, his voice steady and quick. Edgar spoke clearly and made a straightforward case. He took statements directly from the Communist Party's own governing charter and used them like bludgeons. Communists had declared their goal as being "capture" of the bourgeois state through "class struggle," the "conquest" of power, "mass action," and "open combat." Edgar explained how the Party required each member to sign a written statement declaring his allegiance to these principles. The Communist Party, he argued, was "an integral part of the first congress of the Communist International which was formed by the Bolsheviki." He explained how its leaders called themselves "revolutionary socialists," a concept that envisioned "a struggle [that] must go on until the working class, through the seizure of the instruments of production and distribution, the abolition of the capitalist state and the establishment of the dictatorship of the proletariat, creates a socialist system," as he put it.

After Edgar finished and sat down, Isaac Ferguson from Chicago rose to present the case for Pries and the Communists, but he found himself starting in a hole. Ferguson could not dispute any of Edgar's quotations, and he didn't even try. Instead, he brushed them off as mere metaphors. Yes, the Communists wanted to create a Soviet form of government in America, but not through bloodshed, he said. Their ideas were no different from those of Karl Marx, Eugene Debs, and others who had been discussing them peacefully for decades. "Force," the way Communists used the word, meant political action, no different from the mass strikes staged by traditional America labor unions like the Railroad Brotherhoods or

coal miners. Communism had prevailed in Russia in 1917 without bloodshed, Ferguson argued; it was only the counterrevolutionists who started
the killings.

Edgar sat politely and held his tongue as Ferguson presented his case,
but Caminetti, sitting alongside Secretary Wilson at the front of the
room, found Ferguson's argument so irritating that he felt compelled to
interrupt: "Then why is it necessary to talk bloodshed in order to avoid
bloodshed?" he asked, breaking in. "Why not use peaceful language?"
When Ferguson tried to answer, he interrupted again; "Why do you not
proceed by the American means of using the electorate?"

"Because . . ."

"Because—that is not your purpose," Caminetti argued.

Ferguson kept his calm and finished his presentation, but then it was
Edgar's turn to stand up and talk again. Edgar caught Ferguson off guard
by pulling out a copy of a Communist Party handbill that portrayed the
United States government as being "of, for, and by the capitalist class."
Edgar drew gasps from the crowd as he read these words accusingly. Ferguson insisted that the language was not sinister at all, that it barely differed from what Woodrow Wilson himself had said in his own campaign
speeches in 1912 touting his "New Freedom," but his argument drew only
a few laughs around the room.

After the hearing ended, Secretary Wilson went back to his office and
took less than forty-eight hours to draft and publish his formal decision in
the case. It gave Edgar a complete victory. "From the quotations and
numerous other statements in the manifesto," Wilson concluded, "it is
apparent that the Communist Party of America is not merely a political
party seeking control of affairs of State, but a revolutionary party seeking
to conquer and control the State in open combat." As a result, all the
deportation cases, all three thousand of them, stood rock solid.

Edgar had reached a stunning pinnacle in his young career. Just six
months after creating the Radical Division in August 1919, he could look
back at having destroyed the top three radical groups in the country: the
Union of Russian Workers, the Communist Party, and the Communist
Labor Party. He had routed the movement's leadership: Emma Goldman
was deported to Russia, John Reed and Louis Fraina had fled abroad, Benjamin Gitlow and William Bross Lloyd faced criminal charges with long
terms in federal prison. Meanwhile, more than three thousand radicals
sat locked away facing likely deportation. Edgar's first annual report published in December 1919 showed how his Radical Division itself had

blossomed into a bureaucratic juggernaut, the largest unit in the Department's Bureau of Investigation, his card file on suspected Reds bulging with 60,000 names. In late January, Mitchell Palmer topped it all by presenting Edgar with another pay raise, from $3,000 to $4,000 per year, effective February 1.

Edgar certainly gloated over the news. He indulged himself in collecting trophies. "I am endeavoring to place upon the walls of my office here a representative collection of the Communists, and if you could forward to me some of the larger photographs of the leaders of the worldwide Communist movement [seized in the raids], I would greatly appreciate it," he asked his Newark agent Frank Stone in a letter that month, "likewise any interesting banners which could be used for interior decorating would also be appreciated." Another agent already had sent him a collection of buttons seized in one of the New Jersey raids with pictures of Lenin, Trotsky, Karl Liebknecht, Rosa Luxemburg, and other Red celebrities.

All the while, as he racked up his victories, he was developing a harder edge to his attitude toward the Reds. He no longer saw them as curiosities or abstractions. On the same day as Secretary Wilson's decision in the Preis case, Edgar happened to notice a newspaper column, one of the hundreds that crossed his desk, and he clipped it out with a pair of scissors. It had been sent to him by the State Department, and it contained a poem called "An Eye for an Eye," penned by a Russian Bolshevik named Igor Loginov that had been printed in September in *Krasnaya Gazets*, the official organ of the Petrograd Soviet for Workmen's and Red Army Deputies:

> For the blood of those killed in Moscow.
> For the holy blood of communists
> We will destroy the hangman—
> The capitalists.
>
> We will not spare the enemies of labor,
> Make a list of every one of them!
> We shall exterminate the most dangerous.
> They have lived long enough in comfort!
>
> All the handmaids of capitalism
> We shall take as hostages—

We shall not forgive them
But shall crush them like dogs, and throw them into the rubbish
    dish.

Whether Socialist, Revolutionary or Menshevik, if he is caught;
A bullet in the forehead and let it go at that!
Labor, now the master,
Does not need their sort of ballast!

Let our cry reach to all cities,
And also to the far-most villages:
In order to give the final battle to the enemies,
Poor! Be on the lookout!

For the blood of those killed in Moscow,
For the Holy blood of communists
We will destroy the hangman—
The capitalists.

—Iv. Loginov

Edgar immediately sent a copy of it to Caminetti as encouragement to persevere in their fight. "This poem is so indicative of the attitude of the Communists toward the rules of morality and the actual methods by which they endeavor to accomplish their aims," he wrote in a cover letter. Edgar saw it as opening a window into the cruel, cold, violent soul of the Russian Red, and he harbored no visible doubt that this same violent soul lived in the breast of every American communist who mouthed the same slogans.

It was time to finish the job. Edgar now made plans to leave Washington, D.C., and visit Paterson, New Jersey, to tie down one more loose end. Here, after all these months, his agents had unearthed the first solid lead on who actually had planted the bomb at Mitchell Palmer's house the prior June.

· 28 ·

CHEATED

LABOR SECRETARY WILLIAM B. Wilson had no qualms about handing the victory to young Mr. Hoover in the *Preis* case, declaring the Communist Party a menace worthy of deportation under the 1918 Immigration Act. But he detested Mitchell Palmer's gloating, and he chafed at the way Palmer's Justice Department rode roughshod over his own immigration inspectors. A few days after he announced his decision on *Preis*, Wilson received a letter from Palmer congratulating him for coming out the right way: "I consider your opinion the most concise and the clearest expression of the character of the Communist Party of America that has come to my attention," Palmer wrote. This was fine in itself, but Palmer, as usual, found a way to turn the compliment into an offense. "I have been so impressed with the clarity with which your views have been expressed," Palmer's letter went on, "that I feel that much could be accomplished if your opinion could be placed in the hands of all the labor unions in America." The letter then asked Wilson if he had "any objections" to Palmer's printing up thousands of copies to circulate to union halls across the country.

William Wilson erupted. Yes, he certainly did object to such an insulting gesture. "There is no other portion of our community that has so long and persistently opposed revolutionary propaganda . . . as the trade unions of the United States," he wrote back to Palmer, abruptly nixing the idea. "I fear they [the labor union members] would look upon it as a reflection upon their loyalty and patriotism."

Secretary Wilson did one other thing that day. After Wilson had returned to Washington, D.C., from the Christmas holiday a week earlier, John Abercrombie had come to see him and told him how he had changed the Labor Department's Rule 22 to deny immigrants the right to have a lawyer present during the early stages of their deportation hearings —a demand from Caminetti coming just in time for Palmer's Big Raid. Within the day, Wilson issued an order changing the rule back to the way it was before. By then, of course, the raids had come and gone and the damage was done. He had been blindsided again. But he would make very sure that this was the last time.

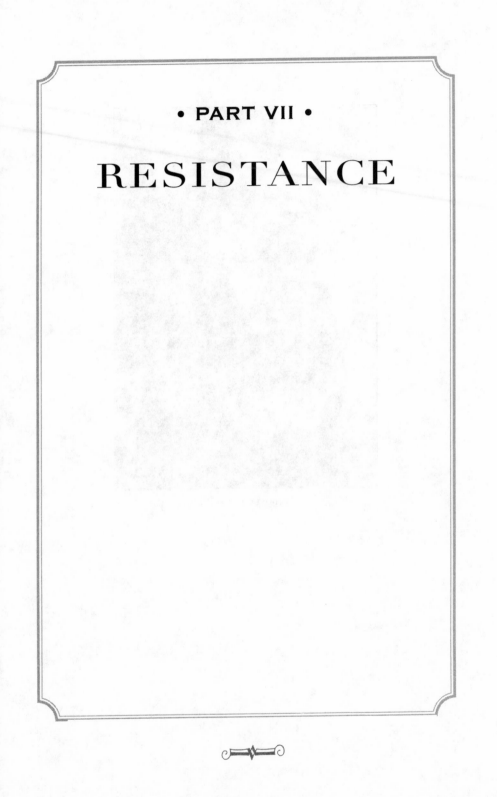

• PART VII •

RESISTANCE

Clarence Darrow in 1922.

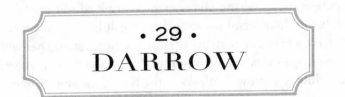

· 29 ·
DARROW

New York City, February 1, 1920

BEFORE THE TAKING of testimony, I want to object to all evidence under this indictment."

Clarence Darrow had a face people didn't forget, a web of lines, creases, and shadows etched in leathery skin, with an oversized forehead under thin brown hair and dominated by squinty blue eyes that stared right back at a person. Millions recognized his face—even here in New York, far from his Chicago home—from newspaper photographs taken during his famous courtroom battles. "[F]irst, the article is not in contravention of the statute"—New York's criminal anarchy law—"and secondly the statute is in contravention of the State Constitution and of the Federal Constitution." Darrow spoke in a slow drawl, a holdover from his boyhood in rural Kinsman, Ohio, but he made his words clear. In court, he saw himself as an actor on the stage who had to deliver his lines with punch and flair. He could be syrupy, funny, engaging, indignant, or homespun as he paced the chamber in a wrinkled suit stretched across hulking broad shoulders, long arms dangling at his sides ready to grab an elbow, shake a hand, or, with an attractive woman, startle her with a hug.

But the judge today was not impressed. "Motion denied on each of the grounds," Justice Bartow S. Weeks of the New York State Supreme Court declared. He rapped his gavel on his wooden desk, its firm slap silencing the room. "Do you desire to say anything further?"

The State of New York had charged his client, Benjamin Gitlow, with criminal anarchy based on Gitlow's having published an article, "The Left Wing Manifesto," that, according to the charges, "advocated . . . the duty, necessity, or propriety of overthrowing [the government] by force or violence." Clarence Darrow had no love of Bolshevism, and he didn't especially like Gitlow. Still, he jumped at the chance to defend this case. He had agreed to come from Chicago before even meeting his client. To him, this case went far beyond any one person. Benjamin Gitlow had simply written a magazine article. He had voiced an opinion, albeit a stupid one, but if that were a crime then half the country would be in jail. He had not killed anyone, thrown any bombs, nor led any armed uprisings. He hadn't robbed a bank or given secrets to the Germans, or even taken an illegal sip of beer under Prohibition. To Darrow, Gitlow's Communist Labor Party looked more like a clutter of cranky eccentrics than of dangerous terrorists.

But that's what made the case appealing. With Gitlow, Clarence Darrow was defending the right to speak, however inflammatory or eccentric the thought.

Darrow had built his legal career from the start on defending outcasts and eccentrics. Moving to Chicago as a young lawyer in the 1880s, he became the city's corporation counsel and made his first public splash by helping to defend zealous young Patrick Eugene Prendergast, who had walked into the office of Chicago mayor Carter Harrison, pulled out a gun, and shot him dead after Harrison had refused to give him a political job. A court had already sentenced Prendergast to death by the time Darrow got involved to help argue his insanity plea, too late to do any good, but it set him on the road to be what a future law partner would call Attorney for the Damned.

The next year, in 1894, working as a lawyer for the Chicago and Northwestern Railway at the height of the great Pullman strike, Darrow shocked his company employers by switching sides. He quit his job and went over to represent the striking workers and their leader, Eugene V. Debs, the future Socialist candidate for president of the United States. Darrow counted Eugene Debs one of his few real heroes. "He was an intelligent, alert, and fearless man," he wrote. He defended Debs throughout the Pullman struggle as Debs ultimately went to prison for violating a federal injunction. Over the next two decades, Clarence Darrow became the favorite lawyer for radicals in trouble. He won an acquittal for I.W.W. president Bill Haywood in his Idaho murder trial, and for Amalgamated Woodmakers Union leader Thomas I. Kidd in his criminal conspiracy trial growing out of an 1898 Wisconsin strike. He convinced a presidential arbitration panel in 1903 to award 100,000 Pennsylvania coal miners a 10 percent pay raise, an eight-hour day for some work categories, and millions of dollars in back pay. He even gave Emma Goldman behind-the-scenes help in preparing the appeal of her wartime espionage conviction.

Darrow faced his biggest personal crisis after traveling to California in 1911 to defend the McNamara brothers, two union activists accused of dynamiting the Los Angeles Times building and killing twenty people in the explosion. Darrow pleaded them guilty, but then prosecutors turned around and slapped him with a criminal indictment for jury tampering in the case. Darrow insisted he was innocent and won an acquittal in a first trial on the charges, but a second trial on related counts ended with a hung jury and many former colleagues assumed him guilty. He returned to Chicago disgraced and dejected. "I had no money left, and had already borrowed about twenty thousand dollars from friends in various parts of the country," he confided. He gave up his law practice for a time and supported himself by giving lectures at Chicago's Garrick Theater on topics ranging from Nietzsche to religion to the purpose of life.

When he finally did return to legal practice, he billed himself as a pure criminal defense lawyer with no tie to the labor movement. He defended Chicago politicians like alderman Oscar DePriest and police chief Charles Healy, both indicted for corruption, and got them acquitted. Darrow received a thousand-dollar fee in Healy's case, and many rich paydays soon made him wealthy again. He defended celebrity criminals like Reinhold Faust, Chicago's notorious "Opera Bomber," who had planted dynamite in the Auditorium Theater and then tried to extort $100,000 from two local bankers by threatening to do the same to their homes. "I do not believe Faust could be proved legally sane, but neither do I believe he is exactly right mentally," Darrow explained in pleading him guilty. He defended swindler "Yellow Kid" Well of cheating a Fort Wayne businessman out of $15,500. "I am not holding up my client as a saint. I would have to go quite a way to find a saint. All of these men were out for a pot of gold," he told reporters. "Darrow impressed on juries that it was not always easy to distinguish between right and wrong," his partner, Peter Sissman, observed of him. "His skepticism was so genuine that he imbued juries with it."

Darrow stayed active in politics, and reformers still loved him for his wit, though they found his cynicism infuriating. He was a man who didn't drink but still supported the wets. "Life drifts on just the same," he wrote a friend in December 1919, "always working, always trying to save someone from the mob, some of the time succeeding but turning more pessimistic and contented to dwell as the days go on." Now, he had a new victim to try and save from the mob: Benjamin Gitlow, the founding ideologue of the American Communist Labor Party.

Clarence Darrow had learned discipline in his sixty-two years of life and four decades trying cases in court. He had studied the New York criminal anarchy law and decided on a strategy. It required keeping the trial short. Darrow recognized that here, in Judge Weeks's courtroom, he held a weak hand. His only chance, he'd decided, was to convince the jury to ignore both the law and facts, and, particularly, his client. Darrow knew exactly how these jurors would see Benjamin Gitlow: as an immigrant-raised Jewish communist rabble-rouser demanding "dictatorship of the proletariat" and smashing of the bourgeoisie, exactly the kind of far-out dangerous Red spook that drove the country to hysteria. Given the chance, they would hang him before breakfast.

As the trial began, Judge Weeks called on Darrow to present his opening statement, but Darrow, sticking to his plan, said he had none. Then, to speed things up further, he offered to concede the key facts in the case. "I rather gathered from the opening statement [of the prosecutors] that counsel expected to spend more or less time showing the legal responsibility of [Mr. Gitlow] for the article published. I want to say that, so as to save time, that my client was the business manager and on the board of this paper and there will be no attempt on his part to deny legal responsibility for it. He was on the board of managers, he knew of the publication, in a general way and he knew of its publication afterwards, and is responsible for its circulation." Then he sat down.

But, unfortunately for Clarence Darrow and his client Gitlow, Darrow was not the only veteran grandstander in the courtroom that day with a strategy to win this case. Alexander I. Rorke, the assistant New York district attorney, knew his business, too. Rorke had won convictions sending at least two other criminal anarchists to prison during the past few months. He knew the judge, the city, and he had his own sense of theater. Rather than keep things short, Rorke, as lead prosecutor, wanted to stretch them out. Before asking this jury to send Benjamin Gitlow to Sing Sing prison for twenty years, he needed to convince them that Gitlow was big enough, bad enough, and important enough to deserve it. So Rorke chose to put on a show. He ignored Darrow's offer and proceeded to spend two full days presenting the crime. He called eight witnesses, including the printer who had mass-produced 15,000 copies of *The Revolutionary Age* with its incriminating article. He also called a stenographer for a leading communist insider who described the Party's backroom operations, and he called Clarence Converse, an undercover federal agent who infiltrated the Communist Labor offices to buy a copy of the magazine and saw Gitlow lurking around inside. Rorke then read aloud from Gitlow's now-famous "Manifesto," dwelling on its use of words like "conquer" and "smash" and "dictatorship" and "strike" and "revolution." To demonstrate how dangerous these ideas were, he produced a witness from Winnipeg, Canada, who described the general strike that had paralyzed that city in mid-1919, a labor dispute escalating into revolution, just as Gitlow's article mapped it out. It had happened in Russia, in Canada, and, if evil men like Gitlow had their way, it would happen in the U.S.A. Nobody was safe so long as he went free.

Rorke could have finished his case in half an hour. Instead, he took his time to paint the portrait of a dark conspiracy, with paranoid people hatching evil plans in secret.

Clarence Darrow barely said a word to interrupt Rorke's melodrama. He sat fidgeting at the defense table, oblivious to the newspaper reporters, detectives, politicos, and sightseers packing the court trying to get a look at him, let alone Gitlow fidgeting at his side. He scribbled a note or two to the attractive red-haired woman sitting behind him in the front row, his wife, Ruby, who traveled with him on cases like this and acted as his private secretary. Darrow had met Ruby in Chicago in 1899—she was sixteen years younger than he—and he married her a few years later. She was his second wife. His first, Jessie Ohl from Ashtabula, Ohio, had left him earlier in an amicable divorce, saying she hated big city Chicago. Darrow preached "free love" in his lectures, and he had at least one long-term amorous affair with a vivacious young writer named Mary Field. He still sent her letters long after they'd broken off the liaison.

Benjamin Gitlow had been the star catch of New York's November raids. With a hint of danger surrounding it, his trial became a popular downtown carnival. Jury selection already had stoked the drama, with Rorke at one point asking a potential juror if "a threat of revolution or a general strike" would affect his judgment in the case—suggesting that dangerous Reds could launch violent reprisals if Gitlow were convicted. Darrow objected, Judge Weeks reworded Rorke's question, and the juror said "no." It still sparked headlines in the local press. Police searched everyone coming into the courtroom lest some radical try to make trouble. Darrow, for his part, had asked each prospective juror about his views on sociology and religion, or political events like the recent ouster of five members of the Socialist Party from the New York State Assembly. "The most important point to learn is whether the prospective juror is humane," Darrow wrote once in a magazine article on trial tactics. "This must be discovered in more or less devious ways. As soon as 'the court' sees what you want, he almost always blocks the game."

When Rorke finished presenting his prosecution case and the defense's turn came, Darrow stuck to his plan. He stood up, faced the judge, and rested without calling a single witness. He denied none of Rorke's evidence and didn't even bother to produce a friend to vouch for Gitlow's good character. What difference would it make? Benjamin Gitlow had written the damning article, he was proud of it, and he had no intention of walking away from it. And it was only after he and Rorke had finished with their cases that Darrow could have his chance to appeal to the jury in the form he always liked best: a stirring summation speech. But now, it was his client that got in the way.

∘━━✦━━∘

Benjamin Gitlow didn't seem to understand that he had Clarence Darrow, America's most accomplished defense lawyer, ready to plead his case for him. Instead, Gitlow insisted on talking to the jury himself. Why? For one thing, he apparently did not exactly like or trust Clarence Darrow, despite the fact that his Communist Labor friends were paying Darrow's top-dollar retainer. "He was not enthusiastic about the case," Gitlow complained, describing how they first met when Darrow arrived in New York a few days before the trial. "'Oh, I know you are innocent, but they have the country steamed up. Everybody is against the Reds,'" he recalled Darrow's telling him. "He seemed not a little frightened when I told him I intended to stand by every Communist principle and to defend my position regardless of the consequences," Gitlow recalled.

That being the case, Darrow told Gitlow there would be no use in his taking the stand to testify; he would only irritate the jury. But Gitlow refused to be silent at his own trial. He insisted at least on giving a speech, to which Darrow had shot back: "Well, I suppose a revolutionist must have his say in court even if it kills him."

But there was a deeper reason as well behind Gitlow's distrust. Clarence Darrow, despite his reputation as America's foremost labor defender, had broken with his leftist friends in 1917 over the most divisive ideological issue of the day: America's entry into World War I. Every socialist worth his salt had opposed the war, but Darrow backed it to the hilt. "Peace will come when the German military machine is destroyed," he declared in a 1918 article. "The earth is not big enough for peace and Prussian militarism at once." Darrow even avoided defending conscientious objectors early in the war and joined a traveling group of American dignitaries visiting Europe in 1918 to bolster troop morale.

Darrow's unapologetic patriotism made him a Washington favorite, and after the war it protected him from any suggestion of being Red or radical despite his long ties to labor. But it also left bad blood in leftist circles, causing even his hero, Eugene Debs, facing Espionage Act charges in 1918, to refuse Darrow's offer to lead his defense. Debs by now considered Clarence Darrow a sell-out, too money-hungry and militaristic to represent his pacifist views.* Most recently, Darrow had turned his cynicism even against Russian Bolsheviks. "They are fanatical idealists, dreamers, extremists, if you will, but they are consistent and honest in their own way," he wrote in early 1919. "The bolsheviki are conducting one of the most remarkable experiments in the history of the race. Personally, I do not look for even a moderate success. . . . Their failure will be tragic, not comic."

Benjamin Gitlow knew all about Clarence Darrow's apostasy and he didn't like it one bit. Darrow might know the law, but, on anything else, Gitlow felt perfectly prepared to speak for himself. So as the time came to make summation speeches in Gitlow's criminal anarchy trial, Clarence Darrow found himself in the odd position of being overruled by his client. He stood up before Judge Weeks and announced this latest twist. "Your Honor, the defendant wishes to make a short argument to the court."

---

*Darrow claims he used his wartime access to top officials to urge them to protect civil liberties, but with little effect. "I talked with the President, principally on the philosophy of freedom of the press," he confided later about a mid-1918 trip he made to Washington. "[President Wilson] said there was no way of defining exactly the line [but] that they were trying to win the war and at the same time preserve liberty." After the World War, he visited Mitchell Palmer at the Justice Department to plead that Debs be freed from his ten-year Espionage sentence, but Palmer refused, and so did the president.

"In addition to the argument of counsel?" Judge Weeks asked, surprised. "It is very unusual to allow a defendant who has not taken the stand, to address the jury. I know of no case in which it has been permitted." Darrow knew this was a bad idea and perhaps he hoped the judge would simply forbid it. Not only would Gitlow showcase his odious ideology but, as a legal matter, Gitlow would be handcuffed in defending himself. Since Gitlow had not testified as a witness under oath nor been subject to cross-examination by prosecutors, Judge Weeks therefore would have every right to stop him from saying anything of substance. Still, Judge Weeks decided not to get in the way. "I do not feel that it should be refused at this time," he ruled, but warned Gitlow that he had no right whatever in addressing the jury to say anything not based on evidence already presented in the case, and told him that "upon the first violation of this privilege [your] right to address the jury will at once be suspended."

So Darrow sat back and watched as his client rose to speak. Gitlow, stockier and several inches shorter than Darrow, squirmed noticeably as he stood up with all eyes in the courtroom turned squarely toward him. "An audience never frightened me," Gitlow confided later about that day, "but here in court it was different. I could feel that the room was supercharged with hostility."

"Gentlemen of the jury, I am charged in this case with publishing and distributing a paper known as the *Revolutionary Age*," he began, "a broad analysis of conditions, economic conditions, and historical events in the world today. I as one maintain that in the eyes of the present day society I am a revolutionist. I desire complete, fundamental. . . ."

But Judge Weeks cut him off before he could get a single coherent thought out of his mouth. "Mr. Gitlow, you are not permitted to state what your views are or what you think," he scolded. "You must confine yourself to an argument based upon the testimony in the case."

Gitlow tried again, this time turning to theory. "What is capitalism?" he asked the jury, and answered his own question by pointing to "this enormous amount of wealth [and] enormous poverty and degradation of the masses." He pointed to the recent World War. "What did we find? We found millions of workers facing one another, and being slaughtered on the fields of battle [over] territory, desired privilege in monies and ore concessions. . . ."

But Judge Weeks stopped him again. "I must interrupt you, because you are stating as facts matters which are not facts of record in this court."

Darrow, watching Gitlow's frustration with the judge, rose to his feet and tried to support him."Your Honor, he has a right to explain the meaning of it."

"No, sir, he has no right to explain the meaning of the manifesto, because he is not subject to cross examination." The judge, of course, stood on a correct legal point, and Darrow sat down.

And so it went, a full hour of bickering between judge and defendant, interspersed with Gitlow's meandering expositions on theoretical Marxism. He ended with a flourish: "I am not going to evade the issue. My whole life has been dedicated to the movement which I am in. No jails will change my opinion in that respect. I ask no clemency. I realize that as an individual I have a perfect right to my opinions. . . . Capitalism is in a state of sorry collapse [and] has brought untold misery and hardships to the working man that thousands of men in this democratic republic are in jails today on account of their views, suffering tortures and abuse and nothing. . . ."

But the judge broke him off in mid-stride. "Again the defendant must cease from making statements," he snapped. "There is no evidence before the court that anyone is in jail or suffering tortures and abuse."

"It was obvious that the judge wanted to break up my talk," Gitlow grumbled later, "disconnect my thoughts and finally spoil whatever effect a continuous well-thought-out speech would have upon the jury." When Darrow got up to try and repair the damage, Gitlow still hadn't finished grumbling. "I knew it was to be one of his flowery appeals to the jury," he recalled. "Upon my insistence, his speech also included a defense of the right of revolution and an attack upon the hysteria which was sweeping the country."

Clarence Darrow finally had his turn. He had prepared carefully for this moment, and he knew his target. Clarence Darrow went to considerable lengths to nurture his reputation as cynic, skeptic, atheist, and doubter, but it was because this cynicism reflected the one thing he believed in most deeply: human frailty, and its necessary corollary, human tolerance. That would be his appeal this day.

"The defendant here on trial is a communist. Everybody in the world has more or less a feeling of distrust and aversion to doctrines which are new to them, and to people that are strangers to them," Darrow at last began to speak, standing before Judge Weeks in his Manhattan courtroom, engaging the jurors with glances from his deep blue eyes and gestures with his hands, sometimes leaning over the rail to look a juror straight in the face, but always projecting his voice across the packed chamber. "But I do know from my own experience in courts, that tolerance is one of the rarest virtues that you find in man. . . . [Gitlow] and his associates are not conspirators. They have done nothing in secret and in private. In the broad light of day they have flung their banner to the breeze, and invited all who would, to come. . . . They have not worked in dark alleys and behind closed doors. They are not cut-throats and burglars, midnight assassins."

Darrow kept his message simple: Gitlow might be a fool, but he was nobody to fear. His ideology, communism, was not so scary. He compared it to the ways of the early Christian apostles who held their belongings in common. "There is nothing strange or weird or unusual about the word," he said. As Gitlow used it, it was simply a dream "of a time when there will be no more poor and no marvelously rich, of a time when we would see some other ideal to worship than cash," and "If you take the dreams away from a man, you take the best part away. . . . It is a creed. That is all. Nothing but a creed. Which they have the right to hold, the same as any other man has a right to hold." Gitlow's manifesto might be misguided, but it was based on that dream. "As long as men speak, they will talk a lot of nonsense, and here and there some sense. . . . And if any man among you had been sent to jail for the nonsense you had spoken you wouldn't be on the jury."

Even that word "revolution" had less to it than met the eye. It meant "fundamental," not necessarily violent. "I am not afraid of the French revolution. I am glad it happened," he told the jurors. "We had the strike in Switzerland and the strike in Belgium. For what? To give suffrage to women. . . . They believe that they should conquer and destroy the power of the state. What of it? Our earliest traditions are for that right."

Then Darrow got to his real enemy. The country had gone crazy with fear. It was this fear that was the problem, not Benjamin Gitlow. "If [Abraham] Lincoln would have been here today, Mr. Palmer, the attorney general of the United States, would send his night riders to invade his office and the privacy of his home and send him to jail." Fear had turned normal, sensible people into idiots. "Do you think that a handful of people can destroy the United States? Utterly absurd. What do you think of this mad fear which would hail a man into court for a thing like this? Which would raid homes and destroy property, because of this fear of existing things?" Clarence Darrow looked the jurors in the face and asked them to free Benjamin Gitlow and reject the whole basis of these Palmer Raids. "I ask you, gentlemen, by your verdict today, to do your share, which is not small, to preserve that freedom, which is the heritage of you and of me alike. I thank you."

He had spoken for almost three hours. His plea filled fifty pages in the trial transcript and left him exhausted. But it seemed to have been a waste of time. The jurors took just three more hours to make up their minds. They found Gitlow guilty on all counts and Judge Weeks sentenced him to five to seven years doing hard labor at Sing Sing.

Darrow wasn't surprised. Gitlow, standing at his side, noticed his reaction. "Darrow did not even want to hear the verdict. He knew what to expect," the defendant wrote. Darrow told reporters afterward that he would appeal the case, and he complained that Judge Weeks had tilted the jury by comments he made just before their deliberations, but he knew better. Darrow left New York City disgusted and returned directly to Chicago. He understood why he'd lost the case. Part of it was his client; Gitlow had hanged himself with his own big mouth. "It was believed that Gitlow's 'Red' speech to the court had something to do with hastening the conclusions of the jury," the *New York Times* reported. But mostly, it was the Red Scare itself, turning reasonable people into fanatics. "[I]t's a hell of a world with very little to recommend it," Darrow wrote to Mary Field on returning to Chicago, still oddly inclined to spill his inner feelings to his former lover. He summed up his role in the case using a German slur: "Was beaten in N.Y. Every juror was a Milkinhein or near it and the judge was a fiend and there was no chance."

Darrow had little time to rest. The Red Scare had made him popular again among his former radical friends, dozens of whom sat in prisons facing anarchy charges. State prosecutors were in the process of arresting some 1,400 people, aliens and citizens alike, under state sedition laws, and would convict about 300 of them during 1919 and 1920, mostly in Illinois, New York, and California—all with the help of Palmer's Justice Department. Darrow already had two more trials like this one slated in his calendar. One involved a glassblower in Rockford, Illinois, named Arthur Person, arrested in January and set to face a jury in April. The other involved a whole school of bigger fish, twenty original Communist Labor Party founders like Benjamin Gitlow, indicted *en masse* and fingered as having led the party's convention in Chicago the prior summer, including the strangest duck of all, William Bross Lloyd. Darrow shuddered at the thought of how he would explain Lloyd to a jury. If he'd had to color Benjamin Gitlow as a misguided fool, how on earth could he possibly present Chicago's Millionaire Socialist?

○━━◆━━○

Back in New York City, Alexander Rorke savored his victory over
Clarence Darrow in the Benjamin Gitlow case, and soon he started
preparing for his next criminal anarchy trial, this one against James
Larkin, the celebrated Irish radical. As a first step, Rorke contacted his
best source for information in Washington, D.C., that bright young man
at the Justice Department, Mr. Hoover, who had been so helpful behind
the scenes in helping him build his case against Gitlow. He wrote Hoover
a letter asking him for help in finding background on James Larkin's
birth, family, activities in Ireland, and criminal record.

Edgar, receiving the letter in Washington, got right on it and asked the
State Department to get involved as well. "It is highly important that this
[information] be procured in order that the proceedings may be successful," Edgar wrote to his contact there. Rorke had done well, and he
appreciated it. Edgar could now put one more trophy up in his office.
Another Red, Benjamin Gitlow, had been taken down, and not even
Clarence Darrow had been able to stop it.

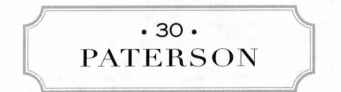

· 30 ·
PATERSON

EDGAR HAD NEVER been on an actual raid before, out with his agents in the line of fire, sharing the jitters, the adrenaline, the excitement of it all. Tonight, he and all the men carried pistols that felt cold against the skin of their hands.* It was a small operation—just one city—but dangerous and important. Paterson, New Jersey, a gritty industrial town across the Hudson River from New York City, was home to the Italian L'Era Nuova anarchists, and Edgar had arrived there by train from Washington that afternoon carrying arrest warrants for thirty-three of them. "[L'Era Nuova] might truly be termed the 'terrorist' group of America," he told Caminetti in asking for the warrants. "I intend to be at Paterson on the night when the arrests are to be made," he explained, despite what he called the "great danger." His agents expected all the suspects to be armed and violent, prepared to kill to avoid capture. "Courage is [a] mental and spiritual discipline," Edgar would write a few years later, after

---

*Congress did not officially authorize Bureau agents to carry firearms until 1934, but it did not forbid them from carrying their own weapons on dangerous assignments, as they did here.

he had become famous. "It is the fear that does not succumb to fright in time of peril." Now, in Paterson, he would put his own courage to the test.

They struck on Valentine's Day, February 14, 1920, a Saturday night. Edgar and his men set out in the darkness in groups of six, backed by Secret Service agents, American Legion volunteers, and half a dozen newspaper reporters who came along to watch. They rode in black sedans and used sleds to glide silently over the narrowest snow-clogged streets. One after another, they hit their targets: the old warehouse that the L'Era Nuova group used as its office, the nearby office of the Francisco Ferrier Association, and the homes of the top radical leaders. They raided a print shop owned by Benjamin Mazotta, a L'Era Nuova stalwart, and found printers there secretly running off copies of an underground I.W.W. handbill called "The Truth About Centralia." Every prisoner they took that night was armed, most carrying automatic pistols. Still, Edgar's men never fired a shot. At each stop, they barged in with guns drawn, never giving their target the chance to draw his own weapon. A *New York Times* reporter described it this way: "Just as official vigilance seemed to be relaxing and a feeling of new security was stealing over the Reds, a hundred agents stole into this city and plucked, one after another, almost the whole of the L'Era Nuova devotees."

Edgar's men nabbed twenty-nine suspects that night, including Ludovico Caminita, the group's leader and editor of its Italian-language newspaper *La Jacquere* ("The Massacre"), a fluent, vitriolic writer who had ended a recent column with a warning: "the tamed lion hatches in his brain plans of revenge." As a bonus, they found hiding in one Paterson house a renegade I.W.W. official from Philadelphia who had been missing since the January raids along with a large stash of internal I.W.W. records. Edgar and his men took their prisoners to the local bureau office and questioned them until well past midnight. "I was present at the examinations of all of these persons and believe that one of the worst groups in the country has finally been apprehended," he wrote to Caminetti, and asked that bail be set at $10,000 for each top leader—an amount certain to keep them jailed indefinitely. "[They] admitted freely that they had been anarchists for many years, were still anarchists, and were preaching anarchy."

But the most important find came at the end. In searching Mazotta's print shop at 298 Straight Street, they found in a back corner a pile of pink stationery that appeared to match perfectly the paper used seven months earlier for the circular "Plain Words" found outside Mitchell Palmer's house the night of June 2, 1919, when self-proclaimed Anarchist Fighters had bombed his home and almost killed Palmer, his wife, and his daughter. This pink paper established a direct link between these L'Era Nuova radicals and the June 2 bomb plot. Edgar instructed his agents to send two dozen sheets immediately to the Bureau of Standards in Washington, D.C., to compare with samples from the original bomb sites. It promised to be their first big break in cracking the case.

It had taken Edgar's men months of hard detective work to make this discovery, starting with a subtle clue: Of all the targets in the June 2 bombings, one stood out as different from the rest, the house of Max Gold, president of Paterson's Suanaha Silk Mill. Unlike the others, Gold held no position in government, and his name rarely appeared in newspapers, but his silk factory had been the scene of violent strikes, and recently he had fired two employees in labor disputes. Both of the fired men belonged to L'Era Nuova. Over the next few months, Edgar's men investigated this group and found it to be dangerous and extreme.

L'Era Nuova was founded in Paterson in 1898 by Gaetano Brecsi, an Italian anarchist who would soon return home and achieve fame by assassinating Italy's King Humbert I, shooting him three times in the chest on July 29, 1900, as the king entered his carriage after watching a gymnastics match in the Italian Alps town of Monza. Another member, Paulo Cuabello, bragged to friends that he had assisted in the 1894 assassination of French president Marie François Sadi Carnot by helping Sante Caserio, the actual killer arrested after stabbing President Carnot in Lyons. L'Era Nuova had kept its violent edge all these years. Federal agents raided and closed down its Italian-language newspaper during World War I, but it had recently started up again with a print run of three thousand copies. An undercover agent from the Justice Department's Newark office infiltrated the group for the first time in October 1919. "It is well known that the most dangerous anarchists in the country have their headquarters in and around Paterson, N.J.," Edgar had reported to Palmer at the time.

Now, the morning after the raid, Edgar stayed in Paterson long enough to watch as seventeen handcuffed L'Era Nuova prisoners were marched through the snowy streets to the railroad station where police loaded them into cars bound for Ellis Island. Afterward, he sent the prisoners' names to the State Department to check with Italian authorities whether they had criminal records there as well. Then he spent time with newspaper reporters making sure they appreciated the story's main point: LINK RAID EVIDENCE WITH PALMER BOMB, the *Newark Evening News* headlined; RED RAIDS YIELD BOMB PLOT CLUE, led the *New York Times*; BOMB PLOT JERSEY MADE, echoed the *Los Angeles Times*.

Edgar thrived on days like this. Beyond the sheer thrill of the night raid, he increasingly appreciated the connections he felt himself forming with the field agents. These were special friendships. He and his men comprised an all-male club in which they shared a rare common bond. Edgar always backed up his men in any argument or bureaucratic tussle. When New York agent Clarence Converse—who had testified weeks earlier in the Benjamin Gitlow case—was hospitalized in March with appendicitis, it was Edgar who wrote him a personal note on behalf of the Department. During the night raid in Paterson, Edgar stuck close to a junior immigration inspector named William Fader who helped in the arrests and then stayed up till nearly dawn to interrogate prisoners, Edgar at his side. Edgar made a point to commend him in a special citation to Caminetti: "I personally was present during the examination of the anarchists taken into custody and noticed that Mr. Fader was not only performing the duties of an inspector that evening, but was actually taking a personal interest in the investigation and examination of the anarchists," he wrote. "I feel that it is only proper that the splendid services performed by him be called to your attention."

Two weeks later, Edgar rode the train from Washington back up to New York City for the next step in the investigation. His mission this time was to question Ludovico Caminita, the L'Era Nuova leader captured in the Paterson raid being held in an isolated cell on Ellis Island. He intended to learn what Caminita actually knew about the June 1919 bombings.

Edgar had little experience interrogating tough customers like Caminita—after all, he was a Washington bureau chief—but he had advantages. Ellis Island was a cold, forbidding place, windswept and isolated, its detention halls intimidating in their size and silence. Edgar used this edge and soon found a way to get his man talking. "I told Caminita at the outset that he had been accused by certain Italians of being the head of the June 2nd bomb plot," he reported. "This seemed to anger Caminita exceedingly, and I told him that unless he came across with all the information he had that I thought the evidence was sufficient to send him to the penitentiary for twenty years." But Edgar soon recognized that threats would not be enough. "[Caminita] is a very high-class Italian and cannot be handled in any third degree manner," he explained. Instead, he found a personal weakness. "He has a boy about ten years of age in whom he has centered his affection, and it is through this boy by playing on Caminita's emotions that much information had been obtained." Did Edgar threaten to harm the boy? Or play on Caminita's fears of being separated from his son for twenty years should he be sent to prison, having him grow up without a father? The record doesn't say.

In any event, Caminita soon started talking. He insisted he played no role in the June 2 bomb plot, but he happily pointed a finger at the people he thought had, a group of anarchists based in Lynn, Massachusetts, led by a man named Luigi Galliani. He also mentioned the names of two Galliani followers he was familiar with, both based in New York City where they worked as printers: Robert Elia and Andrea Salsedo. Salsedo, a thirty-eight-year-old originally from Pantallera, Italy, a small island near Sicily, served nine months in the Italian army during the World War and had returned recently to the United States.

Ending the interview, Edgar immediately obtained immigration warrants for Salsedo and Elia, and had them both picked up by New York City police. The police took them to the Justice Department's office on Park Row where Edgar's men held them on the pretext of their having violated New York State's Sullivan Act by carrying concealed weapons, though they never arraigned either suspect on this or any other charge. These two suspects led to another, Gaspare Cannone, a New York-based Italian who had sent Elia a postcard. They arrested Cannone outside a Brooklyn bookstore where he picked up his mail, though Cannone's friends managed to give the agents a good scare. "[W]e were followed by a large and threatening crowd of people some of whom were blowing police whistles," one agent said, describing the arrest. "[I]t was necessary for us to hire an automobile in order to safely conduct the prisoner to the Bureau."

Edgar reported news of the breakthrough to headquarters in Washington and Mitchell Palmer was thrilled. Big Bill Flynn, the headline-grabbing Bureau of Investigation chief and still Edgar's boss, decided to take personal charge of the case. He raced up to New York City to question Salsedo and Elia himself. After having made such a visible initial splash with the original investigation of the June bombings, Flynn had suffered nine months of public embarrassment over his failure to break the case. Now, thanks to Edgar, Flynn had the chance to save his own reputation. From his years as New York City's detective chief, Flynn had plenty of practice in conducting third-degree interrogations—beating and terrifying a suspect until he talked, or tricking him by mixing kindness with threats or blackmail, all behind closed doors and far from the eyes of judges and lawyers. He would crack Salsedo and Elia soon enough. Success would electrify the country, even if the bombings ended up not being the work of radical Russians as he'd originally claimed. Flynn knew that success covered many sins.

· 31 ·
CANDIDATE

O N MARCH 1, 1920, Mitchell Palmer made it official. He announced in Pittsburgh that he was tossing his hat in the ring as a candidate for president of the United States. He took off on a whirlwind tour of Kansas, Kentucky, and Illinois to rally support. "I am strong for reducing the high cost of living," he told one cheering crowd after another. He proclaimed that "America Must be Up and Doing." Touting himself a friend of working men, despite his tough stands on the steel, coal, and police strikes, he said, "We cannot deny that in the United States many classes of labor have been ground down in an un-American fashion by conscienceless employers who suck their own profit out of industry and nothing else," using words sure to please even the most fervent socialist. "All my political life I have been fighting for labor. I was a strike leader once."

Palmer had a problem, though. His Red Raids, so popular in January, had started to produce a backlash. "[T]he pendulum of public opinion swings in the United States, as it does in most countries," he told a group in Richmond, Virginia, acknowledging the shifting tide. Union members despised him for the smear tactics he used against strikers, and so, too, did a growing number of ordinary voters squeamish over his brutal roundups and mass detentions and increasingly sympathetic to the sob stories they heard from victims. Palmer's friends sent him warnings, including a typical letter he received from one in Minnesota that month describing growing public distaste toward the whole idea of separating men from their families. The letter included a clipping from the *St. Paul Daily News* with the headline:16 AMERICAN-BORN CHILDREN FACE WANT IF FATHERS ARE DEPORTED, showing a photograph of a mother and her three youngsters, poor, scruffy-looking people but proud and modest. "Probably they won't starve," the article read. "But they will undoubtedly be separated and the clean little home given up. . . . Their father a communist, but a good father. . . ." Palmer recognized the danger. Give your enemy a human face, and he becomes all that much harder to hate or fear.

And there was another concern. American women would vote for president for the first time in 1920, and nobody knew yet how they would act in the voting booth. Would they pick the same candidates as their husbands or brothers? Would they follow some other, more unpredictable pattern? Who could tell?

Over the next few weeks, Mitchell Palmer took no chances. He set up campaign shops in a dozen states and named chairmen in every Pennsylvania district. He nailed down pledges of support from party leaders starting with national chairman Homer Cummings and dozens of Democratic National Committeemen. He called in political debts from all the people he'd placed in high-paying jobs as politically appointed United States attorneys and Justice Department officials, and others he'd done favors for as wartime Alien Property Custodian.

On the stump, Palmer tried to broaden his appeal to consumers and wage earners by announcing that his Justice Department had launched over a thousand cases against profiteers for jacking up prices of food, fuel, clothing, shoes, paper, and other necessities. To woo newspapers, he even launched a probe into the skyrocketing cost of newsprint. He saw positive signs wherever he went, big crowds, money coming in, and politicos falling into line.

Backlash or not, Palmer's campaign seemed to be coming together, and it was not lost on his young aide heading the Radical Division that if the boss actually managed to become president, he might very well bring Edgar along with him to the White House as an aide, perhaps give him a top job in the Justice Department, or maybe make him a judge. Edgar believed he'd be able to write his own ticket. Red Raids aside, Palmer was sitting pretty. It was his race to lose.

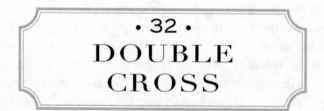

· 32 ·
DOUBLE
CROSS

L OUIS POST NEVER really tried to control the chaos of papers that
littered the top of his desk at the Labor Department. Post enjoyed
wading through this blizzard of letters, manuscripts, and clippings, scribbled notes for his books and articles, the way other people enjoyed a day
of baseball, a night of jazz, or a weekend romp at Coney Island. Today,
though, he didn't mind being interrupted. Peering up through his thick
wire-rimmed glasses, he noticed how John Abercrombie, normally gray
and gloomy, came in with a bounce in his step. Abercrombie had news,
he told Post, grim news, good news. Louis Post could only guess what it
was. Sit down, he told him. What news could possibly be good these days?
Palmer's raids had humiliated their office, the country verged on madness,
and an American adult couldn't even buy a legal glass of whiskey to
drown his sorrows. And inside the Labor Department, Caminetti, the top
Red Raider, stalked the hall with an unbearable strut.

To Louis Post, the only silver lining in all this was that at least it wasn't
his problem. It was John Abercrombie's job to decide deportation cases at

the Labor Department and deal with the fallout from Palmer and his raids; Post could happily avoid any daily involvement in the mess.

March was always a pretty month in Washington, D.C. This year, spring flowers had begun to explode in color—pink and white cherry blossoms, yellow daffodils, and purple crocuses, and Louis Post enjoyed them all. He knew this certainly would be his last spring in Washington as a government official. November's presidential election would bring a new replacement in the White House for sick, crippled Woodrow Wilson. A new crop of political appointees would follow. Louis Post would be able to walk away from all this silliness, concentrate on writing his articles, giving his lectures, and tinkering with his books.

But that's what the news was about, John Abercrombie told him. John H. Bankhead, the seventy-seven-year-old United States senator from Alabama, had died that very day. For John Abercrombie, Bankhead's death created an opportunity, an open seat in the United States Senate, and Abercrombie had decided to go home to Alabama and run for it.

On its face, it made good sense. Abercrombie had won two terms as a U.S. congressman from Alabama before World War I and still had plenty of friends there from his time as University of Alabama president and state education director. But frankly, Abercrombie cared less about winning the seat than about seizing the chance to leave Washington. He had reached the end of his patience with the Labor Department. He was sick of the arguments with Caminetti and the stress over the Red Raids. He intended to quit, and this was his opportunity. He planned to leave Washington as soon as he could arrange it, he told Post, and take an extended leave of absence until at least May 11, when Alabama held its primary election. After that, he would resign outright.*

Louis Post gasped at the news. He understood the point exactly. With Abercrombie gone, he, Louis Post, would become acting secretary of labor and the responsibility for dealing with the deportation cases would fall squarely on him. Secretary Wilson, their boss, still spent weeks away from the office tending to his sick wife and his own poor health. For the next month at least, Post would be left running things totally on his own. He'd have no way to avoid the problems short of quitting himself.

---

*Abercrombie would withdraw from the Senate primary contest after a few weeks, realizing he had no hope of beating long-term Alabama Democratic congressman James Thomas Heflin, who would go on to win the seat. Abercrombie would settle for being appointed state superintendent of education, a post he had held earlier, between 1898 and 1902.

But change also meant opportunity. And if the thought gave him a cold sweat, it didn't last long. After thinking it over a moment, Post had to admit finding a certain appeal in the dilemma. Being in charge, totally on his own, meant having power, the freedom to make decisions. There were things he could do with it. Take the whole Red Raid business. Louis Post had hated it from the start: the hysteria, the mass arrests, the arrogance, and his own shame at being involved in it. At seventy-one years old, he didn't have to worry about making enemies or taking risks. Given the chance to manage the immigration portfolio his own way, Louis Post had no doubt he could do it right. At least, he would try.

Four days later, on March 5, John Abercrombie made his decision official with a public announcement. He came once more to visit Louis Post in his office, and this time he brought along Caminetti to tell them both that he was turning over the immigration portfolio. Post spent little time talking to Caminetti that day. Instead, he thanked them both politely, sent them away, and then took the next few days to make a quick survey of the communist deportation cases piling up in John Abercrombie's office. What he found shocked him. It was worse than he'd imagined. And what he chose do to about it next would shock Caminetti even more.

⚬━✦━⚬

Edgar learned within hours about the changeover. Most likely, Caminetti himself picked up the telephone to tell him. Edgar knew that Caminetti hated Louis Post, and he understood the reasons. Despite all his months of trying to win friends in the Labor Department, Edgar never seemed to get anywhere with Louis Post. Post never gave him the time of day. There is no record of Post and Edgar ever sharing a conversation or trading any but the most curt, formal letters. As early as January 1920, Edgar had heard rumors of possible links between Louis Post and the I.W.W. and asked a few of his agents to check them out. They responded by sending Edgar copies of seized I.W.W. letters mentioning Post's name in connection with meetings between Chicago lawyer and muckraker Lincoln Steffens and an I.W.W. organizer named George Andreytchine, proving that Post was at least "accessible to the I.W.W.," as one of the agents put it.

Edgar feared the worst, and it took him only a few weeks to see his fears confirmed. He began hearing complaints about strange goings-on at the Labor Department. They were freeing Red suspects, dropping cases, and canceling warrants. Edgar asked Caminetti about it, but Caminetti seemed increasingly lost and shut out. In mid-March, Edgar decided to test the waters. Weeks earlier, when he first learned that immigration inspectors were finding Justice Department evidence insufficient in many deportation cases, Edgar had worked out an arrangement with Caminetti to forbid Labor Department inspectors from releasing any suspect without first notifying the Justice Department and giving them the chance to bolster the case. At the same time, Edgar instructed his own agents never to recommend the freeing of any radical in any situation before first checking personally with him. Now, Edgar sent Caminetti a list of forty-one prisoners arrested in January whose cases had been cancelled without his receiving even the courtesy of a telephone call. Had the arrangement been dropped? Edgar demanded an explanation.

Caminetti reported back a few days later that Louis Post had snubbed him. He had cancelled the cases and refused to reopen any of them without a formal request directly from Mitchell Palmer.

It didn't take Edgar long to put the pieces together. He had been double-crossed. He sat down at his desk and hammered out a six-page, single-space typewritten letter to Caminetti blasting the Labor Department for breaking its word. Louis Post's freeing of Red suspects without first contacting the Justice Department was "wholly inimical to the interests of the Government," he argued, listing twenty-eight cases he considered particularly egregious because the prisoner either admitted being a communist, paid dues to the Party, or attended meetings. *What was wrong with this Louis Post?* he wondered. Didn't he know that his country was at war? What if one of these Communists he freed so cavalierly turned out to be a bomber and killed a dozen innocent people the next time he had the chance? Or shot a veteran of the World War, as had happened in Centralia, Washington? How could he take the chance? Had this Louis Post no sense of responsibility? "I must say that I am entirely at a loss to understand the action of the Department of Labor in these cases," he wrote.

By late March, the trickle of dropped cases had become a flood. Edgar had no idea how many warrants Post had actually cancelled, how many Reds he had freed, and on what possible legal basis. Nobody was telling him; the door was slammed shut.

Edgar could be very stubborn at times, and he wasn't afraid to show it even against the most dominating person in his life, his mother. His nieces Anna and Margaret both remembered incidents around this time when Edgar and his mother matched their towering egos in epic conflicts within the small confines of their home on Capitol Hill. "There was never any real fighting," Anna recalled years later. "Nanny always liked to leave the shades down all through the back and front parlors. So it was always a very cool, dark atmosphere when J. E. came home in the evening. He simply would go around and raise the shades and go up to his room." Margaret remembered how they had crossed swords even over something as simple as breakfast. "His favorite breakfast was a poached egg on toast, and if that egg was broken, he wouldn't eat it. It went back to the kitchen and another egg was prepared. This was pretty funny, because he'd eat one bite of it, then cut it up and put the dish on the floor for [the dog] to finish up."

Now, suspecting that his Red crusade was being undercut by a smug bureaucrat in the Labor Department, Edgar gathered his wrath. Louis Post might think himself safe in his high office, but Edgar had no intention of letting him get away with what he'd done. A distraction erupted in Edgar's office on April 6, just as he was learning about Louis Post's treachery, a crisis on yet another front. An urgent wire had arrived telling him to drop everything and get on an overnight train to Boston. Things had gotten out of control there in a *habeas corpus* case, and they needed Edgar in court the next morning.

First things first. Louis Post would have to wait a few days. But when Edgar got back to town, Post would get what was coming to him. Edgar would see to it.

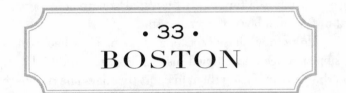

· 33 ·
BOSTON

EDGAR BOARDED THE overnight train on Tuesday, April 6, 1920, carrying a suitcase with a few notes and a change of clothes. It took ten hours to reach Boston from Washington, and he used the time sitting alone to read, think, and steal a few hours' sleep. The next morning, he stepped out on the platform at South Station and found Boston's two top federal prosecutors waiting there to meet him: United States Attorney Thomas J. Boynton and his assistant Louis Goldberg. They took him to breakfast and showed him the Wednesday morning newspapers. Edgar must have grinned ear to ear at what he saw. Every single one featured a story about him, one more glowing than the next. EXPERT ON REDS COMING HERE, shouted the *Boston American* on its front page. "John E. Hoover is the man, it was disclosed, who had direct charge of the Red raids all over the United States early in January." The *Boston Post* called him the one who "directed all the activities of the United States government against radicals during the past two years." So, too, the *Boston Evening Globe:* MAN HERE WHO DIRECTED NATIONWIDE RAIDS, read its headline.

Edgar had left Washington a frustrated government bureaucrat. He arrived in Boston a law enforcement star.

He couldn't enjoy himself for long, though. They had work to do. As Edgar sipped coffee and nibbled his egg, Boynton and Goldberg briefed him on the problem facing them in court that day. The trial in the *habeas corpus* case, the one brought for the prisoners on Deer Island, had gone wildly off course. On the first day of testimony, lawyers for the prisoners had embarrassed the government and threatened to blow the case wide open. First, they got an immigration official named James Sullivan to admit that he jailed over a hundred suspects at Deer Island before having a single warrant for any of them, and that he hadn't even bothered to apply for any warrants by telegraph until five days later—meaning he'd had no legal authority to hold them during this period. The judge himself, George W. Anderson, had confronted Sullivan over the $10,000 bail he charged certain prisoners, far more than they could afford to pay. "You knew these people were all wage-earners?" Judge Anderson had asked from the bench. "Well, didn't it occur to you that $10,000 might be the equivalent to a denial of liberty?"

"No, Your Honor," Sullivan had mumbled sheepishly, denying the obvious.

But an even worse blow-up came in the afternoon when lawyers for the prisoners called as a witness George Kelleher, the Justice Department's bureau chief in Boston, and squeezed him to disclose agency secrets. Tensions reached the breaking point when Judge Anderson interrupted to ask Kelleher how many of his Boston-based Justice Department agents actually had taken part in the raids, and Kelleher refused to answer.

"You will answer that question," Judge Anderson had demanded.

"I decline," Kelleher had said.

Judge Anderson, not used to being defied by government witnesses in his courtroom, threatened Kelleher with a contempt citation, but Kelleher just nodded. "I decline to state the number of men," he repeated.

After a brief recess, Louis Goldberg, the assistant U.S. Attorney, had tried to smooth things over by suggesting that they wait until he could consult with his superiors at the Justice Department in Washington, but this idea only made the judge angrier. "Do you mean to infer that a chief in Washington can rule in this court?" he asked. They recessed again, then Boynton himself stood up. "In view of the information desired I should like to ask the leniency of the court . . . in order that I have the opportunity to communicate with the Department of Justice in Washington."

Anderson finally relented, and so the urgent telegram went out to Washington for Mitchell Palmer to send his top radical expert, Mr. Hoover, to come help. The message was clear: Either give Kelleher permission to answer the question, or be prepared to take the heat for refusing.

Edgar, hearing this story, admired the sheer brass of his bureau chief George Kelleher for standing up to the judge and saying *no* to his face. Kelleher was no fool; he was a graduate of Brown University, Georgetown University Law School, and a former federal prosecutor. Best of all, he knew how to keep secrets. Edgar liked this man Kelleher; he decided he deserved his help.

But that wasn't all. There was another problem. How had the lawyers for the prisoners suddenly gotten to be so smart that they could seize control of the trial and run the government in circles? To answer this, Boynton and Goldberg now had to give Edgar an introduction to the secret world of Boston backroom politics. Goldberg explained how he happened to belong to a small, exclusive group called the Harvard Liberal Club that included many of Boston's top lawyers. Goldberg had attended the club's meeting a few weeks earlier on the night that Judge Anderson himself, now presiding over this *habeas corpus* case, had given a speech blasting Mitchell Palmer and his Red Raids as "hysterical" and "appalling." Since then, tensions had grown worse. Henry J. Skeffington, Boston's tough-talking federal immigration commissioner who operated the Deer Island prison, gave a speech to the Massachusetts Press Association where he shook his finger at the Harvard crowd directly: "I'll take great pleasure in getting some of these Harvard Liberal Clubs myself," Skeffington had said. "Some of the Harvard Liberal Clubs which have been raising so much Cain around here—well, if I have a warrant in my pocket I'll take pleasure in getting them." What exactly he meant by "getting" them, Skeffington didn't say, but when Liberal Club members read his speech in the newspapers, they took it as a threat. They demanded that Skeffington be fired. "He has lost his head, has proved incompetent and has brought your administration into disrepute," club president William P. Everts charged in a letter to Labor Secretary William Wilson.

Now, at the *habeas corpus* trial, Skeffington sat technically as the defendant, Anderson the presiding judge, and the fallout from the argument could be seen in the lineup of faces at the lawyers' tables. Representing the prisoners, in addition to two local attorneys they'd hired originally, sat two well-known professors from Harvard University Law School, the real brains behind the *habeas* team. They appeared as *amici curiae*, "friends of the court," serving without pay at the request of their real-life Liberal Club friend Judge Anderson. One was Zechariah Chafee, a first amendment scholar, and at his side sat the popular, politically connected friend of leftists and Supreme Court justices, Felix Frankfurter. Everyone in court knew that, more than anyone, it was Felix Frankfurter calling the shots.

Reaching Boston's federal courthouse that morning, Edgar must have marveled at the crowd of people clamoring to get into Judge Anderson's chambers. The presence of two celebrities, himself and Frankfurter, made this trial a hot ticket for hundreds of curiosity seekers: newsmen, academics, prisoners' families, and even a group of Harvard law students who came to watch their professors. They packed the seats and jammed the lobby waiting for space to open up in the courtroom. One of those waiting to get in that morning was Mrs. Jesse Wilson Sayre, the glamorous blue-eyed blonde daughter of President Woodrow Wilson himself. Sayre, beyond being the president's daughter, was also the wife of Francis B. Sayre, a Harvard Law School professor. She stood in line like everyone else, wearing a dark coat with gray fur trim and a pretty blue straw hat. She waited for half an hour before a guard recognized her and cleared a seat for her. "I am very much interested in these cases," she told the handful of newsmen who buttonholed her during a recess. "I believe it is the duty of everyone to inform one's self on such matters. I am especially interested in deportation cases and wanted to hear the testimony." Besides, she said, she knew Felix Frankfurter, her husband's friend, just as everyone else around Harvard knew the friendly, outgoing Felix. Asked if she held "liberal views," she just laughed.

Once inside the courtroom, Edgar noticed eyes on him from all around the chamber: "Considerable comment has been made by lawyers and others in attendance . . . on the appearance of extreme youth of John E. Hoover," a *Boston Post* reporter noted. "Despite his boyish looks, however, I am informed that Mr. Hoover is regarded as one of the ablest men connected with the department in Washington. He has been kept very busy since his arrival explaining that he is not a relative of the former food controller," future president Herbert Hoover, who had held the post of Federal Food Administrator during the World War.

But "boyish looks" or not, Edgar soon made it clear who gave the orders at the government lawyers' table. On the very first question of the day, resolving the prior day's argument over Kelleher's refusal to answer Judge Anderson's question on the number of agents involved in the January raid,

Edgar gave his signal and peace was restored. "I wanted to say that no disrespect was intended for the court yesterday," lawyer Thomas Boynton announced, rising from his seat to do the talking. He offered to have Kelleher answer Judge Anderson's question privately in the judge's chambers, and Judge Anderson agreed. Once this was done, they moved ahead. Edgar never rose to speak formally himself but instead sat and whispered to the other lawyers. Still, several observers noted how his presence affected the quality of the government's strategy, "whose wits were reinforced for the first time by the presence of John E. Hoover, special assistant to the Attorney general, who engineered the 'Red' raids," said the *Boston Globe*.

Judge Anderson now turned to the next potential bombshell. Somehow, the prisoners' lawyers had managed to get their hands on a copy of a private letter from Justice Department officials in Washington, D.C., to Boston bureau chief Kelleher giving him instructions for the January raids. Frankfurter offered it into evidence, and Judge Anderson directed that a clerk read it out loud. Louis Goldberg, the assistant U.S. Attorney, objected, but Anderson overruled him. Edgar, sitting at the government lawyers' table, cringed at the spectacle. He had written these instructions himself a few weeks earlier, and here they were being read aloud in this roomful of strangers, leaking the government's secret tactics to the enemy. Had he no right to privacy? Worst of all was hearing his own name mentioned in it: "On the evening of the arrests . . . I desire that you communicate by long distance to Mr. Hoover on matters of vital importance," the clerk read from the letter, and again, "I desire that the morning following the arrests you should forward [reports] marked 'Attention of Mr. Hoover.' . . ."

After the clerk finished reading the letter and Boston bureau chief George Kelleher took the witness chair again, Edgar watched as Felix Frankfurter rose to start his cross-examination.

Edgar had never met Felix Frankfurter before this day and knew only vaguely of his reputation. Watching him, Edgar might have been struck by Frankfurter's owlish face and his small, five-foot-five-inch frame, or the faint echo of a foreign accent in his voice. But what Edgar mostly saw was an articulate, composed, experienced litigator, much smarter, more polished and better prepared than others he'd faced in courtrooms or debates—perhaps the kind of lawyer Edgar himself aspired to become in the future. Today, though, Frankfurter was the enemy.

"How many men were in your arresting force?" Frankfurter stood like the law professor he was grilling a first-year student, his words clear and precise. Kelleher answered matter-of-factly: between three hundred and five hundred, including federal agents and police. "Were they the only ones? Were there any volunteers?" For transportation purposes only, Kelleher admitted, private citizens who drove automobiles for them. "And the agents searched those arrested?" *Yes,* Kelleher said. "How many men were released that night for want of evidence?"

"That is impossible to tell. Each agent had a weeding out process of his own; that is, weeding out the aliens from the citizens, and so forth."

"Why did you pick up any citizens?" Frankfurter asked.

"Well, it was done by mistake, if at all." No one missed the point. In a few brief, almost casual exchanges, Frankfurter had led Kelleher to admit an eye-popping list of illegalities: warrantless arrests, warrantless searches, unauthorized use of nondeputized agents, and he had barely gotten started. As Frankfurter laid it out, Edgar saw the newspaper reporters scribble it all down word for word.

❦

Felix Frankfurter had gotten the urgent telephone call from Judge Anderson on this case just a few weeks earlier. "I went [to Anderson's office] and he told me, 'Important *habeas corpus* cases are before me [and] the lawyer who represents them is plainly inadequate,'" he wrote later. "'He's doubtless a conscientious fellow, but not equal to the problems presented in the cases.'" Anderson wanted Frankfurter to appear free of charge. "Would you do that?" he asked. Frankfurter hesitated, but not for want of a fee. Lawyers who defended Reds these days routinely found themselves being smeared along with their clients, and Frankfurter had twice already barely escaped losing his job in the past few months over these types of run-ins. Even the prestigious *New York Law Journal,* in talking about a recent I.W.W. case, had cautioned attorneys against defending suspects whom it considered traitors. "Lawyers especially may well consider most seriously whether they should give legal aid to such dangerous adversaries to our government and of our fundamental rights and liberties," it warned in an editorial.

Still, Anderson pressed him to take the case. The stakes were high. Not only did fifty-three suspects still sit behind bars on Deer Island in late March 1920 as most of those freed on bail still faced deportation, but a bigger contest was under way in the country as well over the raids. Felix Frankfurter understood this. If Mitchell Palmer could get away with his mass arrests and brutal treatment of people—citizens and immigrants alike—based on nothing more than guilt by association with vaguely defined "communists," then civil liberties had a bleak future in America. Certainly, this fight was just as important as any of the others he had risked his job over during the past year. Yes, he told Anderson, he would do it, but only so long as he could bring along his Harvard colleague Zechariah Chafee as his expert on the First Amendment. Now, he stood in Anderson's courtroom making his stand. Critics would call him a Red one more time, but let them. He had survived these storms before. In fact, one reporter noticed how Frankfurter even made a point to wear a pinkish-red necktie that morning.

"As a matter of fact, there was a considerable proportion of United States citizens [among those arrested], wasn't there?" Kelleher tried to deny it but, before he could speak, Frankfurter pulled out a newspaper clipping from Lynn, Massachusetts, reporting that thirty-eight out of the thirty-nine prisoners taken there had been freed almost immediately, almost half because they were citizens, and none had even been Communist Party members. Kelleher said he had only a "very general" awareness of the situation there.

"What authority had you in your pocket for those arrests?"

"The instructions from the Department at Washington that warrants awaited some and that Communists could be held and warrants obtained by telegraph," Kelleher said. Arresting citizens without warrants? Arresting anyone without warrants? Again, he had made his point. Kelleher had no authority to make the arrests, and had not even made a theoretical case for the Constitutionally required "probable cause." All he had was a note from a bureaucrat in Washington telling him to go ahead.

Frankfurter's purpose in these questions went far beyond winning freedom for the Deer Island prisoners. He knew that Americans had no sympathy for immigrant Reds, and he wasn't likely to change their minds. But however much they might hate radicals, Frankfurter still believed that most Americans valued the rule of law, or at least they resented it when government officials appeared too power hungry. If he could show that the Justice Department had repeatedly broken the law in conducting these raids, the people might listen. To Frankfurter's mind, the chief victims were not the Reds themselves but, instead, the law and the Constitution. If an aggressive attorney general like Palmer could ignore it whenever he had a wave of public passion on his side, the law meant nothing.

"Weren't prisoners searched without warrants?"

"That is true, according to our instructions." Kelleher answered. It was one more violation to add to the list.

"And in those original instructions, it was left to the discretion of the officer as to a warrant?"

"That is true."

"Did you find any instruments of violence on the people, such as bombs, guns, and what not?"

"Nothing in particular, excepting a knife-gun, an ingenious device designed, by the release of a blade, to propel a bullet from the end of a knife."

"Were prisoners brought in in chains?" Frankfurter knew that everyone in Boston had seen the newspaper photos of Red prisoners being marched through the streets in shackles and handcuffs en route to Deer Island. Kelleher could not deny it nor even try to justify it.

"I have no knowledge of such a thing. But I know precautions were necessary in bringing in larger numbers over great distances," he said.

Frankfurter then turned to what had been the most explosive part of the instruction letter from Washington that the clerk read a few minutes earlier, the part dealing with secret spies: "If possible you should arrange with your under-cover informants to have meetings of the COMMUNIST PARTY and the COMMUNIST LABOR PARTY held on the night set [for the raids]," the letter had read, suggesting that Justice Department *agents provocateurs* actually ran the Communist organizations. "As a matter of fact, you had reason to know that these meetings of the Communist parties would be called for the night of January 2, didn't you? . . . You even stimulated the calling of these meetings, didn't you?"

"That is a possibility, but I can't say personally," Kelleher said, damning himself once more with an off-handed admission.

Judge Anderson now interrupted from the bench. "Do you know when government participation in these parties began?" he asked. "Have you any personal knowledge of the extent of Government participation in this district?" No, Kelleher said.

How many undercover agents did he have working under him? "They are a floating population, Your Honor," Kelleher went on. "For instance, if I wanted a Russian worker for any special purpose, we might get him from New York for that case. . . . I have made it a point to get men who have not been connected with any private detective agency. Many of our men are lawyers and university graduates." Their goal was to observe, he insisted, not to make trouble.

"Well," Judge Anderson replied, "in these times of hysteria, I wonder no witches have been hung during the last six months." An eerie silence hung over the courtroom for a moment as every reporter jotted down what Anderson had just said. His remark would appear in newspapers across the county, a federal judge comparing Palmer's Red Raids with the Salem witchcraft trials.

Felix Frankfurter finished his grilling of Kelleher after a few more questions and then sat down. He would take turns with his fellow professor, Zechariah Chafee, questioning other officials the rest of the day. But the damage had already been done.

<hr />

Edgar watched in silence, sitting at the government table and whispering occasionally to the other lawyers, as Kelleher, his best bureau chief and a man who knew how to keep secrets, fell into trap after trap. Edgar could not help but notice how chummy things were between Judge Anderson and his two Harvard Liberal Club friends, Frankfurter and Chafee, the judge taking turns with the lawyers mocking Edgar's operation. He saw how Frankfurter flitted about the room, sharing private jokes and asides with the lawyers, charming even Edgar's own federal prosecutors Boynton and Goldberg. To his eye, this was no fair courtroom. It was a joke, a setup from start to finish, a stacked deck, and the judge's wisecrack about hanging witches was sheer grandstanding. By Friday, Edgar had seen enough. He went home to Washington. Goldberg contacted him the next week and asked him to come back to Boston and testify in the case. Edgar refused. There was nothing else he could do in Boston in that kangaroo court. Felix Frankfurter might have won today's battle, but Edgar would not let him win the whole war.

Besides, he had another fight to finish. On the same day as he watched Frankfurter skewering his bureau chief Kelleher on the witness stand, Edgar had gotten word that Louis Post had thrown one more fistful of sand in the government's gears, canceling a deportation order in a test case. If this stood, it meant that a thousand others would be thrown out with it. This, too, must not stand. For Edgar, it was a confusing and frustrating moment, attacked on all sides, betrayed and mocked. But he remained confident. He could always count on Mitchell Palmer. Palmer would know what to do.

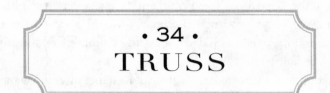

· 34 ·
TRUSS

Louis Post had gotten right down to business. Starting almost immediately after John Abercrombie left town in early March to run for the Alabama U.S. Senate seat left vacant by the death of Senator John H. Bankhead, Post took a quick inventory of the deportation cases sitting in Abercrombie's office. Now, as acting secretary, he could handle them as he pleased. He was ready to fight.

What surprised Post, though, was just how few cases actually had reached Abercrombie's office at all. Counting in his careful way, the numbers just didn't add up. Abercrombie had issued over four thousand deportation warrants during the January raids, Palmer's agents had made thousands of arrests, and immigration inspectors had conducted hundreds, perhaps thousands of hearings, but the actual number of cases sitting in Abercrombie's office waiting for decision by early March totaled just a few dozen. Where had the rest gone? It didn't take long to solve the mystery. Caminetti was holding the case files, stacked in piles in his office. This was his way of keeping the prisoners under lock and key indefinitely, and hiding any defects in the evidence. As their cases sat in limbo, hundreds, perhaps thousands of accused men rotted in prison, unable to raise bail. Meanwhile, unlike the quick deportation of Emma Goldman four months earlier, no actual ships had been lined up to send any of these supposed communists back to Russia, Italy, Poland, or anyplace else.

And Louis Post knew another dirty secret. Under the law, Caminetti actually had no authority to control these case files. The Immigration Act gave the inspectors the power to conduct hearings, and then it gave the secretary of labor or his designee the power to issue final rulings. Caminetti, as commissioner general of immigration, had assumed the role over the years of studying each case and making a recommendation, but this had no legal basis. It was only a custom. Post decided to settle this whole affair once and for all in the only way possible, by using the law to cut Caminetti out of the action.

Within a few days of taking charge, he mobilized his small office staff, his private secretary, Hugh Reid, his confidential clerk, Lillian Conrad, and a messenger. As a first step, to see how the prisoners actually were being treated, he asked the head of the Labor Department's Investigation and Inspection Service, Engelbert Stewart, to make a discreet tour of the detention centers at Boston's Deer Island, New York's Ellis Island, and Detroit's Federal Building. Stewart's report confirmed his worst fears. In Detroit, where eight hundred men and women had been stuffed into a single unlit, unventilated, unsanitary corridor for six days, Stewart reported the scene "could not have been worse and practically everything that has been said about the case is true." In Boston, he reported seeing a three-foot high pile of discarded chains and shackles that were used earlier to march prisoners through the streets.

Next, Post prepared himself to deal with the main issue, the case files. He started by sending Caminetti a demand to turn over every single deportation case under his control, whether or not he had finished writing a recommendation. "I undertook to clear the commissioner general's room of the scores upon scores, and scores upon scores of accumulated records that had come up from the different stations under those warrant cases—men arrested back in the fall and still in jail in March and no hearing had; or at any rate, no action," Post explained later. Once he finally got his hands on them, he started reading some of Caminetti's recommendations and comparing them with the actual evidence in the case records. In case after case, he found the recommendations to be based on pure fantasy. "I went, in any case that seemed important at all, to find out whether I was getting a proper recommendation," he explained. Time after time, he found he was not.

All through March, Louis Post and his assistant, Hugh Reid, spent days at a time locked behind closed doors reading these case files. "At first I scrutinized all the records personally," Post explained, though he soon discovered a pattern and started relying on Hugh Reid to filter them first. Post jotted down a list of principles he would follow in resolving these cases. It went like this: He would view membership in the Communist Party as sufficient cause to deport an immigrant—that was the law, after all—but only if the membership was real, conscious, and knowing. Either the prisoner must have signed a membership application himself or, if someone else signed it for him, there had to be evidence that he gave clear authority and understood what it meant. If the prisoner had withdrawn from the communists in circumstances showing good faith, or if his membership application had never been accepted, he would not count it. He refused to recognize what he called "automatic" memberships, where a chapter of the Socialist Party had been transferred en masse into the Communist Party without checking first with its individual members. Post also decided to ignore any statements made by a prisoner while he was denied access to a lawyer, or any evidence seized from his home without a warrant.* And he gave an extra benefit of the doubt to prisoners who could show general good character and to fathers or mothers of children born in America where their deportation would split the family.

By the end of March, Post had decided over fourteen hundred cases, canceling the warrants in about 80 percent of them for lack of evidence. He had no illusions about how angry this would make Caminetti and his friend Hoover at the Justice Department, let alone Mitchell Palmer. If his

---

*The Exclusionary Rule, which forbids the use of evidence against a defendant if obtained in an improper search, was already an established principle in 1919 and generally applied in federal courts. But its application to deportation cases remained unsettled. The Supreme Court traditionally held deportations not to be criminal trials demanding full constitutional protections, making it acceptable to allow such shortcuts as warrants by telegraph, limited rights to counsel, and hearings by agency officials rather than Article III judges with life terms. Louis Post pointed to two recent federal court cases to support his decision to exclude improperly obtained evidence, but one of those, Re Jackson, came only from a trial-level court, and the second, United States v. Silverthorne, 251 U.S. 385 (1920), did not involve deportations. Even Oliver Wendell Holmes recognized the problem. "On the deportation of aliens, the [critics] ought to remember that the decisions have gone very far in giving to government a right to do as it damn chooses. I speak from ancient memory," he wrote to Felix Frankfurter in December 1919. The exclusionary rule would not be applied to state-level cases until the Supreme Court's 1961 decision in Mapp v. Ohio, 367 U.S. 643.

decisions stood, Post would effectively stop Palmer in his tracks from deporting these aliens, the heart of his anti-Red crusade—right in the middle of Palmer's presidential campaign. He knew he was picking a fight with a bully, that Palmer would use every weapon to beat him in the public press, on Capitol Hill, and in any other sandbox he could find. To defend himself, Post knew his only chance would be to throw the first punch, to get out his side of the story. He had to explain himself and, from his years in politics and journalism, he knew the best way was to find a single, clear, sympathetic case of some poor working stiff who never made trouble, never stole a dime, but who got caught up in this Red Scare dragnet by mistake, incompetence, or overkill, and to throw it in the public eye.

It was about this time that he came upon the case of Thomas Truss. Truss, an immigrant from Lublin, Poland, lived in Baltimore with his wife and three American-born children, two sons and a daughter, and worked as a coat presser. He had joined the Amalgamated Clothing Workers union and his co-workers elected him their chapter president. He was an elder at the local St. Paul's Polish Presbyterian Church, and several church leaders vouched for his good character. Truss had joined the I.W.W. once in 1911 to get a job at a clothing factory but then quit two years later. He had applied for American citizenship but his paperwork got stalled someplace through no fault of his.

Justice Department agents had arrested Truss in January 1920. They raided his home, took him to a police station with no warrant, questioned him without a lawyer, and accused him of belonging to the Union of Russian Workers and the Communist Party, making him subject to deportation. Then they first got a warrant from Washington and turned him over to the Immigration Bureau. Truss paid his bail of $1,000 and returned to his family, but only after spending a full week in jail. When Louis Post looked at the actual evidence that Justice Department agents had presented to support their case, he shuddered at how flimsy it was. Thomas Truss had never actually joined the Union of Russian Workers. Instead, he had once joined a Russian workers' education and mutual benefits society. When that group later merged into the Union of Russian Workers in 1918, Truss dropped his membership. As for the Communist Party, Truss had gone to one organizational meeting—little more than a pep rally—during the summer of 1919 *before* the Party had even been formed. Truss had permitted an organizer to include his name on a list of prospects, and the Communists had mailed Truss a membership card when they came into existence in September 1919, but the local group never accepted the Party's radical charter.

That was it. There was nothing more. "Examination of this record makes it evident that [Truss] is not a Communist. Neither is he an anarchist. He is the opposite of an anarchist, namely, a socialist," Post concluded.

Louis Post now put pen to paper to draw his battle line. "[A]s this case appeared to be typical of most of those in which I had cancelled warrants of arrest, I [have] accompanied my decision with an extended explanatory statement," he wrote. He laid out the facts of Thomas Truss's arrest and explained why he felt Truss was no radical. Any technical membership he might have had in any radical group was purely by accident, not conscious choice. To decide it any other way would amount to "disregarding every principle of personal responsibility," he insisted. He listed the principles he used in deciding these cases, personal signature, ignoring automatic memberships, and the rest, and he explained each one in detail.

Then he got to his real point. Having reviewed well over a thousand of these Palmer Raid cases, he could report with full confidence that it was all a lie. The vast majority, he wrote, were "working men of good character, who have never been arrested before, who are not anarchists or revolutionists, nor politically or otherwise dangerous in any sense. It is pitiful to consider the hardship to which they and their families have been subjected during the past three or four months by arbitrary arrests, long detention in default of bail, beyond the means of hardworking wage earners to give, for nothing more dangerous than affiliating with friends of their own race, country and language, and without the slightest indication of sinister motive, or any unlawful act within their knowledge or intention."

Louis Post finished writing his statement and released it to the newspapers immediately without showing it first to Caminetti. Several quoted it at length. WILL DEPORT ONLY REAL COMMUNISTS, the *New York Times* ran as its headline. OFFICIAL SPEAKS FOR RAIDED ALIENS, echoed the *Christian Science Monitor*.

Then, later that afternoon, Louis Post sat down alone at his desk and scribbled out a letter to his longtime friend and sponsor, William Jennings Bryan, the three-time failed candidate for president of the United States and one-time secretary of state, an ally who likewise had known dramatic ups and downs in his career. "I hardly know how to answer your question as to whether the political outlook seems any brighter to me than to you," he wrote. "My impression is that it does not look very bright to you, and as to myself the whole thing is in such a muddle that I doubt if I should be able to tell whether any given outlook is bright or not. . . . At any rate, I do not recall any period in our history which the present political situation has so much resembled as that of the middle [eighteen] fifties," the time leading up to the Civil War. "The only real difference seems to me to be the greater magnitude and more complete mystification of the present situation."

After he finished, Louis Post enjoyed the quiet. The storm would come very soon.

· 35 ·

PLAIN WORDS

U P IN NEW YORK City, chief detective Bill Flynn finally made a breakthrough. He took full credit for it, pointing to his clever manipulation of Robert Elia and Andrea Salsedo to make Salsedo finally talk. "They were well treated, regularly fed in public restaurants, taken out for exercise, permitted to occupy separate clean beds at night in a clean room, and given ample opportunity to wash and bathe and change linen and were never examined or interrogated without their lawyer being present," he reported to Palmer's assistant John Creighton. Flynn persuaded Salsedo and Elia to stay at the Justice Department's Park Row office, both for their own safety and to allow Flynn's men to keep an eye on them. He kept their location secret from all but a few agents and Salsedo's lawyer and wife. He set up cots for them to sleep on and assigned guards to shadow them day and night, walk with them to the Battery for exercise, eat with them in restaurants or feed them in their rooms.*

Soon, under Flynn's coaxing, Salsedo began to spill. Talking through a translator—he understood only a few words of English—Salsedo admitted being connected to the Galliani anarchists in Lynn, Massachusetts, and even identified some of the group's members from photographs. He admitted printing the pamphlet "Plain Words" found at the June 2 bombing sites. He said he got the print order for the pamphlets from Nicola Recchi, a member of Galliani's gang. "Salsedo was shown a copy of 'Plain Words' and admitted this to be a fact, and confessed his own participation," John Creighton reported. "Elia confirmed the fact that Salsedo delivered a package of these leaflets to Recchi, who took away with him the original manuscript."

It was a breathtaking lead, and it meant that earlier reports tying the "Plain Words" leaflet to exiled Communist Party leader Louis Fraina were simply wrong. Galliani himself, leader of the Lynn anarchists, already had fled to Italy as had Recchi, but they could be extradited, and other bombers might still be in reach. Salsedo held the key. He was the only witness. The whole case rested on his continued willingness to talk.

Flynn decided to take no chances. He convinced Salsedo and Elia to remain at the Park Row office indefinitely. He never formally arrested them, but he never let them out of his sight or away from his guards. He made them prisoners, one way or another. Besides, Salsedo seemed in no hurry to leave, despite his growing despondency and signs of tuberculosis. He may have feared that Galliani's men already suspected him of talking too much and wanted to shut him up permanently. His life could be in danger. To Flynn, it was just a matter of time before Salsedo wrapped up the whole case. Certainly, the bombers would not have trusted the job of printing "Plain Words" to anyone but a trusted friend. Once the case was solved, then they could worry about Salsedo's health and the legal niceties. In the meantime, they needed Andrea Salsedo where they could find him and control him.

---

*Flynn apparently decided to try a tougher approach on Gaspare Cannone, the third Italian arrested with Salsedo and Elia in connection with the June bombing case, questioned down the hall at the Park Row office. Cannone, in a later sworn statement, would claim he was beaten, kicked, and taunted by three agents, called a "damned liar" and "son of a bitch" when he denied knowing about the bombings, made to sleep in a bare jail cell with no bed or blankets, and, when he refused to sign a prepared statement admitting he was an "anarchist," that his signature on the document was forged.

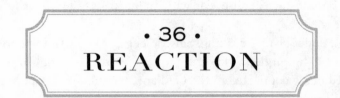

· 36 ·
REACTION

EDGAR HAD PLENTY of time during the ten-hour train ride home from Boston to read Louis Post's opinion in the *Truss* case. His eyes drank in its eight pages of small type, what he saw as its tortured logic and condescending tone. How absurd! How laughable! Post was taking a treacherous Red and turning him into a victim, making Edgar's agents— men who risked their lives for their country—look like liars and bunglers, all based on nothing more than a few nitpicks in the evidence. Edgar recognized the name Thomas Truss. Edgar himself had forwarded the message from his Newark office back in January requesting the arrest warrant for this Truss, fingering him as belonging both to the Communist Party and the Union of Russian Workers, two of the country's worst radical groups, making him doubly deserving to be deported under the 1918 statute.

Rather that mistreating this Thomas Truss, one of Edgar's agents in Baltimore had even gone and visited Mrs. Truss while her husband was in jail to make sure she had coal for the winter and money to feed their children, and he had arranged with the Baltimore Welfare Association to help the family if needed. Who was Truss to complain with his sob stories?

To Edgar's mind, it was one more double-cross. If Louis Post stuck to his logic in the *Truss* case, then any malicious radical could hide behind some technicality and escape justice. What an outrage to the country. Here was Louis Post, an obscure, unelected, foggy-headed intellectual oblivious to the danger, single-handedly undermining the Justice Department's crackdown on anarchy, giving courage to the country's Bolshevist enemies. And he was a liar, too. The Labor Department had promised to cooperate with Justice in this project. Post had broken the deal, plain and simple, and dressed it up in fancy language.

Edgar wondered what had become of his country these days. In the three years since he had joined the Justice Department in 1917, he had known America on a constant war footing, never resting, ever vigilant and prepared to smash its enemies, be it Germany's kaiser or postwar communists. Just three months ago, in January, the whole country applauded Palmer. "The raids . . . certainly met with unusual success," Edgar had bragged in a note to his Justice Department superiors just in February. It had been "the first attempt of its kind [and] conducted so far as I know with no adverse criticism." Now, in the wink of an eye, leaders turned soft, and the public grew indifferent. Edgar saw turncoats all around him. Felix Frankfurter and Judge Anderson were only the latest. Take Francis Fisher Kane, the Philadelphia federal prosecutor who quit his job in January to protest the raids. Just two weeks after leaving the Justice Department, Kane had gone on a speaking tour, courting groups like Philadelphia's City Club and Young Democracy Club by criticizing his former colleagues with what Edgar considered pure pandering. "We have never reached the truth by censorship," Kane told one audience. "If you suppress meetings . . . then people will go to the garrets and places unknown to the police, and you will be creating real danger."

Even more disappointing for Edgar was John Lord O'Brian, his one-time mentor at the Justice Department's War Emergency Division who had hired him back in 1917, promoted him four times, then recommended him to Mitchell Palmer. O'Brian had left Washington and returned to his private law practice in Buffalo in March 1919, but in early 1920 he, too, became a critic. In January, O'Brian had denounced the New York State

---

*Leading opposition to the ouster, which even Mitchell Palmer decried as excessive, was Charles Evans Hughes, a former New York governor, Republican presidential nominee, and Supreme Court Justice, and future Chief Justice. Hughes sent an open letter to Assembly Speaker Thomas Sweet on January 10, 1920, calling it "absolutely opposed to the fundamental principles of our government, for a majority to undertake to deny representation to a minority through its representatives elected by ballots lawfully cast."

legislature's decision to oust its five Socialist Party members,* and then had given a speech to the Maryland Bar Association calling the raids themselves a "rare evil . . . flatly at variance with American standards" and run by "some anonymous subordinate administrative official in Washington." How insulting it all was. Edgar had once counted O'Brian a friend and a role model. Edgar knew firsthand that O'Brian had gone even farther during the World War in cracking down on dissent. Now, wasting no time on sentiment, he promptly assigned an agent to start keeping tabs on John Lord O'Brian and set up a file on him: Old German 384125. "Information received from confidential informant states that the above [O'Brian] who was formerly connected with this department is an active person in radical circles to the extent of sending several checks to the PEOPLES FREEDOM UNION, #138 West 13th Street, New York City (Roger Baldwin, Treasurer) an organization formed for the purpose of defending radicals now held by the Federal authorities," the agent's initial report disclosed.

Could Edgar have missed the irony in this? Here he was, setting up a dossier on O'Brian, the very same person who as Edgar's wartime boss had approved the creation of these Old German files in the first place.

Reaching Washington, Edgar hurried from the train station across town to the Justice Department building on Vermont Avenue. Here, he found Caminetti waiting to join him in commiserating over their situation. To Caminetti, this was personal. Louis Post had given him a cold bureaucratic slap in the face, seizing his files and clipping his power. Soon, another ally joined them, this one from Capitol Hill: Congressman Albert Johnson, chairman of the House Immigration Committee. Johnson represented a district in Washington State, scene of the Seattle general strike and the Centralia killings, and had been a stalwart supporter of the raids. Back in December 1919, Johnson had even joined Edgar in New York City to celebrate the sailing of the *Buford* and wish Emma Goldman a *bon voyage* back to Russia. Caminetti already had started slipping immigration case files secretly to Johnson to use against Louis Post.

Congressman Johnson suggested that they launch a quick preemptive strike, and he volunteered to take the first shot. On Monday, April 12, 1920, just three days after Edgar's return from Boston, Johnson mounted the floor of the House of Representatives and proceeded to open fire. "[I]t is my opinion that the Department of Labor is being bored from within," he charged, and accused Louis Post of planning to release 95 percent of all the Reds nabbed in the January raids. To prove that Post had sold out to his country, Johnson gave his own example of what he considered an outrageous excess: Paul Bosco, a Russian immigrant and convicted wartime seditionist who had served two years at the federal penitentiary in Atlanta and had declared in open court: "When I come out of prison, I hope to see the red flag flying above the Stars and Stripes." This was the kind of criminal that Louis Post had freed from jail, over the objections of every lawyer in the Immigration Bureau.

The other congressmen listened in disbelief. Who was this villain Louis Post? Most had never heard of him. Why hadn't someone fired him? Couldn't they do something? Why not strip him of his power? The drumbeat against him had started.

In mid-April, Mitchell Palmer came back to Washington from his latest presidential campaign swing, and Edgar made a point to see him as soon as he returned to his office. He found Palmer worried. Long before the advent of reliable opinion polls, Palmer had made himself an expert at reading the tiniest changes in public moods. What he saw worried him. The Red Scare had cooled. Americans in April 1920 looked out at a far less scary world than they had just a few months earlier. American soldiers had mostly left Soviet Russia by late 1919, ending their brief intervention there. Communism had failed to sweep Europe as revolutions in Germany and Hungary collapsed. And the 1919 steel, coal, and police strikes in the U.S. had failed. Fears of subversion melted like the winter snow. The World War was over and people finally allowed themselves to think about happier things. Peace had its pleasures.

The same week that Edgar and Felix Frankfurter had faced each other across Judge Anderson's Boston courtroom in the *habeas corpus* case, Boston's own *Evening Globe* had topped its front page with a headline on a totally different subject: SUNDAY SPORTS BILL SIGNED. Babe Ruth's upcoming debut with the New York Yankees, Jack Dempsey's upcoming fight against Frenchman Georges Carpentier, grumbling over Prohibition, and anticipation over the newest ladies' skirts and bonnets, all seemed more interesting to most Americans than fretting over Reds. In his presidential campaign speeches, Palmer noticed how he now drew far bigger applause by criticizing coal companies, sugar processors, and milk suppliers for high prices than by attacking radicals.

Palmer had staked his name on his Red Raids and spent years building a reputation as a man who got things done. What he needed was a fresh chance to fan the flames and get people angry again.

He didn't have to look far. That same month of April 1920, as Palmer and Edgar faced their crisis over the raids, a wave of wildcat railroad strikes hit the country. The Pennsylvania Railroad abruptly shut down, leaving 35,000 commuters stranded, followed soon by the Erie and Lackawanna, two major New York lines, and smaller strikes in Syracuse, Chicago, and Dayton, Ohio. Officials warned of food shortages if the work stoppages lasted long. The national railroad unions disowned these strikes and blamed them on local hotheads, but Palmer read the reports from Edgar's Radical Division and he saw behind them a different culprit: a Red conspiracy led by the I.W.W. Here was his villain.

Palmer raced over to the White House and held an urgent *tête-à-tête* with hard-liners in President Woodrow Wilson's inner circle, including private secretary Joe Tumulty and Postmaster General Albert Burleson. They quickly decided what to do. "We have been warning the country against the activity of radicals, but we have been accused of 'seeing things' and exaggerating," an unnamed Justice Department official told the *Washington Star*. It was time to mobilize public opinion. Woodrow Wilson had not attended a single cabinet meeting in the seven months since his thrombosis attack in September 1919. Here was a good chance for him to step forward and show that he could still lead the country. The president decided to call one now, scheduled for the next day. Its first item of business would be the railroad strike and the Reds.

AIDES HAD TO place Woodrow Wilson in a chair behind a desk before anyone else arrived for the meeting at 10:00 A.M. that morning, Wednesday, April 14, 1920, in order to hide the fact that the president could not stand up or move much of his body. Wilson was a damaged man, his face sagging to one side, his skin pale and clammy. As he sat there, another aide announced the name of each cabinet member entering the small study near his bedroom on the upper floor of the White House, so Wilson wouldn't stumble trying to remember the man's name or face. Each cabinet member came up to him and shook his hand. Navy Secretary Josephus Daniels recalled Wilson that day as being "bright & cheerful." Palmer was more direct. He told a friend later that the president "seemed mentally all right but physically he was in bad shape [and] looked like a very old man and acted like one. He shook hands but did not move his left arm." The president's wife, Edith, and his doctor, Admiral Cary Grayson, sat watching the whole time, ready to step in and call off the whole affair should Wilson show any sign of discomfort.

Once the cabinet secretaries took seats, the president tried to break the ice by telling a joke. "I felt it well to put our heads together, not as the Chicago Aldermen who did so when they wished to make a solid pavement," he said. A few of them chuckled.

Any warmth among these cabinet members had vanished long ago. They eyed each other suspiciously. Just a few weeks earlier, Wilson had forced his secretary of state, Robert Lansing, to resign in an ugly exchange of finger-pointing. Wilson had distrusted Lansing at least since early 1919 when Lansing, at the height of the Versailles Treaty negotiations, had criticized Wilson's League of Nations in a private conversation that then leaked out on Capitol Hill. "Were I in Washington I would at once demand his resignation!" Wilson had fumed to Joe Tumulty in Paris at the time. "That kind of disloyalty must not be permitted to go unchallenged for a single minute."* Then, in early February 1920, Wilson had accused Lansing of disloyalty again, this time after Lansing called cabinet members together to meet several times during the president's illness. "I received . . . a letter from the president indicating that he did not consider it proper for the Cabinet to meet except at his personal summons," Lansing wrote colleagues.

But when the White House made this new charge public, it raised embarrassing questions about Wilson's own mental clarity. Hadn't the president known about these cabinet meetings? Hadn't Joe Tumulty, his trusted personal secretary, even attended several of them? The controversy left Mitchell Palmer in a particularly awkward spot. Back in October 1919, during the coal strike, Palmer had publicly justified his own tough stand by pointing to the president's agreement with decisions from one of these meetings. "I outlined to [the president] everything that the Cabinet had done and what it contemplated doing, all of which the president approved," Palmer had told reporters after visiting Wilson in his White House sickroom, a quote that critics now happily unearthed.

And there was another sore point. Palmer was actively running for the 1920 Democratic presidential nomination, and his chief rival was the

---

*Wilson's myopia over the League of Nations and lingering distrust of anyone who questioned his stance, the real heart of his controversy with Lansing, continued to color his attitudes in early 1920, months after the Senate had killed the treaty. In January, Edith Wilson had sent a note to Palmer's colleague Albert Burleson, the postmaster general: "At the President's request, I am sending you the enclosed list of Senators who hindered or did not assist the ratification of the Treaty. He asks that you be kind enough to go over it for him with Senators Hitchcock and Underwood, and that after you have done so let him know your joint judgment in answer to these two questions: (1) Is it fair? (2) Is it complete?"

president's son-in-law, former treasury secretary William Gibbs McAdoo. Both Palmer and McAdoo scoured the country for support, but President Wilson so far had refused to endorse either of them or to take his own name out of the race. Palmer complained about the situation to Colonel Edward M. House, the president's confidante. "The President's silence is particularly embarrassing to him and to McAdoo," House confided, but Wilson seemed oblivious. Finally, another cabinet member, Interior Secretary Franklin Lane, had quit in early February to take a high-paying job with the Pan-American Petroleum Company, giving the look of one more rat deserting a sinking ship.

So now, in April 1920, with Wilson still incapacitated, the cabinet members sat around his desk in the small study for their first meeting in seven months and tried to pretend everything was normal. They had work to do, and Palmer took the lead. As the president sat quietly, his attorney general laid out in no uncertain terms that he believed these wildcat railroad strikes endangered the country, and he pointed his finger directly at the culprits: Bolshevists and the I.W.W. His Justice Department agents had confirmed their complicity, he insisted. These radicals had to be stopped.

Most of the other cabinet members simply nodded or took notes, assuming that Palmer knew what he was talking about. But not everyone went along. Labor Secretary William B. Wilson, who had gotten out of his own sick bed to attend this meeting, disagreed. These railroad men faced tough times, low wages, and a skyrocketing cost of living that made it hard to feed their families. That's what caused this strike, he argued. The railroad men simply wanted better pay, and they had every right to demand it through a legal work stoppage. Washington should keep its nose out of the affair.

But Palmer wasn't finished; he had another bone to pick. The problem was not just the Reds. Pointing at Secretary Wilson, sitting just a few chairs away from him, Palmer insisted that Wilson was in no position to argue; because his own Labor Department shared the blame. It was shielding communist enemies. Wilson's deputy, Louis Post, had undermined the government's crackdown on radicals by dropping cases against hundreds of Red immigrants who should have been deported. Many of the Reds behind this railroad strike would be back in Russia by now if only Louis Post had not gotten in the way. Post had to be fired.

William B. Wilson had seen plenty of backstabbing smears during his twenty years in politics, but he found it hard to recall any other such appalling lack of courtesy as this attack by Palmer, right in front of the president. No, he insisted, Louis Post should not be fired. He was following the law and making sure that only *real* communists were deported, not just any law-abiding person who happened to disagree with the government. Palmer jumped in to argue back, and he and Wilson soon were shouting at each other across the room. Navy Secretary Daniels, sitting between them, tried to distill the argument in his notes: "Palmer said if Post were removed from office it would end the strike. WBW[ilson] thought it might aggravate it."

President Woodrow Wilson, sitting at his desk trying to follow the conversation, seemed bothered by the shrill voices. His wife, Edith, interrupted from her seat off to the side. "This is an experiment, you know," she told them; they ought not to stay long. The president's doctor, Admiral Cary Grayson, agreed.

But Woodrow Wilson now wanted to speak. He got the group's attention. Navy Secretary Daniels's diary is the only direct source for what he proceeded to say: "[The president] told Palmer not to let the country see red." That was all. What did this mean? Was he telling Palmer to stop his raids, or tone down his rhetoric, or stop fighting against the Labor Department, or release some of the Red prisoners, or to go easy on Louis Post? Woodrow Wilson did not elaborate. Like a sphinx, having uttered his epigram, he sealed his lips. If this was Woodrow Wilson's way of protesting that he was unaware of the Red Raids until this moment or that he disapproved of them, he was far from clear about it. Palmer, for one, took the president's response as a green light to go forward and attack the Reds he saw lurking behind the railroad strikes, and nobody else present in the room contradicted him at the time.

The conversation moved on, but nothing was decided, so the two adversaries, Palmer and William Wilson, each felt free to do as he pleased. The president ended the meeting after a few more minutes. "Cabinet officers declared the president had been in excellent humor and laughed and joked with them," one White House official told the *Boston Globe* after the session. "It did him good," his doctor, Cary Grayson, added.

Later that afternoon, back at the Justice Department, Mitchell Palmer invited a handful of newspaper men to his office and bared his teeth. These wildcat railroad strikes were the product of one big radical plot: "In a word, this is the latest manifestation of the working out of the program of the international Communist to capture industrial and political power, overturn the government, and obtain the dictatorship of what they are pleased to call the proletariat, and transplant to this country the chaotic conditions in Russia," he told them. The I.W.W. and communist leaders had planned the whole thing in a series of meetings at New York's Continental Hotel and Chicago's Great Northern. "The basic agitation of these leaders was the destruction of the railroad brotherhoods, the removal of their union, and the [creation of] One Big Union"—the I.W.W. Mitchell Palmer intended "to arouse the American people to a sense of the dangers [and] to appeal to the patriotism of the misled workers who have participated in this strike without realizing its significance," he said. And what's more, he insisted, he had just met with President Woodrow Wilson and the entire cabinet, and they all stood squarely behind him. "People said I was seeing red," Palmer insisted, "but what I said was going to take place has come to pass" in the form of these strikes.

The news hit like a thunderbolt in headlines across the country. A few labor leaders like American Federation of Labor secretary Fred Morrison tried to excuse the railroad stoppage as "just a plain, ordinary strike for more pay. . . . The absolute failure of the attorney general to grasp the true situation is amazing." But when workers returned to their jobs a few days later and trains started running again, Mitchell Palmer declared victory, claiming he had beaten the Reds once more.

That done, it was time to deal with that renegade in the Labor Department, Louis Post.

Mitchell Palmer once again had a plan, and he spelled it out for his young protégé, Hoover. Edgar grasped it easily. Post had to be removed, or else he could block the Red deportations indefinitely. And if neither President Wilson nor Secretary Wilson was prepared to fire him, Palmer had no choice but to go over their heads. There was another power in Washington, D.C., one that was less squeamish about this kind of dirty work: Congress. There lay the power of impeachment, and they could use it in this case. They would isolate Louis Post, disgrace him, and eliminate him.

The orchestration was quick. Palmer, Edgar, and Caminetti spread the message all over town. They snapped their fingers, and friendly congressmen popped up to do their bidding. Ohio representative Martin Davey, who had sponsored Palmer's antisedition bill in January, stood up on the House floor on Wednesday, April 14, 1920, and opened a barrage of attacks. "We have there in the Department of Labor a man whose sympathies evidently are with the enemies of our Government," he announced. "The hand of the Attorney General [in deporting radicals] has been made impotent by the friend of the revolutionists and that enemy of our Government, Louis F. Post. . . . I can say with authority that if this man Post had not stood in the way of the Attorney General there would not have been in this country certain men who are leading the railroad strike."

Edgar, working behind the scenes, turned his agents loose to find any dirt possible on Louis Post. His New York office reported that Post in 1904 had signed an affidavit supporting the good character of an anarchist named Turner who was later deported. A Chicago agent claimed that Post had sent red stickers to arrested communists telling them to fight their deportations by filing *habeas corpus* petitions. He also claimed that Post was a 50 percent owner of the *New Republic*, apparently confusing the *New Republic* with Post's own magazine, *The Public*. Edgar created an Old German file for Louis Post, and ultimately his system would contain fifteen typed index cards on him, each one listing multiple cross-references, plus two more cards on Post's wife.

At the same time, Palmer directed his prosecutors across the country to ignore Post's decision in the *Truss* case and to keep pushing to deport as many radicals as possible. "Ruling in Truss case by Assistant Secretary of Labor [Post] should not be position taken by you," he wired one U.S. Attorney in response to a question. He turned to Kansas congressman Homer Hoch to sponsor an actual impeachment resolution. "Assistant Secretary of Labor Post, by his attitude toward the law and by his action in specific cases, has virtually nullified the law against alien reds and anarchists," Hoch announced introducing his bill.

Palmer did not even try to hide his fingerprints. He and Edgar left calling cards all over Capitol Hill lining up support. Congressman after congressman mentioned Edgar or Caminetti by name in their speeches. "This young man, Hoover, went over there and tried the case [of one Red prisoner]," Kansas congressman Jasper Tincher told his colleagues. "He was thoroughly familiar with the facts and he begged the department [of Labor] to hold this man because he was a vicious organizer." Another impeachment backer, New York congressman Isaac Siegel, said "it is frankly admitted by everybody that there exists a sort of open hostility between the Department of Justice, Mr. Post, and Mr. Caminetti in regard to all these alien deportation cases. . . . It is frankly admitted by Mr. Hoover, Assistant Attorney General, that both he and the Department of Labor can not reach any agreement."

Rumors began popping up around Washington that even Post's boss at the Labor Department would soon have his head on the chopping block. CABINET CLASH MAY FORCE OUT WM. B. WILSON, headlined the *Washington*

Herald, quoting what it called "a source instantly authoritative" and citing Wilson's recent clashes with Palmer.

Palmer gave the order, Edgar spoke, and Congress listened. By the end of April, they had set all the wheels turning. It was just a matter of time, or so they hoped.

One night soon after Mitchell Palmer's performance at the contentious cabinet meeting, President Woodrow Wilson sat in his bedroom in the White House in front of a lit fire and shared an after-dinner cup of tea with Admiral Cary Grayson, his doctor and friend. According to Grayson's diary notes, the conversation turned to politics, the 1920 presidential race, and the attorney general. "Mitchell Palmer talks too much," the president told Grayson in that strained, scratchy voice he'd acquired since his illness. "His ambition is to keep before the public; after it is over here, go to N.Y. & practice law. Why he would not accept Secy War— was on account of being a Quaker. I should not have offered it. That was one on me."

These idle words from the sick president, irritated at his pushy attorney general but unable, or unwilling, to restrain him, amounted to little more that night than a simple rumination before he drifted off to bed. But if Mitchell Palmer still hoped to win the president's blessing in his bid for the White House in return for years of loyal service, he would be disappointed.

· 38 ·
COMMUNIST LABOR

HOW DIFFERENT IT was this time. Edgar once again stood before Labor Secretary William B. Wilson in the wood-paneled Labor Department conference room packed with lawyers, ranking officials, and newsmen. He had come back to argue yet another legal case crucial to the Red Raids. Dressed in a dark suit, white shirt, black shoes, and bright tie—presumably any color except red—his wavy black hair accentuating his big, boyish eyes, Edgar's good looks and straight posture made him stand out among the gray old men. This time, Secretary Wilson had agreed to hear a test case on whether the Communist Labor Party met the legal standard to be considered a radical organization under the 1918 Immigration Act, making its members subject to deportation. Wilson had already decided this issue once when he allowed hundreds of warrants to be issued against Communist Labor members for the January raids, but now he had agreed to reconsider the matter.

Why? Edgar had no doubt that these gray old men, his onetime friends at the Labor Department, had all turned yellow.

Edgar could not help but notice Louis Post sitting at Wilson's right hand at the head table, Post's face hidden behind his Trotsky-like beard and thick glasses. Did Edgar even bother to shake hands with this man whom he considered a double-dealing turncoat who stood accused by Congress of Red sympathies? In the weeks before this hearing, Post had freed every one of the 140 Communist Labor members still behind bars, charging no bail whatever. Caminetti had objected, but Post overruled him. To Edgar, this figured to be yet another kangaroo court, just like Judge Anderson's courtroom in Boston.

Making matters worse, Judge Anderson had just issued a preliminary ruling in the Boston *habeas corpus* case the prior Thursday, ordering that thirteen Red prisoners on Deer Island be immediately freed on bail of just $500. He used the occasion to criticize the whole operation. "A more lawless proceeding is hard to conceive," he'd snapped at prosecutors in open court. "I can hardly sit on the bench as an American citizen and restrain my indignation. I view with horror such proceedings as this. . . . This case seems to have been conducted under the modern theory of statesmanship: Hang first and try afterward."

Now, standing in front of Secretary Wilson at the Labor Department, Edgar had to go through all the motions again. The latest test case involved a thirty-eight-year-old immigrant from Germany named Carl Miller, who had been arrested in Denver in the January roundup and admitted belonging to the Communist Labor Party. His case raised only one question: Did the Party advocate the violent overthrow of the United States government, making membership in it a deportable offense for noncitizens like Miller? If yes, then the deportations of the 140 Communist Labor members could go forward. If no, then all these cases would be dropped, and the Reds turned loose to wander the streets and throw their bombs. To Edgar, this was the choice.

As he had before, Edgar led off the debate by standing up and, in his crisp, clear, staccato voice, ticking off a long list of incriminating statements from the Party's charter and manifestos: its bragging over its connection to Moscow's Third International, its goal to "conquer" and "capture" political power, its aim to "abolish" capitalism and use "mass action" to spark revolution. They were no different from all the other communist groups, he insisted, "a band of cut throat aliens who have come to this country to overthrow the Government by force." They and others like them had represented 50 percent of the influence behind the recent steel, coal, railroad, and police strikes. Then he finished and sat down.

This time, though, the communists had come better prepared to present their case. When their turn came, Secretary Wilson gave the floor to Swinburne Hale, a veteran, topflight New York litigator who had served as a captain in army military intelligence during World War I. Educated at Harvard and the son of a University of Chicago Latin professor, Swinburne Hale had become a leading Justice Department critic over the past year, testifying before Congress against the adoption of peacetime sedition laws. He had defended two radicals against criminal anarchy charges in New York City—he lost both cases—and even helped to raise bail money for the Communist Labor Party founder, Benjamin Gitlow. Hale shared his New York law office with no less a Red than Isaac Schorr, the lawyer who gave Edgar such headaches by showing up at Ellis Island after the November raid and coaching the communist prisoners to stop talking and launch a hunger strike.

Swinburne Hale presented the case for the Communist Labor Party today. Hale, too, had studied the Party's literature, having learned a trick from Edgar's earlier cases. Polished and urbane, he took the floor and presented his own litany of small but, he argued, important differences between the Communist Labor Party and the Communist Party. Communist Labor members signed no pledge of allegiance to party principles and its platform never called directly for armed bloodshed. Then, picking up a copy of Judge Anderson's new decision in the Boston *habeas corpus* case, Hale launched out in another direction. Not only was the Justice Department's case weak, he argued, but it was a fraud. And here was proof. He began to read aloud from Anderson's opinion: "The evidence here is clear that the Government operates some part of the Communist party," it said, referring to its use of undercover *agents provocateurs* to call Party meetings.

Edgar could not believe his ears. Was Hale calling him a liar? Not just Edgar alone, but his whole Justice Department? Had he been talking to Felix Frankfurter? Were all these liberal lawyers working together? Edgar jumped up from his chair and interrupted. Judge Anderson was wrong, he insisted. He had twisted the truth; his statement was "an unjustifiable misconception of facts," he said, that even "the most perverted mind" could not have drawn from the evidence. The Justice Department had no secret *agents provocateurs*, at least not in the ugly way Judge Anderson meant it.

But Swinburne Hale, too, had come prepared. He pulled out a second document, a copy of the "instruction" letter to George Kelleher, the Justice

Department's bureau chief in Boston, the same letter that Felix Frank-furter had introduced in evidence in Judge Anderson's courtroom in Boston, telling Kelleher to "arrange with your undercover informants" to call meetings for January 2, the night of the raids. Hale now started to read aloud from the letter, just as the clerk had done in Boston. Edgar objected again. The letter meant nothing, he said. January 2 was a Friday, and communists always held their meetings on Friday nights.

Secretary Wilson banged his gavel. He would not let this hearing become a free-for-all. "Criticism of the methods of the Department of Jus-tice or defense of those methods [does] not come within the purview of this hearing," he told the lawyers. They should stick to the point.

Hale finished and sat down, giving Edgar the chance for another response. He rose to his feet and, in his methodical way, began by reading a few more inflammatory Communist quotes into the record. It all went smoothly until he came to one by Louis Fraina, the longtime leftwing firebrand who had edited *The Revolutionary Age* and drafted the Commu-nist Party's platform in 1919 before fleeing the country in December. This time, it was Swinburne Hale who jumped to his feet and objected. Here was your *agent provocateur*, Hale insisted: Louis Fraina. Fraina was an undercover agent for the Department of Justice. The Justice Department had used Fraina as a stooge, planted him in the Communist Party to con-coct these wild incriminating statements, and now was using them as reason to deport innocent people.

Edgar normally prided himself on his self-control, but this last outburst by Swinburne Hale touched a raw nerve, perhaps aggravated by weeks of stress. Edgar certainly knew the stories about Louis Fraina being a Justice Department spy. It was one of Edgar's own agents who originally planted it, and Edgar had fired the agent over the incident. Everyone knew this story was fake. The communists themselves had cleared Fraina of these charges months ago. So why would Swinburne Hale repeat this fabrica-tion here and now in a public hearing? Was he lying on purpose? Was he deluded? Did he think Edgar was stupid? Was he trying to trick him? Edgar's face must have hardened into a chilling stone façade at that moment. "Are you prepared to prove that statement?" Edgar said, standing in his place at the front of the room, turning on Swinburne Hale. "The man who will say that Fraina was, or is, or will be an agent of the Department of Justice has uttered a deliberate and malicious false-hood, and the man who makes such a statement is a liar."

Swinburne Hale stood speechless. Publicly calling a man a liar in most of America in 1919 still amounted to daring him to pick up a gun or put up his fists, but Edgar hadn't finished yet. He faced Hale squarely. Substantiate the statement within ten days, he demanded. If not, he said, Palmer would "call upon [you] publicly to do so."

Once again, Secretary Wilson banged his gavel. He refused to allow a brawl in his conference room. He demanded both lawyers step back from the brink. Edgar took a breath, and so did Hale. Hale sat down, and their argument was over. None of it did Edgar any good. After it ended, he went back to the Justice Department to fret. Newspapers headlines captured the tension that day. [HOOVER] MAKES HOT REPLY TO BOSTON JUDGE, led the *Boston Globe*; CHARGE AT DEPORTATION HEARING SHARPLY CONTRADICTED BY DEPARTMENT OF JUSTICE; UGLY WORD USED, added the *New York Tribune*.

Secretary Wilson this time took ten days to announce his decision. It was a total reversal. He found the Communist Labor Party *not* to be a radical organization under the 1918 Immigration Act, invalidating all the deportation orders based solely on membership in it. The Justice Department had failed to show that the Party intended to overthrow the government by force. "If the American people are left free to discuss and decide the questions facing themselves for consideration from day to day, uninfluenced by the threat of violence," Wilson concluded, "they can be relied on to protect themselves from any false philosophies, wild-eyed revolutions, or dictatorships of any kind." Edgar did not believe it for a minute when Wilson claimed later that he never consulted Louis Post in deciding this case. Edgar could only shake his head. He had been cheated again, and another 140 Reds would go free.

One day around this time, Edgar took a pair of scissors while sitting at his desk and clipped a photograph from a newspaper of Louis Post smiling back from the page. Edgar pasted it into his scrapbook, then he took a red pencil and colored in the background all around Post's head to form a red halo. Next to the photograph, he typed a poem. It was called "THE BULLY BOLSHEVIK" and it started like a nursery rhyme:

> The "Reds" at Ellis Island
>   Are happy as can be
> For Comrade Post at Washington
>   Is setting them all free.

The poem had no signature. Maybe Edgar wrote it himself; maybe he didn't. Either way, he liked it enough to save it. It must have made him laugh, and laughter was far too rare a tonic in his life at this point.

THE BULLY BOLSHEVIK
Disrespectfully dedicated
to "Comrade" Louie Post.

The "Reds" at Ellis Island
   Are happy as can be
For Comrade Post at Washington
   Is setting them all free.

They'll soon be raising hell again
   In every city and town
To bring on Revolution
   And the USA to down.

But Uncle Sam will clinch his fist
   And rise up mighty strong
Take hold of Comrade "Louie"—
   Send the "Reds" where they belong.

It's awfully nice of Comrade Louie
   Of his position to make the most
The "Reds" all cheer when er they hear
   That sweet sounding name "Ach Louie dear."

But don't forget, he'll get his yet
   For this is the land of the brave
He'll fail in his plan to rescue
   Not one of the "Reds" will he save.

And when he's lost his nice fat job
   And is looking around for work
They'll ask him to come to Russia
   With the Bolsheviks he'll lurk.

Nick Lenine will gladly greet him
   In dear old Petrograd

He'll be a "Bullsheviki" sure
    Because he got in bad.

His whiskers they'll grow longer
    On the "Bullsheviki" bull
If you don't believe me, watch them
    After he has lost his pull.

So then all hail, dear Comrade Post!
    With all his ways so tricky
And ponder well, that it was only he
    Who saved the "Bullsheviki."

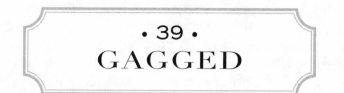

· 39 ·
GAGGED

L OUIS POST TRIED to be brave about his pending impeachment. He
told reporters he welcomed the chance to clear his name. A few
friends quietly called on him to lend support. Inside the Labor Department, Secretary Wilson promised to help him, and he said he considered
his own record to be under attack along with Post's. "If an impeachable
offense has been committed, I am responsible for it," he confided in a
letter to Felix Frankfurter. But Louis Post knew the score. Mounting a
defense against impeachment charges could cost thousands of dollars—
money he did not have. He would need a top-notch lawyer, and he
refused to accept free handouts. "Several offers of financial support came
to me, but they were from friends no abler financially than I," he confided. "Yet the alternative was to make my defense unsupported and
unadvised." He would be alone, facing the combined power of Congress
and Palmer's Justice Department. They would beat him bloody and
exploit any slipup. To fight seemed hopeless, but, to seventy-one-year-old
Post, it would be even worse to end his career humiliated in this way.

Meanwhile, he watched his reputation being ripped to shreds in the daily newspapers and on Capitol Hill. He found himself a pariah in Washington, D.C. Old friends snubbed him at restaurants and avoided him on the street.

The leaders of Congress decided to assign his impeachment to the House Rules Committee, not the Judiciary Committee that normally investigated these types of charges. The Rules Committee, a political body, would have a freer hand to vilify Post in public hearings without addressing any concrete facts. Louis Post had written over a dozen books in his lifetime and hundreds of magazine articles. He knew his enemies would use these against him. One congressman scoured his *Ethical Principles of Marriage and Divorce* and claimed to find a passage promoting free love and divorce on demand, painting Post a laughable philistine as well as a Red. Another congressman uncovered a letter to him from Emma Goldman, the arch-villain herself, written in July 1916 and containing a handwritten note from Post saying that Goldman's views were "worthy of full credence."

Post made no apology for his note regarding Emma Goldman. He admitted he had known her over the years. "She was a woman of veracity; no one ever questioned that," he explained. If they wanted to hang him over this letter, then let them try—just so long as they gave him a chance to explain.

The Rules Committee held its first hearing on the impeachment in late April. They didn't invite Post. Instead, they invited all of Post's Capitol Hill enemies and let them blacken his name with terrible stories about him. Congressman Albert Johnson led things off by unveiling a new report prepared by his Immigration Committee accusing Post of systematically going over the head of Caminetti to protect dangerous radical thugs. "In my opinion, the public is not seeing red without a reason. It is seeing its laws violated by public officials in behalf of aliens who have contempt for this Government, who are trying to overthrow it. . . . Personally, I can not believe that Secretary Wilson knows what sort of boring from within is going on within his department, and I do not believe Secretary Wilson knows of the situation and its dangers." Congressman Homer Hoch, author of the impeachment resolution, testified as well, citing thirty-eight specific cases where Caminetti had recommended deportations and Post had blocked them.

After the hearing, the Rules Committee leaders met behind closed doors and agreed on a plan that seemed to put a final nail in the coffin.

Instead of pursuing formal impeachment charges against Post, they would vote to "condemn" him. This would force his resignation without their ever having to see him or hear him. "Post, they say, can force an investigation under impeachment proceedings of each of the 5,000 deportations," one Committee member told the *New York Times* in justifying the decision. In effect, they would keep Post from having the chance to speak for himself. They would silence him, denounce him, and give him the bum's rush out the door.

Not a single member of the committee spoke up against the idea.

Louis Post watched all this with growing alarm. In his forty-year career, he had seen political bosses do their worst from New York to Chicago to the Reconstruction South, but these slanders and machinations smelled more like New York's Tammany Hall than the U.S. Congress. And he could do nothing to stop them. Finally, a ray of hope came his way through Ernst Gundlach, a wealthy Chicago friend whose father had founded the Gundlach Optical Company and who now ran a large advertising firm. Gundlach came to see Post in late April and offered to float him ten thousand dollars to mount a defense. Gundlach could afford it. He had worked with Post at the Labor Department during World War I as an unpaid consultant, and he found the whole Red Scare disgraceful. Post finally accepted the offer and, with Gundlach's money, he promptly hired himself a lawyer, in fact a very good one: Jackson H. Ralston, a Washington veteran and author of two legal textbooks who had argued cases in the United States Supreme Court, the Hague Tribunal on International Disputes, on Capitol Hill, and in local courts all around the District. Ralston knew the Washington power game as well as anyone.

Post and Ralston put their heads together and came up with a plan. First, they had to force Congress to give Louis Post his day in court. Defying protocol, he had Post write a letter to Rules Committee chairman Philip Pitt Campbell demanding, not asking, to testify: "I cannot believe that it is seriously intended by the Committee on Rules to violate all the precedents of Congress and the spirit of American law by closing this hearing when only one side has been heard [and] before an opportunity to make my defense or even to be heard in my own behalf." But instead of sending the letter to the chairman, Ralston first gave copies of it to his own friends in the newspaper business. This way, the press would print it even if Congress tried to bury it.

The strategy worked. Newsmen confronted Chairman Campbell over the issue the next day on Capitol Hill, and caught him off guard. Campbell "reiterated that the committee did not intend to call Mr. Post as a witness, but that he would be heard whenever he presented himself," a *Boston Globe* reporter wrote. But Campbell quickly realized he'd been outfoxed and changed his tune: "the committee never intended to deny him an opportunity to be heard," he told the same newsmen the next day. Maybe Campbell was lying, but his committee quickly slated a public hearing for Thursday, May 7, featuring just one name on its witness list: Louis Post.

Meanwhile, Post could take comfort in the few public voices that did speak up in his behalf. Former president William Howard Taft told the *New York Times* he agreed with Post's logic in the *Truss* case. "Mr. Post has kept his head clear and his heart true in the midst of an epidemic of hysteria and panic fear," wrote Francis Fisher Kane, the former United States Attorney from Philadelphia who had quit his job in protest over the raids. The *New Republic* weighed in with a column, "On Behalf of Louis Post," suggesting that, between Post and Mitchell Palmer, Congress was impeaching the wrong man. Even philanthropist George Peabody wrote Post a letter telling him to stand firm.

Louis Post would have his chance to testify, but he would have to carry the day alone. That suited him fine.

ᴏ⤙ᴏ

Judson King made a career out of sticking his nose into other peoples' business. "Blue-eyed, large-toothed, and bald; university-trained, a reformer, and a practical politician"—that's how muckraking reporter J. R. Hildebrand described him. Judson King had founded the National Popular Government League in 1913 and ran it as executive director. The League was a bipartisan club that pressed upright causes like the referendum and recall, the short ballot in city elections, tougher campaign finance rules, and recognition of state granges and direct legislation leagues, a throwback to Woodrow Wilson's early progressive days.* Lately, its main function had been to host weekly lunches at Cushman's Restaurant on

---

*These signature reforms of the Progressive Era all were designed to remove political power from state officials and place it in the hands of voters. The referendum allowed voters in states where it existed to enact new laws by direct election, rather than going through their legislatures. The recall allowed voters to remove unpopular officials before their terms ended, a tool used most recently in the high-profile 2003 removal of then-California Governor Gray Davis. The short ballot was a reform to prevent urban political machines from confusing voters into voting the "straight ticket" through overly complicated ballots.

Fourteenth Street where friends drank martinis, traded gossip, and heard like-minded speakers talk about topics like the League of Nations, the labor crisis in England, the food monopoly, or the Peacetime Sedition Bill. A former newspaperman, King loved this work, lobbying state legislatures and Capitol Hill offices, arranging lunches and dinners, and enjoying the Washington social scene.

Now, Judson King looked around the table in his cramped office in the Munsey Building in downtown Washington and saw twenty nervous men staring back at him. They spoke in whispers. Jackson Ralston and Swinburne Hale, both of whom represented targets in the recent raids, led the conversation. Most of the others insisted on keeping their names secret. Ralston referred to them later only as "gentlemen interested in maintaining the liberties of the people." Each had taken a risk coming to this meeting. King had called them together to ask them to mount a protest against Mitchell Palmer's abuse of power: the raids, the Red Scare, Palmer's own propaganda, and now what Ralston described as Palmer's "vicious and uncalled for attacks [on] Louis F. Post." If word got out, these men had no doubt Palmer and his bullies would get revenge, smear them in the newspapers, make them lose their jobs, or even put them in jail.

What could they do? Judson King and Jackson Ralston knew the answer and soon they all agreed. They would broadcast the truth and beat Palmer at his own publicity game. They could compile evidence of enough Justice Department lawbreaking to shock the country and expose it to as wide an audience of Washington *cognoscenti* as possible. They agreed on a plan: Ralston and Hale would take the lead in assembling firsthand accounts of eye-catching abuses, and King would then package them into a hard-hitting exposé. Then, to sign it and give it weight, they would assemble a group of distinguished lawyers with spotless reputations.

It would take weeks to get this job done, and they would not finish on time to help Louis Post in his confrontation with the House Rules Committee. But King, Ralston, and Swinburne Hale saw a bigger game afoot. If people like them sat silent, Mitchell Palmer could well become the next president of the United States, and his raids could set a new dismal standard for American justice.

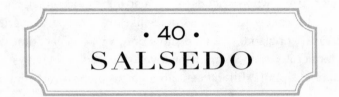

· 40 ·
SALSEDO

EDGAR GOT THE news by telephone from New York City. Andrea Salsedo, the anarchist printer whom his agents had been holding at their Park Row office in lower Manhattan, had gotten up during the night, tiptoed silently across the room, opened a window, slid himself outside into the darkness, and jumped fourteen stories to his death. Salsedo had been so quiet in committing suicide that even fellow suspect Roberto Elia, sleeping on a cot next to him, never knew he had gone. Salsedo had been the Department's sole witness in the June 2 bombing case, and guards had been ordered to watch him constantly, but they made a mistake. They let him and Elia sleep on their own. Their room was on the fourteenth floor of a skyscraper office building. Where could they go? It was only when a policeman discovered the body splattered on the concrete sidewalk below and came running upstairs to ask if anyone had jumped out a window that the Justice Department guard came bursting into Salsedo's room and found his cot empty.

Edgar's men had been holding Salsedo for seven weeks by then and never charged him with a crime. Now, the policeman who found the body would report the suicide and tip off every beat newspaper reporter at police headquarters. The papers surely would pounce on it, and explaining it would be hell. Edgar knew they'd look silly claiming they had been holding Salsedo of his own free will. Why then would he kill himself? Bill Flynn, still in New York, tried to limit the damage by corralling a reporter from the *New York World* and convincing him that Salsedo had been terrified that fellow anarchists might try to assassinate him, but few others took the bait. Salsedo's own lawyer, N. C. Donato, muddled the story the next morning by telling newsmen that his client had been a prisoner, didn't speak English, and suffered from tuberculosis and despondency.

Even worse, Salsedo's suicide left Edgar's investigation of the June bombing of Mitchell Palmer's house in shambles. Without Salsedo's testimony, they had nothing. John Creighton, sent by Palmer to gauge the damage, summed it up this way: "every physical clue [from the June 2 bombing] has been run out to the last possible extreme, resulting in the discovery of the man that printed the circular 'Plain Words,' the probable discovery of the man who was killed at the house of the attorney general, the inference that the plot originated with members of the Galliani group of which Carlos Tresca is now the principal leader, and that the perpetrators of the crime have succeeded in leaving the country with the possible exception of one or two, who are unknown to us, and that the principal source of information is now closed by virtue of the suicide of Salsedo." In other words, the criminals had made a clean getaway, and the Justice Department had no direct evidence against anyone.

After all the hoopla, the Red Raids, and the months of gumshoe work, Palmer, Edgar, Flynn, and their whole Justice Department team had bungled the single most important investigation under their charge.

Edgar knew they were going to take a beating on this. Palmer had stirred the pot again in late April 1920 by warning that Reds were planning a new wave of riots and assassinations timed for May Day, the international worker's holiday. New York City authorities had panicked and called out the entire police force to defend the city that day. Philadelphia, Washington, D.C., and Chicago officials all had placed extra guards around public buildings and homes of top figures, and Chicago police arrested 360 suspected radicals and jailed them for the full twenty-four hours. But May Day came, nothing happened, and the newspapers this time erupted in ridicule. "Everybody is laughing at A. Mitchell Palmer's

May Day 'revolution,'" announced the *Boston American*. RED PLOT FELL
FLAT, headlined the *New York Tribune*.

MAY DAY REVOLUTION DANGER ONLY IN PALMER'S EYE.

Everybody is laughing at A. Mitchell Palmer's May Day "revolution."
*The joke is certainly on A. Mitchell Palmer, but the matter is not
wholly a joke.*
*The spectacle of a Cabinet officer going around surrounded with armed
guards because he is afraid of his own hand-made bogey is a sorry
one, even though it appeals to the humor of Americans.*
*Of course, the terrible "revolution" did not come off. Nobody with a
grain of sense supposed it would.*
*Yet, in spite of universal laughter, the people are seriously disgusted with
these official Red scares.*
*They cost the taxpayers thousands of dollars spent in assembling soldiers
and policemen and in paying wages and expenses to Mr. Palmer's
agents.*
*They help to frighten capital and demoralize business, and to make
timid men and women jumpy and nervous. . . .*
*The whole thing is a mixture of personal cowardice and cheap depart-
ment politics.*
*What Mr. Palmer is trying to do is to distract public attention from his
miserable failure to reduce prices and jail profiteers.*
                                        —Boston American, May 4, 1920

Edgar saw the handwriting on the wall. That day, he scribbled a note
to Frank Stone, his bureau chief in Newark, New Jersey, and told him to
start cutting his losses on the last few Red deportation cases still pending
before Ellis Island immigration inspectors. "I desire that you communicate with [the chief Ellis Island inspector] and endeavor to arrange
whereby the weak cases will be eliminated, and those cases in which the
evidence is conclusive will be speedily disposed of."

During these times of trial and testing, Edgar seemed to nourish himself by the sheer act of self-discipline, the long hours at his desk, and by
the sheer exercise of power, be it the routine of approving expense
accounts or hiring stenographers, or the growing muscle he flexed over

the lives of total strangers. By now, his power went far beyond the Justice Department. Even the State Department, before approving any passport or permit for an immigrant to leave the country, felt obliged first to ask Edgar for his blessing. They send Edgar the names of all the applicants, he would check them against his mountain of index cards, and then he would give his own nonreviewable thumbs up or thumbs down.

For instance, Edgar worked frantically on May 6, the day before Louis Post planned to deliver his testimony to the House Rules Committee. Edgar spent hours that day going door to door on Capitol Hill visiting congressmen to prepare them for the confrontation, arming them with facts and questions, talking to newspaper reporters, trading notes and telephone calls with Caminetti, and keeping Palmer posted every step of the way. But even that day, Edgar found time to sit down at his polished mahogany desk and indulge himself in three of these State Department requests, one after the other, like three courses of a gourmet meal.

The first request dealt with a man from Des Moines, Iowa, named Martin M. Johnson, who had applied for a passport. "I find in my files a report regarding this subject," Edgar wrote. Johnson had run for mayor of Des Moines in 1918 as a Socialist. In a speech at the time, Johnson opposed American involvement in World War I and said, "As far as standing by the President is concerned, I believe we should stand for justice to the workingman first." An undercover agent had heard the speech and filed a report on it—he considered it treasonous. "In view of these facts it is recommended that the application of this subject for a passport be denied." Johnson had violated no law, made no threat, committed no treason or sedition. Still, Edgar considered him subversive. Case closed. The second one involved a Samuel Schwartz from New York City. For him, too, Edgar had a file that contained a report from an undercover agent. It showed that Schwartz had once belonged to a labor union that one time considered going on strike. The union held a meeting to discuss it, and, according to the undercover agent's report, a man named Wohle spoke up and said, "By all means we should adhere to Bolshevism as this is the only thing for the workmen," and then a few minutes later Schwartz had said, "Wohle is right." Schwartz, too, was a subversive. Passport denied.

Only on the third file did he relent. This one involved a New York City resident named Moissay Oglin. "I find in the files of this Department a number of reports regarding this subject. However, the reports state that subject, while a writer and speaker on the question 'Why was Bolshevism possible in Russia,' it was entirely from an educational standpoint and at no time radical. It is, therefore, recommended that the Application of this subject be approved."

Nowhere in the rules of the United States government did it mention that applicants for passports had to survive a loyalty test imposed unilaterally by a zealous young upstart in the Justice Department named John Edgar Hoover based on the extensive files he kept of raw, unsifted gossip. But this was the effective test in America in May 1920.*

When he finished that day, Edgar went home to the small house on Capitol Hill where he lived with his mother and his depressed, emaciated father. If he followed his normal routine, Edgar either went to bed early or else he sat downstairs by the fireplace with his mother, Annie Marie Scheitlin Hoover, and confided his secrets. He would have told her that the next morning, his enemy, Louis Post, would appear before the House Rules Committee and slander him and Palmer in front of all the newspaper writers, discredit his Red Raids, and perhaps cripple Palmer's hopes for gaining the 1920 presidential nomination.

And he would have told her something else. Edgar had learned that week of a conspiracy, a group of liberal lawyers who had gotten together, hiding behind the façade of a do-gooder group called the National Popular Government League, that was planning to slap at him in a sneak attack. He could never let his guard down. There always seemed to be people ready to attack him and defend the criminals.

Whatever he told her, his mother, Annie Marie Scheitlin Hoover, would have understood. Her son Edgar was her prize.

---

*The 1920 *Annual Report of the Attorney General* notes that the Justice Department's Bureau of Investigation conducted field and file searches on about 800 passport and 75 permit applications per day that year, including "searches in the indexes," but these were couched in terms of issues generated by the resumption of travel after World War I—a process that would be reported as ceasing once a formal peace resolution was adopted in March 1921—and not related to the work of Edgar's Radical Division.

• PART VIII •

EXPOSURE

I see no impropriety in suggesting that with effervescing opinions, as with the not yet forgotten champagne, the quickest way to let them get flat is to let them be exposed to the air.

—Supreme Court Justice
Oliver Wendell Holmes,
January 12, 1920

· 41 ·
DAY IN
COURT

H E WAS A "short shaggy dark haired figure," as one reporter
described him, sitting at the far end of the committee table, talking
in a flat, scratchy voice, his eyes peering through thick glasses, his wrinkled hands fumbling piles of notes. But once he began, Louis Post held
center stage for over ten hours, and he never let it go. This was his one
chance to speak, and he defied anyone to take it away from him.

The House Rules Committee met on the top floor of the Capitol
Building in a small corner room with tall windows looking out over green
shade trees and red rooftops of Capitol Hill. The chairman, Kansas
Republican Philip Pitt Campbell, was a round-faced, congenial man and
father of three daughters. He presided from the head of a long table under
cut-glass chandeliers, the walls adorned with oil portraits of solemn gray
eminences, the faces of congressmen past. Joining Campbell at his side
was Edward Pou, the committee's senior Democrat, a tall, thin, bespecta-
cled North Carolina lawyer whose navy flier son had died in action in
northern France during World War I. The committee's twelve members,

a few clerks, Post, his lawyer, and the few dozen newsmen and friends who came to watch more than filled the chamber to overflowing, an intimate space for the pre-radio, pre-television Congress to do its work.

The newspaper reporters came because they expected to see blood spilled. For weeks, they'd been told stories about this spineless, faceless bureaucrat named Louis Post who sold out the country to communists. But from the moment Chairman Campbell said, "I will ask Mr. Post to come forward" and Post took his seat at the table, they saw something very different. Louis Post came out swinging. "I hope the chairman will understand me and not misunderstand me," Post said in a clear, confident tone, brushing aside questions over his unusual demand to testify as being "of small importance." Then he turned to Immigration Chairman Albert Johnson's recent report. "The one striking point, the one striking fact about [it] is that whoever drafted, whoever proposed it had a very slight idea of even the procedure with reference to the arrest and deportation of aliens."

From that point on, Louis Post lectured the committee like a college master tutoring a class of dullards. He taught them the basics of immigration law: the difference between "exclusion" and "expulsion," the lines of authority, the legal tests. Then, building on facts and logic, he demonstrated how Caminetti, Palmer, and Congressman Johnson each had twisted the truth, violated statutes, and defied basic sense. For three hours on Friday, May 7, and for seven more hours on Saturday, May 8, he answered question after question, and the newsmen marveled at how his seventy-one-year-old mind never seemed to fail him.

Post started with Caminetti, the immigration chief, and painted him as a bumbling usurper. He showed how Caminetti needlessly delayed hundreds of deportation cases as men waited in prison cells, despite the fact that Caminetti had no legal right to decide any of these cases. His rulings were "often at variance with the evidence," Post charged, and "[he] had no such authority as he was assuming." As for Caminetti's secret sharing of Labor Department files with Capitol Hill friends, he said: "The commissioner general [Caminetti] had no more right than messenger boys have to let files go out."

Then he turned to Mitchell Palmer and the raids, and made them look laughable, a vast overreaction based on shadows and spooks. Out of the thousands of prisoners arrested in January 1920, only about fifty ever gave any sign of wanting to overthrow the government by force, Post said. All the rest had simply been innocent pawns caught in the dragnet. He showed the absurdity in one simple fact, that virtually none of these so-called dangerous radicals carried a weapon. "With all these sweeping raids all over the country, there have been three pistols, I think it is, brought to our attention," he said, prompting belly-laughs in the room. "Three pistols, two of them .22 caliber. Now I do not know whether a .22 caliber is for a homeopathic pill or a cannon ball." Finally, he quoted chapter and verse from the statute books to prove that Palmer's Justice Department had no legal power—"Not the slightest"—to get involved in deportations at all. The whole operation had been outside their jurisdiction.

Even the Red Scare hoopla, Post argued, came largely from Palmer's own Justice Department publicity shop working with what he called "two-salary newspaper men," meaning reporters taking under-the-table money to write slanted stories. When Chairman Campbell acted surprised at such a thing, Louis Post's eyes twinkled, and he turned it into a joke: "I am glad to know it is news; but you must have been asleep at some stages of the game, sir," he said. "I think, Mr. Chairman, some people are losing sight of the difference. It is unfair . . . to assume everybody whom a [Justice Department] detective charges with culpability shall, therefore, be deported, and whoever stands in the way . . . be denounced as a defender of Reds."

But Louis Post spent most of his testimony that day explaining each of the dozen or so individual cases that congressmen had pointed to as examples of his coddling Reds. He took two hours on Thomas Truss alone and explained, in detail, each of the rules he laid out for making these decisions: requiring evidence that the immigrant actually knew he belonged to the Communist Party, or refusing to consider evidence seized without a warrant. He drew gasps by pointing out how even the House Immigration Committee, in its recent report, had selectively omitted printing the evidence in key cases, presenting only the Justice Department charges and Caminetti's slanted cover notes. Now, to make the point as clear as possible, Post insisted in each case that the committee should print the entire record of evidence, including the full transcript of the deportation hearing, on each case before he would discuss it.

For instance, on Paul Bosco, that fearful-sounding Russian who had become a staple in speeches by congressmen for saying, "When I come out of prison, I hope to see the red flag waving above the stars and stripes," Post showed how this terrifying bogeyman was nothing but an image made of hot air. Yes, Paul Bosco, working as a glass cutter in West Virginia, had been convicted of sedition during World War I for distributing Socialist

Party leaflets and, yes, on being sentenced by the judge to ten years in prison, he lost his temper and made the hot remark. But this single temper tantrum and nothing else was the sole basis for labeling him an "anarchist" and marking him for deportation. Yes, Post admitted, he granted Paul Bosco a new hearing, and when the hearing came and the inspector asked Bosco what he thought an "anarchist" was, Bosco gave an answer that could have come straight from Thomas Jefferson: "I do not believe in the overthrow of law, but whenever the laws are against the people I see no reason why the people should not resist their enforcement by force," he told the inspector. "I say this because the Constitution of the United States gives every man of the United States a right to express his opinion."

In another case involving a Russian named Ivan Dudinsky—also a staple of congressmen's speeches—Post admitted that, yes, he gave the man a new hearing and reduced his bail from $10,000 to $1,000, but then he went on to show how the main piece of damning evidence presented against Dudinsky had been an angry letter from Mr. Hoover at the Justice Department. Prior to his deportation hearing, Dudinsky repeatedly had asked for a lawyer and been denied one, was never allowed to question his accusers, and was threatened with clubbings when he asked to see his arrest warrant. "Evidently the bail demanded was not to ensure the appearance of the accused, but to keep him locked up," Post argued. "I am ready to meet any impeachment charge for reducing bail."

Committee members kept trying to trip him up, but Louis Post refused to yield, even to Chairman Campbell. "I was about to say, when you interrupted me, Mr. Chairman," he said at one point, or, "Will you permit me to do the testifying at this moment, Mr. Chairman?" he said at another. When Campbell at another point tried to press him over what he called "high brow" or "Harvard and Yale" anarchists—a sideways slap at Felix Frankfurter—Post refused to go along. "Suppose you give names," he insisted. "I can answer better if you give names." The Chairman backed down and declined to provide any.

The committee invited Albert Johnson, the House Immigration Chairman, to come and join them at one point in grilling the witness, but Post easily threw Johnson on the defensive. He accused Johnson to his face of producing a one-sided report showing "gross ignorance of the law." When Johnson tried to squirm away by inviting Post to testify at his Immigration Committee some time in the future, Post declined: "Mr. Post has been ready to come before your committee for six months at least," he said, referring to himself in the third person, "you are rather late in extending me an invitation." When Johnson tried to excuse his delay by pointing to Secretary Wilson's recent illnesses, Post corrected him again: "I was speaking of the time when you came into my office last summer or last fall—I have forgotten which it was—and when you said we were going to have a hearing, and when you rummaged through and got the papers." After a few of these exchanges, Johnson kept his mouth shut.

But mostly, Post won the committee over with his humor and story-telling. When he started at one point to explain the multilayered meaning of the word "anarchist," he happily let Campbell and Pou play his foil. "I suppose we are all anarchists to a certain extent," Post explained. "I am quite sure I do not have to have any law or police force to prevent my picking anybody's pocket, and I have no doubt that is true of everybody here and true of the vast number of people."

"I ask to be excused from being called an anarchist in any sense," Congressman Pou chimed in.

"I excuse you, sir," Post said, sparking rounds of laugher in the room.

"Thank you," the congressman said to a few more chuckles.

But Post had made his point. "I was using the term [anarchist] in the Proudhon sense and not in the sense of those gentlemen who do their debating with epithets instead of arguments."

The most telling moment of the day came near the end when Edward Pou, the senior Democrat who had a reputation for taking security issues to heart after losing a son in the World War, asked Post to explain his own political background for the committee. "Mr. Secretary, your political convictions have been represented in all sorts of ways, so that I believe I will give you an opportunity to say what your politics are, if you desire to do so."

Louis Post responded with a long, meandering narrative of his own unique life odyssey, starting with his early days carrying a torch for James Buchanan in the 1850s, then his travels to the violent Reconstruction South in the 1860s, to his crusades against New York's Tammany Hall in the 1870s, his romance with Henry George's single tax, and his flirtation with the Greenback Labor Party in the 1880s, and up to the present. When he finished, Congressman Pou asked him what he thought of the Immigration Act itself. Were it up to him, Post said, he would require proof of an overt act of violence before deporting anyone.

"There is just one other question that I wanted to ask you," Pou went on. "You realized, of course, Mr. Secretary, that all of these rules that you have laid out [in the Truss case] operate to make it more difficult to deport the alien?"

"Every rule in the interest of personal liberty makes it more difficult to take personal liberty away from a man who is entitled to his liberty."

"I want to say, Mr. Secretary, that my feeling is that in what you have done, speaking for myself, I believe you have followed your sense of duty absolutely," Pou said.

Chairman Campbell, too, needed no more convincing. By the end of the second day of testimony, he felt at ease with this shaggy little dark-haired man sitting across the table and closed with a friendly joke. "Whatever else we have done today, Mr. Secretary, I think we have violated the 8-hour law, and I am very jealous of law violations," he said with a wink, to which Post reassured him: "No; we are still within the law, Mr. Chairman. We have been here only 7 hours, less the time we took for luncheon. I want to express my appreciation, Mr. Chairman, for the courtesy I have received since I have been here."

Post had charmed them, and he had won over the reporters, too. The long-hostile *Spokesman-Review* of Spokane, Washington, proclaimed the next day: "Post hurls broadside at foes, in self-defense—Wins round one—Lands 'terrific wallops' on critics of his policy in 'deporting reds'—Is 71, full of fight." The *Christian Science Monitor* made his point as well: "Mr. Post said it was his duty to decide cases on the evidence, not on the memoranda prepared by the Commissioner-General or anyone else," it reported. The truth be known, Louis Post had enjoyed the whole thing, a fair fight where he finally could punch back. "I am glad that my recent experiences have amused you," he told a friend in a letter a few days later. "They have been the kind that should have amused you, and which on the whole amused me, too."

<hr>

Edgar sat through all ten hours of Louis Post's performance in the cramped Rules Committee room. He found it egregious, vindictive, and not amusing at all. He listened to how Post made his Justice Department look like a gang of corrupt goons, and he saw the smirks it had brought to the faces of the congressmen. Edgar kept a low profile, but at least one reporter from the *New Republic* seemed to spot him lurking around the hearing room: "Agitated gentlemen kept going into corners and emerging with a new question from another side of the room," she wrote. If Edgar looked agitated, he had good reason. Louis Post had hurt them. He had to be rebutted.

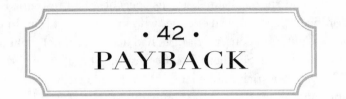

· 42 ·
PAYBACK

EDGAR HAD LEARNED by accident about the conspiracy. An envelope had arrived at the Justice Department in early May containing
two printed flyers, both under the letterhead "National Popular Government League" with a threatening hand-scrawled note: "This may interest
you Palmer. Those who trample on and ignore law are the real anarchists." One of the flyers carried the title "What we would prove concerning attack upon Honorable Louis F. Post" and it explained how the
League had assembled a group of what it called "distinguished attorneys"
to investigate the conduct of Attorney General A. Mitchell Palmer. The
second flyer asked League members to contribute toward a $3,000 pub-
licity fund. It was signed "Judson King, executive secretary."

Edgar had laid this envelope aside at first. But with Louis Post's hearing
over, he picked it up again. It was time to raise the issue with the attorney
general.

He found Palmer full of fight, just back from another campaign swing,
when he went to see him in his office after the Louis Post hearing. All

that winter and spring, Palmer, in his speeches, had restrained himself from lashing back at political enemies who kicked dirt at him. In January, a group of California conservationists had accused him of making secret deals to enrich the Southern Pacific Railway by allowing it to seize 160,000 acres of oil-rich public lands in California estimated to be worth a half-billion dollars, causing the company's stock to jump 14 points in a single morning. In March, critics pointed to Palmer's approval of a Louisiana sugar processor's deal to fix prices at 17 cents per pound and accused him of protecting profiteers. Now, in May, a local Pennsylvania political rival—Philadelphia Municipal Court Judge Eugene Bonniwell—was charging Palmer with blackmail, of using federal prohibition agents to squeeze Pennsylvania saloon keepers and liquor distributors into donating cash to his presidential campaign.

Palmer denied all these charges, but they came at a bad time, just as labor unions were lining up against him, speaking out over his Red Scare strikebreaking. The American Labor Party, the Chicago Federated Union, and the American Federation of Labor all debated resolutions in 1920 calling for Palmer's ouster as attorney general. Even a few business leaders like steel magnate Charles Schwab had now denounced Palmer for his Red Raids. And another critic, Congressman George Huddleston (D-Ala.), openly mocked him over it. "A well-informed gentleman from New York City said to me that a great many of those who were arrested did not so much as know the difference between 'bolshevism' and 'rheumatism,'" he told colleagues.

Now, Louis Post's damaging testimony was the last straw. Palmer had received a letter that week from Rules Committee Chairman Philip Pitt Campbell telling him that, in his view, Post's allegations of Justice Department lawbreaking were so serious that Palmer had no choice but to respond. "Should you desire a public hearing before the committee to refute the charges that have been made, I shall be glad to arrange for such a hearing at your convenience," Campbell wrote.

Palmer agreed. He had to fight back, and he knew this would be different from his usual Capitol Hill appearances. To answer Louis Post, Palmer could not simply rely on his backslapping and shoulderpushing. He needed to prepare himself solidly to slap down all these charges. He listened to Edgar as his young aide explained how Post had made the raids look silly and barbaric, picking them apart with his specific cases and anecdotes, like his claim that only three guns had been found out of thousands of suspects. Already, Post's lawyer, Jackson Ralston, had sent Rules

Committee Chairman Campbell a list of thirteen questions to raise with Palmer should he appear publicly, covering a laundry list of embarrassments, from the handcuffing of prisoners in Boston, to the arrests of American citizens under immigration warrants, to the Andrea Salsedo suicide.

Now, this latest threat from the National Popular Government League raised a whole new set of questions. Who were these self-anointed "distinguished lawyers" who had the audacity to investigate the attorney general of the United States? Edgar could guess at some of the names, like Swinburne Hale, Ralston, or Felix Frankfurter. But were there others? And what were they up to? Palmer needed to know, and Edgar had to find out.

After talking it over with the attorney general, Edgar went back to his office and decided to get to the bottom of things. He had at his fingertips the single most powerful machine in existence to answer his questions: the investigative muscle of the Department of Justice. On May 8, the day after Louis Post's hearing, he decided to unleash the bloodhounds. He called into his office one of his Washington-based agents, a man named Ahern, handed him the materials from the National Popular Government League, and told him to get busy: "I place these in your hands for a discreet and thorough investigation of all essential facts," he wrote him in a memorandum. "You should report fully on Judson King. The Bureau desire[s] to know who they are and what they are doing, and to obtain full information concerning the National Popular Government League. The inquiry should be directed, if possible, without precipitating issue."

This was just a first step. As Ahern got started, Edgar also raised the issue with Frank Burke, the Bureau of Investigation's deputy director, and Burke sent a coded telegram to Boston to open a probe there as well. "Forward detailed report of information [in] your file upon Felix Frankfurter, and others associated in [the *habeas corpus*] trial," he instructed Boston bureau chief George Kelleher. Edgar also called on his friends at Military Intelligence for help. "I would appreciate it if you could supply this office with a summary of the files in Military Intelligence upon the following subjects," he wrote to General Marlborough Churchill, the director, and listed five targets: Felix Frankfurter, Zechariah Chafee, and Laurence Brooks, all of Harvard Law School, plus Louis Post and the Interchurch World Movement, a group that had criticized Palmer's response during the recent steel strike and had commissioned a study of the January raids as well.

When he didn't hear back instantly, Edgar sounded the alarms again. "Please personally make investigation [of] Frankfurter, Brooks, Chafee, including circumstances surrounding their employment or participation in cases before Anderson," he had Burke telegraph Kelleher. "This information desired earliest practicable date."

The question of whether it was legitimate at all to use Justice Department agents to spy on "political" enemies like Judson King or Felix Frankfurter never seemed even to come up as an issue in these conversations. Neither Edgar nor anyone else at the Justice Department or Military Intelligence seemed to give it a thought. They all jumped at the commands. It made a natural, logical progression: from tracking criminals, to tracking Reds, to tracking lawyers, to tracking anyone who criticized the Justice Department, or anyone who criticized the attorney general. Palmer and his men protected the country, and anyone who questioned them was helping criminals. Why not use the government's spy machinery to stop them?

And sure enough, spying got results. Within two days, Military Intelligence reported back to Edgar that it had two items in its files on Felix Frankfurter: a program from Frankfurter's 1919 Armistice Day speech at Faneuil Hall in Boston and a report on Frankfurter's work for the Amalgamated Clothing Workers Union, a group that Military Intelligence considered a radical front. It also produced a fat file on the Interchurch World Movement and one of its leaders, the Reverend Doctor F. M. Crouch: "Dr. Crouch is intensely Socialist and believes Bolshevism is preferable to Capitalism," it confirmed. Edgar set up a file on this Interchurch World Movement with its own index card and code: Bureau Special File 207588.

But it was his own men who dug the deepest. Agent Ahern quickly handed off the assignment to another Washington-based agent named Kemon, and Kemon went to work on the National Popular Government League. "The League conducts conferences, dinners and luncheon forums wherein national popular government subjects, etc., are discussed," he wrote in his initial report. He produced for Edgar a full list of the League's officers, committees, members, and recent lunch speakers. He shadowed its director, Judson King, and reported that King belonged to the Bannockburn Golf Club and was "married [and] about 45 years old, about 5 feet, 9 inches tall; weight, 155 to 60 pounds; dark complexion, hair and eyes; clean shaven; and careless of dress."

But this, too, was just the start. Kemon visited the Munsey Trust Company, the bank where the League kept its financial accounts, and here he confronted the bank's vice president demanding to see the League's back statements. He had no search warrant, just his gruff personality, but that

was enough. "Mr. Pope [the bank vice president] stated that under the circumstances he was forced to give our department information regarding
Judson King and the NPGL," Kemon reported, "but that it was 'nothing
but political bumbombe;' that there was nothing the matter with King,
that he was simply 'a nut' with political phantasies [sic] and he would grab
at any new issue that might bring the league and himself into publicity."
Kemon, using the bank's data, analyzed the League's finances over the past
four months and produced lists of the bills it paid and the people who gave
it contributions.

A separate report from a New York–based agent confirmed that "the
National Popular Government League is trying to raise money for the
defense of that notorious friend, aider and abettor of anarchists and criminals, Louis F. Post." Edgar created a file on this National Popular Government League with its own index card and code: Old German 379228.

Soon, his agents were sending him information by the bucketful. By
May 29, Edgar's Boston-based team had assembled thick background
dossiers on Felix Frankfurter, Roscoe Pound, Swinburne Hale, and
Zechariah Chafee—all contained in reports titled "radical matter."
Boston bureau chief George Kelleher compiled a twenty-two page, single-
space letter documenting all the radical activities of each one, starting
with Frankfurter and going back to a 1918 report from the American Protective League that fingered Frankfurter as an "alien enemy." Kelleher's
letter cited an agent who witnessed Frankfurter's Armistice Day speech
and concluded that Frankfurter sympathized with draft dodgers and seditionists and was "still voicing opposition to the government—not to its
prosecution of treasonable offenders." Another agent visited the National
Civil Liberties Bureau office in New York City and walked away with a
fistful of pilfered papers, including letters to Frankfurter from 1918 asking
his help on I.W.W. cases.

Edgar read them all, but they only frustrated him. All these men—
Frankfurter, Chafee, Ralston, Francis Fisher Kane, Roscoe Pound, even
Judge Anderson—had plenty in their backgrounds to paint them Red,
but they'd been careful. Not one of them had opposed the country's entry
into World War I, several had held high government posts, and none ever
said anything directly unpatriotic or radical. As lawyers, they defended
what Edgar considered the worst communist thugs, but they kept their
own skirts clean.

In a moment of caution, Edgar chose not to open a separate file on
Felix Frankfurter with its own index card. Instead, he kept all the reports

on Frankfurter, Chafee, and the others in the National Popular Government League file. This way, he alone would know where to find them, and
perhaps he could hide them from anyone else.

The month of May in Washington usually was a fun time, the start of
summer, with baseball, picnics, movies, and outdoor concerts. But Edgar
had no time to enjoy it. His daily grind sapped him of every ounce of
energy. He lived behind his office desk and thought about little else even
when he did go home at night. "[A]n unexpected request upon the part
of the attorney general for certain data has taken a considerable amount
of time to arrange," he confided in one letter that month, explaining his
late answer. Still, by late May, like Sisyphus rolling the boulder up the
mountain one more time, he had prepared for Palmer a lengthy testimony
to present to the House Rules Committee designed to land a knockout
punch on Louis Post and restore the honor of the Justice Department.

But the danger remained, those liberal lawyers at the National Popular
Government League. Despite all his snooping, Edgar still had not gotten
a fix on their game.

HOW DO YOU plead?" Oscar Hebel, the presiding judge of the Cook County Criminal Court, asked the defendants. His Honor looked like a shriveled little cherub with pink cheeks set against his gray hair, black robe, and small eyes, seated at his oversized desk beneath an oversized American flag brought in for the occasion and placed just behind him where photographers could not fail to capture it in their shots. Each defendant stood and answered, one after the next.

"Not guilty," said L. E. Katterfield.

"Not guilty," said Jack Carney.

"Not guilty," said Perry Shipman.

"Not guilty," said Ludwig Lore.

"Not guilty," said Arthur Proctor, L. K. England, Oscar Owens, Neils Kjar, Karl Sandburg, Oscar Jesse Brown, N. J. Christianson, Samuel Ash, James Meisenger, Samuel Hankin, John Vogel, Morris A. Stolar, Charles Krumbein, Max Bedacht, and Edwin Firth.

"Not guilty," said William Bross Lloyd, Chicago's Millionaire Socialist. Flashbulbs went off as newspapermen snapped his picture.

Clarence Darrow was glad to be back in Chicago here in this court-house on North Clark Street. Darrow craved the noise here, the sounds of street cars, elevated trains, honking horns, and kicking horses from outside on the street. From inside, he heard the voices—the whispers, shouts, laughs, and cries—echoing off the granite floors and high corridor ceilings. How many hundreds of cases had he argued in this building? Here, Darrow knew the faces, the favorite wisecracks, even the secret sins of most of the newsmen, the lawyers, the clerks, barbers, and street ped-dlers, and the criminals who haunted this place. This was home. Sitting at the defense table, passing a note or two back to his wife, Ruby, planted a few rows behind him, Darrow could not remember the last time he shared the spotlight in a trial with so many other high-powered lawyers and defendants. The Grand Jury had charged every single Communist Labor Party officer it could find in the state of Illinois, thirty-nine alto-gether, in a single big indictment citing the Illinois Overthrow Act—its peacetime sedition law—claiming they had conspired to advocate the overthrow of the American government by force. A dozen or so of these communists had flown the coop, disappearing to Mexico, Canada, or Russia. Two others had turned chicken and agreed to testify for the state.

That left twenty defendants, who sat packed like herrings today in the courtroom, all being prosecuted together in a single grand carnival of jus-tice. Maclay Hoyne, the Chicago state's attorney who six months earlier had defied Mitchell Palmer to launch his own Red Raids on New Year's Day, had conceived this circus. Hoyne billed it as the biggest conspiracy case in Chicago since the Haymarket anarchists of the 1880s, a surefire publicity lightning rod out of every politician's fondest dream. To carry the load, Hoyne fielded a team of five prosecutors led by a special counsel named Frank Comerford, who had just returned from six months studying Bolshevists in Soviet Russia and Poland. Comerford announced that he planned to call three hundred witnesses, and Maclay Hoyne made it known he would spare no expense to put these criminals behind bars.

Darrow would have laughed at this hubris had he not been so fearful they would get away with it. Darrow had reason to worry. To start with, he had disagreements even within his own defense team. William Bross Lloyd, besides being the only defendant with his own butler, his own chauffeur, his own money manager, and his own mansion in Winnetka, insisted on hiring his own lawyers for the case as well: left-wing veterans William S. Forrest and William Cunnea. Darrow alone represented all the others, though he had no problem with Forrest or Cunnea. He knew both these men and liked them. He particularly enjoyed Cunnea, "a typical radical Irishman," as one correspondent for the radical magazine, *The Liberator,* put it, "thickset . . . but very magnetic and likeable as he stands there conferring with the other two, whispering out of the corner of his mouth." Cunnea had argued Eugene Debs's case at his 1918 Espionage Act trial and he shared Darrow's delight for politics, running a close second against Maclay Hoyne as a Socialist Party candidate for Illinois state's attorney in 1913.

Darrow even had no problem personally with Maclay Hoyne; in fact, he liked the grandstanding state's attorney. When Hoyne ran for mayor of Chicago in 1919, Darrow backed him and even wrote a newspaper column headlined "Hoyne, Only Hope in Mayor's Race," calling him intelligent, honest, fearless, and independent. Hoyne and Darrow had faced each other in dozens of criminal trials, and Darrow tried to avoid bragging that he won most of them.

But William Bross Lloyd was another matter. As obnoxious clients went, Lloyd was far worse even than Benjamin Gitlow in New York City. Lloyd was spoiled, pampered, and self-righteous, a purist who believed his own speeches. Back in 1918, at the height of the World War, when Darrow voiced his support for American involvement, Lloyd had made a public stink over it by sending Darrow an open letter mocking him as "a Tolstoyan nonresistant shouting for war and a philosophical anarchist supporting the government that wages it." He even threatened Darrow with excommunication from his own left-wing clique, saying: "I want to repeat to you what a prominent Socialist said to the United States District Attorney of the district in which he lived: 'You will want to live in [your home town] after the war is over. Don't forget to live and act during the war so that you can live here after it.' Yours very truly [signed] William Bross Lloyd."

Now, with the tables turned, this same William Bross Lloyd, who thought nothing of attacking Clarence Darrow for speaking his mind in 1918, smugly expected Darrow to help him defend his own free speech and keep him out of prison. Lloyd, of course, snubbed Darrow at every chance and made it clear that Darrow did not speak for him, only for the others. But Darrow knew this was hogwash. These twenty defendants all stood in the same shoes. If one fell, they all fell.

Still, Clarence Darrow felt upbeat that spring of 1920 once he'd returned from New York, after losing the Benjamin Gitlow case. For one thing, in April, he won a clean victory in Rockford, Illinois, for Arthur Person, a communist arrested there during a January raid and charged under the Illinois Overthrow Act. Person, a working man who spent twenty years beveling glass in a factory to feed his wife and three children, was the type of defendant Darrow preferred. "I believe in a government for the working people, of the working people," Person had told federal agents after they arrested him. To Darrow, these words sounded musical: "Why, that is almost the exact language Abraham Lincoln used!" he told the jury. "Lincoln would be under indictment here, too, if he were living now and could talk." It had been easy to convince them that Arthur Person had committed no crime.

But his new crop of clients was a different matter. Darrow had no doubt what the jury would think of them. These Chicago communists, who relished their tough radical talk, mostly had never done hard physical work in their lives. Instead, they spent their days writing magazine articles, organizing factions, and haggling over theories. They were intellectuals, and the jury would despise them as dilettantes, spoiled, arrogant, and traitorous.

Darrow knew that, as a matter of pure abstract theory, he could win this case easily. The Illinois Overthrow Act made it a crime to advocate using violence or lawbreaking to overthrow the government. But, arguably, these Communist Laborites backed "force" only in the sense of worker strikes—not armed rebellion. Even Labor Department secretary William B. Wilson in Washington, D.C., had ruled that month that the Communist Labor Party failed to qualify as a radical organization under the 1918 Immigration Act. None of his clients had so much as tossed a pebble against the state, despite all their talk—except perhaps for Lloyd's throwing a punch or two at a Chicago policeman. The indictment charged them with conspiracy, a crime that required showing what the law called an "overt act" to achieve its goal. But these Communist Laborites had never actually lifted a finger.

Yes, they all attended the Communist conventions back in August and cheered the hot rhetoric, but the other evidence was all fluff. For instance, Hoyne's prosecutors pointed to a red flag that police found hidden behind a bookcase when they raided Oscar Owens's house to arrest him in January. "That is my flag. Some day it will be your flag when people understand us better," Owens had told them, and "might made right, because an organized group of sufficient numbers had power to enforce its rule." Owens had also written a letter to John Reed about his pianist son: "I want him to be a musician of the revolution [to] contribute to the overthrow of the God damn system that makes slaves and prostitutes of the masses." Another of the twenty, Arthur Proctor, owned a bookstore in Chicago, he allowed the Communist Labor Party to meet there, and he sold books by Lenin and

Trotsky alongside radical magazines like *The Revolutionary Age*, *The Class Struggle*, and the *Communist Labor News*. Suspicious? Unpatriotic? Maybe. But none of this suggested violence. Still another of Darrow's clients, a man named L. E. Katterfield, had received over 21,000 votes running for governor of Illinois as a Socialist in 1916; he was hardly someone trying to overthrow the ballot system.

Instead, the prosecutors built their case around William Bross Lloyd and his fire-breathing speeches, and lumped the rest in with him. "You want to get rifles, machine guns, field artillery, and the ammunition for it; you want to get dynamite," Lloyd had told a crowd in Milwaukee a few months earlier. "Dynamite the doors of the banks to get the money to finance the revolution." His hot rhetoric—fighting words—meant little, but Darrow knew it would scare the socks off any sane juror, and the prosecutors would have no trouble smearing the whole group with Lloyd's inanity. Theory aside, fear and emotion would make it nearly impossible to win this case. His clients were Reds, as Red as the red flags they waved. Mitchell Palmer and his Red Scare were the real enemy, the way they turned normal, rational people into narrow zealots.

So Clarence Darrow settled in. Once all the defendants pleaded not guilty, Judge Hebel ordered them to start the next phase of the trial, picking a jury. Darrow decided to lay down his marker right from the start. When Frank Comerford, the special prosecutor, asked one of the first prospective jurors a loaded question, Darrow attacked. "Do you believe any one has the right to advocate a general strike for the purpose of seizing private property and eventually overthrowing the government by unlawful means?" Comerford asked. Darrow jumped to his feet in an instant. "You might as well ask if any one has the right to call a prayer meeting for the purpose of overthrowing the government by unlawful means," he shouted, holding his suspenders by his thumbs, standing at the defense table, looking "bulky, bronze, and wrinkled," as one reporter described him. Comerford withdrew his question and, after that, Darrow was "on his neck at every word," another reporter wrote.

The rest of the country might be moving past the Red Scare and starting to enjoy the Jazz Age and the fun times of summer. Most of the deportation cases had been dropped; immigrant prisoners had gone home to their families to get on with their lives. But these twenty defendants still faced twenty years in prison. Clarence Darrow was left to clean up the mess.

· 44 ·
TWELVE
LAWYERS

FELIX FRANKFURTER LEFT Boston after the *habeas corpus* trial ended in April 1920 and Harvard Law School classes broke for the Easter holiday. But instead of going south to vacation with his new wife, he traveled west to Rochester, New York, then a cold industrial town dominated by the Eastman Kodak camera company and other optical works. Sidney Hillman, president of the Amalgamated Clothing Workers Union, was trying to unionize a factory there but had been slapped with an injunction. He asked Felix Frankfurter to help him fight it, and Frankfurter came at the first chance. "I'm in this typically colorless American city—esthetics is certainly not one of their wants—on a very interesting labor litigation," Frankfurter wrote to Oliver Wendell Holmes from his hotel room.

Even if he hated the city, though, Frankfurter could not complain about the way Sidney Hillman pampered him there. On Frankfurter's arrival, Hillman introduced him to a rally of striking workers as a hero, "the man who went before Judge Anderson in the federal court and secured an indictment against the Department of Justice for lawbreaking and who has defended the Communists who have rights as citizens, no matter to what party they belong." The crowd exploded in cheers, and Felix Frankfurter flashed a wide, toothy grin—facts that did not go unnoticed by the Justice Department agent assigned to shadow Felix Frankfurter wherever he went.

Frankfurter won the case in Rochester after a two-week trial, and he returned to Harvard just on time for classes to resume. Reaching his office, he found a package waiting for him from Washington, D.C. He'd been expecting it. It came from Judson King, head of the National Popular Government League. Frankfurter opened it and found inside the page proofs for a small pamphlet titled "Report on the Illegal Practices of the United States Department of Justice," accompanied by a note from lawyer Jackson Ralston. "Those of us having the matter in charge in Washington are desirous of giving the pamphlet to the newspapers no later than early Saturday morning so that complete publicity may be obtained through the Monday morning papers," it explained, and asked that he look it over quickly. Would Frankfurter be willing to sign it? He should telegram his answer as soon as possible.

Felix Frankfurter read the stack of page proofs, and he liked what he saw. The Report consisted of a seven-page cover letter addressed "To The American People" and sixty pages of exhibits: photographs, affidavits, and court papers, all bound together in a small book. Its opening read like a Bill of Indictment from a grand jury: "Under the guise of a campaign for the suppression of radical activities, the office of the attorney general, acting by its local agents throughout the country, has committed continual illegal acts," it began. "Wholesale arrests both of aliens and citizens have been made without warrant or any process of law; men and women have been jailed and held *incommunicado* without access of friends and counsel; homes have been entered without search-warrant and property removed; other property had been wantonly destroyed; workingmen and workingwomen suspected of radical views have been shamefully abused and maltreated." Then, like an indictment, it listed six specific counts: "(a) Cruel and Unreasonable Punishments, including all the beatings, violence, and brutal imprisonments during the raids; (b) Arrests without Warrants; (c) Unreasonable Searches and Seizures; (d) Provocative Agents, (e) Compelling Persons to be Witnesses against Themselves, and (f) Propaganda by the Department of Justice." Each of these counts represented a violation of statute or the Constitution by the top policeman in the country, Attorney General A. Mitchell Palmer. It ended with a nod to Louis Post, "to whose courageous reestablishment of American Constitutional Law in deportation proceedings are due the attacks that have been made on him."*

To support these charges, Ralston and Swinburne Hale had compiled a stack of sworn eyewitness statements, mostly from victims of the November 1919 assault on the New York Russian Peoples House and the Hartford City Jail during the first big raid. As a case study, it included an account by Gaspare Cannone, the Italian seized in Brooklyn in connection with the June 2 bomb investigation, who told of being jailed without a warrant and questioned by three detectives who kicked, punched, and clubbed him in the process. As proof of his maltreatment, it contained photographs showing Cannone's black eye and facial bruises after the beating along with writing samples to demonstrate how one of the detectives had forged Cannone's signature on his so-called confession.

Felix Frankfurter recognized that some of its strongest material in the package came straight from his own Boston *habeas corpus* case, including excerpts from his courtroom grilling of Boston Justice Department bureau chief George Kelleher. "Hale & Ralston have spent a month on this work," Judson King insisted. "It is bullet proof!—and cost money as well as time." Frankfurter took his copy of the draft report and walked down the hall to talk it over with his Harvard colleague, Zechariah Chafee, who also had received a package from Washington. They both saw it as a chance to vindicate their work in the Boston case. "[W]hy, the thing seemed to us an opportunity to let people know just what we were doing," Chafee explained later.

Felix Frankfurter had no illusions about the dangers of getting involved in this undertaking. Mitchell Palmer would be furious, and he would certainly fight back. Just recently, Frankfurter had seen another close friend of his vilified as being too soft on Reds, none less than Oliver Wendell Holmes, a sitting Supreme Court justice. The attack came from John Wigmore, the professor at Chicago's Northwestern University Law School whose 1904 four-volume *Treatise on Evidence* had become a standard text. Wigmore had served as a judge advocate colonel during World

---

*Frankfurter knew Louis Post from World War I when he worked at the Labor Department as a mediator and chaired the War Labor Resources Board: "He was a single-taxer, a very kind and thoughtful man," Frankfurter wrote of him. On hearing of the impeachment, Frankfurter had promptly sent Post a telegram offering to represent him free of charge before the U.S. Congress, but Post declined for the time being until he could figure out his finances, then instead hired local attorney Jackson Ralston.

War I and written a stark censure of Holmes's free-speech dissent in the *Abrams* case titled *"Abrams v. U.S.: Freedom of Speech and Freedom of Thuggery in War-time and Peace-Time."* Holmes's loose attitude toward free speech was naïve, Wigmore charged, and his dissent in *Abrams*, had it ever been adopted by the Court, "would have ended by letting our soldiers die helpless in France," he argued. "If a company of soldiers in wartime on their way to the front were halted for rest in the public highway, and a disaffected citizen, going among them, were to begin thus to harangue: 'Boys! This is a bad war! We ought not to be in it! And you ought not to be in it'—the state would have a moral right to step promptly up to that man and smite him in the mouth."

"The poor man has not yet come out of his uniform," Felix Frankfurter reassured Holmes in a letter. "I'm rather sad about Wigmore—it's the kind of recklessness that he not infrequently manifests. Some of your brethren [on the Supreme Court] are fear traders and their distilled fear they call 'constitutional law.' I thank all the gods that be that you're on the bench."

Publicly charging Mitchell Palmer with his own brand of lawbreaking, at a time when he still had goons at his command ready to go out and raid leftists across the country, would be dangerous. "The clash between 'fear' and 'faith' is a pretty far-reaching one in personalities," Frankfurter confided to Holmes. "For instance, our attorney general, Palmer, sees spooks everywhere—and thereby helps not a little to create them." Still, he, Chafee, and Harvard Law School dean Roscoe Pound all decided to take the plunge together. They all answered *yes* to Judson King. Each would sign the report.

⊂══╪══⊃

No one had seen anything quite like it before in America: twelve of the country's most prominent attorneys accusing the attorney general of breaking the law he was sworn to enforce. Judson King could not have been happier at the reception. He released the report on Friday, May 28, four days before Palmer was set to testify before the House Rules Committee. King sent hundreds of copies to newspaper editors, judges, church leaders, civic groups, congressmen, and senators. "The venture has been a fine success from the point of view of press publicity," King reported to Swinburne Hale, "requests for the pamphlet are turning up from all over the United States." Frank Walsh, one of the signers, called it "a 'gut shot'! ... Nothing could be added to it, and certainly nothing taken away." The list of people Judson King finally convinced to sign it read like a virtual

Who's Who of American law, including five professors or deans of leading
university law schools and three former ranking federal officials:

1. R. G. Brown, attorney, Memphis, Tennessee;
2. Zechariah Chafee Jr., professor, Harvard Law School;
3. Ernst Freund, professor, University of Chicago Law School;
4. Felix Frankfurter, professor, Harvard Law School;
5. Swinburne Hale, attorney, New York City;
6. Francis Fisher Kane, former United States Attorney, Philadelphia;
7. Alfred S. Niles, former judge and professor, Maryland University
   Law School;
8. Roscoe Pound, Dean, Harvard Law School;
9. Jackson H. Ralston, attorney, Washington, D.C.;
10. David Wallerstein, attorney, Philadelphia;
11. Frank P. Walsh, attorney, New York City and Kansas City; and
12. Tyrrell Williams, Dean, Washington University Law School in
    St. Louis.

Edgar saw the report for the first time on May 28, the same day that it
came out in the newspapers. Of course, nobody at the National Popular
Government League had bothered to send the Justice Department an
advance copy. This gave Edgar just four days to read it, digest it, and prepare a response. Palmer was up to his eyeballs in fighting off attacks that
week. The Louisiana sugar price-fixing deal had reared its head again
with Republican congressman George Tinkham demanding Palmer resign
over it. Separately, a Senate investigating committee had opened hearings on the Pennsylvania campaign blackmail charges. And now these
twelve self-described "distinguished" lawyers had finally shown their
hand.

In just three weeks, Democrats would meet in San Francisco at their
national convention to pick their nominee for president of the United
States, and Palmer still hoped to win that contest. First, though, he had
to answer Louis Post and these twelve lawyers.

Edgar flew into a frenzy of activity over the next four days. He pressed
his field offices to produce thirty affidavits, mostly from agents accused
of brutality by the twelve lawyers, in each case denying or downplaying
the charge. His agents in New York City denied committing any violence
in their raid on the Russian Peoples House in November 1919. If any

violence did occur, they insisted, it must have come from the New York City police or the Lusk Committee. Edgar compiled evidence to show that none of the Department's undercover men were *agents provocateurs* in any evil sense but just honest, hardworking confidential investigators. He prepared outright denials of beatings, threats, and inhumane imprisonments. As for the claim by Gaspare Cannone that an agent had forged his signature to a confession, Edgar prepared an answer expressing outrage, saying the Department of Justice would fire any agent it caught forging a document, but that it had seen no evidence that any such thing had occurred.

At the same time, Edgar pushed his bureaus in key cities to provide numbers and stories showing how the raids had been well managed, smoothly run, and humane.

The testimony that Edgar and the Justice Department staff ultimately prepared for Palmer ran 209 pages long, a *tour de force* answering almost every charge made by Post and the National Popular Government League, calling them all a pack of lies, while also exposing the Red Menace and the danger of international communism. That done, Edgar now could only sit back and watch. The rest was up to Palmer, the politician. This was Palmer's Raid, Palmer's presidential campaign, and Palmer's moment to perform.

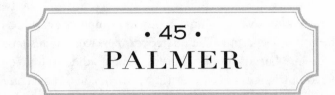

· 45 ·
PALMER

CHAIRMAN PHILIP PITT Campbell called the Rules Committee to order promptly at 10:00 A.M. with a sharp rap of his gavel. Edgar watched as Mitchell Palmer practiced his trademark charm making his way to the witness chair, slapping the congressmen's shoulders, sharing a laugh with the news reporters, winking and smiling at the clerks. Palmer took his seat, and Edgar slid in beside him, close enough to pass him a note, whisper in his ear, or kick him under the table. Edgar had sat through plenty of congressional hearings, but today was the first time he would be expected to speak out loud if Palmer or a congressman asked him a question. "Mr. Attorney General, we will hear you," Chairman Campbell announced, bringing silence to the room. The committee's focus was no longer on Louis F. Post and his impeachment. Instead, it titled its hearing: "Charges Made Against Department of Justice by Louis F. Post and Others." Mitchell Palmer was on trial this day, June 1, 1920, one day short of the anniversary of the bombing of his house.

Palmer opened his briefcase and removed his 209-page prepared testimony. But instead of following the custom of summarizing it briefly and then taking questions from congressmen, a chance to interact with them, engage them, and explain himself in his own words, Palmer began to read. He read and read and read some more. He read for five hours that day, followed by three more hours the next day. "I declare these charges are outrageous and unconscionable falsehoods," he began, calling Louis Post a liar, a Red, and a traitor. Palmer's presence at the table, his broad shoulders, wide face, and booming voice, seemed magnified by the smallness of the room. But mostly he kept his eyes lowered to the pages in front of him, his voice locked in the mechanical cadence of the prepared script. "I had hoped that it might never be necessary for me to indulge in any criticism of another officer of the Government and I would not do so now had Mr. Post not seen fit to publicly, by himself and his attorney, make these false and slanderous charges against me," he read. "[By] his self-willed and autocratic substitution of his mistaken personal viewpoint for the obligation of public law; by his habitually tender solicitude for social revolutionists and perverted sympathy for the criminal anarchists of the country, [Post has] defied the rules of evidence . . . flouted the judgment of a committee of the Senate [and] shown constant favors to violators of the law and their attorneys, refusing even common courtesy to the Department of Justice."

Palmer used the material that Edgar had collected in his secret investigations to recast Louis Post's life as a study in Red: his ties to Emma Goldman, his leftist magazine, *The Public*, with its articles glorifying anarchists and liberals. Palmer quoted columns Post had written as far back as 1902 and 1905, one showing him sticking up for a radical newspaper shut down by the government, another of him justifying the assassination of a Russian czarist official. "From this point of view Mr. Post became, although I do him credit to say unconsciously, a factor in the revolutionary plan and he has demonstrated that status beyond shadow of chance for contradiction." Louis Post had twisted the deportation laws to protect criminals, and all this time his country faced danger from worldwide communism and its cutthroat leaders in Bolshevist Russia. "For peace they would sacrifice honor and provinces. For bread they would murder and destroy government. For land they would steal even the plate from the churches," he said of Lenin and his ilk; "the world is on fire with this infamous Red stuff. . . . I am not an alarmist or even a pessimist. But I have my eyes open."

Palmer tied it all together: the railroad, coal, steel, and police strikes, the raids, and the radical immigrants—all inspired by these Bolshevik Reds. "If there is any doubt of the general character of the active leaders and agitators amongst these avowed revolutionists, a visit to the Department of Justice and an examination of their photographs there collected would dispel it. Out of the sly and crafty eyes of many of them leap cupidity, cruelty, insanity, and crime; from their lopsided faces, sloping brows, and misshapen features may be recognized the unmistakable criminal type."

He spent all of the first morning talking about communists and their criminality. Then, in the afternoon, he turned to his enemies, starting with what he called "our so-called 'liberal press'" who'd been taken in by the Bolsheviks, missing the fact that they were, in his words, "the most brutal, the most corrupt, the most wickedly fatuous insurrection of mob ignorance in all of history." Now, these same naïve fools took it on themselves to criticize the Department of Justice. "My own life is daily threatened," Palmer insisted, a not so subtle reference to the bombing of his house a year earlier. "We have been condemned for making what are called wholesale raids. If there be any fault in that, I accept the responsibility for it. We made simultaneous arrests, because we wanted in good faith to carry out the purpose of Congress." If there were "one or two isolated cases of unethical action," as he put it, they were rare and isolated, and any charge that he was making political hay out of his anti-Red crusade was "a deliberate and base falsehood [coming] from the pale-pink parlor bolsheviks and from the mouths of the friends of the radicals."

Palmer flatly denied Louis Post's laugh line that only three tiny pistols had been found on the thousands of people seized in his raids. He pointed to Newark, New Jersey, where the L'Era Nuova anarchists had kept twelve rifles, two revolvers, and four bombs. His men had taken three guns in Providence, three more in Philadelphia, three revolvers and a shotgun in Hartford, five in Cleveland, five in Chicago, and one in Toledo. These numbers, too, might sound trivial, perhaps no more than the number of guns one might find in any typical cross-section of Americans in 1920, but, to Palmer, this comparison missed the point. The numbers showed that Post "was absolutely in error when he made the somewhat facetious remark." Palmer defended his confidential agents as "men of splendid character, of unusual intellectual attainments and of a wonderfully high order of physical courage, who take their lives in their hands daily in association with the criminal classes."

By the end of the first day, Mitchell Palmer had cast himself as a hero, a victim, a patriot, and a willing slanderer. He had spoken three hours before a single congressman dared to interrupt and ask a question. After five hours, he had barely reached the midpoint of his prepared text. When Chairman Campbell reconvened the committee the next morning, Palmer launched in again, this time turning his guns on the new report of the National Popular Government League and its twelve lawyers. "I do not know all of these gentlemen," Palmer said, but "these twelve men who claim to be lawyers [had] accepted at full value every statement made by these ignorant aliens." Palmer reduced their whole effort to a question of loyalty. "Are you going to believe the sworn statements of sworn government officials or are you going to take the word of aliens for all the charges made of illegal practices by the department. I say the whole report simmers down to this."

Then he presented all the evidence that Edgar had prepared over the past four days, the sworn statements, memos, testimony extracts, and the rest. Palmer had investigated every single charge in the report except for two of them, he insisted, and found them all to be rubbish—sour grapes from criminals. As for these twelve lawyers themselves, he couldn't resist rubbing their noses in their Red connections. "We find several of them appearing as counsel for communist and communist labor party members at deportation hearings," he insisted. "I have difficulty in reconciling their attitude with that of men who have sworn to uphold the Constitution of the United States."

"I think the public is entitled to know what is going on in the country," Mitchell Palmer at last concluded. "I have tried to tell them. I have told them the truth. I have received for it vilification, abuse, and ridicule, but I propose to continue."

Edgar sat at Mitchell Palmer's side during the entire two-day performance. This whole time, he uttered only six words for the record—"No, sir; it has not" and "Yes"—all in response to two direct questions from Palmer. How much of Palmer's tough talk came directly from Edgar's pen is impossible to tell, but Louis Post would later claim that Edgar's Radical Division—what he called Palmer's "secret-service auxiliary"—wrote most of it. But even beyond Palmer's words, Edgar's fingerprints dominated the official hearing record, including the forty-page *Record of the Activities of the Radical Division of the Bureau of Investigation of the Department of Justice*, the dozens of affidavits contradicting the National Popular Government League report, the five hundred pages of exhibits, including the full text of Edgar's briefs against the Communist and Communist Labor

Parties, histories of the L'Era Nuova group and the recent strikes, and the reams of radical literature seized in the raids.

After Palmer left the hearing room, the Rules Committee members met privately and decided not to take any action that year on the proposed impeachment of Louis Post. That simple shrug of the shoulders decided the issue. Louis Post would not be impeached. He could stay in his job and continue to block the Red deportations as long as he pleased, at least until the next election. To historian Robert K. Murray, the congressmen, after hearing the loud harangues from both sides, "[i]ndeed . . . did look very much like a person who had picked up a hot poker and was trying to find a place to put it."

Critics jumped on the fact that Palmer failed to win a knockout. "If Attorney General Palmer had in hand any real defense against the charges brought against him, he would not have required 30,000 words in which to set it forth," the New York Evening Post jabbed. Swinburne Hale, after taking time to study Palmer's testimony closely, took a tougher line. "Palmer's defense," he told friends, "was compounded of false testimony and equivocal boasting. There are some raw bits of perjury in the affidavits presented by him. . . ."

But this was not the end of it. Mitchell Palmer still had one more chance to make his case, in San Francisco. He could still work his will and certainly would be able to fire Louis Post once he was elected president of the United States.

• PART IX •

VERDICTS

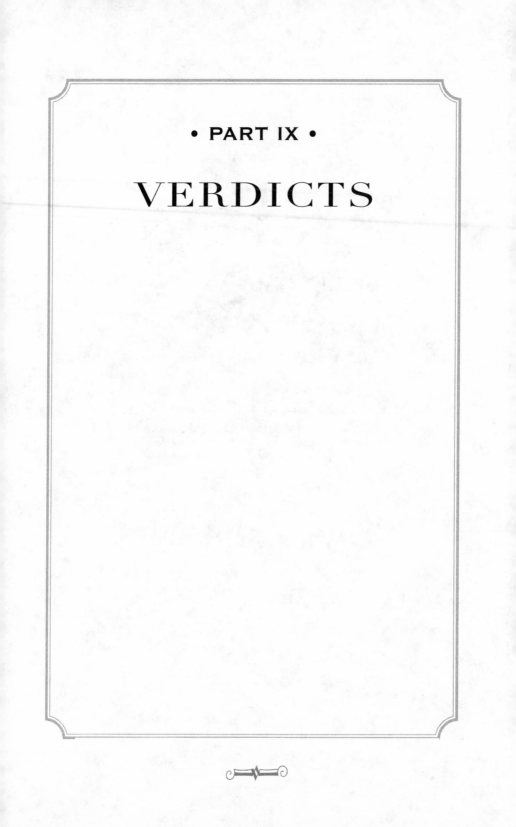

"As Gag-Rulers Would Have It." The figures on the left represent Honest Opinion, Free Speech, and Free Press. *Jersey City Journal*, in *Literary Digest*, February 7, 1920.

· 46 ·
POLITICS

O N June 5, 1920, four days after Mitchell Palmer finished
defending himself to the House Rules Committee, Congress quit
for a six-month recess. Its members declared their work done, then closed
their doors and left town. It was just in time. June in Washington, D.C.,
meant summer, hot, sticky days, thick, humid air, unsleepable nights, and
no relief. Modern air-conditioning would not make Washington a year-
round livable city for another three decades. Schools and offices closed,
and anyone with a few days off and a few dollars in his pocket boarded a
train, boat, or motorcar for vacation.

Summer 1920 was special. It was the first one since 1914 that felt like
peace: no European War, no race riots, no massive labor strikes, no
soaring inflation, and no anarchist bombs. The country seemed determined to have fun, and Washington offered plenty for those who stayed
behind. There were baseball doubleheaders at Griffith Stadium, swimming in the Tidal Basin or at Great Falls Park, horse racing at the Pim-
lico track, and dancing galore. Jazz filled the air, the new sound of the new

decade. Records played crisp, happy tunes like "Oh! By Jingo," "Profi-
teering Blues," and "Ching-a-Ling's Jazz Bazaar." Glen Echo Park offered
dancing under the stars—fox trots, cat steps, and two steps—in an open
pavilion and the best amusement rides outside Coney Island and Atlantic
City. The Rock Creek Café touted its Four Piece Colored Orchestra and
steamboats left nightly from the Seventh Street wharf for jazz moonlight
cruises down the Potomac River to Chesapeake Beach and back.

At local theatres, crowds flocked to see Helen Keller, billed as "The
Famous Blind, Deaf, and Formerly Dumb Girl," appearing onstage with
her teacher, Anne Sullivan, in a musical cabaret called *Vanity Fair*.
Douglas Fairbanks swashbuckled across the silent film screen in *The
Mark of Zorro*, and Balusco's theater offered an all-Yiddish rendition
of *Tevya the Milkman*. Sports drew the biggest crowds, both locally and
globally: baseball, golf, tennis, canoeing, horse racing, yachting, and
the Olympic Games held that summer in Antwerp, Belgium, the first
since the start of World War I. Fans by the tens of thousands mobbed
the Indianapolis Speedway that month and thrilled to the spectacle of
Gaston Chevrolet at a jaw-dropping speed of 88.16 miles per hour winning the eighth annual 500-mile motorcar race, which had been suspended for two years during the World War. At the ocean beaches,
bathing beauties were the rage. New Jersey's Atlantic City would soon
launch a new pageant called Miss America featuring pretty girls in
skimpy swimsuits to keep vacationing tourists in town for an extra two
weeks past Labor Day.

For those who didn't like sports, there was shopping. Women flocked
to stores that summer to buy skirts with hemlines nine inches above the
ankle. They cut their hair short and wrapped their bodies in flowing satin
and silk tunics and shawls in bright yellows, blues, and whites. Stores featured Japanese crepe kimonos with floral designs in pastel blues, pinks,
and lavenders. Automobiles, too, came in a dazzling range of flavors:
roadsters, town cars, and open sedans, Packards, Dorts, Dodges, West-
cotts, Arrowlines, Franklins, Lexingtons, Overlands, and Paiges.

Edgar entered this new decade in his prime of life, smart, young, full of
energy, and on the rise. But he made an odd fit: a fussy teetotaler who
turned his nose at cards and free thinking. He wore the latest men's fashions, dressed like a dandy in white linen suits and spats, and he loved
sports. Later, he would make himself a regular at boxing matches, horse
races, and major league baseball games. He smoked cigarettes just like the
film stars, a Turkish brand called Fatimas, although jazz never fit his

musical taste. His niece Margaret remembered his listening to records by Enrico Caruso, the Italian opera virtuoso. As for dancing, Edgar never quite fit it in. A dance card from one of the social nights he attended at Central High School as a teenager contained not a single name of a female classmate.

It's not that women found him unattractive. Just the opposite. But other than his mother and his secretary, Helen Gandy, Edgar showed no interest in them at all. "I think he regarded women as a kind of hindrance. You know, they sort of got in the way when you were going places," his niece Margaret recalled of her uncle J. E. Later, Edgar would describe his view of them in surreal terms. "I have always held girls and women on a pedestal," he told an interviewer in 1939. "If I ever marry and the girl fails me, ceases to love me, and our marriage is dissolved, it would ruin me. My mental status couldn't take it, and I would not be responsible for my actions." If any of this made Edgar feel odd or abnormal, he didn't show it. If his aloofness toward girls and women was the angst of a young man who preferred the company of other young men, he never mentioned it. Like everything else, he hid it all by burying himself in his work.

For Edgar, the biggest draw that summer of 1920 was something quite different; 1920 was a presidential election year, and Edgar was a ranking official at the Department of Justice and a personal protégé of one of the leading candidates. It had been a remarkable blossoming for him. Just eight years earlier, in 1912, when Woodrow Wilson won his first election as president, Edgar was a seventeen-year-old senior at Central High School; the closest he got to the action that year was marching with his high school cadet corps in the inaugural parade. Four years later, in 1916, when Americans reelected Wilson on his platform to keep the country out of war, Edgar was still studying law at George Washington University, a full year shy of graduation. This time, in 1920, he could be a player.

June was political convention month. The Republicans went first, meeting in Chicago, and included women as delegates for the first time, since women's suffrage was now the law. They took ten ballots to nominate for president Warren G. Harding, a first-term United States senator and local newspaper publisher from Marion, Ohio. Harding stood six feet tall, had a handsome face, a firm handshake, distinguished gray hair, and spoke in a soothing baritone. People said he looked like a president, and he had already given his signature speech for the campaign: "America's

present need is not heroics but healing; not nostrums but normalcy."
After two years of World War and two more years of postwar race riots,
Red Scares, labor unrest, deportation raids, and White House histrionics,
"normalcy" sounded pretty good.

To complete the ticket, Republicans chose as their vice-presidential
nominee Massachusetts governor Calvin Coolidge, hero of the Boston
police strike. Otherwise, strikingly absent from speeches at both parties'
conventions were any explicit mentions of the Red hysteria that had hypnotized the country the past year. Instead, Harding's platform touted free
speech, opposed violence, and took a clear swipe at Palmer and his Red
Raids, which it referred to simply as "the vigorous malpractice of the
Departments of Justice and Labor." Times had changed. "[T]oo much has
been said about Bolshevism in America," Harding told supporters.

Next came the Democrats, who planned to meet in San Francisco in
late June. Without Woodrow Wilson, Democrats had no clear leader.
Twenty-four different candidates vied for votes on the first ballot, but talk
centered on three top contenders: William Gibbs McAdoo, the suave
Wall Street financier and wartime treasury secretary; James M. Cox, the
governor of Ohio and antiprohibition "wet"; and A. Mitchell Palmer, the
sitting attorney general and sponsor of the Palmer Raids.

Even now, after all the controversy, Palmer strutted the stage a formi-
dable candidate. He carried strong support from New England, Illinois,
and Georgia, plus home state Pennsylvania and a scattering of delegates
nationwide. "Since the nomination of Coolidge, the drift has been decid-
edly toward Palmer," an Atlanta Constitution analyst wrote that month,
pointing out how Palmer benefited from the Republican's decision to
ornament their national ticket with Calvin Coolidge, whose popularity
was based squarely on his anti-Red stance in the Boston police strike.
Nobody was more anti-Red than Palmer. It made a neat package. "Whoever nominated Harding did the Democrats a great favor," Palmer told
the Washington Post with a straight face. "He is a typical reactionary, and
a colorless candidate at that."

For Edgar, the Democratic convention in San Francisco provided him
his summer adventure, a chance to leave overheated Washington and
tour the country. In other years, he vacationed with his parents or ran off
to organize deportation raids. In 1920, he decided—or perhaps was
ordered by Palmer's top staff—to head out west and work for his candidate. Edgar had never seen California. He left Washington in mid-June
and traveled by train, marveling at the vistas of desert, mountains, and

farm fields gliding past his window. In Cleveland, El Paso, and Los Angeles, he took time to stop and visit the local Justice Department offices there. He hobnobbed with agents and chiefs, listened to their stories and gripes, shook their hands, shared their company for dinners and coffees.

Edgar took a full week to reach San Francisco, where tens of thousands of delegates and politicos jammed the city's hotels and eateries. This was the first major party convention held west of the Mississippi River, and Palmer's campaign set up its headquarters at the imposing St. Francis Hotel on Powell Street, one of the few structures to survive the 1906 earthquake. A reporter described Palmer's suite as an endless circus, "redolent with flowers, plastered with posters, littered with literature and loud with enthusiasm." Bands, vocal quartets, and stump speakers entertained visitors day and night. "One is greeted with tremendous enthusiasm on entering the Palmer camp," another wrote. "A hearty handshake and an openhanded smash between the shoulder blades is the least one may expect." Palmer's team plastered the neighborhood around the San Francisco Civic Auditorium, where the convention would take place, with billboards showing Palmer's stern face looking down on passersby, one hand holding a book, the other pointing a finger. "The Fighting Quaker—laying down the law," read the caption.

Rivals poked fun at the image and especially the nickname, calling Palmer either the "Quaking Fighter," the "Fighting Quacker," or the "Quaking Quitter."

Edgar checked in at headquarters and quickly immersed himself in the pageant. It remains a mystery what precise role he played. He admitted spending three days in San Francisco and venturing into the convention hall at least once for forty-five minutes, though he denied engaging directly in politics. That left plenty of gray area. Edgar by then knew all the tricks on how to keep his name out of unwanted newspaper stories, though he couldn't hide completely. "[Palmer's] friends have been exceedingly active and a large squad of office holders appear to be on the go day and night in an effort to corral delegates for him," a newsman for the *New York Times* wrote, pointing to the many Justice Department hacks working the convention crowd. The spectacle of Justice Department men stalking the halls, taking names of delegates, coming so soon after the Red Raids, gave many people the chills. Some referred to them as "secret agents." A *Boston Globe* analyst, after canvassing the hall, described Palmer's appeal as based on "official favoritism and terrorism" and concluded, "here he is with more delegates enrolled in his support than any other man, and yet no one really wants him or expects him to be nominated."

Palmer also shared a special problem with William Gibbs McAdoo, the former treasury secretary. As loyal cabinet members, both claimed Woodrow Wilson's mantle in the presidential contest, and both were embarrassed by Wilson's utter silence on their behalf. The president not only refused to endorse either Palmer or McAdoo, but he also refused even to take his own name out of contention, making Palmer and McAdoo appear disloyal whenever either one campaigned. "McAdoo has been to see the president recently five times and not once has the president given him an interview," presidential stenographer Charles Swem wrote in his diary. "The President won't speak to Mitchell Palmer in Cabinet." McAdoo, who had become the president's son-in-law after marrying Wilson's daughter Nellie in a 1915 White House ceremony, found the standoff especially awkward. "Every family visit which Mr. McAdoo and his wife, the President's daughter, paid the White House, was distorted in the newspaper reports," Joe Tumulty recalled.

Party leaders begged the president to signal his preference before the San Francisco balloting, but he refused. Instead, he took every opportunity in private conversations to belittle the front-runners. When U.S. senator Carter Glass of Virginia stopped by the White House to visit the president *en route* to San Francisco, he tried to draw Wilson out on the issue by mentioning that he thought Palmer would make a good president but a weak candidate because he had offended so many groups. "Exactly, hence his nomination would be futile," Wilson shot back. And as for Governor Cox, the president said, "Oh! You know Cox's nomination would be a fake."

As late as mid-March 1920, Woodrow Wilson, emotionally spent and physically broken, still saw only one deserving hat in the ring for the White House that year, his own. He confided to his doctor, Cary Grayson, that he still imagined the convention being deadlocked and turning to him, Woodrow Wilson, to save it. "In such circumstances I would feel obliged to accept the nomination even if I thought it would cost me my life," he told Grayson. McAdoo responded to this uncomfortable standoff by refusing publicly to acknowledge his own candidacy, though he never actually dropped out. He declined to enter any state primary, and five days before the San Francisco convention he announced he was not running for president, even as his political managers continued to collect hundreds of vote commitments from friendly delegates.

For Edgar, attending his first political convention, these machinations must have seemed bizarre. But wherever he went in San Francisco, he heard the same talk. Party regulars admired Mitchell Palmer
and respected him. One Washington State delegate described him
as "a brilliant man, a great orator, and really is presidential timber."
But the controversy surrounding the Red Raids crippled his chances.
"All these charges that various persons are making against him seem
to be taking effect," Kansas party boss Joe Taggart confided. As biographer Stanley Coban later put it, "the Red Scare had petered out;
apparently most Americans wanted to forget the experience, but
Palmer's enemies remembered." Samuel Gompers, who came to town
representing the four million members of the American Federation of
Labor, told anyone at the convention who would listen that Palmer
was simply unacceptable. In fact, Palmer was the *only* unacceptable
Democrat to his union.

In the three weeks since Palmer's appearance before the House Rules
Committee, this situation had only grown worse. Felix Frankfurter,
responding to one of Palmer's remarks at the hearing attacking his representation of Red clients in court, issued a hot public telegram from
Harvard accusing Palmer of demagoguery. "You are quoted as having
difficulty in reconciling the attitude of lawyers who appear as counsel
for alleged communist party aliens in deportation cases," Frankfurter
wrote, his words printed in many major newspapers. "May we respectfully ask you, the official head of the bar of the United States, to state
since when it has become otherwise than ethically proper and profes-
sionally right for members of the bar . . . to challenge through the
courts administrative actions exceeding the bounds of law and fairness?
Is this your position? Do you mean that these aliens are not entitled to
counsel?"

Palmer responded with his own typical belligerence, shooting back his
own public telegram accusing Frankfurter of foul play, making "utterly
false charges" and using shady courtroom tactics in the Boston *habeas
corpus* case. Worse news came on June 25, just three days before the formal
opening of the convention, when Judge George W. Anderson issued his
final decision in the Boston case, a blistering condemnation of the raids as
an abomination of justice. "A mob is a mob whether made up of government officials acting under orders of the Department of Justice or of criminals, loafers, and the vicious classes," he concluded. Of the fourteen
prisoners still being held on Deer Island six months after the episode,

Anderson freed them all: ten because they had been denied a fair trial, and the rest because he found that the Communist Party itself did not fall under the 1918 Immigration Act since it never actually threatened to overthrow the government by force or violence.* This one-two punch from Frankfurter and Anderson, coming just as delegates were gathering for the convention's opening sessions, left Palmer looking weak, shrill, and a bit scary.

The San Francisco Civic Auditorium, a vast, square-shaped arena, was transformed into a dazzling spectacle of sound and light for the convention as it opened on Monday, June 28. A sea of ten thousand faces flooded the arena's floor, the walls decorated in flags and banners, all red, white, and blue. Palmer chose Pennsylvania state party chair John H. Bigelow to place his name in nomination, and Bigelow delivered a speech depicting Palmer as the country's protector against what he called "the hydra-head of anarchy and revolution." "True Americanism must be on guard," he berated the delegates. "Therefore your candidate must be [an] intrepid defender of your institutions, a courageous crusader in the cause of law and order [and an] ardent advocate of Americanism." To second his nomination, Palmer tapped Mrs. Florence Brown Cotnam of Little Rock, Arkansas, a veteran suffragette, president of the Arkansas League of Women Voters, and the first woman to speak in the Arkansas General Assembly. These choices painted a pretty picture for the delegates: Palmer, the hard-line patriot, was also a progressive.

It seemed to work. On the first ballot, Palmer polled a strong 254 votes, running second only to McAdoo's 266, with neither coming close to the 729 votes needed to win the nomination under the Democrats' traditional two-thirds rule. "Our forces are firmly intact," Palmer's floor manager, Virginia delegate Charles Carlin, told newsmen. On the second ballot, McAdoo and Palmer both gained, polling 289 and 264, respectively. The convention then adjourned for a good night's sleep.

The Democratic convention in San Francisco in 1920 would take forty-four ballots over four days to pick a nominee, making it the

---

*A Federal Appeals court would later reverse the portion of Anderson's ruling saying that the Communist Party fell outside the 1918 Act. See 265 FR 17 (1922). The Justice Department would not appeal the portion of the decision finding violations of due process of law, a fact that Frankfurter would construe as an admission of guilt. Anderson would make his personal views on communists known two years later in a letter to Senator Walsh, calling them "nothing but a negligible set of theorists emitting crusade rhetoric . . . one of the many rampant absurdities of our modern thinking, or lack of thinking."

fourth-longest up to that point in American history.* On Saturday, July 3, the delegates cast their votes twenty times, in one roll call after another, from early morning until almost midnight, all the while singing songs, staging parades, and sharing endless gossip. Governor Cox took the lead and Palmer fell to third place as tensions mounted between Palmer's and McAdoo's camps: "The Palmer managers are resentful and unforgiving," a *Boston Globe* reporter wrote after talking with them, pointing to McAdoo's waffling over whether he was a candidate and his hogging of the Wilson Administration mantle. The delegates took a break for the July Fourth holiday, then cast eight more ballots the next morning. McAdoo took the lead again on the thirtieth ballot, but Palmer refused to quit. Late that night, Palmer enjoyed one last surge on the thirty-sixth ballot when ten Illinois delegates jumped his way in an attempt to break the deadlock, but things fell apart after that. A third of his votes abandoned him on the thirty-eighth roll call. On the next, the thirty-ninth, his total slipped to 79.

During a recess well past midnight, a delegation of party leaders came to see Palmer in his St. Francis Hotel suite. Palmer had kept the door closed and himself out of public sight during the convention—normal courtesy by a candidate of the era. Now, he listened wearily as party elders told him to give up. Palmer took a scrap of paper and scribbled a note on it, addressed it to his floor manager, Charles Carlin, and gave it to a messenger to be hand delivered. When Carlin received it on the convention floor, he immediately gained recognition and read it aloud to the crowd: "[Mr. Palmer] is not willing to delay the proceedings further and authorized me to finally, positively and absolutely release every delegate pledged to him, that the convention may proceed to nominate the next President of the United States." Cheers rose from around the arena.

Palmer had lost, but only after fighting an epic battle. After he dropped out, the deadlock broke quickly. On the forty-fourth ballot, Governor Cox polled 699 1/2 votes and the convention agreed to nominate him by acclamation. Bitter over the loss, Palmer could still cheer Cox's choice for vice president, thirty-eight-year-old Franklin Delano Roosevelt, the handsome socialite assistant secretary of the navy, Palmer's

---

*The longest to date had all been Democratic: Woodrow Wilson's in 1912 at 46 ballots, Stephen Douglas's in 1860 at 59 ballots; and Franklin Pierce's in 1852 at 49. The longest Republican convention was James Garfield's in 1880 at 36 ballots. The Democratic contest in New York City in 1924 would be the longest ever, taking 104 ballots to nominate John W. Davis.

neighbor on R Street who came to help him the night the Anarchist Fighters blew up his house.

⚬━◆━⚬

Edgar had left San Francisco long before the finale. He had disappeared from sight around the time balloting began on July 1. It's not exactly clear why. He might have sensed the coming defeat, or Palmer's managers might have told him to leave town because they feared his face at the convention would scare away labor support, being too vivid a reminder of the Red Raids. Or Edgar simply might not have planned on the affair lasting so long. Whatever the reason, he checked out of his hotel, left the convention, and boarded a train. He took his time going home, stopping along the way in Seattle, Spokane, Dubuque, and Helena, Montana. He claimed to have nearly reached Chicago by the time news flashed across the wires that Governor Cox finally won the nomination.

Reaching Washington, he waxed philosophic. "I have just returned from my trip West and must say that I am an absolute convert to the wonderful climate and scenic beauties of the West, particularly California," he wrote to a friend in New York City. "While my trip was rather short and hurried and full of business, yet I feel that I have gained a liberal education in taking it." Edgar had seen the country, seen politics, and seen his own future thrown into disarray.

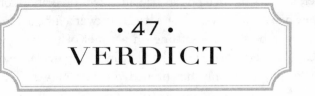

· 47 ·
VERDICT

D O YOU SEE the defendant William Bross Lloyd?" Marvin Barnhart, the assistant state's attorney, asked the witness.

Certainly. Everyone knew Chicago's Millionaire Socialist. "The second man on the end of the chairs." The witness, George F. R. Cummerow, special agent of the Department of Justice, pointed across the courtroom at the handsome man with the thinning gray-blond hair and expensive suit who sat in a corner of the defendants' dock.

"State whether all the men you see here now, you saw at that convention, whether you can give their names or cannot?" Barnhart asked, pointing to the whole group of twenty defendants.

"I possibly saw most of them."

Clarence Darrow jumped up. "Object to that," he snapped.

Judge Oscar Hebel agreed. "Strike it out," he ordered. The answer was too vague.

Darrow sat down, sprawling his tall, gangly frame across the wooden chair. The trial by now had lasted almost three months in the stuffy chamber; lawyers and defendants had all grown tired and short-tempered. First, they had spent fifty-two days haggling over a jury, questioning 1,359 potential members before settling on a panel of twelve, including five union card-holders. Prosecutors had begun taking evidence on July 11, a hot, sticky day that only heightened the raw nerves. They produced twenty-eight witnesses and fifty-two exhibits and, as expected, aimed most of it at William Bross Lloyd, their flashiest target. They called Lloyd's business manager to demonstrate how wealthy he was. They called three different stenographers, who recorded his incendiary speeches in Wisconsin and Chicago, so they could dwell on the precise language he used in calling on workers to seize machine guns and dynamite to storm the halls of capitalism. They called the policeman who arrested Lloyd for causing a commotion on Chicago's State Street by waving a red flag from his car, and then the reporter who visited Lloyd's home in Winnetka and interviewed him there after the January raids to describe Lloyd's disappointment at not being arrested and his threat that American workers would rise up in bloody violence on a par with the French Revolution or World War I. They called a New York City detective who recognized Lloyd as one of the suspects he saw while raiding a meeting of New York socialists, placing him shoulder to shoulder with convicted criminal anarchist Benjamin Gitlow and communist fugitives John Reed and Louis Fraina.

They could have stopped right there and rested their case. But instead, to dramatize the danger of how Lloyd's radical talk could lead to radical action, they called Ole Hanson, mayor of Seattle during the 1919 general strike and self-proclaimed hero of the affair. Hanson described how unions had shut down the entire city while spouting Bolshevik rhetoric. He quoted one leader as saying: "If we cannot overthrow [the government] by the ballot route, we will overthrow it by the bullet route."

Darrow, who stalked the courtroom in shirtsleeves and suspenders, complained this was all hearsay, but Judge Hebel let it in. So Darrow, to counter it, used his cross-examination of Hanson to ridicule him on the witness stand, forcing him to admit that he had made $60,000 in speaking fees by going on the lecture circuit to grandstand his largely fictional heroics. "Gas was left flowing, electricity was left running, telephones were running and everybody was fed; the only man creating any disturbance was Ole Hanson," Darrow told the jury, mocking the former mayor. "Now, that is Ole; that is Ole Hanson, the cheap vaudeville performer."

Lloyd and the other defendants remained free the whole time during their trial, though they hardly got to enjoy the Chicago summer. The

Communist Labor Party almost bankrupted its treasury paying their bail bonds and had to launch a heated fundraising drive just to stay solvent and pay Darrow's legal retainer.

But the star witness for the prosecution was George Cummerow, provided courtesy of A. Mitchell Palmer and his Justice Department. Cummerow, a federal agent, had attended the Communist Labor Party's founding convention in Chicago the prior summer and taken copious notes on all the overheated speeches, the resolutions, and, most importantly, the names of people in the room. His testimony filled fifty-one pages of trial transcript, documenting how all twenty defendants had been there, played active roles, joined committees, sang songs, and spouted manifestoes. This was the dark conspiracy to overthrow the United States government. Now, Marvin Barnhart, one of the assistant prosecutors, led Cummerow in identifying a few more of the men sitting nervously in the defendants' seats. Cummerow pointed to Ludwig Lore, "the gentleman with the black mustache sitting in the back," he explained, and then Oscar Owens, "the first man facing this way, with his arm up, with his glasses." He had seen them at the convention too.

"Do you know the defendant Katterfield?" Barnhart asked, trying to complete the list.

"The last time I saw Katterfield he had a mustache."

Darrow jumped up again. "Just a minute, I ask that that be stricken." Again, Judge Hebel agreed.

Barnhart reworded his question. "At the time of the convention was the defendant Katterfield smooth faced, or did he have a mustache?"

Darrow interrupted again. "Have you any more guesses? That is not Katterfield."

Barnhart looked confused. He thought it was. "I move that the observation of Mr. Darrow be stricken out."

But before the judge could say another word, Darrow broke in again. "Just a minute. Let him stand up." He pointed to the defendant in question. Judge Hebel agreed and the man stood up. "What is your name?" Darrow asked. "Hankin," the man said.

Darrow could feel smug for a moment. He'd won a small victory. No, the man was not Katterfield. Yes, Darrow had made the prosecutor look silly. No, Cummerow's memory, his ability to attach names to faces, was less than perfect. "I can recognize their faces, but not their names," he admitted. But Darrow's larger point, that the jury should ignore this witness, failed miserably.

"Step down and look over those defendants and point out such as you recollect in that convention and participating in it," Barnhart asked the witness. Darrow objected, but this time Judge Hebel sided with the prosecutor. Cummerow rose to his feet, stepped across the courtroom from the witness chair to the defendants' seats, and tapped the shoulders of half a dozen more of them. No, he could not remember all their names, but he remembered their faces. "All these men were at the convention."

Clarence Darrow sat down. It was pointless, this nitpicking at the prosecution. The witness, Cummerow, was telling the truth. Every single one of Darrow's twenty clients had attended that Communist Labor Party convention. That was the problem. The twelve jurors saw them exactly for what they were: communist diehards. And, to the jurors, this made the defendants despicable human beings: revolutionaries bent on destroying their homes, mockingly unpatriotic and, worse still, effete intellectuals, writers, bookstore owners, leaflet printers. None of these Reds had ever gotten his hands dirty working in a factory, digging for coal, forging steel, or working a packing plant. Who were they to shoot their mouths off about the working class?

Darrow could rant all day about technical flaws in the prosecution case, but hate, fear, and envy were against him in this courtroom. Not one of the jurors missed the fact that William Bross Lloyd wore the best-tailored suit in the courtroom, owned three homes, and employed a chauffeur to drive his car.

Darrow and his defense cocounsels, of course, had their own message that they had begun drumming in from the beginning of the trial. Lawyer William Forrest went first, calling Lloyd and the others "these twenty cowards." "Is this cowardly cripple Owens [a defendant] responsible because that other coward, William Bross Lloyd, wrote a letter?" he asked. "Wherever there are strikes you will find some loud mouthed Socialists saying things that should not be said, but is that unlawful?" Then he went for the kill: "Because Attorney General Palmer sought to ride into the presidential chair by raising a hullabaloo against 'reds,' these men are arrested. Is the poor man to be convicted because he believes he is not getting his share of the good things of the world?" Darrow followed this same line in his own opening speech. "[T]hese poor deluded clients of mine," he moaned. If anything, they belonged in an insane asylum, not the penitentiary.

After Cummerow finished his testimony, identifying all twenty communists and telling the whole story of the conventions, the prosecution rested its case. Darrow then wasted little time on a defense. He called only three witnesses, all from Seattle, to explain that the Seattle strike actually had been a mild-mannered affair—no violence, no upheaval. Then he rested. He called no witnesses to vouch for the defendants' good character, their alibis, their hopes for a better world—nothing. As with Benjamin Gitlow in New York, Darrow decided that the less said about these eccentric misanthropes, the better. His best chance would come at the end of the trial when he could talk directly to the jurors and appeal to their better nature.

The great Communist Trial became popular entertainment in Chicago that summer, far better than the city's baseball team, the "Black Sox," who had earned that nickname for the unspeakable crime of throwing the 1919 World Series, revealed during that same summer. Maclay Hoyne ultimately would indict eight players on the team; they would all be acquitted the next summer but banned from baseball for life.

Still, Chicagoans knew all about Clarence Darrow and his dramatic jury appeals. Typically, they lined up hours in advance to hear him deliver one in a big case, and this would be no exception. "The state's attorney will argue today, followed by Clarence Darrow tomorrow," the *Chicago Daily Tribune* announced in early August. "Throngs filled the courtroom. The heat did not stop them," the same reporter noted when the day finally arrived. "They wanted to hear Darrow."

"Gentlemen of the jury: I have for a good many years been arguing cases in court and, in my own way, as a lawyer, asking jurors to forget their prejudices and their feelings," he began in his Midwest drawl, thumbs fastened to his suspenders, pacing back and forth, leaning his body over the rail to talk directly into the juror's faces, just close enough to look them in the eye and make them squirm. He never spoke from notes, even for speeches lasting ten hours or longer. "I must say that in all my experience, which covers forty-two years, it seems to me I never saw a case where every cheap feeling has been appealed to. . . . Gentlemen, from the beginning to the end there has been no attempt at fairness; there has been no effort to see that these defendants had a trial as should be had in an American court, or in an Indian court, or in a cannibal court." Then, stretching out his arm to point to the defendants sitting stuffed together in the front rows, he turned his own earlier rhetoric upside down: "[T]hey have been called cowards for doing what not a single lawyer in this case would do, to stand up against a mob. They are not cowards enough to beg, and if you want to convict them for this, then convict them. . . . I will

submit this case squarely to this jury to see what you are going to do in
the cause of freedom of speech. . . ."

This was his theme. These defendants were hotheads, but they threatened nobody. And the only reason they were on trial was because a few
politicians were trying to exploit peoples' fears to win votes on Election
Day or break the local labor unions. "Here are twenty men whom you can
put in jail if you want to," he said, voice rising in indignation, arms
aflutter, pacing, racing. "But do you think you can stop Bolshevism that
way? Does the state's attorney think so? Do those in back of the State's
attorney think so?"

This last remark caused a stir. Frank Comerford, the lead prosecutor,
jumped up from his seat. "I object, your Honor, to these insinuations that
there is 'something back' of this case," he shouted. Comerford, hired as a
special counsel to argue the prosecution, had his own dashing presence,
"the Beau Brummel of the occasion," journalist Austin Simons wrote to
describe him in *The Liberator*. "Someone must have told him he resem-
bles a movie star—he dressed and deports himself as though he had some
particular one in mind." Comerford had traveled to Poland and Russia
after World War I to study Bolshevism and write articles about it for the
Chicago Tribune. He considered himself an expert and, since coming
home, gave public lectures on what he had seen there, ripe with stories of
atrocities and evil Red conspiracies. Frank Comerford bristled at any suggestion that he was merely the pawn of some local business thugs trying
to bust a union. "Furthermore, I denounce these statements of Mr.
Darrow as willful, malicious, ugly lies."

This argument had been brewing for weeks in the stuffy courtroom. It
quickly degenerated into a free-for-all. William Forrest, Darrow's co-
counsel, jumped to his feet as well. "I know from my own knowledge that
Mr. Darrow's statement is true," he insisted, and launched into his own
litany of charges that Chicago industrialists had put up $40,000 to
finance the city's local Red Raids, a fact disclosed in the newspapers six
months earlier. Judge Hebel banged his gavel. He demanded order and
instructed his bailiffs to hustle the jury out of the room so they could hear
no more of this. Then he demanded the lawyers behave themselves.

The storm settled down as quickly as it started. Back on good behavior,
the jury back in the room, Darrow took the rest of that day to finish up.
He spent hours analyzing the evidence, but he never strayed far from
his single theme: "I don't know whether Bolshevism is right or wrong. I
don't know whether or not communism will work. But I do know that

capitalism doesn't work," he said, addressing the bitter conflict of ideologies that had caused such a fright across the country.

Comerford used this opening to try one more time to get Darrow's goat by interrupting him in mid-thought. "Will you please tell us, Mr. Darrow, what legal methods there are for changing the government except the ballot?"

It was an obvious trick question, designed to make Darrow admit his clients had no intention to follow the normal rules of democratic government, but Darrow had his own lifetime of scars on this particular issue, having stood with Eugene Debs during the 1894 Pullman strike, among many others. "Oh, the ballot, the ballot! You make me sick!" he snapped back. "The ballot never got anybody anything. As if we did nothing but vote and sit around waiting for the next election! . . . Men have a right to urge their fellow workers to quit work until laws are changed. It will be done more and more in the future. How did we get the eight-hour day in the railroad industry? Vote for it? No! The men threatened to strike: then the politicians passed the law. . . . When people give up the right to strike and depend solely on the ballot, they're lost. . . . You get what you want only when you go out and fight for it."

Back in his own rhythm, he finished with a flourish. This case was about human nature, nothing more nor less. "I know that freedom produces wealth and that wealth destroys freedom. I know that the nation that is not watchful of its liberty will lose it." Then, "I urge you to stand for the right of men to think; for the right to speak boldly and unafraid; the right to be master of their souls, the right to live free and to die free." Then he sat down exhausted. He was finished.

Darrow fidgeted in his chair all the next day as Frank Comerford summed up the case for the prosecution. Comerford rang every patriotic bell he could chime. "Like Francis Scott Key, who watched all night to see if the flag still waved, the people throughout the entire country are awaiting your verdict to see if our flag is still waving," he told the jurors. "If the verdict is not guilty they may as well tear down Old Glory and hoist in its stead a red flag, symbol of anarchy, and join the communist party. Go to Arlington and take out the bodies of our soldiers dead. . . . Do all these things if you find them not guilty." He closed by reciting the four stanzas of "The Star Spangled Banner." He didn't actually sing them; he just read them. The rocket's red glare. The bombs bursting in air. And the rest. Then he, too, sat down.

The trial had lasted three full months, from May through August 1920, spanning two thousand pages of transcript and 485 pages of briefs. After all that time, the twelve jurors took less than a single afternoon to reach a decision. They announced their verdict in open court as Darrow stood quietly alongside his twenty clients: Guilty. Every one of them. Judge Hebel then meted out the sentences. For William Bross Lloyd and six of the others, it was one to five years in Joliet Prison plus fines of up to $2,000. For the rest, it was one year in the Cook County jail.

One of the newsmen who sat through the entire ordeal, a reporter for *The Nation*, raced from his seat after the verdict was read out to ask one of the jurors why he'd voted to convict. The juror conceded he heard no evidence of any "overt act" as the law required, but "we were certain that had the defendants carried their revolutionary program to its logical conclusion, or had it run its course a state of anarchy would have been brought about." Another said: "This is our country. It is the best country in the world. . . . If others do not think it is good enough for them, let them get out and stay out." The reporter threw up his hands. "Obviously, in such a state of affairs, a trial of eighty-four days is [a] pure waste of time on the part of everyone concerned," he wrote.

But Clarence Darrow seemed satisfied. He had given his clients the chance to make their stand and, under the circumstances, they got off lightly. Judge Hebel could have sent them all to Joliet for twenty years. Benjamin Gitlow in New York had already begun serving his own five-to-seven year sentence in Sing Sing. Emma Goldman had been deported for life, Louis Fraina was in hiding, and Eugene Debs was serving up to ten years behind bars in Atlanta. In fact, to the extent that the entire past year's Red Raids had all been one big exercise in guilt by association, he lamented the thousands of innocents who suffered by their accidental associations with the likes of a few bigmouths like Lloyd, Oscar Owens, Katterfield, Ben Gitlow, and Louis Fraina. To Darrow, it was their silly vitriolic talk that brought down the wrath of Palmer on innocent and guilty alike.

But, then again, that was the whole point. These firebrands had every right to be wrong or stupid or incendiary. That's what free speech boiled down to, the ability to think and not have the government shut you up whenever it didn't like what you said. Sometimes, those ridiculous, naïve, idiotic notions from the lips of fools turned out to be the most sublime truths of all.

Besides, Darrow had reason to hope that his clients would never serve these sentences. This was still Chicago. Politics reigned, and moods changed. Walking out the courtroom door, he passed Frank Comerford standing around talking to a few reporters. They had no hard feelings. "I lose a $10 hat to you as the matter stands," Darrow told him, "but I'll bet you $100 we get a reversal [on appeal]."

"You're on," Comerford said with a wink.

Clarence Darrow never had any sour feelings toward state's attorney Maclay Hoyne for bringing this prosecution and turning it into a circus. He even supported Hoyne for re-election again, in 1920. "Every one knows that Mr. Hoyne is fearless and honest," he announced in a press release. But this trial, coming on top of the Ben Gitlow trial in New York, on top of the raids and the hysteria, could not help but deepen his contrarian attitude. "People are getting more cruel all the time, more insistent that they shall have their way," he scribbled in a note to Mary Field on Thanksgiving Day that year. "I have grown quite convinced that the happiest time of the human race was in Barbarism and likewise convinced that we are going back to it. . . . I presume when the Soviets get to boss the world they will snuff out what little freedom is left. The fact is that I am getting afraid of everyone who has conviction."

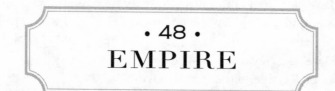

· 48 ·
EMPIRE

B ACK HOME IN Washington, D.C., Edgar had plenty to worry about. His San Francisco adventure had taught him a hard lesson in politics. Having hitched his star to a single candidate, he now faced the consequences. A. Mitchell Palmer, having lost his chance for the presidency, left San Francisco a discredited lame duck, rebuffed by his party, and soon to be retired. The final nail in Palmer's political coffin came shortly after the convention when he announced plans to campaign for Governor Cox, the party's nominee for president, but quickly dropped them when Cox said his help was not wanted. Palmer might be "high-minded" and "conscientious," Cox told reporters following him on the campaign trail, "Yet there are matters in his administration [of the Justice Department] which I do not endorse." Candidate Cox no longer considered the Red-baiting A. Mitchell Palmer the face he wanted to show the country.

So Palmer went home to tiny Stroudsburg, Pennsylvania, where he would spend the summer nursing his wounds. Palmer would be only forty-nine years old on leaving the government—plenty of time, he hoped, for another career.

Edgar had no such luxury. As Palmer's protégé, people identified him not only with the man personally but also with his signature exploit, the suddenly unpopular Red Raids. In a few months, Palmer would be gone, and a new administration would take control in Washington. What treatment could Edgar expect to receive under a President James M. Cox or a President Warren G. Harding, both of whom had publicly disavowed his handiwork? The winner would install his own new attorney general with his own friends needing jobs. Edgar could expect nothing better than the fate of any other political hack: to be tossed out the door. That was how the game worked. Being just twenty-five years old, he had to think about his future.

This would have been a good time for him to look for a new job outside the government. And with his experience, Edgar could have made himself an attractive catch to any Washington law firm looking for a go-getter young associate. But if the thought of leaving the Justice Department ever entered his mind, he never pursued it. Work had become his obsession and he now dived in again, working harder than ever.

Recriminations came quickly. Barely a week after Edgar returned from San Francisco, a Senate investigating committee launched hearings into charges that Mitchell Palmer had abused his Justice Department office in running for president. The allegations ranged from influence peddling— releasing federal prisoners, granting pardons, and preventing indictments of large companies in exchange for political favors—to putting campaign aides on the federal payroll, to ordering the Department to wrongly pay travel expenses for officials taking political trips. Senator William Kenyon (R-IA), the committee chairman leading the probe, summoned a Justice Department clerk to Capitol Hill that week and questioned him publicly about dubious travel vouchers he had approved. One of the first names to come up on the list was that of Palmer's young Radical Division chief, Mr. Hoover. "Was there a Red outbreak on the Pacific Coast about that time?" Kenyon asked with a smirk.

Yes, the clerk said, the Department paid Edgar $155.32 in expenses for his June trip to San Francisco after he, the clerk, subtracted for tips Edgar paid to a waiter and to a Pullman porter that he considered excessive.

Edgar learned about this disclosure from a *New York Times* reporter who covered the hearing and called him for a comment. "All I can say is that any inference that I went to San Francisco for political purposes or that the vouchers for my journey were for other than strictly official business is without foundation," he insisted, jumping at the chance to defend himself. "My journey to the west was entirely official. I was engaged wholly in conference with officials of the department on strictly departmental work in connection with the investigation of Red activities." Why did his official business require him to spend three days hanging around a political convention? The reporter never pressed this point, and, true or not, the *New York Times* printed every word of Edgar's explanation. Senator Kenyon never challenged the account, apparently dropping the issue. But Edgar saw the deeper meaning in the attack: his power was being chipped away inch by inch in small, irritating ways.

First went his budget. For the first time in his three-year government career, Edgar found himself strapped for funds and forced to freeze hiring in his office. "I might state that no new appointments are being made, in view of the fact that our appropriation was smaller than we had anticipated," he wrote to one disappointed applicant. Then, the Department made him cancel all his office newspaper subscriptions except for a handful from major cities. In September, they assigned him the distasteful job of examining the budgets of each of the Justice Department solicitors detailed to other government agencies. "In going over the personnel assigned to your office, I note that there is an employee by the name of Mrs. R. G. Walsh, employed as a typist, with compensation at $1,000," he wrote to the Post Office Department's solicitor that month, for instance. "I regret that I find it necessary to dispense with the service of Mrs. Walsh at the present time," he explained, and suggested the solicitor combine her work with that of another typist.

A few weeks later, a Justice Department functionary informed Edgar that his office was being cut off from its newspaper clipping service. "[T]he Department, as far as is known, has authorized no special clipping service for the Radical Division," he said. Even the clerks now assumed Edgar was a short-timer who would soon be out the door.

But instead of letting go, Edgar dug in. He had plans for his bureaucratic empire, and he seemed oblivious to the fact that, in a few months, he might no longer be there to run it. He renamed his office: from the Radical Division, it became the new General Intelligence Division, a loftier title that placed him on a par with the War Department's Military Intelligence. To match this new name, he decreed himself a bigger mandate. As he put it in his 1920 annual report, his new, expanded office would cover "not only ultraradical activities but also the study of matters of an international nature, as well as economic and industrial disturbances incident thereto." Nobody questioned his power grab; he just did it. And Palmer, still the attorney general, backed him.

The Red Raids might be over, but Edgar showed no sign of giving up his spying on anyone in the country whom he considered a possible subversive. His index-card system for tracking suspects ballooned to over 200,000 cards by late 1920 and would reach a mind-boggling 450,000 cards by late 1921. Edgar assigned a staff of specially trained assistants just to handle it on a full-time basis. His office files bulged with photographs and descriptions of thousands of people and material on every known radical group, big and small, foreign and domestic. His bureaus routinely sent agents to take stenographic notes on left-wing speeches and collected 625 newspapers in 26 languages and prepared biographies on hundreds of left-wing authors, publishers, and editors. He received weekly reports from his bureaus across the country that covered the activities not only of local communists but also of Japanese, Mexican, and African-American groups, organizations of World War I veterans, and of liberals like the American Civil Liberties Union.

Edgar ran it all with meticulous care, and pushed even to expand his reach overseas. In July 1920, he worked with the State Department and the International Red Cross to arrange a prisoner swap, offering to release ten Russian immigrants jailed under the Espionage Act in exchange for ten Americans held in Moscow by Soviet authorities. In August, he asked the State Department to investigate an overseas American diplomat in Rotterdam, Holland, accused of supplying false papers to help Bolshevik couriers enter the country. In September, he launched an operation in Mexico aimed at an East Indian man identified only as "Roy" spotted attending a communist meeting in Europe and planning, according to Edgar's sources, "[to] attempt to return to Mexico with funds for agitation in the United States among the negroes."

It became common knowledge that he patrolled the world from his Justice Department office on Vermont Avenue. "That A. Mitchell Palmer, attorney general of the United States, is the head of a vast underground organization of international intelligence agents was learned by Universal Service today through a diplomatic source," the press service reported in mid-August in a dispatch from Paris.

Edgar sat atop it all, and Palmer continued to reward him. In October 1920, a month before Election Day, he gave Edgar another pay raise, from $4,000 to $4,500 per year. Why would he even think of wanting to work anyplace else, or do anything else, other than being boss of his own grand self-created global intelligence machine?

Two hot new books swept the country that summer: *This Side of Paradise* by F. Scott Fitzgerald and Sinclair Lewis's *Main Street*, classics of the emerging Jazz Age. But Edgar had no time for them. His crusade was his life. Instead, he got a copy of the book *Faccia a Faccia col Nemico* ("Face to Face with the Enemy") written by Luigi Galliani, the anarchist leader from Lynn, Massachusetts, whose group had included Andrea Salsedo and Roberto Elia. He requested a copy of *Military Law and Precedents* from Military Intelligence and, from the State Department, twelve copies of the pamphlet "The Jewish Peril" or "Ten Protocols," versions of the discredited but still popular *Protocols of the Elders of Zion*, which Edgar devoured. Even knowing it was a hoax, he found the *Protocols* so fascinating that he asked the State Department to check on whether six particular Bolshevist leaders were in fact Jewish. He collected a photographic history of Bolshevist atrocities compiled by the State Department and shared it with congressmen to use in their anti-Red speeches.

But as he built his empire all that summer, the situation still galled him. The collapse of the deportations and the charges of lawbreaking in the Red Raids had tarred him as a failure. To Edgar, this seemed unfair. Of the 5,000 or so suspected Reds his agents detained between November 1919 and January 1920, only a handful remained in jail. The rest were free now, either by Louis Post's cancellation of their warrants or by the prisoners themselves finally paying bail. Only 591 had been found deportable by the Labor Department and, of these, only a few dozen actually had been shipped overseas since the *Buford* sailed in December 1919, and, unlike Emma Goldman, none to Russia.

Instead, Edgar now found himself being pestered over how to clean up the loose ends. What, for instance, should they do with all the material seized in the raids, not just the tons of confiscated radical literature but also personal items: money, jewelry, small change, photos, and clothing? The fact was, his agents had committed a sizeable amount of petty theft in rounding up suspects, picking pockets, stealing watches, seizing small valuables. "I have several communications from various cities indicating a concerted movement on the part of attorneys for various aliens, making a demand upon the Department for the return of all property, including literature taken," one Department lawyer complained to Edgar that summer. Edgar wanted to keep the radical literature, but fretted that he had no legal basis since the cases had been dropped. He worried about running afoul of the law again. "I would . . . appreciate a suggestion from you as to the advisability of holding the minutes and records of [radical] organizations," he asked one Department lawyer. "I personally can find no authority [for it, and] there is no provision for confiscation or holding of the same, so far as I know."

After weeks of arguing, he finally agreed to donate much of the Red literature to the Library of Congress. His General Intelligence Division kept the rest.

At the same time, though, Edgar saw evidence crossing his desk every day that, by his own narrow yardstick, his Red crackdown had succeeded beyond his most zealous hopes. They had decimated the communist movement in America. Almost every major radical leader of 1919 was in jail, facing charges, living underground, or had been chased from the country. His reign of state terrorism had worked. He had scared the wits out of the communists, driving them into hiding or quitting, at least temporarily. A typical report from Grand Rapids, Michigan, for instance, told him that the Communist Party there was now "very inactive, and I have been advised that they do not hold any meetings at this time." Thirty-six of its fifty-one members had been arrested and, even though only two were deported, the others all kept their heads down and their hands clean. "As a matter of fact, the raids did have a devastating effect on the domestic radical movement," historian Robert K. Murray concluded in the 1950s. "It was true that for many weeks after the government action the radical press ceased its activities and meetings of the Communist organizations were suspended." Benjamin Gitlow saw the effect even from his prison cell in Sing Sing. "These raids were very costly to the movement. They struck at its very heart and terrorized the foreign-born membership. Thousands of members dropped out," Gitlow recalled. Those who remained active went underground, using false names and meeting only in secret.

To Edgar, the fact that literally thousands of innocent people had been swept up in the process, arrested, jailed, and harassed for no legally valid reason, seemed beside the point, a forgettable detail.

Meanwhile, the presidential election unfolding that summer and fall between the two Ohioans, James M. Cox and Warren G. Harding, appeared dull and vacuous. Governor Cox criss-crossed the country giving speeches, traveling 22,000 miles and talking up Woodrow Wilson's League of Nations and other progressive causes. The Republican, Harding, mostly stayed on his front porch in Marion, Ohio, as his campaign pounded the drums of "Back to Normalcy" and "Down With Wilson." The press tried to spice things up with traditional mudslinging. Harding spent much of his time avoiding charges that he had an

African-American ancestor in his family tree. Political enemies circulated thousands of leaflets showing a photograph of the White House
over the caption "Uncle Tom's Cabin?" along with a genealogical chart
tracing Harding's bloodline to a reputed West Indian. When a reporter
cornered Harding on the issue at one point and asked him directly if he
had African blood running in his veins, Harding evaded the question.
"How do I know?" he said. "One of my ancestors may have jumped the
fence." None of the mudslinging against Harding yet mentioned the
names of Nan Britton and Carrie Phillips, two women with whom
Harding later would be accused of having extramarital affairs.

The Socialist Party, for its part, nominated Eugene V. Debs for the fifth
time as its candidate for the presidency. Debs ran his campaign from the
Atlanta prison cell where he was still serving his ten-year sentence for
speaking out against the wartime draft.

For a moment, it looked like the old Red hysteria might erupt all over
again and eclipse the campaign small talk. On September 16, a large
explosion erupted in New York City's financial district, on Wall Street,
just across the sidewalk from the office of mega-banker J. P. Morgan and
a stone's throw from the New York Stock Exchange. Coming just before
noon as office workers flooded the street, it killed twenty-nine people
instantly—mostly clerks, messengers, typists, and neighborhood street
repairmen—sent two hundred more to hospitals, broke windows all
through lower Manhattan, and burned office workers six stories above
street level. At the spot of the explosion, police found only the remains
of a horse and wagon, suggesting a TNT bomb. Mitchell Palmer raced to
New York City along with his Bureau of Investigation chief, Big Bill
Flynn, and together they told newsmen the blast had to be a new radical
attack. Based on what evidence? They had no good answer.

Had this blast occurred at the height of the Red Scare panic a year earlier, Palmer's charges would have carried the day. But not this time. "Capitalism is untouched. The federal government is not shaken in the
slightest degree," the Cleveland Plain Dealer reported, reflecting the prevalent mood. "The public is merely shocked, not terrorized." Instead, people
kept their eye on the political campaign, the bathing beauties, baseball's
World Series (Cleveland's Indians facing Brooklyn's Robins), and the
latest jazz records. Life had become too good, too busy, too interesting to
get caught up in another big scare. The crime itself was never solved.

Election Day came, and Warren Harding won by a landslide. He outpolled James Cox by 16,152,200 to 9,147,353 votes, while Debs got

Wall Street after the September 1920 explosion.

915,000 votes. Republicans trounced Democrats at every level, fattening their majorities in Congress with ten more seats in the Senate and sixty-one more in the House of Representatives. It was the final repudiation. The country wanted no more of Woodrow Wilson, A. Mitchell Palmer, or anyone connected to them.

And where did that leave John Edgar Hoover? Even now, with his fate apparently sealed, Edgar made no apparent effort to look for a new job. Instead, he used his December 1920 Annual Report to Congress to declare the Red Raids a success. He cited an internal report to the Third International meeting in Moscow concluding that the raids had resulted in "the wrecking of the communist parties in this country," and he highlighted his proxy victories in state court prosecutions, singling out "the conviction of 32 members of the Communist Labor Party, including William Bross Lloyd, by the Illinois State authorities." Edgar made the section covering his General Intelligence Division the longest, most detailed part of the entire document. He wanted nobody to miss it. This was his calling card.

And that wasn't all. Before the year was out, Edgar made a point to cross the name of one more top Red off his target list by winning the deportation of Ludwig Martens, the Soviet Envoy to the United States, personally arguing the case in front of Labor Secretary William B. Wilson. By this time, December 1920, Great Britain, France, Italy, and Germany all had opened commercial ties with the new Bolshevik regime. But America had not. In the United States, foreign policy was being run not by diplomats in the State Department, but by Palmer and his Red fighters. Ironically, Martens, in his deportation hearing, was represented by Thomas Hardwick, the former United States senator from Georgia whose home in Atlanta had been the first to receive a bomb sent by anarchists through the mail, in May 1919. Its explosion had blown off the hands of his housemaid and caused an early spike in anti-Red hysteria. Hardwick as a lawyer now represented not only Ludwig Martins but a host of other communists as well. Still, voters in Georgia had elected him governor in November 1920 in a hard-fought contest where Hardwick's Red connections were thoroughly aired. He won anyway. Voters just didn't care enough anymore about Red leanings in a politician or in anyone else.

When Ludwig Martens left the country in January 1921 for his trip back to Russia, he took with him his entire staff and their families, closed the door of the Soviet Bureau, and turned over his portfolio to lawyer Charles Recht, who became as close to an ambassador as Russia would have in the United States until 1933 when President Franklin D. Roosevelt finally granted formal diplomatic recognition to the Soviet regime.

But Washington was not done yet with A. Mitchell Palmer. The election was over, but Congress decided in December 1920 to come back to town for a lame duck session. Palmer would have to confront one last enemy before being allowed to walk away quietly. And for one last time, he would need young John Edgar Hoover to pull him through.

· 49 ·
WALSH

S ENATOR THOMAS J. WALSH, Democrat from Montana, had always
liked Mitchell Palmer. After the June 1919 bombing of Palmer's
house, Walsh was one of the first to show up and help him, telling
friends he had no sympathy, as he put it, for "the murderous acts of
scoundrels who profess to represent the laboring men of the country [and]
whose conduct is calculated to bring the legitimate labor organizations
into disrepute." Walsh happily joined Palmer in defending his drive to
crush radical agitation in late 1919 and early 1920, even at the cost of
limiting free speech. "If you care to address me further on this subject I
am going to ask you what you would do about the circulation of literature
. . . in which murder and assassination are counseled for the purpose of
accomplishing what is described as revolution?" he asked home state
critics. "I am very sure there are no farmers and very few workmen who
are advocating or advising the overthrow of our government by force or
violence, by murder and assassination, or by physical injury to property,"
he told others.

But Thomas Walsh was no yes-man. A United States senator since 1913, Walsh represented Montana, a rugged mining state, and he kept himself at arm's length from the state's largest political Goliath, the Anaconda Copper Company. Walsh often sided with miners in disputes with it, and he publicly condemned the 1917 lynching of I.W.W. organizer Frank Little by company-backed vigilantes. "Walsh was no backslapper.

He neither smoked nor drank, and his humor was very dry and rarely expressed," his Montana colleague Burton K. Wheeler said of him.

By late 1920, Senator Walsh had second thoughts about Palmer's Red Raids. As the senior Democrat on the Senate subcommittee that oversaw the Justice Department, Walsh followed the Raids closely, and they began to remind him of how the Anaconda Copper Company bullied its workers back home in Montana. He read the charges of violence and lawbreaking by Justice Department agents presented by the National Popular Government League in its Twelve Lawyer report, and he found them alarming.

Senator Thomas J. Walsh of Montana.

Where was Congress in this affair, he asked? Why hadn't the Senate spoken up on it? Walsh tracked the House Rules Committee impeachment hearings on Louis Post and was incredulous that the Rules Committee members refused to take a stand or ask any questions about what went on inside the Justice Department itself.

So on December 10, 1920, four weeks after the presidential election, Senator Tom Walsh decided to start his own investigation. He mounted the floor of the United States Senate, presented a copy of the Twelve Lawyer report and asked that it be referred to the Senate Judiciary Committee for action. Nobody objected. "[E]ven the most conscienceless and blood thirsty murderer has rights under the law," Walsh insisted, "even bolshevists and anarchists have certain rights under the law."

That done, Walsh got in touch with Judson King, the National Popular

Government League's executive director, and asked for his help. King was delighted. He contacted Felix Frankfurter's Harvard Law School colleague, Zechariah Chafee, who promptly agreed to come to Washington to testify at any upcoming hearing and then prepared for Walsh an eight-page digest of Justice Department lawbreaking. Others of the Twelve Lawyers volunteered to testify as well, including former Philadelphia federal prosecutor Francis Fisher Kane and Washington University Law School dean Tyrrel Williams, both signers of the original report. Then, a few weeks later, King presented Senator Walsh with a fiery new document approved by his Twelve Lawyer committee, this time taking Palmer's June 1920 testimony before the House Rules Committee and knocking it down point by point. "The present Attorney General will soon relinquish office, but the precedent he has set will remain," it argued. Walsh agreed. If Palmer and his Justice Department actually did all the things they were accused of, then Palmer deserved impeachment, maybe even prison, and so would any future attorney general who followed his example. Palmer's sins had to be exposed.

And so on January 19, 1921, A. Mitchell Palmer, with only six weeks left in office, came marching once again up to Capitol Hill to answer for his role in launching the Red Raids.

The Senate Judiciary Subcommittee met in a snug corner suite on the ground floor of the Capitol Building just down a small staircase from the Senate chamber with windows facing down Pennsylvania Avenue toward the White House, an expanse of pretty green lawn in the foreground with trees whose naked branches trembled in the January wind. The senators sat at a long, polished wood table beneath cut-glass chandeliers, arched ceilings, and oil paintings of stern-faced former members. Palmer showed little of his normal good humor—the shoulder slapping and wise-cracking—as he threaded his way past familiar faces of newsmen and politicos, taking his place opposite the senators. He brought a full entourage of Justice Department brass with him, including three assistant attorneys general and the head of the Department's criminal bureau, but they were only window-dressing. The only one Palmer really needed, the one he planted in a chair at his side for everyone in the room to see and notice, was Edgar.

Three United States senators sat looking at Palmer from across the table that morning: Walsh, the lone Democrat, and Republicans Thomas Sterling of South Dakota and William E. Borah of Idaho. Sterling, the subcommittee's chairman, quickly handed the gavel across the table to

his Montana friend. "Proceed, Mr. Walsh," he said. Walsh, a tall, digni-
fied man with black hair, narrow eyes, and a thick mustache with curls at
the tips, started in directly. "I would like to ask some questions of the
attorney general with respect to certain matters referred to the Subcommittee," he explained, raising a copy of the Twelve Lawyer report and
laying it on the table between them. Then he extended Palmer a courtesy. "Is there anything that you care to add concerning the matter, and
what was there said?"

"Mr. Chairman, I made a full statement before the Committee on
Rules of the House of Representatives in answer to all the allegations
contained in the so-called report referred to, on or about the 1st of June
1920," Palmer said, as if this entire hearing were unnecessary and just a
waste of everyone's time. "I should like to say . . . that the time has come
when we need something more than blind allegations and assertions by
this self-constituted committee of lawyers." The charges against him were
lies and sour grapes from nobody but lawyers who represented communists, he insisted, a one-sided group with an axe to grind, and based on
uncorroborated claims that he and his colleagues had denied already. "I
have nothing to go on but the reports of Department of Justice agents,
carefully selected men who have sworn to abide by the law and tell the
truth," he told the senators. "I believe the agent. I have no difficulty
about it whatever."

But that wasn't all. Palmer demanded his own investigation. If these
Twelve Lawyers had any new charges to raise against him, let them show
their cards. "Bring in witnesses of this volunteer committee who have
misrepresented the Department of Justice here," he insisted. "That is the
fair, honest and proper thing to do, to bring them here and get the facts."

If Palmer seemed impatient with this revival of the whole affair—these
senators, these old allegations, this new investigation—he had other things
on his mind. Palmer was spending his final weeks as attorney general grap-
pling with a new headache, the thorniest police issue facing the country in
early 1921: Prohibition. The law banning sale and production of alcoholic
drink, in effect since January 1920—a full year now—was causing nightmares for law enforcement across the country. Ordinary Americans bristled
at suddenly being denied their right to a glass of whiskey or a mug of beer.
Violations became so widespread that, already, the Feds had logged over
17,000 Prohibition-related arrests and prosecutions, and the Coast Guard
complained of being outclassed by rumrunners in small, fast boats slipping
booze across the water from the Bahamas and Canada.

Palmer, the stern Fighting Quaker when it came to Reds, had little sympathy with Prohibition. Instead, in his last days in office, he spent his time scouring the statute books trying to find any possible loophole to allow those who wanted a drink to get one. In December 1920, he ruled that the law did not forbid a citizen from enjoying the apple cider he'd made and then consumed at home, even after it became intoxicating from fermentation. A few weeks later, in early 1921, he exploited a gap in the law to create an exemption for doctors to prescribe unlimited amounts of beer or wine for medicinal purposes, served by a pharmacist, opening the door, as Palmer himself put it, to "beer at the [drugstore] soda fountain, but never again beer over the saloon bar." Brewers cheered, but his decision prompted howls from the Anti-Saloon League.

Palmer was also making an effort that month to win the release of Eugene V. Debs from his prison cell in Atlanta, hoping to end his tenure on a high note by taking credit for this one act of postwar, post–Red Scare reconciliation. Palmer argued the case in a cabinet meeting and sent Woodrow Wilson a formal recommendation for a pardon in January 1921. "Debs is now approaching 65 years of age," he wrote the president. "If not adequately, he has surely been severely punished." But Wilson sent his recommendation back with a terse note: "Denied. W. W."

Otherwise, Palmer mostly concentrated on dodging attacks. He still faced charges over his presidential campaign tactics from 1920, his sweetheart deals as wartime Alien Property Custodian, and his intervention in the 1919 coal strike. He hoped to lie low for just two more months, until March 5, when he could walk away from office. His strategy mostly worked, except for the one controversy that had now dragged him back to Capitol Hill for one more round of hearings: the Red Raids.

Palmer already faced lawsuits brought against him by families of two raid victims who died in custody: Mike Marzinik, a prisoner arrested in New Jersey dead from pneumonia while jailed on Ellis Island awaiting his hearing, and Andrea Salsedo, the suspect who jumped to his death from the Justice Department's fourteenth-floor office in its Park Row building in lower Manhattan. Between the two, these suits demanded Palmer personally pay $450,000 in compensation.

Now, sitting before Senator Walsh and his subcommittee, Palmer had barely started talking, telling his side of the story, when the senators began peppering him with questions. Palmer no longer scared people. Having lost his bid for the presidency, followed by his party's loss of the election, he no longer had the means to threaten anyone. Thomas Sterling, the seventy-year-old chairman, himself a one-time prosecutor in the gun-slinging Dakota Territory of the 1880s, broke in to ask Palmer how he had coordinated the January 1920 raids with the Labor Department. When Palmer explained that he had reached an agreement with them, Senator Borah interrupted. "Was the understanding agreeable to the Department of Labor?"

It certainly was, Palmer insisted. And more: "Our written instructions [to field agents]—which I shall leave here with you—were that no arrests should be made without warrants, that no seizure or search should be made without a warrant," a statement directly at odds with the charges in the Twelve Lawyer report.

Sterling broke in again, noting the discrepancy. "Who issued the warrants?" he asked. "The Commissioner General of Immigration?"

Palmer seemed confused at the question. Perhaps he had no patience any longer for people interrupting him, even senators. Either way, he looked quizzically to his side, to Edgar. "It was the Secretary of Labor, was it not?" he asked.

"The Secretary of Labor," Edgar spoke up, sitting straight in his chair, finishing Palmer's thought with no wasted words or embellishments, his face a study in earnest attention.

Sterling pressed on. "Who first decides whether a person should be deported?"

Palmer again looked to his side. Again, Edgar spoke up, his voice as loud as Palmer's if an octave higher and squeakier. "The Inspector of Immigration is the first. A hearing is held before the immigration inspector, who then makes a report to the inspector general of immigration, and the case is then forwarded." Edgar showed no hesitation in talking to these powerful men, despite the tension in the room. In every sense, he had just as much at stake in this hearing as Palmer. Edgar had his own reputation to protect and was glad to make his presence heard. He was defending his future. Besides, he knew the ground rules here. They were all actors on a stage, both he and the senators, and he stuck to his role, the helpful assistant to the beleaguered witness, self-effacing and polite, ready to speak only when spoken to, confident and knowledgeable.

Palmer took the lead again and began describing to the senators how the January 2 raid had been an organizational marvel, a coordinated nationwide operation where his men executed warrants in dozens of cities simultaneously to maximize surprise. He explained how 3,000 warrants were placed in the hands of inspectors, how they rounded up the suspects, overwhelmingly aliens with only a handful of inadvertent exceptions. "Of course, when it was discovered that [any] were citizens, they were promptly released," Palmer said. And where the agents lacked a warrant for a particular suspect, they simply asked for one by telegraph.

This last point again raised eyebrows across the table. This use of after-the-fact warrants by telegraph again seemed to contradict what Palmer had just said a minute earlier. "Were any of these people detained in custody for any considerable length of time who were arrested without warrants?" Senator Borah broke in.

Palmer chose his words to paint the rosiest possible picture. "Not for any considerable length of time," he explained. "These arrests were made in the nighttime, and they were held awaiting the result of a telegraphic request for a warrant, and if the warrant did not come they were released." In this brief sentence, Palmer had utterly rewritten history, erasing from memory all the logistical nightmares Edgar had wrestled with during the weeks after the raids, the hellhole detention centers on Boston's Deer Island and in Detroit's Federal Building, the monthlong backlogs in obtaining warrants, the midnight dragnet arrests of innocent bystanders, the immigrants held for weeks waiting for initial hearings, the dropped cases, the missing evidence, the thefts of property, and all the rest. Then Palmer turned to his young assistant at his side who knew these ugly truths better than anyone else. "We had more warrants that night than we made arrests, did we not?"

This question was a wild distortion of reality, but Palmer was asking him to verify it. Edgar didn't flinch. "Yes, sir," he agreed.

Senator Walsh next took the lead in asking questions and turned immediately to Palmer's assertion that he had instructed his agents to get search warrants. He pointed to the very same sets of instructions that Palmer had laid on the table a few minutes earlier and noted that, when one actually read them, they told agents to obtain search warrants *only* at their own discretion and *only* "where necessary" or "where absolutely necessary"—a very different matter. Walsh then mentioned two documented, eyewitness accounts of abusive arrests and roughing up of suspects.

Palmer again seemed flustered. He grew indignant. "I do not think that you ought to impute to the attorney general a violation of law which justifies his impeachment, and all that kind of thing, because some zealous officers exceeded their authority, or exceeded the law in the prosecution of offenses." This was the only time during the entire day when anyone breathed the word "impeachment," and it had to cause a stir coming, as it did, from Palmer's own lips.

But Walsh wasn't finished. "How many search warrants were issued?" he asked Palmer.

"I cannot tell you, Senator, personally," he answered. Then Palmer gestured again to his side. "If you would like to ask Mr. Hoover, who was in charge of this matter, he can tell you." This, too, was an odd evasion. Was Palmer denying his responsibility, trying to blame an underling for an apparent foul-up? It was the first and only time he ever stated publicly that Edgar was "in charge" of the operation, though it came as no surprise to anyone in the room.

Senator Walsh looked across the table at the bright young man. "Yes?" he said.

Edgar drew himself forward as the senators, the newspapermen, and his Justice Department colleagues all turned to watch him. But unfortunately, for this moment in the spotlight, Edgar had no idea what the answer to Senator Walsh's question actually was. He started to dance. "The search warrants were entirely a matter which the agent in charge of local offices handled," he said.

"You have no record of that at all?"

"No, sir," Edgar said.

"You know nothing at all about it?"

"No, sir."

Walsh had cornered him, almost by accident. There had been no direct demand from Washington for search warrants in the January raids, and Edgar had no way to deny it short of lying outright. To Edgar's mind at the time, in January 1920, it was not clear that the law even demanded them in deportation cases. "Do you really know whether a search warrant ever was issued at all or not?" Walsh asked.

"Yes; I have been advised of many cases where search warrants were obtained."

"Do you know how many searches were made without a search warrant?"

"I do not."

"Do you know that any were made without a search warrant?"

"No sir; I do not."

It was the first time, and perhaps the only time in his life, that Edgar had allowed himself to be trapped this way in public, forced to admit being ignorant of facts central to his operation. Arguably, he had just acknowledged widespread illegality by his own agents acting under his orders.

Senator Walsh turned back to Palmer to quiz him more about his statutory authorities. Then later that morning, he led Edgar down another line of questions about the procedure he used to obtain warrants by telegraph. Edgar this time managed to sidestep the issue by explaining that most of the warrants used by Justice Department agents were issued in advance, not by telegraph, another half-truth hiding plenty of dirty laundry.

He would spend all that morning and afternoon seated next to Palmer being grilled by Walsh and the other senators. At the end of that long day, Walsh let Palmer go, but he announced that his subcommittee was far from finished with this topic. Next, it would call as witnesses several of the lawyers who signed the National Popular Government League's report, starting with Zechariah Chafee from Harvard University Law School. Palmer and Edgar left the room without facing any more questions that day, but they knew they could be called back at any time.

Senator Walsh, for his part, ended the hearing concerned about the mixed outcome. He, too, had a problem and didn't know what to do about it. He had thrown Palmer off guard by pinning him down on his warrantless searches and challenging his half-truths, but Palmer had thrown a damaging counterpunch. When he claimed that the charges against him were biased, he had a point. Every one of the twelve lawyers who signed the National Popular Government League report had some axe to grind. Either they had represented leftists or publicly criticized the raids at the time: Felix Frankfurter and Zechariah Chafee had appeared in the Boston *habeas corpus* trial, Jackson Ralston had counseled Louis Post before the House Rules Committee, Swinburne Hale had argued the Communist Labor Party's case in its deportation hearing, and so on down the list. None could honestly claim true neutrality.

To pin Palmer down once and for all, Walsh needed to find at least one distinguished lawyer willing to come forward with totally clean hands, someone who had never represented communists, anarchists, or labor leaders, whose independence could not be questioned. He raised the problem with Judson King and Jackson Ralston. They talked it over and came up with an idea. Ralston sent a message around this time to Columbia University Law School in New York City. He addressed it to the dean, Harlan Fiske Stone.

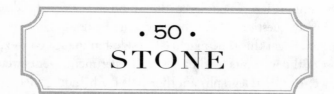

· 50 ·
STONE

HARLAN FISKE STONE had not signed the Twelve Lawyer report. Apparently, nobody ever bothered to ask him. Stone rarely jumped on bandwagons, and he never showed much sympathy for Reds. Big and physical, over six feet tall with wide hands and bushy eyebrows, Harlan Stone was an outdoorsman who loved to hike and fish, though he was an academic at heart. Stone spent his childhood on a farm in New Hampshire, but he hated farming and was expelled by the Massachusetts Agricultural College. After graduating from Amherst, he finally made his home in New York City. He came to New York's Columbia University Law School as a student in 1895, graduated, and became a lecturer, then a professor, then dean, the post he'd held ever since. His legal scholarship won him a perch at the top of the city's legal intelligentsia and made his textbook *Law and Its Administration* a popular standard. Rather than venturing into politics, he used his energy to champion better salaries for professors, better access for students to university libraries, and improvements to the law school's building, Kent Hall. He expanded student enrollment at Columbia and raised the school's stature by luring top professors from Yale, Michigan, and Harvard, and winning new research endowments.

Stone spoke like an academic, too. "When he talks to you he takes off his pince-nez and poises them on the thumb of his right hand," a reporter wrote of him around this time, "and while he talks he never seems to move."

But despite this preoccupation with the academy, Harlan Stone lived in no ivory tower. He experienced the paranoid hysteria of his time. In 1918, Stone had been forced to help his own brother, Winthrop, president of Indiana's Purdue University, defend himself from charges of disloyalty to the country, the kind that could sink careers and reputations. The army had set up World War I training camps on Purdue's campus, and Stone's

Harlan Fiske Stone, with fishing gear, circa 1924.

brother made the mistake of arguing with an army officer over his budget and use of facilities. The officer accused Winthrop Stone of showing contempt for the military, prompting a formal loyalty investigation. Winthrop Stone had to produce dozens of sworn statements from friends, local military officials, and faculty colleagues at Purdue vouching for his patriotism, despite the fact that he had two sons serving in the army and a brother, Lawson Stone, working as a scientist developing gas warfare weapons.

During World War I, as young men went off to the army and enrollment at Columbia University Law School fell by a third, Harlan Stone left the school to take on a special assignment from President Woodrow Wilson. Some four thousand draftees in the army had defied orders and refused to fight, citing religious or moral grounds. The army had no system to deal with these conscientious objectors. Stone's job, as part of a three-man commission, was to weed out the slackers and draft dodgers in this group. He traveled across the country and interviewed hundreds of these young pacifists, many of them already serving sentences in the federal penitentiary in Leavenworth, Kansas. He often urged them to reconsider. One of the draftees he met, a thirty-year-old Tennessean named Alvin C. York, did agree to put aside his religious qualms and became America's most decorated soldier in World War I, Sergeant York. Stone and his commission ultimately convinced some 1,300 others to accept noncombatant service in back offices or military hospitals. They recommended court-martial and prison for only 404 of the rest. But throughout this process, Harlan Stone never showed any sympathy for those who refused to fight solely because they claimed to be socialists, radicals, or anarchists who considered the World War an assault by capitalism against the working class. They might be sincere, but to Stone they remained "the loose-thinking, wild-talking agitator whose dream is a world in chaos that a new Utopia may arise on its ruins," as he put it later. For them, he insisted on "firm but impartial adherence to the law." That usually meant prison.

Even so, the Palmer Raids struck a nerve. Stone recoiled at the turmoil he witnessed around him in New York City. After the January 1920 raids, he complained to friends about rowdy police and out-of-control federal agents. "[I]t strengthens the opinion which I have always held that the power to interfere with the liberty of the individual should never be committed to administrative officers without some provision for review of their action by the courts," he wrote to Columbia University president Nicholas Murray Butler. Stone never spoke about it publicly, though, despite having plenty of chances. In mid-January 1920, Stone joined Charles Evans Hughes, the former United States Supreme Court justice and 1916 Republican candidate for president of the United States, in pressing the New York City Bar Association to denounce the state legislature in Albany for its action expelling its five elected Socialist assemblymen. A few months later, in April 1920, when a fight broke out at a legal conference Stone was attending over a proposal to ban socialists from attending law schools in New York State, he skirted the issue. He opposed the proposal, but he kept his point narrow, arguing that it was too political and would turn the expelled students into martyrs.

Otherwise, he held his tongue, at least in public. Unlike Felix Frankfurter at Harvard, there is no record of professors from Columbia University Law School volunteering to intervene in the legal proceedings against suspected Reds then flooding the courtrooms of lower Manhattan. As a result, Harlan Stone had every reason to be surprised when he received an urgent message in late January 1921 from lawyer Jackson Ralston, representing the National Popular Government League in Washington, D.C., asking him to come to Washington and testify before Senator Walsh's subcommittee against Mitchell Palmer and the raids.

Stone had little to gain by joining this fight. By now, in January 1921, the raids were over, the prisoners mostly freed, and Palmer would soon leave office, but that didn't lessen the risk. Hatred against Reds and anyone connected to them still ran high in America. For Stone to make headlines over it could easily attract enemies and slanders. His own trustees at Columbia University might protest, maybe threaten his academic agenda or even his tenure. This had happened before. One professor at Columbia, named J. McKeen Cattell, had been fired by the university for writing pacifist letters to Congress during the World War. The fact that he also participated in war-related research didn't save him.

Harlan Stone, though, had a careful way of going about things, a calm confidence, and a clear enough sense of right and wrong to shrug off these concerns. He doubtless checked first with Columbia University president Nicholas Murray Butler; then he told Ralston that, yes, he would come. Perhaps he wanted to do it all along and was just waiting to be asked.

Stone planned to travel to Washington for the hearing on Thursday, January 27, 1921, a day devoted entirely to testimony by members of the Twelve Lawyer committee—Zechariah Chafee, Jackson Ralston, and Ernst Freund by letter. But he canceled at the last minute, forcing the subcommittee to adjourn early. When the next hearing day came, Tuesday, February 1, Stone again failed to appear.

What was the problem? There is no indication that Stone had gotten cold feet or deliberately tried to dodge his date with the senators. Instead, far from anything to do with radicals or communists, Harlan Stone had gotten himself embroiled that month in yet another time-consuming fight, this time over a plan he was pushing to force the New York City Bar Association to tighten its rules and require that lawyers attend at least one year of college before joining the profession to represent clients. "New York is more solicitous for the health of its horses and dogs than the preservation of the rights of its citizens," he chided fellow lawyers at one of the meetings on the topic, pointing to a litany of complaints he'd heard about unqualified and unethical attorneys. The conflict over the plan raged all that winter, tying Stone to his desk.

Whether it was this alone, or something as simple as bad winter weather or a last-minute cold, Stone realized that he would not be able to make the trip and decided instead to commit his thoughts to paper. As a result, when Senator Sterling banged his gavel to convene the subcommittee that day, February 1, 1920, Jackson Ralston sat in the witness chair ready to proceed. "Mr. Chairman, we were in hopes that Dean Stone, head of the law school of Columbia University of New York, could be here this morning, but he has informed us that it is impossible, but he sent this note, which with your permission I will read."

Harlan Stone had boiled down his thoughts to a single page devoid of rhetorical flourish, and Ralston proceeded to read it aloud for the senators and newspaper reporters crammed into the small room on Capitol Hill. "It appears by the public admissions of the attorney general and otherwise that he has proceeded on the theory that aliens are not entitled to the constitutional guarantee of due process of law [and] aliens have been deprived of such constitutional guarantees. It also appears that the agents of the Department of Justice in violation of the express provisions of the statute have arrested aliens in deportation cases without warrants." It was that simple. Laws existed, along with requirements in the Constitution, and the attorney general had ignored them.

That, by itself, was the crux of the matter. But Stone went on. To his eye, Palmer's raids were a product of a regime gone wild for lack of discipline. "It is inevitable that any system which confers upon administrative officers power to restrain the liberty of individuals, without safeguards substantially like those which exist in criminal cases, and without adequate authority for judicial review of the actions of such administrative officers will result in abuse of power and in intolerable injustice and cruelty to individuals." He ended with these words, leaving the implication clear: abuse of power by unaccountable subordinates without legal safeguards leading to human misery—that was exactly what had happened here.

Ralston finished reading Harlan Stone's paper in just a few minutes, and the subcommittee consumed the rest of its day in detailed testimony from lawyers in the thick of the action from January 1920: Francis Fisher Kane, Charles Recht, among others. But Stone had made his mark. Of all the witnesses, Stone alone had no dog in this fight, no record of representing leftists, no question of credentials. He was the unbiased referee, and he had blown the whistle on the raids, ruling them clearly out of bounds. A. Mitchell Palmer had no more excuses.

By the time Palmer came back to them, four weeks had passed since his first appearance before the Senate Judiciary Subcommittee in its small room in the Capitol Building. Two weeks remained in Woodrow Wilson's presidency. Wilson already had hosted his entire cabinet for a farewell visit and posed with them all around the cabinet table for a final group photograph. Wilson had been awarded the Nobel Peace Prize for his work negotiating the Versailles Treaty, despite his failure to win ratification for it in his own country.

Palmer by now had announced his own plans to leave the Justice Department as soon as Wilson's term ended. He intended to open a small law office in Washington and to spend more time with his wife, Roberta, at their second home in rural Pennsylvania.

Had he wanted to, Palmer easily could have blown off this final hearing on the Red Raids, sending a deputy like Frank Garvan or Bill Flynn to take his place before the judiciary subcommittee, and spared himself the aggravation. But Palmer had followed the testimony presented to Senator Walsh over the past few weeks, all of which painted him the heartless villain. He had Edgar prepare responses to as many of the specifics as possible, but, beyond that, Palmer had some things to get off his chest. He wanted to clear the air, and this was his last chance. Once he left office in two weeks, nobody would listen to him anymore.

"Mr. Chairman, I am sorry to be compelled to go to the trouble of replying at some length and in some detail to the statements made by varying witnesses who have appeared before your committee, chiefly lawyers, in most cases counsel for some of the persons arrested for deportations," he began that day, Wednesday, February 16. He used the qualification "in most cases" to avoid any mention of the name of the glaring, fatal exception to his point: Harlan Fiske Stone.

This time, instead of his top brass, Palmer brought along Frank Stone and George Kelleher, the special agents who ran his bureau offices and led the raids in Boston and Newark, and, of course, he brought Edgar. With Edgar at his side, Palmer spent hours presenting mountains of affidavits, transcripts, and file memos, trying to convince the senators that his own hands were clean. He repeated his blanket denials and criticized the subcommittee for listening to the lawyers he claimed were biased. Then he introduced Kelleher and Stone so they could tell their own stories. But it made little difference, like talking to a brick wall. The senators and the newspapermen, like most people across the country, had made up their minds by now.

By Friday, February 18, his last day in the witness chair, Mitchell Palmer was slouched, his face heavy with fatigue. He spoke like a man abandoned by time, a walking anachronism. Instead of answering specific charges, he found himself exasperated at having to remind these senators of the whole point behind his anti-Red crusade, a crusade they once supported, launched just eighteen months earlier, in June 1919, the morning after Anarchist Fighters had exploded a bomb in his home. "How soon we do forget!" he told them. The country was in crisis then. "[We] had just passed through a steel strike and a coal strike of great magnitude [in which] leaflets were distributed by the communist parties urging the workers to rise up and seize not only the shops in which they worked, but also the government, and stating to the workers that they must control the State power, the police and the army."

"At that time, in 1919 . . . I say that I was shouted at from every editorial sanctum in America from sea to sea; I was preached upon from every pulpit; I was urged—I could feel it dinned into my ears—throughout the country to do something and do it now and do it quick and do it in a way that would bring results to stop this sort of thing in the United States," he continued. "I accept responsibility for carrying out that policy. . . . I apologize for nothing that the Department of Justice has done in this matter. I glory in it. I point with pride and enthusiasm to the results of that work; and if, as I said, some of my agents out in the field, or some of the agents of the Department of Labor, were a little rough or unkind, or short and curt, with these alien agitators whom they observed seeking to destroy their homes, their religion, and their country, I think, it might well be overlooked in the general good to the country which has come from it. That is all I have to say." With that, Palmer ended his defense.

Just before adjourning the hearing, Senator Walsh turned one last time to Palmer's young assistant. "I would like to have Mr. Hoover tell us about that Rule 22," he said, referring to the Labor Department's deportation procedure that required inspectors to tell suspects of their right to have a lawyer present at the beginning of a hearing, the provision that was secretly changed in December 1919 just before the big January raids. Edgar used the opportunity for one last big evasion. "Now, in as far as the Department of Justice is concerned in the change in Rule 22, it had no part in it whatsoever," he declared. "The rule was changed at the instance of the immigration officers." No matter that Edgar had pushed, cajoled, and pressured them for weeks to change Rule 22, complaining to Caminetti that Red-leaning lawyers had gummed up the works on Ellis Island and had to be stopped. The Labor Department signed the papers, so it was all their fault, he insisted. He had nothing to do with it.

"That is all I care for," Senator Walsh said.

The hearing ended right after that, and Palmer walked out of the sub-committee room satisfied at having explained himself to the country. He could now retire with some measure of peace. There would be no impeachment and no official denunciation of Palmer for his role in the Red Raids. He had stood his ground. Edgar, too, walked out of the room trailing along at Palmer's side carrying the notebooks and briefcases for his boss the way that staff assistants do. He, too, had some satisfaction in the moment; he had been loyal to the end.

· 51 ·
SURVIVOR

WHEN WOODROW WILSON left the White House on Inauguration Day, 1921, he was a crippled man. Walking with a cane, his face gaunt and hair gray, he had to be physically lifted into the back seat of his open limousine next to President-Elect Warren G. Harding for the ceremonial ride up Pennsylvania Avenue. Along the way, he and Harding talked about animals. Harding, feeling nervous, mentioned his fondness for elephants based on his sister's having lived in Siam as a missionary, where she owned one as a pet. When Harding said he always wanted to own one himself, Wilson shot back, "I hope it won't turn out to be a white elephant." On reaching the Capitol Building, Wilson had to be pushed in a wheelchair from the car to a freight elevator that carried him up to the foyer where senators had gathered. One of the first he met here was Henry Cabot Lodge, the foreign relations chairman who had embarrassed him a year earlier by blocking ratification of his League of Nations. "Well, the Senate threw me down before, and I don't want to fall down myself now," Wilson joked.

After signing a few papers, he told Harding that he was fatigued and could not stay for the ceremony. Instead, when time came for Harding to step outside into the sunlight and take the oath of office, Woodrow Wilson left quietly through a side door and rode off to the new home he had purchased in Washington, D.C., at 2340 S Street NW, where he planned to live out his final years.

So ended the presidency of Woodrow Wilson. Warren G. Harding became president that day with an inaugural speech almost entirely forgotten but for the fact that a new contraption, an electric voice amplifier, allowed the crowd outside the Capitol Building to hear its every forgettable syllable. Four years later, on the next Inauguration Day, in 1925, Harding and Wilson would both be dead, Harding's presidency disgraced by the Teapot Dome scandal. Calvin Coolidge would take the oath of office and deliver a speech likewise forgotten but for the fact that it, too, was carried by a new contraption, radio, allowing people all across the country to hear its every forgettable syllable.

Woodrow Wilson and Warren G. Harding riding together
to Harding's 1921 inauguration.

By then, the Roaring Twenties would be in full swing and J. Edgar Hoover would have started his forty-eight-year reign as director of the Bureau of Investigation.

For Edgar, it was a stunning turnaround. To get that job, he had to survive first the Harding takeover, then Teapot Dome, then the reformers.

He managed all three. Presidents came and went; he could work for one just as well as another. Edgar had set his career gyroscope for life. He would not leave the Justice Department till the day he died fifty-one years later in 1972.

As the new president, Warren Harding replaced A. Mitchell Palmer with a new attorney general, his close friend and campaign manager, Harry Daugherty. Daugherty, given the chance, managed to transform the Department of Justice into a brothel of scandal beyond anything seen before or since.

Daugherty, a lawyer and state Republican wire-puller, had first gotten to know Harding back when Harding was publisher of the *Marion Star* of small-town Marion, Ohio. He saw the talent and appeal in his handsome friend. Harding by then had already won a race for lieutenant governor in 1904 and lost one for governor in 1910. Daugherty helped him win again in 1914, this time a race for United States senator. By 1920, Daugherty recognized that Harding could well make himself the next president, and he appointed himself his friend's chief strategist. "I was no amateur at the task which I faced," Daugherty bragged years later. It was Daugherty who created the myth of the smoke-filled room that sealed Harding's 1920 nomination. Asked by reporters in February 1920 how he thought the Republican convention would play out, Daugherty told them: "Well, boys, I'll tell ya what I think. The convention will be deadlocked. After the other candidates have failed, we'll get together in some hotel room, oh, about 2:11 in the morning, and some 15 men, bleary-eyed with lack of sleep, will sit down around a big table. When that time comes, Senator Harding will be selected."

When such a late-night meeting actually did occur in Chicago that summer, Harding was invited to it, and he won the nomination the next day. Political reporters deemed Harry Daugherty a genius and a prophet.

The scandals came a year later, after an initial honeymoon. Daugherty seemed at first a breath of fresh air to a Justice Department exhausted from the Mitchell Palmer days. Daugherty pledged to hire the best people, perhaps even keeping a few Democratic jobholders. In his first few months, he helped orchestrate Harding's pardon of Eugene V. Debs, freeing the venerable Socialist presidential candidate from his Atlanta prison cell in December 1921 after three years behind bars. Daugherty also promised to reorganize the Bureau of Investigation. For this, he hired as its new director an old friend from Ohio, former Secret Service chief and longtime private detective William J. Burns. Burns, a cigar always in

Harry Daugherty, the new Attorney General.

his mouth and a wisecrack at the ready, ran a detective agency with a long checkered record—strike-breaking, jury tampering, and burglary. But this was par for the course, and Burns, too, announced a handful of showy reforms in his first few weeks, including plans to set up a master fingerprint file in Washington, D.C., and a new training school for agent recruits.

Edgar had no hesitation at first about jumping on board with this new crew. He launched a full charm offensive in early 1921, constantly finding ways to impress the new chiefs, especially Daugherty. Everyone in the building knew Edgar as Mitchell Palmer's protégé and anticommunist bulldog, but Edgar found ways to sidestep all this. He repackaged himself for the new regime. Since he lived in Washington, D.C., and was never allowed to vote in elections anyway, he took advantage of this fact and declared himself to be above politics, a professional nuts-and-bolts manager who could run the office and fight crime. Edgar had discovered the art of making himself useful, and soon indispensable—a talent he would practice more effectively than any single other American official of the twentieth century.

Edgar worked long hours and volunteered for assignments. And he had lots of friends happy to vouch for him, congressmen and

William J. Burns, new director of the Bureau of Investigation.

senators, Republican and Democrat alike, plus his contacts in the State Department and Military Intelligence. Harry Daugherty could barely step outside his office to visit Capitol Hill or the War Department without someone tugging his sleeve to tell him about that bright young man in his office, that Mr. Hoover—so competent, hardworking, and dedicated.

Then Edgar played his trump card. Harry Daugherty had no visible interest before coming to Washington in communists or Bolsheviks or the Red Menace. He knew that people were sick of Palmer-era hysterics. But Edgar began feeding him weekly intelligence briefings full of alarming reports on Reds and radicals and their threat to the country, their infiltration of labor unions, their secret meetings, their links to Moscow, their treasonous plots and global ambitions. Just as he scared the country in 1919 and 1920, he now got the attention of the new attorney general. Daugherty became a convert.

As for the Red Raids and all the controversy over Justice Department lawbreaking, Edgar gave a simple answer. Mitchell Palmer had called the shots—he and his top staff—not a small-fry junior staff assistant like himself. He, Edgar, had only done his job. Yes, he did it well, thank you, but he was just following orders. Besides, the clamor soon died down. By August 22, 1921, Edgar had sealed his deal. Harry Daugherty named him the new deputy chief of the Bureau of Investigation. Rather than being fired, Edgar had won himself another promotion. He would work directly under William J. Burns, the new chief, and keep control of the General Intelligence Division, his creation, with its voluminous files and index-card collection.

He thrived at first in the new system. He used his influence to reassemble his personal staff from the old Radical Division. He telegraphed his secretary, Helen Gandy, then away on vacation, to "return to Washington as soon as possible" to join him, and he also got permission to transfer his law school friend, Frank Baughman, into his private office. Burns, the director, a cranky sixty-five-year-old, didn't care for day-to-day details and spent much of his time running his private detective firm— whose control he never gave up, even after taking office. This left Edgar running the office. He strengthened his tie to Harry Daugherty in early 1922 when a crisis hit. Over a million coal and railroad workers walked off the job early that year. Edgar had the answer. "The Red agents of the Soviet Government who had bored into the organizations of our coal miners called a strike," Daugherty explained, describing the affair in language unmistakably Edgar's style. It didn't matter to Daugherty that the

New York Central Railroad cut wages for 43,000 employees that year and the U.S. Steel company imposed three pay cuts during the same period. Edgar had taught him to see Red. And to address the strike, Daugherty tore a page straight from Mitchell Palmer's old playbook. He went to federal court and won an injunction barring it, then he sent out Justice Department agents to arrest 1,200 strike leaders for violating the court order. It was just like old times. A few congressmen leveled impeachment charges against Daugherty in late 1922 for his tough stand, but the charges never stuck.

But then the scandals arrived, and any good times for Edgar ended abruptly.

The collapse came quickly. Harry Daugherty had installed around him in the Justice Department a circle of grafters that came to be called the Ohio Gang. They made their money mostly through kickbacks from gangsters and bootleggers. The ring operated from a townhouse on H Street where Daugherty, a bachelor, lived with another bachelor named Jess Smith, a former Ohio haberdasher with no official title but who always enjoyed direct access to Daugherty, often to the White House as well, and never lacked a seat at the Daugherty poker game. Here, the liquor flowed, and card games ran all night. Another core member of the gang was Gaston Means, a former private detective from Burns's agency with a criminal record and a murder indictment to his credit. Daugherty installed Means as a special agent in the Bureau of Investigation, though he had a wide and unconventional beat. Among other things, Means claimed that he conducted an investigation into the private sex life of President Harding himself, acting at the request of his wife, Florence Harding. Means also claimed to act as liaison between Daugherty and the bootleggers, and admitted to several burglaries while carrying a Justice Department badge.

As for Burns and his much-ballyhooed reorganization of the Bureau of Investigation, this, too, turned sinister. Burns began firing long-time agents and replacing them with political flunkies. Some, he assigned directly to serve paying clients at his private detective firm, often in union-busting jobs. Worse still were the so-called dollar-a-year men: thugs given a detective badge but no salary and no duties. They used the badges to extort kickbacks and collect graft, clearing thousands of dollars a week. Edgar himself recalled some of the stranger outrages, such as a New York theatrical producer given a badge to escort show girls around the Capitol to entertain political friends, and another badge given to a local drunk whom they used, as Edgar put it, "for amusing Department of

Justice officials at noontime on the sidewalk outside the building" by having the drunk perform "ribald songs and recitations."

And when congressmen started poking their noses into his business, Daugherty used the Bureau of Investigation to strike back. At the height of the impeachment debate growing out of his heavy-handed tactics in the 1922 strikes, Daugherty had Burns send Bureau agents to break into the office of Congressman Oscar Keller, a leader of the effort. At one point, Daugherty reportedly even tried to blackmail Mitchell Palmer by threatening to prosecute him for crimes related to his wartime Alien Property Custodian work. They demanded Palmer's help in pressuring Democratic congressmen to oppose the impeachment. "I saw Palmer coming out [of Daugherty's office] frightened to death," Gaston Means testified about the meeting. "You could see it in his face. He was trembling all over."

In mid-1923, Senator Thomas Walsh, who had spearheaded the investigation of Palmer's Red Raids in early 1921, now joined with his Montana colleague Burton K. Wheeler in announcing plans to explore evidence surrounding Warren G. Harding. Harry Daugherty responded by ordering Burns to send Justice Department agents out to Montana to try and discredit the two senators. The agents shadowed Wheeler and Walsh, along with their friends and families, tapped their telephones, intercepted their mail, and burglarized their offices. They found enough dirt to convince a grand jury in Montana to indict Wheeler for influence peddling, though a jury would later acquit him, as would a separate Senate investigation.

In the midst of all this, President Harding died suddenly in August 1923 of a heart attack while on a train returning from a visit to Alaska. According to one of his cabinet members, Commerce Secretary Herbert Hoover, Harding had just recently learned the extent of the corruption around him. Hoover recalled the president's asking him shortly before the trip: "If you knew of a great scandal in our administration, would you for the good of the country and the party expose it publicly or would you bury it?"

"Publish it, and at least get credit for integrity on your side," Herbert Hoover told him, and asked if Harry Daugherty was involved. Warren Harding didn't answer, and his well-timed death became the stuff of conspiracy theories immediately and for decades to come.[*]

---

[*]For the most colorful Harding conspiracy stories, see Nan Britton's *The President's Daughter* (1927) and Gaston Means's *The Strange Death of President Harding* (1930). For the best modern debunking of these conspiracies, see John W. Dean's *Warren G. Harding* (2004).

With Warren Harding out of the way, scandals blossomed like wild-flowers. First came Teapot Dome itself, the revelation that Harding's sec-retary of the interior, Albert Fall, had leased two of the navy's principal oil reserves in exchange for sizeable bribes from oil industry friends. Then came the seamy disclosures about Harry Daugherty's Justice Department, triggered after Jess Smith, Daugherty's housemate and shadowy go-between, shot himself to death with a .32 caliber revolver, leaving a for-tune valued at almost $200,000. Walsh and Wheeler pounced on the affair, calling hearings all the next winter and spring to expose the details. They called Daugherty and Burns separately to come testify on Capitol Hill on charges of misconduct. Each made a point to bring along their most seasoned veteran to sit with them at the witness table, that smart Mr. Hoover. Edgar sat with them just as he had sat with Mitchell Palmer after the Red Raids.

In a snap, the Ohio Gang disappeared. Calvin Coolidge, who suc-ceeded Harding as president, fired Harry Daugherty and brought in his old friend and Amherst College classmate, Harlan Fiske Stone, to replace him. Stone quickly fired William J. Burns, the crooked Bureau of Inves-tigation chief. Gaston Means had been fired months earlier. "Warren Harding had a dim realization that he had been betrayed by a few of the men he had trusted, by men whom he had believed were his devoted friends," Herbert Hoover lamented of the whole sorry story. Harry Daugh-erty would escape going to prison only by the grace of a hung jury in each of two separate criminal trials.

But for Harlan Fiske Stone, as the new attorney general, all this coming and going left him with a big question. Suddenly, he had a key job to fill, the vacant office of Director of the Bureau of Investigation. Though new to Washington, Stone already had seen firsthand how this Bureau had been compromised twice just within the past few years, first by A. Mitchell Palmer in conducting his notorious Red Raids, and then by Harry Daugherty in the latest scandals. Harlan Stone wanted to fix it, to turn this Bureau into an honest, professional, lawabiding force that deserved the public's trust. But to do it, he needed to find the right new person to fill the director's chair.

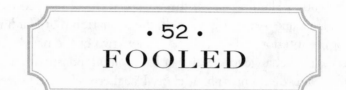

· 52 ·
FOOLED

B Y THE TIME Edgar received the urgent call on Saturday, May 10, 1924, to come at once to see Harlan Fiske Stone, the new attorney general, he had reason to worry. Was Stone going to fire him? He had just fired Edgar's boss, William J. Burns, a few days earlier. Edgar was visibly connected not only to Burns but to just about everything else Stone considered corrupt. Edgar had been Burns's deputy for three years, all through the worst recent scandals, and had sat with both Burns and Harry Daugherty at their Senate hearings. And on top of that, he had been Mitchell Palmer's point man on the Red Raids.

Edgar had never met Harlan Stone until just four weeks earlier when the older man came to Washington to take the job as attorney general for Calvin Coolidge. They were strangers to one another. Edgar knew Stone's handiwork, though. He had been in the room on Capitol Hill back in February 1921 when Senator Walsh's subcommittee was holding its hearings on the Red Raids, the day Harlan Stone's belated testimony arrived hand-carried by Jackson Ralston, who read it aloud to the senators. Edgar certainly remembered Stone's dramatic climax, his warning that "any system which confers upon administrative officers power to restrain the liberty of individuals, without safeguards . . . will result in abuse of power and in intolerable injustice and cruelty to individuals." Even if Stone never meant it personally, how could Edgar miss the fact that he himself fit Stone's description of an unaccountable "administrative officer" better than anyone else in Palmer's camp?

Now, this same Harlan Stone had come to clean house at the Justice Department. Could Edgar expect his name to be anyplace else than on Stone's short list of people to remove?

Edgar's father, Dickerson, had died finally on March 30, 1921, of what the official death certificate listed as "melancholia" and "inanition," eight years after his initial treatments at the Laurel Sanitarium. If accurate, it meant Dickerson wasted away from depression leading to self-imposed starvation. "My mother used to say Uncle Edgar wasn't nice to his father when he was ill," Edgar's niece Dorothy, the daughter of his estranged sister Lillian, told an interviewer years later. "He was ashamed of him. He couldn't tolerate the fact that Granddaddy had mental illness. He could never tolerate anything that was imperfect." But Edgar never spoke about it himself, whatever was the peculiar mix of guilt, shame, confusion, or hurt that lay behind his cold demeanor. He arranged the funeral and had his father buried with Masonic honors in Washington's Congressional Cemetery. He saved a handful of the letters his father wrote him in happier times, full of hugs and kisses for him and Mama. Mostly, he and his mother seemed relieved at no longer having to care for the emaciated dying man with his unpredictable moods, sullen, bitter, often demanding, and rarely normal or pleasant. Now, they could live quietly alone together in the small house on Seward Square.

Edgar's mother stopped wearing black a day or two after the funeral and bought herself several new spring outfits, charging them to her son. To keep her company when he worked late at the office, Edgar bought them a dog, an Airedale terrier, and named him Spee Dee Bozo. It was their first dog; she gave him the run of the house, and they both spoiled him. "I remember [Edgar] used to take Spee Dee for a walk every single evening," his niece Margaret recalled. "He took him with him in the morning when he walked over to Pennsylvania Avenue to get the morning paper. When he came in the front door, he'd roll it up and put it in Spee Dee's mouth and he would roar up the steps and take it to Nanny." But two years later, in 1923, Edgar's older brother, Dickerson, moved his own family out of the neighborhood to rural Glendale, Maryland, depriving Edgar of yet another friendship, that of his niece Margaret.

It's not that Edgar spent much time alone. On the contrary, he always seemed busy. His friends at the Kappa Alpha fraternity voted him their alumni president in 1921, and he became a regular at meetings of the Masons and the University Club as well. He grew inseparable from his office pal Frank Baughman. They went to movies together and sometimes wore matching new suits, always the latest styles. And of course he had his mother. But, mostly, Edgar lived at his desk, at the office, at work. This remained his passion, and this was where Harlan Fiske Stone saw him in April and May 1924, night after night, during his first few weeks as attorney general, as he was still trying to size up the place.

Harlan Stone had left his perch as dean of the Columbia University Law School at the end of the 1923 spring semester, then spent the summer sightseeing in Italy, Switzerland, and England with his wife, Agnes. He returned to New York City to join Sullivan and Cromwell, the large Wall Street law firm, as its litigation chief. He had been in his new job only six months when Calvin Coolidge asked him to drop everything and join his administration. As Stone remembered it, he came to Washington for a White House breakfast one day in early 1924, after which Silent Cal took him to an upstairs study, lit a cigar, smoked in silence a few minutes, then said, "Well, I think you will do."

It meant giving up a $100,000 per year legal practice for a $12,000 government salary, but Harlan Stone packed his bags, left Manhattan and his Riverside Drive home, and took the train south. Reaching Washington, he found himself a newcomer, an outsider. By one account, on his first day as attorney general, he didn't even know how to walk the half-dozen blocks from the White House to the Justice Department's building on Vermont Avenue; he had to ask a guard for directions. Once inside the building, he found himself surrounded by strangers. "I don't know whom to trust," he lamented to a friend. "I don't know any of these people."

One of the first people he did decide to trust was Felix Frankfurter. Stone barely knew Frankfurter at this point, though Frankfurter at least was a professor, an academic like himself. Of all the hundreds of letters Stone received during his first few days on the job, he found Frankfurter's the most intriguing: "[N]othing had been more saddening during the last few years than the betrayal of law by its special custodians at the Department of Justice," it read. Frankfurter made no effort to sugar coat the problem. He pointed to the "unsavory atmosphere" and "professional demoralization" facing Stone in his new office, and warned of what he called a "Herculean job" confronting him. Stone answered right away. "I shall be grateful if at some convenient time you find an opportunity to talk with me," he wrote Frankfurter. "I need all the help I can get."

Felix Frankfurter that spring was busy teaching classes at Harvard Law School four hundred miles away in Massachusetts, but he and Stone quickly sparked up a busy correspondence. They traded letters every few days as issues popped up. Frankfurter had strong views about people. He seemed to remember every corrupt, power-hungry functionary he'd ever crossed swords with at the Justice Department, and he applauded Stone particularly when Stone gave the axe to William J. Burns as head of the Bureau of Investigation. "There can hardly be two opinions about the fact that the spy system in government has been the watershed of the improprieties, illegalities, and corrupting atmosphere of recent years," Frankfurter wrote to Stone that week. "And some of us are not without hope that some of the other officers of the Department of Justice will follow Burns into retirement."

Frankfurter stopped short of listing the names of these "other officers" whose heads he hoped to see roll, but Stone got the point. And anyone close to Burns, Daugherty, or Palmer should go first.

Stone knew that picking his own new chief for the Bureau of Investigation could be the single most important decision he made as attorney general. It had to be the right person, somebody who was loyal, clean, and ready to knock heads. Candidates were scarce. All the recent scandals, from the Red Raids to the Daugherty graft, to the spying on congressmen, to the Burns dollar-a-year men, had cut a wide path. Just about anyone in government who knew detective work had been tainted by one or another. Private detective agencies were even worse, reeking from years of union busting, violence, burglary, jury tampering, and bribery—all common practices. So Harlan Stone began mulling over a different approach. Journalist Jack Alexander, writing in 1937, put it this way: "Unable to find a man who filled the bill to his liking, Stone resolved to look for a promising young man who could be trained along the line of his pet theories."

For Harlan Stone, the professor, his ideal candidate might well be a pupil he could take under his wing and teach. And when it came to promising young men, he seemed to have a very good one sitting right in front of him—if only he could be trusted.

A news reporter who met Edgar in 1924, around the time that Stone got to know him, described him as looking "much like an active young bond salesman" who "dispatches his business with a vigorous air from behind his broad mahogany desk." Edgar tried to make a good first impression on his new boss. He knew he could never win over Harlan Stone with his usual scare stories about Reds or by staged boostering from Capitol Hill or Military Intelligence friends. Instead, Edgar simply started coming to Stone's office to brief him on routine agency work, always in a no-nonsense, matter-of-fact way. Stone noticed something peculiar about him. Burns might be the Bureau's director, but it was this young Mr. Hoover who actually ran it. After Stone fired Burns, he saw Edgar easily fill the void. There wasn't much void to fill. Stone started asking questions about him. He raised the issue, for instance, with Mabel Walker Willebrandt, the trail-blazing California lawyer recently appointed as the first woman assistant attorney general in charge of prohibition, tax, and prison cases. She knew the office scuttlebutt. Edgar, she told him, was "honest and informed and one who operated like an electric wire, with almost trigger response." Stone also heard from Herbert Hoover, the secretary of commerce, who buttonholed him at the White House one day after a cabinet meeting to pass along a tip he heard about him from one of his staff assistants, a fellow named Larry Richey. Richey happened to be friendly with Edgar through their memberships at the Masonic Lodge: "Stone doesn't have to go searching," Richey told him. "He's got the man he needs right there. He's young and he has a good legal background. And his name is Hoover, too."

Harlan Stone was intrigued. One by one, he started to consider each of the damning facts he knew about this John Edgar Hoover, things that seemed to disqualify him immediately, and he found an excuse to ignore each one. On the Daugherty-Burns scandals, for instance, none of the charges of graft or bribery pointed to Edgar, and it was Burns who gave the orders to spy on the congressmen and senators, not his deputy. Edgar's bad blood with Gaston Means, the worst of the Ohio Gang grafters, was legendary. The two men hated each other. Edgar reputedly even refused to allow Means to walk into his office. Means, for his part, gave Edgar a backhanded compliment when he testified to Congress that he never dealt with anyone in the Bureau below Burns on any of the graft or abusive spying.

Could this Mr. Hoover have been actually clean of all the goings-on? There was an obvious hole in this theory. Edgar, as deputy chief, had been Burns's second-in-command through all the episodes: Teapot Dome, the Dougherty scandals, and the rest. He had to know what was happening around him, even if just to stay out of the way. And the fact that Edgar sat with Burns and Daugherty at the witness table at each one's respective Senate hearing showed more than simple loyalty. Edgar shared their secrets, their confidences. Had Stone been more suspicious, he easily could have latched onto any of the stories going around then about Edgar's using his own strong-arm tactics to protect Daugherty, in one case demanding the resignation of a female Justice Department employee after she testified against Daugherty to Senate investigators.

Harlan Stone was no amateur. As a top-flight administrator and lawyer, he knew how to ask questions and get answers. He met with Edgar regularly during this time. Did he confront him on these points? Did Edgar level with him? Did he lie? Did he change the subject?

Whatever the truth, Stone seemed to give him the benefit of every doubt. Stone noted, for instance, how Edgar had ignored the distractions in 1923 to launch an important new case, a federal operation against the Ku Klux Klan. The Klan became so strong in the 1920s as to overwhelm the governments of several southern states and was responsible for dozens of lynchings and murders. At the request of the governor of Louisiana, Edgar and his agents stepped in, and, failing to block the organization itself, they built a case against the Klan's top national leader, Imperial Kleagle Edward Clarke, on white slavery charges, winning a March 1924 guilty plea from Clarke and forcing a $5,000 fine. It might be a slap on the wrist, but it was something.

As for the Red Raids, how could he possibly blame them on young Hoover? Edgar was just twenty-four years old when they occurred, the most junior member of Mitchell Palmer's staff. To suggest that he played any large role in shaping the policy behind them bordered on ludicrous. And Stone was not alone thinking this way. He could have checked with Louis F. Post, for instance. Post, the former assistant secretary of labor, had cancelled over a thousand deportation orders at the height of the frenzy, stood up to Palmer at his impeachment hearing, and was widely celebrated by progressives as the hero of the story. He, too, gave Edgar a pass on the raids. Post wrote a memoir about it titled *The Deportations Delirium of Nineteen-Twenty* that was published in 1923 where he recounted the episode in detail, dwelling on the roles of Palmer, Caminetti, Garvan, and Flynn. But he conspicuously left out any mention—beyond one passing parenthetical— of the young director of the Justice Department's Radical Division. So, too, with John Lord O'Brian, the lawyer who first hired Edgar to the Justice Department in 1917, supervised him at the War Emergency Division, and later joined dissidents in condemning the raids. He considered Edgar blameless. "Personally, I always blamed Garvan for everything connected with the infamous red raids," O'Brian confided to Felix Frankfurter. "Hoover is a conscientious and honest fellow and will carry out faithfully instructions given him by his chief. Under the new conditions in the Department, I think he will do well."

Harlan Stone listened to his instincts, he listened to all the advice, and he ignored all the danger signs. "Young man, I want you to be acting director of the Bureau of Investigation," he told Edgar in his office, on Saturday, May 10, 1924.

If Edgar, sitting across the desk from him, had jumped too quickly at the offer, Stone even then might still have grown suspicious. Instead, Edgar gave the best possible answer. "I'll take the job, Mr. Stone, but only on certain conditions." And what were those? "The Bureau must be divorced from politics and not be a catch-all for political hacks. Appointments must be based on merit. Promotions will be made only on proven ability. And the bureau will be responsible only to the Attorney General."

Harlan Stone was thrilled. This young man put principle first, and he had backbone, too. "I wouldn't give it to you under any other conditions," Stone told him. "That's all. Good day."

All seemed well in the kingdom after that. Stone sealed the bargain within seventy-two hours by issuing a memorandum laying out his vision for a reformed Bureau of Investigation. "A secret police may become a menace to free government," he insisted in its preamble, and he promised to prevent one. He announced that he was taking personal charge of the Bureau and that, under his watch, it would stop its notorious witch hunts. He laid out six concrete operating principles: (a) limit Bureau investigations to actual violations of law, (b) reduce the number of personnel, (c) remove incompetent and unreliable agents, (d) discontinue the "dollar a year men," (e) require that new agents have "good character" and, preferably, legal training, and (f) raise Bureau morale.

Edgar agreed, and he gave every appearance of keeping his word. He went to Capitol Hill and assured skeptical senators that he and Stone meant business. "Instructions have been sent to officers in the field to limit their investigations to violations of the statutes," he told them. In applying these new rules, Edgar refused to be bullied by politicians, and Stone consistently backed him. Stories began making the rounds. One had it, for instance, that when Edgar tried to transfer a politically connected agent to a new city and the agent sent his local congressman to complain about the distant posting, Edgar turned him down to his face. When the congressman then stomped off down the hall to complain to Stone, Stone called Edgar into his office and, with the congressmen standing right there, told him, "I'm surprised you didn't fire the fellow [the agent] at once."

"Everyone says he's too young but maybe that's his asset," Stone told one friend about his new protégé. "Apparently he hasn't learned to be afraid of the politicians." Public reactions mirrored his own. "Young Mr. Hoover . . . has no entangling alliances," wrote Robert T. Small of the Consolidated Press Association around this time. "Among his friends he is known to be as clean as a hound's tooth."

Once installed in his new post, Edgar drew almost universal praise for his reorganization of the Bureau of Investigation under Harlan Stone in the mid-1920s. Even Felix Frankfurter complimented it. Stone insisted that Edgar meet personally with Roger Baldwin, head of the recently formed American Civil Liberties Union and a veteran target of Justice Department harassment. A few days later, Felix Frankfurter reported to Stone from Boston on the fine impression Edgar had made: "at a public meeting here, before a rather unusually thoughtful audience, [Baldwin] spoke in the warmest terms of appreciation not only of your work, but also of Mr. Hoover's conduct of the Bureau of Investigation."

Within six months, by February 1925, Edgar, under Stone's guidance, had transformed the Bureau's agent force to the point that fully half its 352 agents had legal training and most of the rest had academic degrees. Edgar instituted background checks on all new recruits and required they be trained not only on rules of evidence but also on how to act like gentlemen. He instituted surprise inspections of local offices, uniform efficiency reports, and fired scores of unqualified hacks. Between 1924 and 1925, the Bureau shrank from 657 down to 502 employees—all in line with Harlan Stone's plan.

Along the way, Edgar and Stone developed a personal warmth that lasted a lifetime. For the next twenty years, they traded letters and visits. "Having been appointed by you and having received my so-called first experience under fire under your leadership, I have always cherished the privilege and honor of the period that I served as Director under you," he wrote to Stone in 1929. "As a young man, his guiding hand on my shoulder meant so much, his counsel and judgment were always so sound," he wrote to Stone's widow, Agnes, after Stone's death in 1946. Harlan Stone, too, returned the compliments. "[Hoover] removed from the Bureau every man as to whose character there was any ground for suspicion," Stone, by then a United States Supreme Court justice, wrote to Felix Frankfurter in 1933, when Edgar was being attacked politically. "He withdrew it wholly from its extra-legal activities and made it an efficient organization for the investigation of criminal offenses against the United States."

Around this time, Edgar took one other step to demonstrate his clean, new start in life. He clarified his name. His parents always called him Edgar; his nieces called him J. E.; and he signed papers with a random mix of J. E., John E., or John. Then one day, he walked over to open a charge account at Garfinkel's, the upscale Washington, D.C., retail store, but was embarrassed when the store's credit director turned him down, saying he already issued a card to a Mr. John E. Hoover whose credit had gone bad. Edgar explained sheepishly that he was a different person, not the one with bad credit. From that point on, he began signing his name in a consistent new way, as J. Edgar.

He doubtless had deeper motives for the change beyond getting a store credit account. His new name, J. Edgar Hoover, had a striking similarity to that of his earlier mentor, A. Mitchell Palmer. But mostly, it was new and different, a dividing line between then and now. Whatever the ultimate reason, when Harlan Stone announced his new permanent chief of the Bureau of Investigation in December 1924, the newspapers recorded it precisely as J. Edgar Hoover. So it would stay. The metamorphosis ended. The youth vanished; the adult emerged fully formed.

The day after he got the job as acting director happened to be Mother's Day 1924, and Annie Marie Scheitlin Hoover celebrated it by giving her son a gift to mark his new status, a sapphire ring studded with diamonds. Edgar wore it every day for the rest of his life. It was the closest he ever got to an engagement ring.

Only Felix Frankfurter seemed to sense that his new friend Harlan Fiske Stone had made a dreadful mistake. He raised it only once, then dropped the subject. "I know you want to know that we . . . were not happy when we saw the appointment," he wrote to Stone shortly after the news of Edgar's permanent position as Bureau director. Frankfurter pointed to Edgar's connection with A. Mitchell Palmer, his courtroom defenses of the Red Raids, and his demands to the Labor Department for deportation orders. "Nevertheless, my mouth has been sealed about the Hoover appointment, except in talk with Chafee and Brooks, because I feel so deeply about the ends at which you aim in the reorganization of the Bureau of Investigation, that I did not want to set my judgment against yours in the selection of your means." But then he gave Stone his warning: "Hoover . . . might be a very effective and zealous instrument for the realization of the 'liberal ideas' which you had in mind for the investigatorial activities of the Department of Justice when his chief is a man who cares about these ideas as deeply as you do, but his effectiveness might be of a weaker coefficient with a chief less profoundly concerned over these 'ideas.'"

Felix Frankfurter saw Edgar as a functionary, someone who followed orders, able to do the bidding of a Red-baiter like Palmer, a grafter like Daugherty, or a reformer like Stone. But what would happen if he were ever on his own? Who really was this John Edgar Hoover? Did anyone know him? Yes, everyone agreed, he was smart and capable, but did he have a moral compass? Had anyone checked its setting?

Harlan Fiske Stone could have found these answers if only he asked the right questions. There was a clue sticking out the whole time that would have given it away, but apparently nobody saw it. Stone, as part of his reform agenda, made an early point to disband the General Intelligence Division, the office Edgar had nurtured as his personal fiefdom inside the Department of Justice. But Edgar knew it didn't matter. He still controlled the real crown jewels, which he kept intact the whole time under his personal control, untouched, untouchable, and largely invisible. It was his files, the 450,000 index cards with all the names and cross-references and personal dirt about people that could be pulled up at a moment's notice. For Edgar—now J. Edgar—this was the heart of the matter, his power, his spying machine, the truest expression of his compulsive creative genius.

If Harlan Stone had only asked to see the index cards and the files, specifically, for instance, the one for lawyer Isaac Schorr (Old German 377466), or the many for Louis F. Post, or the one for Felix Frankfurter, Zechariah Chafee, Roscoe Pound, and Judson King (Old German 379228), or the one for John Lord O'Brian (Old German 384125), or the one for Chicago prosecutor Maclay Hoyne (Old German 383427), or the ones for the raids themselves bulging with hundreds of notes and letters bearing Edgar's signature demanding more arrests, higher bail, fewer lawyers, and more spying. If Harlan Stone had only seen the files, he would never have been fooled.

This was no bright-eyed innocent he had just hired as Director for Life of the Bureau of Investigation. It was the young man who had evolved to become J. Edgar Hoover.

• PART X •

LEGACY

To DISMISS THE Palmer Raids as a hysterical overreaction to a phantom Red Menace misses the point. Then as now, the country feared terrorism—anarchist bombs and communist treason—and wrestled with one of the most difficult questions a democracy can face: how to balance civil liberties with public safety. A. Mitchell Palmer may have become fanatical, especially after the bomb blast by self-proclaimed Anarchist Fighters destroyed his home and almost killed his family, but his crackdown against Reds in America was applauded by top officials in government, media, business, academia, and religion, almost across the board. These were not ignorant or irrational people. Palmer was a long-time progressive, and he enjoyed the support of most of Woodrow Wilson's cabinet. They all made their judgments about the Red Menace based on what they considered hard evidence: bombings, riots, strikes, and the plain meaning of words spoken by self-proclaimed radical leaders. Palmer, sitting inside the Justice Department, saw the best intelligence available—undercover reports from police, federal investigators, private detectives, and the military. The reports all sounded the same alarm.

Palmer and his team connected the dots as they saw them: communism had triumphed in Russia and was sweeping Europe in a wave of uprisings. American communist leaders, proudly allied to Moscow, announced their own blueprint for a takeover in broadsides such as the "Left Wing Manifesto" that called for mass labor strikes leading to a broad-based insurgency. Sure enough, like clockwork, almost a million coal miners, steel workers, and police walked off the job, while many of their leaders had ties to socialism. Agitation grew louder month by month. Sprinkle in a few hangover anxieties from the recent World War—fears of sabotage, resentment of leftist pacifists, and exaggerated patriotism—plus some stress factors like an out-of-control economy, wide unemployment, skyrocketing inflation, race riots, May Day riots, anarchist bombings, and the Centralia shootings. By late 1919, anyone who didn't see danger on the horizon seemed like a fool.

Nobody knew the future. Was the threat hollow? Honest people could argue the evidence either way. Even if the government in Washington could avoid being overthrown outright, the risk of more violence, riots, strikes, killings and counter-killings, seemed clear, and Palmer took it seriously. Certainly, a crackdown on Reds at that precise moment coincided with a host of selfish agendas: Palmer's upcoming campaign for the presidency and the undisguised zeal of the coal, steel, timber, and other industries to crush their nascent labor unions topped the list. Exploitation of the hysteria by cynics—politicians, newspaper publishers, and corporate oligarchs—was unmistakable. But this did not change the basic equation: A. Mitchell Palmer, as a responsible government official, had a duty to address the danger. He had to do something to protect the public.

That was the easy part, though. The harder question was: Do what? There is a seductive downward spiral in times of crisis from "doing something" to "doing what it takes" to "doing anything." Faced with the 1919 Red Scare, Palmer decided to seize the initiative with a bold first strike. He would send out his men to round up as many dangerous radicals as possible and get them off the street. Those who were immigrants, the large majority, he would hand over to the Labor Department to be deported; the rest, the American citizens, he would turn over to state governments to be prosecuted under state peacetime antisedition laws. Lawyer Charles Recht summed it up neatly: "Their avowed objective was to make these United States lily-white by ridding them of all the Reds and Pinks at one fell blow."

Here, however, came the problem. Whenever any government in any country tries to crack down on an internal threat, especially a poorly defined one, it affects real people, and often the wrong ones. America has rules about this, contained in the Constitution and its Bill of Rights, rules designed to protect a way of life built on free speech, free association, free exchange of ideas, and freedom from government harassment. To put tangible force behind these principles, the Constitution and statutes based on it require the government to follow procedures, such as going to a judge and showing probable cause to get a search warrant or an arrest warrant, providing prisoners a fair trial, including access to a lawyer, or more specialized, modern forms like those under the Foreign Intelligence Surveillance Act, among others. These rules can seem arcane and counterproductive when they occasionally get in the way, stopping police from preventing a crime, helping a guilty person go free, or interfering in the tracking of a possible terrorist. But they serve an essential purpose: they force the government to get its facts straight before it deprives any person—citizen or immigrant—of his or her freedoms, locks them up, deports them, seizes their property, or invades their privacy.

When the government ignores these rules, it not only violates the public trust. It also invites mistakes: fingering the wrong person for a crime, or fingering anyone at all when no crime has taken place. Even worse is when the mistakes are systematic or deliberate, driven by prejudice, vengeance, or politics.

Police work back in 1919 was closer in time and spirit to Wyatt Earp and his 1881 shootout at the OK Corral—an event recent enough to be a boyhood memory for Palmer and his chief detective, Big Bill Flynn—than to anything today. Brutal interrogations, police clubbings and vigilante shootings, dragnet raids, all were common practice. "If I should step on a thug's toe when I was examining him I'd be up for assault the next day," Flynn once joked in explaining how he questioned suspects as a private detective in New York City in the 1920s. "The police, of course, have a little more scope." World War I brought out a still harsher face of this frontier justice: the prosecution and jailing of hundreds under the Espionage Act for the sheer act of speaking out against the government, and the jailing of thousands more in episodes like the Slacker Raids aimed at draft dodgers and the mass detentions of German nationals, so-called alien enemies.

A. Mitchell Palmer, in launching his crackdown against the Reds in 1919, took this embryonic legal system and pressed it to its limit. "Certainly, gentlemen cannot with any seriousness contend that the Government must stand idly by and wait for the actual throwing of the bomb or the actual use of arms in military operation before it can defend itself," he told Congress in 1921. Palmer saw himself in the same shoes as a military commander in the heat of combat. If legal technicalities got in his way, he saw it as his duty to settle any doubt in favor of protecting the country.

Not surprisingly, illegalities piled up from the start. For one thing, the Justice Department itself never had any legal authority to touch this issue. Edgar himself conceded the point in a 1924 internal memorandum where he explained: "activities of Communists and other ultra-radicals have not up to the present time constituted a violation of the federal statutes and, consequently, the Department of Justice, theoretically, has no right to investigate [them]." As for deporting suspicious aliens, the Immigration Acts gave this power solely to the labor secretary, not the attorney general. Had the new rules that Harlan Fiske Stone laid down in 1924 to reform the Bureau of Investigation been in effect in 1919, limiting it to investigations of actual violations of federal law, Palmer's raids never could have gotten started. No violations had been alleged.

Once the raids began, the illegalities snowballed. Warrantless arrests, warrantless searches, beatings, excessively high bail, deplorable jail conditions, stacked hearings, all became common and acceptable. Perhaps the only purely legally conducted aspects of the whole campaign were the state prosecutions of radicals such as Benjamin Gitlow in New York and William Bross Lloyd in Illinois. The New York criminal anarchy statute might smell rotten to modern senses, but Gitlow and Lloyd at least each got a fair trial. "We shall repent in sackcloth and ashes for the injustice we have done to men under this law," Clarence Darrow told the jury in the Lloyd case. Oliver Wendall Holmes agreed. "[I]t is manifest that there was no present danger of an attempt to overthrow the government by force," he wrote when Gitlow's appeal finally reached the United States Supreme Court in 1925. But Holmes was writing in dissent. The Supreme Court back then still found no First Amendment problem with New York's criminal anarchy statute, and it affirmed Gitlow's conviction by a 7 to 2 margin. Holmes's views on free speech would not prevail in American law until the 1930s.

Add to all this one more ingredient: an intelligence failure. Who were these dangerous radicals? Palmer and his circle saw the answer in the swarms of recent immigrants from poor countries, mostly Russians, with socialist leanings and communist ties. But this begged the question. Millions of recent immigrants walked the streets of American cities in 1919, not all of them were socialists, not all the socialists were communists, and not all the communists were bomb-throwing zealots. And some of the most virulent radicals were not immigrants at all but native-born citizens. To identify which people were actually dangerous required cutting through crude stereotypes, but Palmer's Justice Department, even its seasoned veterans, seemed incapable. They often jumped to conclusions before collecting a single fact.* Ignorance, prejudice, and fear all combined to lead them to a conclusion that was simply wrong: that all these

---

*As one result, for instance, the probe into who bombed Mitchell Palmer's house in June 1919 floundered for months because Justice Department agents assumed it to be Russian Reds, despite finding an Italian-English dictionary on the scene. By the time they isolated L'Era Nuova and the Galliani gangs as the likely suspects, most of the guilty had skipped the country.

Russians were Reds at heart and dangerous if given the chance. And anyone connected to the Communist Party certainly meant bad business to the country.

Unable to pick out the dangerous communists, they decided to snag them all.

The result was a civil liberties catastrophe: Between five and ten thousand people—the exact number is impossible to calculate—were rounded up and detained, often beaten and terrified. They were dragged from their homes and families, many taken from their beds in the middle of the night or arrested *en masse* at dances, theatres, or neighborhood clubs, locked up for weeks or months, often railroaded through sham hearings, cut off from lawyers and friends, and kept in decrepit, overcrowded, makeshift prisons. None of these immigrants was accused, much less convicted, of violating any state or federal law. For most of them, no evidence was ever presented beyond the unsubstantiated word of a Justice Department agent on a preprinted form that they belonged to some organization—not that they actually *did* anything or even said anything.

Once the immigration inspectors started asking questions, the truth quickly came out. The large majority of these prisoners had nothing to do with radicalism and posed no threat to anyone. They had been arrested solely based on guilt by association, their supposed connection to one of the newfangled Communist parties, even though the bulk of them had no idea what these parties stood for and often had no idea they were even members. Many thought they had joined a neighborhood social club to enjoy musical concerts, English language classes, or the chance for a pleasant night out with people like themselves—no small thing for new arrivals in a strange land.

By and large, the wrong people had been fingered and punished for a crime that had never been committed in the first place. That's the danger of what can happen when those procedures laid out in the Constitution and the statutes based on it are ignored.

Palmer's sledgehammer approach certainly succeeded in crippling the communist movement in America in the immediate short term. Plenty of suspected Reds were pulled out of circulation. The Labor Department, by the time it finished all the hearings and appeals for all the suspects rounded up between November 1919 and January 1920, ultimately found 820 of them to qualify for deportation under the 1918 Immigration Act. The last large group of them, sixty-two Reds, left Ellis Island for Russia in

March 1921 aboard the steamship Magnolia. These were in addition to
the hundreds of citizens imprisoned under state sedition laws in 1919 and
1920. And this was just the tip of the iceberg. Simply put, the raids scared
the pants off of anyone even thinking of joining the movement. In less
than a year, the combined membership of the Communist and Communist Labor parties plummeted by over 80 percent, from 60,000 down to
less than 10,000. If any real threat of revolution existed in late 1919, it
vanished by late 1920.

But this effect was short-lived. Once the heat was off, the Reds started
coming back, and Edgar began sounding his familiar alarm bells. "Four
hundred and twenty-seven propagandists and couriers arrived from foreign countries during the year ended June 30, 1921," he warned in his
1921 Annual Report, and he later claimed that these Red infiltrators
played a direct role in the 1922 coal and railroad strikes. For Edgar, these
anti-Red alarms would become a constant theme during his five decades
atop the FBI.

A more lasting impact of the episode, though, grew from the revulsion
many Americans felt upon learning what their government had done.

Palmer and his allies came very close to deporting thousands of innocent bystanders, all the immigrants they rounded up between
November 1919 and January 1920. What stopped them? Historians like
to point to the rapid cooling of the American temper after late 1919,
but this, too, misses the point. Unlike the Seventh Cavalry showing up
in the final reel of an old western movie, impersonal forces of history
rarely reveal themselves on time to save the day for real people in
danger. Instead, some individual person usually has to come forward
first and be willing to stick his or her neck out. In 1920, this role fell
to a small circle of lawyers. Louis F. Post dared to cancel the thousands
of deportation warrants, and then talk back to Congress when it tried
to impeach him over it. Felix Frankfurter succeeded in exposing Justice
Department lawbreaking in a Boston courtroom and through the
Twelve Lawyer report. Clarence Darrow defended the most difficult
Communist cases, representing clients in courtrooms thick with hostility, based solely on their right to free speech. Without these and a
handful of others, the tide would not have turned so quickly, and the
damage would have been far worse.

Once it did turn and the truth seeped out, it caused a slow shift in
American legal culture. Americans believed in the rule of law and, once
they knew the facts, they would not tolerate systematic abuses by

government. From this caldron of trauma in 1919 and 1920 emerged a modern concept of civil liberties.* The Red Scare critics emerged to become the new leading lights of American law. Oliver Wendell Holmes's dissenting views on free speech became accepted as judicial dogma in the 1930s and 1940s. Harlan Fiske Stone, having imposed his reforms on the Department of Justice, joined Holmes on the Supreme Court in 1925. Charles Evans Hughes, who led the protests in New York against the state legislature's 1920 decision to expel its five Socialist members, rejoined the High Court as chief justice in 1930, and Stone then replaced him as chief justice in 1941. Felix Frankfurter, too, became a Supreme Court associate justice in 1939. A new organization, the American Civil Liberties Union, emerged in 1920 to defend assaults on the Bill of Rights. Louis Post's guidelines for deciding deportation cases, including his refusal to consider evidence collected from illegal searches or lawyerless confessions, became standard practice.**

By mid-1920, the Justice Department itself adopted a strict policy against bringing Red-related cases under the Espionage Act, even those parts that remained in effect in peacetime. A year later, in 1921, Congress would repeal the 1918 Espionage Act altogether, and leave in its place the weaker 1917 version of the provision.†

---

*Senator Thomas Walsh's 1921 investigation of the Red Raids, intended to boost public awareness and spur reforms, unfortunately foundered in its mission. Walsh's subcommittee produced a 780-page transcript that represents the single most complete public disclosure of the affair. But after that, the senators fell into squabbling. Walsh drafted a report criticizing Palmer, but Thomas Sterling, the subcommittee's Republican chairman, drafted a separate report defending him. In March 1922, they scheduled five different meetings to discuss the two reports, but never made a decision. Finally, in January 1923, three years after the raids and two years after the hearings, the full Senate Judiciary Committee took charge. In a single marathon session, it rejected Walsh's report; it refused even to consider Sterling's competing report, and then it washed its hands of the whole affair, agreeing to a motion that, under the circumstances, it was "inadvisable" to issue any report at all.

**Still, the emergence of a new Red Scare after World War II with its own new federal sedition law—the 1946 Smith Act—caused the Supreme Court to backtrack in *Dennis v. United States*, 341 U.S. 494 (1951), with even Felix Frankfurter concurring in upholding a sentence against a group of communist spokesmen, saying: "the plain fact [is] that the interest in speech, profoundly important as it is, is no more conclusive . . . than other attributes of democracy."

†The Espionage Act, amended several times since then, remains in effect today (see title 18, United States Code, section 793 et seq.), though its use has been sparing. A modern controversy has been raised, however, by recent attempts to apply it aggressively in cases such as *United States v. Steven Rosen and Keith Weissman*, involving two employees of the American Israel Public Affairs Committee (AIPAC), and suggestions that the Justice Department might attempt to apply it to news media outlets as well. See opinion of United States District Judge T. S. Ellis, case 1:05-cr-225, Eastern District of Virginia, filed August 9, 2006.

Eight decades later, as America today wrestles with a new war on terror raising the same complex issues of how to balance civil liberties with public safety, the Palmer Raids stand as a frightful precedent. It's not because the country lost its mind in 1919. Just the opposite. It's because rational, well-informed, well-intentioned people back then, acting under stress in the heat of events, found it so easy to be seduced down the spiral from "doing something" to "doing anything," making a civil liberties catastrophe seem reasonable and acceptable. If they could do it then, what makes today's generation any more immune?

❦

Congress never impeached A. MITCHELL PALMER for launching the Red Raids. Still, Palmer became an isolated figure in Washington after leaving the Justice Department in 1921. He opened a small law office but attracted few clients, the most notable being Edward McLean, the millionaire *Washington Post* publisher who became a minor figure in the Teapot Dome scandal. Palmer spent much of the early 1920s dodging investigations. Congress launched a probe into decisions he made as attorney general favoring the Southern Pacific Railway, and the litigation over his actions as Alien Property Custodian during World War I dragged on through the decade. He did manage to dodge the two lawsuits brought against him by families of victims from the Red Raids, but only after paying a small fortune in legal fees. A federal judge threw out the $100,000 suit brought by the wife of Andrea Salsedo, the man who killed himself by jumping out the window of the Justice Department's fourteenth-floor office in lower Manhattan, finding no convincing evidence that Palmer personally caused the death. Similarly, Mrs. Mary Marzinik, who sued Palmer for $350,000 over the death of her husband from pneumonia while he was being held at Ellis Island, dropped her case a few months later when witnesses refused to appear.

Personal tragedies soon darkened Palmer's life. His wife of twenty-two years, Roberta Bartlett Palmer, died suddenly in January 1922 from what doctors could diagnose only as complications from an illness she'd contracted the prior summer. She was just fifty years old. Palmer suffered a heart attack a few months later while playing golf near Palm Beach, Florida. He remarried the next year a Mrs. Margaret Fallon Burrell, widow of a wealthy New York manufacturer. With her, he traveled to France, Italy, and Holland, and spent his winters in Boca Raton, playing golf and enjoying dinner parties with old political friends, but his health never fully returned.

Palmer came out of his political exile only once, in 1932, to help Franklin Delano Roosevelt, his former neighbor who was then running for president of the United States. Roosevelt asked Palmer to help him draft a platform to present to the 1932 Democratic National Convention and Palmer produced a conservative document calling for balanced budgets and Woodrow Wilson–style civic reforms. Roosevelt used it to win the nomination, though he ignored it upon reaching the White House. In forming his initial 1933 cabinet, though, Roosevelt dealt Palmer a deep insult by choosing one of Palmer's worst critics, Senator Thomas Walsh, the one who led the Senate investigation into the 1920 raids, as his first attorney general. Walsh, though, never had the chance to take the job, dying in a train accident en route to Washington to accept it.

Palmer's friendship with Roosevelt cooled after the snub. In early 1936, Palmer felt well enough to spend ten days hiking in the Adirondack Mountains, but then, after returning home, he suffered one last heart attack and died soon after, on May 11, 1936.

Palmer's Red Raids ended up costing him the 1920 presidential nomination and ruined his reputation. He took full responsibility for them, though. By doing so, he saved his president, WOODROW WILSON, from being blamed for one of the worst abuses of his presidency. Wilson loyalists created a myth that the president had nothing to do with it, and didn't even know about it until long after the fact. The raids were "a matter which has been a great grief to Mr. Wilson's friends," one of them, philanthropist George Foster Peabody, wrote to Senator Walsh in 1921. "Doubtless you know even more surely than I that Mr. Palmer was without Mr. Wilson's active sympathy," Peabody argued, and he claimed that Wilson would have fired Palmer over the episode but for his bad health. This fairy tale was almost certainly wrong. Woodrow Wilson never showed the slightest sign of desire to fire Mitchell Palmer either before or after the raids, and his attack of thrombosis did not occur until well after the Red hysteria reached full boil in 1919, by which time planning for the raids was well underway. Nor is there any reason to think that Palmer, a longtime ally, would have hidden his intentions from Wilson. The president's warning to Palmer in April 1920 to "not let the country see red" came with no particulars and no explanation.

If Woodrow Wilson did not know about the raids, it was only because he kept himself ignorant, not because Mitchell Palmer refused to tell him. Wilson either did not ask or did not listen, being too preoccupied with world affairs, his League of Nations, or his imagined place in history. He died in February 1924 in his home on S Street, just around the corner from Palmer's house, bringing down the final curtain on the era.*

As for the ANARCHIST FIGHTERS who bombed Palmer's house in June 1919, nobody was ever prosecuted for the crime despite the most massive federal investigation ever conducted up to that point. The leading suspects, members of the Galliani anarchist gang of Lynn, Massachusetts, all escaped. "There's no evidence for conviction without a confession," Chief Detective Bill Flynn commiserated in 1922. "The whole gang is out of the country now. They left at once as stowaways, and so on. As the thing now stands our work is almost wasted." Only two of Galliani's followers ever ended up standing trial, and they were probably the two least deserving of it. Nicola Sacco and Bartolomeo Vanzetti came to New York City to check on Salsedo after his arrest in March 1920, but after failing to see him they returned home and soon were arrested themselves for the murder of a paymaster at a shoe factory in nearby South Braintree, Massachusetts. Sacco and Vanzetti insisted they didn't commit the crime, and each produced witnesses to swear they were someplace else when it occurred, but the jury convicted them, and the judge sentenced them to death. The trial had a political tone, there were signs of sloppy police work, and the whole situation had a bad odor. Skeptics concluded the two had been framed by police because of their anarchist views. Their execution in 1927 became a heated international *cause célèbre*. Making the legal case for those trying to save Sacco and Vanzetti from the electric chair was the familiar professor from Harvard Law School, Felix Frankfurter.

ANTHONY CAMINETTI, the Immigration chief at the Department of Labor who conspired with Edgar to set the Red Raids in motion in late 1919, managed to avoid taking any blame for them in the congressional hearings afterward. Instead, Caminetti left the country in late 1920 for an extended tour of Europe, visiting England, France, Belgium, Holland, Poland, Czechoslovakia, and Yugoslavia. He came home in January 1921 with a new message. America had to close the doors for good on mass immigration. Caminetti claimed to see a looming nightmare during his overseas trip: hordes of Europe's poorest outcasts clamoring to reach

---

*When Palmer was sick one time, Joe Tumulty, his friend and one-time ally in the Wilson White House, sent his wife a letter to cheer her up. "Ask Mitchell if he heard about [Wilson]'s arrival in Heaven," Tumulty wrote. "St. Peter interrogated him about the Fourteen Points and said, 'Woodrow, your Fourteen Points sagged a bit down below.' Woodrow turned to St. Peter and said, 'Your own Ten Points haven't been much of a success down there.'"

America. Immigration from Europe already had rebounded sharply after World War I. More than 560,000 newcomers passed through Ellis Island in 1921, approaching levels not seen since 1914. Steamship lines announced that their lowly steerage bunks were booked solid a full year in advance.

Caminetti's words struck a chord. "This flood of cheap foreign labor is a menace to American prosperity and American standards of living," the *Chicago Daily Tribune* editorialized. Congressman Albert Johnson, chairman of the House Immigration Committee, agreed. When one business leader suggested that immigration might help the country's economy, Johnson slapped him down: "Do you want to let the scourings of the sewers of Europe be poured into the United States?" he asked. General Leonard Wood, a leading Republican presidential contender in 1920, echoed the point: "We do not want to be the dumping ground for radicals, agitators, Reds, who do not understand our ideals."

Six months after Caminetti returned to Washington, Congress passed the Emergency Immigration Act of 1921 creating country-by-country quotas, calculated at 3 percent of the number of people from each country living in the United States in 1910, a formula designed to limit the admission of Russians, Eastern Europeans, and Italians. In 1924, Congress closed the door further, adjusting the country quota formula back to demographic data from 1890 and, beginning in 1927, limiting immigrants overall to 150,000 per year. As a result, Italy saw its yearly quota slashed from 42,057 under the old law to 3,845 under the new.

The waves of mass immigration that recast American life during the late nineteenth and early twentieth centuries came to a halt.

CLARENCE DARROW defended more communists and leftists than anyone, but Edgar seemed not to have resented him for it. In his 1958 book, *Masters of Deceit*, Edgar described him simply as the "famed Chicago criminal lawyer" and praised him for his work in 1931 in helping to defend the Scottsboro Boys in Alabama.

In the mid-1920s, Darrow undertook a series of cases that solidified his status as America's most celebrated trial lawyer. In 1924, he defended Nathan Leopold and Richard Loeb, two wealthy Chicago teenagers who admitted murdering their fourteen-year-old cousin in an attempt to commit a perfect crime; Darrow saved them from the electric chair in an epic appeal against the death penalty. In 1925, he traveled to Dayton, Tennessee, to defend the right of John Scopes to teach evolution, facing William Jennings Bryan in the circus-like Scopes Monkey Trial. And in

1927, he defended Ossian Sweet, an African-American doctor charged with murder for shooting a man when a mob tried to drive Sweet from his Detroit home. Darrow won him an acquittal from an all-white jury.

Edgar seemed to have nothing but admiration for him. The FBI later would open a file on Darrow, but only to hold a few magazine articles Darrow wrote on courtroom strategy that Edgar used as speech material

FELIX FRANKFURTER never learned the full extent of the secret dossier Edgar compiled against him. When President Franklin Roosevelt considered sacking Edgar in 1933, it was Frankfurter, at the request of Harlan Stone, who vouched for him with the new president and helped save his job—despite his reservations over Hoover's original appointment in 1924. Years later, in 1961, word of the existence of a forty-year-old letter from Edgar accusing Frankfurter of "communistic propaganda activities" leaked out of the National Archives. Frankfurter, by then a Supreme Court Justice with twenty-two years' tenure on the bench, angrily confronted him over it. Edgar, who by then had survived thirty-six years himself atop the FBI, denied the letter's authenticity. "I stated I sign my name 'J. Edgar Hoover' and this letter is signed 'J. E. Hoover,'" he explained to Frankfurter in a note. He was almost certainly lying; the letter apparently predated Edgar's name change by at least two years. Still, he insisted it was a fake, and Frankfurter had no basis to call this denial a lie.

Frankfurter escaped any direct reprisal for his role in exposing Justice Department lawbreaking in the Palmer Raids, but his Harvard colleague ZECHARIAH CHAFEE was less fortunate. A member of the Harvard Board of Overseers, using materials compiled by Edgar's Justice Department office, filed charges against Chafee with the university in May 1921 to get him fired. He called Chafee academically unfit to teach, citing errors in one of Chafee's *Harvard Law Review* articles attacking convictions under the 1917 Espionage Act. The university decided to force Chafee to defend himself in front of a special blue-ribbon panel of Law School alumni, resulting in what became known as the Trial at the Harvard Club in May 1921. The panel included New York State Appeals Court chief justice Benjamin Cardozo, federal judges Augustus N. Hand and James H. Morton Jr., and three Massachusetts state judges. It cleared Chafee by a single vote, but not before Chafee, the scion of a wealthy Rhode Island family made rich by its iron-manufacturing business, delivered a stirring final plea: "My sympathies and all my associations are with the men who save, who manage and produce. But I want my side to fight fair."

Chafee's nephew, John H. Chafee, would serve as United States senator from Rhode Island from 1976 though 1999. His grandnephew, Lincoln D. Chafee, would hold the seat from 1999 through January 2007.

BENJAMIN GITLOW served only three years of his seven-year sentence for criminal anarchy at Sing Sing prison. New York governor Al Smith ultimately pardoned him and suffered no visible political damage as a result. This came after President Warren G. Harding had already pardoned Eugene V. Debs with no political backlash. Gitlow ran for vice president of the United States on the Communist Party line in 1924 and 1928, sharing the ticket both times with the Party's presidential candidate, William Z. Foster, leader of the ill-fated 1919 steel strike.* Gitlow visited Russia in 1929 and met Joseph Stalin, though Stalin found Gitlow too much a free thinker and ordered him expelled from the party. Gitlow, for his part, would publicly renounce Communism in 1939, mocking his former creed as "an ideological system that strongly appeals to the gullible and, especially, ignorant masses." In 1951, he would even write a letter to J. Edgar Hoover, the man who helped send him to prison in 1920, praising him for his anticommunist work and offering to meet him in Washington to help him ferret out subversives.

EMMA GOLDMAN reached Russian soil in December 1919 after embarking on the *Buford* following her deportation from Ellis Island. She quickly lost her enthusiasm for the Bolsheviks after seeing firsthand the brutality of Lenin's regime, the forced labor, political repression, military brutality, and secret police. This was no workers' paradise. She managed to leave Russia after two years, made her way to France, and produced two books whose titles made her feelings clear: *My Disillusionment in Russia* (1923) and *My Further Disillusionment in Russia* (1924). Edgar never lost an ounce of his spite against Emma Goldman. He bragged about his role in deporting her in 1919, and he undoubtedly took pleasure watching her eat her words about the Soviet Bolsheviks. When Goldman repeatedly asked permission to visit America during the 1920s and 1930s to see her family, Edgar consistently blocked her as a security threat. As a result, she returned only twice, both times over his objections. Once was to give a lecture tour in 1934 speaking against Hitler and fascism, limited to ninety days under strict surveillance. The other was in May 1940 after she died

---

*In August 1920, the Executive Committee of the Communist International, meeting in Moscow, instructed the American Communist and Communist Labor parties to end their split and merge by the end of the year, which they did.

of a stroke in Toronto, Canada, and immigration officials allowed her body to reenter the country to be buried in Chicago's Waldheim Cemetery. Her grave can be found there today on the Cemetery's "Dissenters Row" near the tomb for the Haymarket anarchists.

WILLIAM BROSS LLOYD, Chicago's Millionaire Socialist, refused to renounce his communist creed until the 1940s. But, as Clarence Darrow predicted, he never served his prison term. In 1922, Illinois governor Lennington Small pardoned Lloyd and all the other remaining defendants from the 1920 Chicago communist trial. Small, too, suffered no visible political backlash for the decision.

LOUIS F. POST left the Labor Department in 1921 to live quietly with his wife in Washington, D.C.* He spent much of the next two years writing *The Deportations Delirium of Nineteen-Twenty*, pub-

"Somewhere in 'Free' Russia," a 1920 satire on Emma Goldman's exile. *Literary Digest*, October 9, 1920.

lished in 1923. Still healthy at seventy-five years old, he went on to give speeches, write articles, and dabble in all sorts of causes. He headed a local Coal Consumers League and a National Association Opposed to Blue Laws, and became a favorite booster for Robert LaFollette in his 1924 Progressive Party presidential campaign. "If our young men were giving as much attention to politics as they give to sports, we would have a better government," he joked at one campaign stop that year. "Political issues are at least as important as baseball." He knew this was a hard sell during the same summer that Babe Ruth hit forty-seven home runs and swimming star Johnny Weismuller, the future Hollywood Tarzan, won three gold medals at the Paris Olympic Games. Post later joined Felix

*Post had to survive one last attempt by J. Edgar Hoover to get him fired in 1920. Late that year, Hoover helped the American Legion produce its own damning report on Post, insisting on his removal. They presented it to the White House, but the White House decided to hand it off to Labor Secretary William B. Wilson. Wilson answered the Legion by calling Post "among the ablest and best administrative officers in the Government service . . . one of the truest Americans I have ever come in contact with."

Frankfurter in his drive to win a pardon for Sacco and Vanzetti, seeing in their case the same threat to free speech as the 1920 Raids had posed. He died the next January in Washington, D.C., at seventy-eight years old.

Given the singular role he played in facing down Mitchell Palmer at the height of the Red Scare, including his defense against impeachment charges, it is striking how utterly history has forgotten Louis F. Post. There is no government building named for him, no monument, nor even a full biography. Post himself might not have cared. As he saw it, he was simply doing his job and following the law. But if a key legacy of the Palmer Raids is the example set by those who had the backbone to stand up against government abuse when it counted, Louis Post's absence is a costly blind spot in the country's national memory.

⊙━━◆━━⊙

By contrast, nobody has forgotten J. EDGAR HOOVER.

Edgar entered the Justice Department in mid-1917 as an impression-able, ambitious, hard-working perfectionist straight from law school, a youngster who was eager to impress his bosses. By the time he took com-mand of the Bureau of Investigation in 1924, seven years later, he had hardened into a bureaucratic veteran. Of all the experiences shaping him during these formative years, none loomed larger than the Red Raids. This operation propelled him onto a national stage at just twenty-four years old, and he seized the opportunity with energy and drive. It was the crucible in which Edgar came of age. Over the next five decades leading the FBI, he never lost the anticommunist religion or his sense of entitle-ment in bending the rules to save the country from whomever he consid-ered subversive.

But J. Edgar Hoover was precisely the wrong person for this job, and his choice to lead the operation in 1919 was Mitchell Palmer's biggest single mistake. If balancing individual liberties with public safety in times of crisis is one of the most difficult jobs a democracy can face, Palmer gave free reign in managing this uniquely sensitive task to an inexperienced, zealous rookie. Despite his clear genius for organization, Edgar lacked the other essential qualification for the job, the life experience and human context to appreciate the responsibility that came with power.

Edgar did not invent the Red Raids or the Red Scare. He got his first hands-on training in government law enforcement at the height of World War I, a time when locking up dissenters was everyday business, scare talk of saboteurs was taken as gospel, and wartime security always trumped individual rights. Mitchell Palmer had already decided on a national crackdown against Reds in 1919, based on the 1918 Immigration Act, before he chose Edgar to lead it. By then, the atmosphere of police repression and anti-Red frenzy was already well entrenched. "Much sedition is heard and tolerated in the name of free speech," the New York Times expressed it in a typical piece in March 1919. "Aliens who belong to a society of revolutionists are not entitled to any tenderness from the Government." The experienced hands at the Justice Department, Edgar's supervisors and role models, all agreed on the concept. Edgar never questioned it. He soaked in their attitudes like a sponge, adopted them as his own personal beliefs, and got the job done beyond their wildest dreams.

J. Edgar Hoover in 1919, at twenty-four years of age, operated under a weight of mental demons that could have paralyzed a weaker person: guilt over having avoided military service in World War I; shame and more guilt surrounding his father's mental illness; anxiety over perhaps being a gay man—if in fact he was—in a time and place where this was unthinkable; pressures from his dominant mother; the isolation of living at home with his parents; and on and on. How these forces shaped his subconscious, we can never know. But one result was clear. He made his job his favorite refuge, and he turned it into a bludgeon to assert control over this one possession uniquely his own.

Beneath it all, what made him dangerous was the fact that Edgar was so extraordinarily gifted. His organization, drive, and focus won him repeated promotions, making him the best possible underling. Once Palmer gave him the order to round up and deport Reds, Edgar made it a reality. Without Edgar, Palmer's raids at most would have been a muted, watered-down affair, not the blockbuster, headline-grabbing production they became. The problem was that Edgar did his job too well. He took a bad plan and pushed it to the extreme, then failed to recognize the problems when it went off course. Done modestly, targeted at known dangerous leaders and a handful of key violent followers, a microversion of Palmer's Raid, without the overkill and fanfare, could have been a healthy remedy to the excesses of 1919. After all, the bombings did occur. But instead, the reality of Palmer's vision, magnified by Edgar's hypercompetence, became a horror.

Years later, Edgar would insist he was appalled on first learning the extent of the violence, the beatings, the inhumane treatment of suspects. "I was sent up to New York later by assistant attorney general Garvan and reported back that there had been clear cases of brutality in the raids," he told an interviewer from Look magazine in 1955. "They arrested a lot of people that weren't Communists." But at the time, in 1920, he showed no remorse, no sign of recognizing that anything was amiss, even after hearings made it clear that few of those arrested had posed any real danger to the country.

As late as June 1920, after most of the Red Raid prisoners were freed, the Twelve Lawyer report was out, and Palmer was suffering daily attacks over the abuses, Edgar still seemed unable to grasp the problem. "I must state that I am at a complete loss to understand why aliens who are charged with a violation of the anarchist deportation statute are permitted to examine official files when government officers charged with the enforcement of the laws are refused such permission," he confided to Caminetti that month on hearing about one particular case in Detroit. The fact that the alien, as a defendant facing deportation, had a right to see the evidence against him seemed never to enter Edgar's mind, except as a nuisance. Instead, still young, raw, full of fight, and with a chip on his shoulder, he was ready to take criticisms as personal attacks, and criticisms of his work as attacks on the country. In his eyes, dissenters became enemies, and lawyers representing communists became accomplices to treason.

There were at least five people in the Justice Department who outranked Edgar at the time: Bureau of Investigation chief Bill Flynn, his deputy Frank Burke, Assistant Attorney General Frank Garvan, Palmer's assistant, John Creighton, and Palmer himself. But none of them objected. Instead, they let Edgar call the tune from below. The problem was visible even to an outside lawyer like Jackson Ralston. "I believe that Mr. Palmer was played upon," Ralston told Senator Walsh's subcommittee during its 1921 hearings. "You find a growing—there was under him a growing—department of investigation. That department of investigation had to justify its existence." Reminded that the Bureau of Investigation existed long before Mitchell Palmer's time, Ralston hit the key point: "Yes, it has, but not in its present—not as it is today." Edgar had fundamentally changed it.

Edgar projected a confidence and earnestness that drew people to him. Even enemies and opposing lawyers often respected him for it. They rarely distrusted his motives, though often they came to regret it.

Senator Burton K. Wheeler of Montana, for instance, had every good reason to despise J. Edgar Hoover. Wheeler, after he announced his plan to investigate the Teapot Dome scandals in 1923, suffered vicious harassment at the hands of Bureau of Investigation agents—wiretapping, burglary, and a trumped-up indictment—all during the time that Edgar served as the Bureau's deputy director. Still, when Wheeler was handed the chance to get his revenge a decade later, he declined. Franklin D. Roosevelt, on becoming president in 1933, asked Wheeler if he had any objection to Edgar's staying on as Bureau director in the new administration, handing Wheeler the ability to end his career on the spot. Instead, "Hoover got wind of this talk and came to see me," Wheeler recalled, writing about the incident in 1962. "He insisted he played no part in the reprisals against me. I had no desire to ask for Hoover's head on a platter—and I'm glad I didn't."

Morris Katzeff, one of the lawyers who helped Felix Frankfurter during the Boston *habeas corpus* case in 1920, went further. He wrote a letter to a leading congressman in 1940 denying that Edgar had any hand in the Red Scare abuses. "I spoke to Mr. Hoover once or twice at Washington in 1920 about the manner in which the raids were carried out, the utter lawlessness of the entire transactions, and I do recall distinctly that he deplored these conditions as much as did counsel for defense," Katzeff insisted. To Edgar himself, he wrote: "[Y]ou had nothing to do with the irregularities and harsh treatment of the aliens suspected of being Communists." It was a total lie, but Katzeff believed it—or at least pretended to—and Edgar let him.

Edgar, for his part, managed to find a soft spot only for a select very few of his adversaries. Beyond Clarence Darrow, there was Charles Recht, the lawyer who defended a string of communists in 1920 including Soviet emissary Ludwig Martens. Recht recalled how he sat cramped together with Edgar at the lawyers' table during dozens of courtroom sessions that year. "After months of such physical proximity it became difficult for either of us to evince personal hostility toward each other," he wrote in his unpublished memoirs. He got to enjoy joking with Edgar about their odd relationship. Recht described how during a recess in one Communist trial, he took a witness outside the courthouse for a taxi ride through New York's Central Park so they could talk privately, but, along the way, he noticed they were being followed. "Next day in Court I said facetiously to Hoover: 'Did you have a good drive through the Park?'" They both laughed. Years later, after Edgar became head of the FBI, he wrote Recht a letter saying, as Recht remembered it, "that despite our bitter opposition in the Court hearings he had a high regard for me as a lawyer."

But this was an exception, and they were few. More typical were the grudges, the lifetime hatreds against anyone who dared to cross him. Edgar came to distrust liberals as a group. He took to mocking John Lord

O'Brian, his onetime Justice Department mentor, as a "pseudo liberal," his lowest slur for someone he considered a highbrow phony, and he made a point to mispronounce the word as "swaydo." Edgar's vindictive streak reached grotesque heights with Felix Frankfurter and the twelve lawyers who signed the National Popular Government League report in 1920. He wrote poison pen letters about them. "I am informed that Roscoe Pound, of Harvard . . . is a behind-the-scenes socialist, who puts on one face to the Harvard faculty, etc., and another to his chums," he said in one addressed to House Immigration chairman Albert Johnson. "My impression is that [Chicago Law School dean Ernst] Freund is also red, but I have not yet run this out and probably it will be found that everyone in the gang is, unless poor [former Philadelphia federal prosecutor Francis Fisher] Kane is excused on the ground of lack of mental balance, which he certainly has not got."

Edgar used his power to have Felix Frankfurter stalked as if he were a wanted criminal. When one of his agents got wind of a telegram Frankfurter sent to a prominent congressman in June 1920 suggesting that the congressman investigate Palmer for abuses of power, Edgar went into a rage and called out the dogs. "I am in receipt of information that Felix Frankfurter is contemplating sailing abroad at the end of the week," he alerted the State Department. "I have not been informed of his destination or what the purpose of his trip may be, but I thought that this information might be of interest to you in view of the activities of this subject in this country."

Had Frankfurter been a less prominent person, Edgar might have gone further and asked the State Department to pull his passport, but they got the message. "I would advise you that the subject [Frankfurter] is sailing on the *Lapland* or *Rotterdam* this Saturday, as American delegate to the International Zionist Conference," they reported back promptly. They would keep an eye on him.

Given the chance by Harlan Fiske Stone in 1924 to make a clean start in his career, Edgar once again seized the moment. Starting with his reorganization of the agent force that year, he built his Bureau of Investigation into a showpiece. He laid down rules requiring each new agent to be expert in law or accounting and to meet strict standards for dress, deportment, and personal conduct. He championed a scientific approach to crime fighting, instituting uniform crime reports, establishing a national Crime Laboratory and a National Academy, and conceiving new tools like a public list of most-wanted criminals. His flagship was the nationwide

Fingerprint Division he created for both Feds and local police to use in identifying suspects. By 1931, he could boast of it as the largest in the world with ten million sets of prints; by 1974, it would top 159 million sets, covering a large majority of the American population. "There is a feeling in the underworld that they cannot get away, and that has been brought about largely through the establishment of the identification division," he told Congress in the mid-1920s.

When a wave of kidnappings, bank robberies, and racketeering swept the country in the early 1930s, Congress and President Franklin Roosevelt turned to Edgar and his Bureau. They expanded its powers and budgets to fight the crime spree, and the Bureau responded with a parade of high-profile successes: the capture of the Lindbergh baby kidnapper, the killings of bank robber John Dillinger, murderer "Baby Face" Nelson, and gangster-killer "Pretty Boy" Floyd, and the capture of kidnapper George "Machine Gun" Kelly. James Cagney became the first major Hollywood movie star to play a Bureau agent in the movies in 1935, the same year that Congress renamed it the FBI. Cagney's film was called G-Men, a name that stuck to FBI agents after they spread the story of "Machine Gun" Kelly pleading during his 1923 arrest: "Don't shoot, G-Men; don't shoot." Edgar installed a publicity team in his Washington, D.C., office that took this image, the clean-cut, heroic crime-fighter, and made it a national brand, with G-Men radio shows, pulp novels, magazines, toys, bubblegum cards, and copycat films, all orchestrated by J. Edgar Hoover. In 1936, a magazine called The Feds featured J. Edgar as Public Hero No. 1. A few years later, the Big Brothers of America named him, with no intentional irony, Big Brother of 1951. The George Orwell dystopian classic 1984 had been published just two years earlier, in 1949.

Young boys across the country soon dreamed of joining the team, and the FBI could cherry-pick the best. At one point, its admission acceptance rate for new agents rivaled that of an Ivy League college, choosing just seven out of every hundred applicants.

Along with the agency, Edgar used his publicity machine to build an image for himself as a patron saint for detectives, a virtual monk living a vow of abstinence, sacrificing wealth and family, to devote his life to law enforcement. Edgar never married, despite brief flirtations in the 1930s with actress Dorothy Lamour and Lela Rogers, mother of actress Ginger Rogers. Edgar lived with his own mother in the same house on Seward Square until she died in 1938. Edgar was forty-three years old and, by then, he had started his lifelong relationship with Clyde Tolson, his closest friend, whom he hired in 1928 and made FBI deputy director. He and Tolson traveled together on vacations and official business, shared lunch each day, rode to work together each morning and home each evening, and often wore matching suits. Edgar would leave Tolson the bulk of his estate when he died. If they did have a sexual relationship, as is widely believed though never established, it was discreet, stable, and disciplined, as was everything else about J. Edgar Hoover.

His only other lifelong partner was Helen Gandy, who remained his secretary and executive assistant at the FBI for fifty-two years, longer than all but a handful of marriages. After his death in 1972, it was Helen Gandy who secretly shredded or disposed of J. Edgar's most sensitive personal files, even as the new acting FBI director, a Richard M. Nixon appointee named L. Patrick Gray, stood in the very same room trying to occupy the office.

Edgar mostly stayed away from tracking radicals and communists during the late 1920s and early 1930s. But in 1934, President Franklin D. Roosevelt saw war on the horizon and worried that Nazis connected to Adolph Hitler and communists linked to Joseph Stalin might form dangerous subversive cells in the United States. That year, he asked the FBI to start monitoring Nazi groups operating in the country. Then, in August 1936, he called into his office the now middle-aged J. Edgar Hoover, a paunchier, grayer, cagier man, for a private briefing on communist activities as well. Edgar had never totally taken his eye off the Red Menace. His friends at Military Intelligence—which spied on American citizens at home until the 1940s—kept him supplied with the latest updates. As a result, when Franklin Roosevelt raised the issue, Edgar was ready to barrage him with purported evidence on communist infiltration of the International Longshoreman's Union, the United Mine Workers, and dozens of other labor organizations in addition to several government departments. Roosevelt, alarmed, asked if he could develop a fuller picture of the threat. But this time, it was Edgar who demurred. "Mr. President, there is no government agency compiling such general intelligence," he recalled telling Roosevelt, raising some of the legal issues that got Mitchell Palmer in trouble back in 1920. "Of course, it is not a violation of the law to be a member of the Communist Party and we have had no specific authority to make such general investigations."

Edgar had learned his lesson. The American public was fickle and likely to turn against wide-scale government snooping. Any such program had to have some veneer of legality and be kept secret, never disclosed or discussed. President Roosevelt solved the immediate problem with clever lawyering. He asked Secretary of State Cordell Hull to make a formal request for an investigation under the obscure provisions of a 1916 Appropriations Act. This was enough to put Edgar back in business.

All through World War II, he expanded the FBI's intelligence and counterespionage operations to cover fascists, communists, and wartime dissenters. Even actress Mary Pickford, America's Sweetheart from the silent screen era, earned herself an FBI file in 1944 after a friend reported her for making pro-Japanese remarks after a few drinks at a Hollywood dinner party. Later, with the onset of the Cold War and a new Red Scare, this time led by United States Senator Joseph McCarthy (R-Wis.), Edgar took the lead and expanded his spy network. In March 1947, he announced to the House Un-American Activities Committee that "the deceit, trickery, and lies of the American communists," as he put it, were just as serious as any threat from Russia. When Senator McCarthy launched his abusive public hearings to expose alleged communist sympathizers, Edgar backed him up. "The FBI kept McCarthy in business," then-FBI assistant director William Sullivan explained in the 1970s. "We gave McCarthy all we had . . . even while [Hoover] publicly denied that we were helping him." Edgar made a big splash over the FBI's arrest in

J. Edgar Hoover in 1935, demonstrating FBI firearms training.

Hoover in the 1960s, after four decades in office.

1950 of Ethel and Julius Rosenberg, two Communist Party members ultimately convicted of stealing design plans for the atomic bomb and
passing them to Russia, in what Edgar called "the crime of the century."
Both of the Rosenbergs were electrocuted in 1953.

Edgar's FBI files soon bulged with surveillance reports on luminaries
from First Lady Eleanor Roosevelt, to philanthropist John D. Rockefeller
III, to scientist Albert Einstein, from President John F. Kennedy, to
actress Marilyn Monroe and scores of other celebrities. He had obscenity
files, sex files, clearance files on governmental appointees, delicious dirt
and blackmail on half of official Washington at the snap of his fingers. By
1960, the FBI had 432,000 open files on subversives and, beginning in
1956, it expanded these operations through a new program called COIN-
TELPRO that grew in the 1960s to include extralegal break-ins, buggings,
and sabotage of anti–Vietnam War protestors and civil rights leaders like
the Rev. Martin Luther King Jr.

J. Edgar kept a tight lid on all these secrets. "[He] required that Bureau
officials obtain his written approval before conducting any sensitive investigation," professor Athan Theoharis has written in explaining Hoover's
system, "and then report, also in writing, what they discovered and how
they secured the information." To safeguard these files, and ensure they'd
never fall into the hands of Congress, a court, or some overcurious attorney
general, Edgar evolved a complex web of systems and subsystems. He kept
certain records in his own office where Helen Gandy could watch them
personally. These were deemed "official and confidential." More sensitive
files were separated out and deemed "personal and confidential," and all of
these were kept separate from the official files of the FBI.

All the while, he maintained his own rarified profile as a national icon.
He seemed immortal as the decades rolled by, from the 1940s to the
1950s, 1960s, and 1970s. presidents came and went, but not J. Edgar
Hoover. He would serve eleven of them, from Woodrow Wilson to
Richard M. Nixon, and eighteen attorneys general from A. Mitchell
Palmer to John Mitchell. Whispers always followed him, suspicions about
his dark side, but they never got far. "One hears in Washington that
Hoover has secret dossiers on all left-wingers and is just awaiting a chance
to clap them in concentration camps," Jack Alexander wrote as far back
as 1937. "Hoover poo-poos such stories." But if anyone tried to tarnish J.
Edgar's well-polished image, particularly by suggesting that his relationship with Clyde Tolson might be more than platonic, he made sure they
received a blunt threat from a tough-talking FBI official. It always

worked. By then, he had built the FBI into a $330 million annual budget with a staff approaching 20,000.

Only after he died did the truth come out. Newspapers ran stunning exposes about the longtime FBI director, how he kept secret files on presidents, congressmen, cabinet members, and movie stars. After President Nixon's resignation in the Watergate scandal, Congress launched a massive probe into intelligence gathering by both the FBI and the Central Intelligence Agency, led by Senator Frank Church (D-Ida.) and Congressman Otis Pike (D-NY) in 1975. These investigations revealed that Hoover's FBI had harassed and spied on Americans since the 1930s using illegal wiretaps, bugs, and break-ins. Another new attorney general, this one Edward H. Levi under new president Gerald R. Ford, demanded a new set of reforms to reign in the agency.

Today, all the dirt is public. Edgar's files, with few exceptions, are open for any American to come and see at the National Archives in Washington, D.C., and College Park, Maryland. They make endlessly fascinating reading and paint a stark portrait of absolute power breeding absolute corruption. J. Edgar Hoover today, a figure of fact, myth, and speculation, stands as perhaps one of the most hated men in American history. John Lord O'Brian, the Justice Department lawyer who first hired him in 1917 and promoted him repeatedly, was asked about this by a television interviewer in 1972, after Edgar's death. O'Brian said: "This is something I prefer to whisper in dark corners. It is one of the sins for which I have to atone." Edgar's legend—a plausibly gay man who harassed gays, a possible descendant of an African-American who harassed civil rights leaders, a top law enforcement official who placed himself above the law, all making him out as something approaching a monster—is a far cry from the young eager beaver who came to work at the Justice Department in 1917, ready to make a good impression and save the country from subversives.

But Edgar did not step into the world as an evil autocrat. This side of him was shaped in large part by the events and attitudes that engulfed him during his formative years, his coming of age. And to the extent that our modern war on terror is paralleling the attitudes of the 1919–1920 Red Scare, we have to wonder: How many young J. Edgar Hoovers are we creating today?

His name still stands carved on a marble slab on the front of the FBI headquarters building in Washington, D.C. So it should stay. J. Edgar Hoover is the reality behind the institution, its true founding spirit for good and ill. Removing his name wouldn't change that. But rather than a tribute, his name there should serve as a warning, particularly to the dedicated professionals who work inside. There is danger in the power they wield, the license they carry to intrude into people's lives. Theirs is a special public trust, one that was abused in the past by that man named J. Edgar Hoover. They have the duty to make sure it is not abused again. That is the most important legacy of the Palmer Raids.

NOTES

(For abbreviations and coded references to hearings or manuscript collections, see Sources.)

1. DENIALS

1   "He told me brusquely . . ." Toledano, p. 71.See also Whitehead, p. 67.
1   "Then he said to me '. . . .": Toledano, p. 71.See also Whitehead, p. 67.
2   "When I became Attorney General, . . .": Mason, p. 149.
2   "I don't know whom to trust; I . . .": Mason, p. 150.
5   "limited strictly to investigations . . .": Theoharis, p. 85.
5   "a man of exceptional . . .": Mason, p. 152.
5   Hoover's homosexuality: see Summers p. 254, Theoharis (1995), and Hack, p. 271–274. African-American ancestor: see McGhee, Secrets Uncovered.
6   Stone had submitted public testimony: see Stone testimony, Palmer hearing, 1921, pp. 270–280.
7   "[H]e was just a kid . . .": Carusi interview in Demaris, p. 57.
7   "vicious and false . . ." "in the illegal methods . . .": Toledano, p. 60.
7   Roger Baldwin . . ."unwilling part": Memorandum supplied by L.B. Nichols to Dr. Alpheus Thomas Mason, August 8, 1950, p. 9. NARA, RG 65; File 62-8782.

2. BOMBS

12   Washington's West End: Today, the West End had moved further west. Modern Washingtonians know the neighborhood as including the larger area between P Street, Twenty-second Street, Rock Creek Park, and Pennsylvania Avenue, NW.
12   "I heard a crash downstairs . . .": Chicago Daily Tribune, June 3, 1919.
13   "I had just placed my automobile . . .": Chicago Daily Tribune, June 3, 1920.
13   "The world has come . . .": Roosevelt and Shalett, p. 59; Gentry, p. 75.
13   "an embrace . . ." "Whatever are you doing . . .": Roosevelt and Shalett, p. 60; Collier, p. 255.
13   "I went over to the attorney general's home . . .": Chicago Daily Tribune, June 3, 1919.
13   "Say, I never knew before . . .": Roosevelt and Shalett, p. 60; Gentry, p. 75. Alice Roosevelt Longworth, Theodore Roosevelt's daughter, who also lived in the neighborhood, came by the scene that night as well and observed that Palmer's house looked "as if it might fetch loose at any moment." See Weimer p. 7.
13   "I'm glad you are here"; "I believe that the man with the bomb . . .": Washington Evening Star, June 3, 1919.
14   "I hope sincerely . . .": Chicago Daily Tribune, June 3, 1919.

15   "[The bomb] blew in the front . . .": Chicago Daily Tribune, June 3, 1919.

15   Civil War . . . World War II . . . : In those conflicts, American military fatalities were 558,000 and 405,000, respectively.

17   "I could not, without . . .": Letter from Palmer to Wilson, February 24, 1913. Wilson papers, LC.

17   "Palmer's first choice . . .": McCombs, p. 163.

18   "Many of the German-owned industrial concerns . . .": Palmer, Scribner's, July 1919, p. 17.

18   Slacker Raids: Generally on the slacker raids, see Theoharis pp. 104–105.

19   "Palmer, our friend in 1912 . . ."; "Palmer is young, militant . . .": Letters from Tumulty to Wilson, January 12, 1919, and February 1, 1919. Wilson papers. LC.

19   "Palmer . . . recommended that fifty-one prisoners": Letters from Palmer to Joe Tumulty, April 4, May 9, 10, and 15, 1919. Wilson papers, LC; Annual Report of the Attorney General for 1919, pp. 25–27; Hoyt p. 28.

19   Gregory . . . review of political prisoner: see letter from Gregory to Wilson, March 1, 1919.Wilson papers, LC.

19   "The master class has always . ." :see Debs v. United States, 249 U.S. 211 (1919), and Ginger, pp. 375–377.

20   "Reds Directing Seattle Strike . . ."; "From Russia they came . . .": Murray, p. 65.

21   "riots savaged Toledo, Ohio": see Chicago Daily Tribune, June 4, 1919.

21   "American soldiers . . . dumped chaotically": Chances for an orderly transition to a peacetime economy vanished after the War Department scrapped its demobilization plan and Congress cut funding of the U.S. Employment Service by 80 percent that year, both as cost-cutting moves.

22   "Letter to American Workingmen": V. I. Lenin, "A Letter to American Workingmen," August 20, 1918, Lusk Committee files, Albany. See also Washington Evening Star, June 20, 1919.

24   "weak, vacillating . . ."; "I hope Washington . . .": Murray, p. 72.

24   "The Department of Justice . . .": From Report by Special Agent Feri Weiss, June 3, 1919.NARA, M1085, file BS 211793.

24   "A fitter in one of the shops . . .": Letter to Mrs. Palmer from Mary Lownden, quoted in letter from John Creighton to W. M. Offley, June 9, 1919, in NARA, RG 65, M1085, OG 367962.

24   "I stood in the middle of the wreckage . . .": Palmer testimony, Palmer hearing, 1921, p. 580.

25   "The outrages of last night . . ."; "These attacks by bomb throwers . . .": Washington Post and other newspapers, June 4, 1919.

25   "Attorney General Palmer's courage . . .": New York Times, June 4, 1919; Hoyt, p. 33.

25   "Free speech has been outraged . . .": Washington Post , June 4, 1919.

25   Every true American citizen . . .": Letter from Tull to Palmer, June 4, 1919, NARA RG 60, file 202600, Palmer file.

26   "Mr. Garvan, in my judgment. . . .":Palmer testimony, June 13, 1919, in Appropriation hearing, 1920, p. 305.

27   1915 espionage case: see Washington Post, October 26, 1915; New York Times, November 2, 1915.

27   counterfeit . . . silver certificates: Boston Globe, August 17, 1916.

27   "I place a conservative estimate . . .": Los Angeles Times, April 7, 1918.

27   Flynn . . . crime novels: see, for instance, The Eagle's Eye: The True Story of

the Imperial German Government's Spies and Intrigues in America, 1919; and *The Barrel Mystery*, serialized in *New York Times*, July 16, 1911; and *Washington Post*, April 19, 1914.

28 "*Mr. Flynn looks you in the eye . . .*": *Los Angeles Times*, April 7, 1918.

28 "*[A]s he told me, . . .* ": Palmer testimony, Appropriation hearing, 1920. p. 306.

28 "*extraordinarily susceptible to the fear . . .*": Coban, p. 207.

28 "*perfectly splendid*": Palmer testimony, Appropriation hearing, 1920, p. 306.

28 "*I am really quite as much . . .*": Palmer testimony, Appropriation hearing, 1920, p. 304.

28 "*A sifting process . . .*": Clipping in NARA RG 65, M1085, file BS 211793.

28 "*precautionary measures.*": *Boston Daily Globe*, June 19, 1919.

29 FN: "*preventive detention . . . recent proposals to expand*": see, for instance, Rosenzweig and Carafano.

29 FN: "*Chicago . . .*" "*idlers . . . to see why . . .*": *Boston Daily Globe*, February 13, 1919.

29 "*Cleveland . . . arrested twenty-eight men*": Memorandum from Cleveland Immigration Inspector in Charge to Commissioner General of Immigration, June 6, 1919.NARA, RG 85, File 54235/36.

29 "*Philadelphia . . .*"; "*suspicious liquid*": *Washington Post*, June 14, 1919.

29 "*holding him under . . .*"; "*By my own right . . .*" : Ralston testimony, Palmer hearing, 1921, pp. 247–254.

29 "*We know the source . . .*": *Washington Post*, June 19, 1919.

30 "*either made by a Russian . . .*": Report by Pittsburgh agent R.B. Spencer, June 5, 1919, in NARA RG 65, M1085, file BS 211793.

31 "*I am convinced that the pink circular . . .*": Report by Boston agent Weiss, June 3, 1919, in NARA RG 65, M1085, file BS 211793. Weiss claimed that he showed a copy to a socialist being held in a Boston jail: "after reading the same, [he] stated: 'Well, that is no Louis Fraina,' but later on [he] admitted that it certainly appeared identical with other writing of Fraina." Weiss also went undercover to the Boston socialist party office on Washington Street. "Now they are getting their own medicine in return for what they have been giving the poor classes," one former official there told him. See also reports from Boston agents Harold Zorian and William J. West, June 14 and 20, 1919, in NARA RG 65, M1085, file BS 211793.

31 "*It should be noted that Fraina . . .*": Report by Boston agent Weiss, June 3, 1919, in NARA RG 65, M1085, file BS 211793.

31 "*[T]he Jews had a six day meeting . . .*": Reports by Boston agent Weiss, June 3 and 10, 1919, in NARA RG 65, M1085, file BS 211793.

31 "*The theory that [the attacker] was an Italian . . .*": *Washington Post*, June 4, 1919.

32 "*There is a great deal of talk . . .*": *Chicago Daily Tribune*, June 27, 1919.

32 "*Palmer . . . tip . . . bomb in the House of Representatives*": see Memorandum from Creighton to Flynn, June 18, 1919, in NARA RG 65, M1085, file BS 211793.

32 "*Cleveland . . .*": "*armed parade . . . as part of plans . . .*": Newspaper clipping in NARA RG 65, M1085, file BS 211793. Similarly, an attack in New York City that week on the Pershing Club on Madison Avenue was stopped only when an alert guard opening a postal package noticed it contained explosive black powder. *New York Times*, June 18, 1919.

33 *"Martens . . . testify"*: see Martens testimony, Executive Session, June 12, 1919. Lusk Committee files, Albany.

33 *"We have received so many . . ."*: Palmer testimony, Appropriation hearing, 1920, p. 304.

33 *"thus giving them an opportunity . . ."*: Reports by Boston agent Weiss, June 3, 1919, in NARA RG 65, M1085, file BS 211793.

34 *"aliens . . . in Pittsburgh . . . released by Labor Department"*: Letter from Pittsburgh Special Agent in Charge R.B. Spencer, June 3, 1919, in NARA RG 65, M1085, file BS 211793.

34 *"Immigration Act . . . strengthened it in 1918"*: see Section 4287 of the Immigration Act as amended by Act of October 16, 1918.

34 *"[T]he deportation statute ought . . ."*: Palmer testimony in Appropriation hearing, 1920, p. 307.

35 *"[a] drastic policy of deporting . . ."*: *Washington Post*, June 19, 1919.

35 *"If we can . . . round up . . ."*: *Chicago Daily Tribune*, June 27, 1919.

35 *"There is no room, . . ."*: *New York Times*, June 18, 1919.

36 *"For Attorney General: My heartfelt congratulations . . ."*: Telegram from Wilson via Tumulty to Palmer, June 4, 1919.Wilson papers. LC.

36 *"[W]e have every reason . . ."*: *Chicago Daily Tribune*, June 27, 1919.

36 *"Congress . . . agreed. . . . Who could argue . . . with Mitchell Palmer?"*: When one senator, New Jersey Republican Joe Frelinghuysen, tried to challenge Palmer at a hearing that week over allegations of abuse in Palmer's wartime office, Palmer's friends had a field day mocking him in the press: "[T]he very night that the republican senators stayed the confirmation of this cabinet official . . . an anarchist, an alien to American institutions, attempted the life of the attorney general, and had his own body blown into fragments in the attempt," wrote syndicated columnist James Hollomon. "Politics!" see generally Palmer nomination hearing, 1919, and *Atlanta Constitution*, June 6, 1919.

3. EDGAR

40 *Edgar . . . hired . . . a few weeks earlier:* The exact date is unclear. John Lord O'Brian remained at the Justice Department at least until April 2. See letter from O'Brian to Harry Weinberger, April 25, 1919, Emma Goldman papers, Delaware.

40 *"Palmer's . . . mail system . . . irritated clerk nagged"*: Memo to Hoover from J. T. Suter, July 6, 1919, NARA.RG 60, file 202600.

40 *"Edgar . . . to John Creighton . . . formal notes . . . Respectfully"* : see, for instance, Memorandum to Creighton from Hoover, June 14, 1919; RG 65, file BS 211793.

40 *lead . . . by North Carolina U.S. Senator Lee Overman:* see Memorandum from Hoover to Flynn, July 30, 1919; Report by Dayton, Ohio agent Claude P. Light, July 20, 1919, both in RG 65, file BS211793.

41 *"I think that early in his career . . ."*: Fennell interview, in Demaris, p. 8.

42 *"theory . . . African-American mother . . . African-American ancestor"*: McGhee, pp. 205–216; 226–228.

42 *citywide competition:* see *Washington Herald*, May 19, 1913, clipping in Hoover Scrapbooks, 1913-1972; NARA RG 65, Director's Official

Records and Memorabilia, Box 1. For childhood materials generally, see Hoover Center collection.

43 *"'Speed' is one of the best . . ."*: Toledano, p. 41.

43 *"He was one of the world's . . ."*: Margaret Fennel interview in Demaris, p. 23.

43 *"Is that noise a lion . . ."*: Toledano, p. 39.

43 *"The saddest moment of the year . . ."*: Toledano, p. 40.

44 *"I'm sure he would be the chief librarian . . ."*: Washington Post, February 25, 1968, in Gentry, p. 67.

44 *"From the day he entered the Department . . ."*: Alexander, II, p. 21.

44 *"scare stories . . . German spies . . . glass in wheat and flour"*: New York Times, February 22, 1918.

45 "I discovered he worked Sundays and nights . . .": O'Brian interview in Gentry, 69.

45 *"At the end of the war . . ."*; *"I took that up . . ."*: O'Brian interview, in Gentry, p. 74.

45 *pay raise, from $2,000 to $3,000* : NARA, RG 65, class 67 (personal matters), Redacted Personal Case Files of Former FBI Director J. Edgar Hoover, 1920–1977.

46 *"I knew he had a nervous breakdown . . ."*: Margaret Fennell interview, in Demaris, p. 8.

46 *"Sir: The Department is in receipt . . ."*: Letter to DN Hoover from Hastings, April 6, 1917, Hoover Center collection; Margaret Fennel interview in Demaris, p. 5.

47 *"Yesterday I saw . . ."*; *"Love to all . . ."*: Letters from Dickerson Hoover to J. Edgar Hover, Undated, and April 29, 1904. Hoover Center collection.

48 *"Don't study too hard"*: see, for instance, letters from Dickerson Hoover to J. Edgar Hoover, September 8, 1912 andundated, 1916.Hoover Center collection.

48 *"So glad to hear . . ."*: Letter from Annie Hoover to Hoover, October 9, 1905.Hoover Center collection.

48 *"Mrs. Hoover . . . kept alive the disciplinary tradition . . ."*: Alexander, II, p. 21.

48 *"How is the attorney tonight?"*: Theoharis and Cox, p. 52.

48 *"I have wheeled Edgar . . ."*: Washington Post, October 7, 1934.

49 *"I cried and cried . . ."*: Margaret Fennel interview in Theoharis and Cox, p. 40.

49 *Edgar . . . Alice . . . engagement*: Summers, p. 31.The source for this story is Helen Gandy, who reportedly told it seventy-one years later in 1988, shortly before her death and sixteen years after Edgar's death. She reportedly never revealed Alice's full name.

4. BUREAUCRATS

51 *"I have observed . . ."*: Memorandum from Wilson to Palmer, June 10, 1919. NARA, RG 85, File 54235/36.

52 *"[A]ny alien [found to be unqualified] . . ."*: Section 19 of Immigraiton Act of 1917, as amended in 1918. See also Louis Post's explanation in Post hearing, June 1920, pp. 61–64.

52 *"The work was extremely disturbing . . ."*: Post (1923), p. 149.

53 *"a government agency for keeping . . ."*: Lombardi, p. 132.

54 *"His table was piled mountains high . . ."*: Howe, p. 255.

56 *"When the Attorney General gives orders . . ."* *"Mr. Attorney General, not*

only is there no . . .": This incident is told by Louis Post, having heard it from Parker. Post (1923), pp. 56–57.

57 *"Rule 22":* On this, see memorandum from Caminetti to Garvin, June 20, 1919, NARA, RG 85. File 54235/36.

57 FN: *Federal Courts in 1919 held . . . :* see, for instance, *Fong Yue Ting v. United States,* 149 U.S. 698 (1893); *The Japanese Immigrant Case,* 189 U.S. 86 (1902); *Yick Wo v. Hopkins,* 118 U.S. 356 (1886); *Whitfield v. Hanges* 222 FR 745 (1915); and Post hearing, June 1920, p. 222.

57 *"The bomb explosion in front . . .":* Post (1923), p. 55.

58 *"the important work to be done . . .":* Memorandum from John Lord O'Brien to Attorney General Gregory, December 14, 1917, NARA, RG 60, file 190470.

5. RACE RIOTS

62 *"[Y]ou should have heard . . .":* Letter from Annie Hoover to Hoover, September 4, 1912. Hoover Center collection.

6. RADICAL DIVISION

63 *"I never cared for them":* Washington Post, October 7, 1934.

63 *gruesome murders . . . Floyd Allen:* see *New York Times,* March 15, and May 18, 1912, *Washington Post,* April 23, 1912, and *Boston Globe,* September 12, 1912, and letter from Annie Hoover to Hoover, September 16, 1912, in Hoover Center collection.

64 *Edgar . . . grand vision:* Technically, he now wore two hats now at the Justice Department. As chief of the Radical Division, he answered to Bureau of Investigation Chief Bill Flynn. And as a special assistant to the attorney general, Edgar continued to report directly to Mitchell Palmer, Flynn's boss. In reality, this left him mostly on his own with no single primary supervisor. Edgar could always play one off against the other, and avoid having either boss, Palmer or Flynn, pull the reins too tightly.

64 *"[I]t was the original intention . . .":* Memorandum Upon Work of the Radical Division, August 1, 1919 to October 15, 1919, from Hoover, p. 8, NARA, RG 65, in Emma Goldman papers, Delaware.

64 *"Young Hoover was instructed . . .":* Whitehead, p. 41. See also AG Annual Report, 1919, p. 13: "Although ordinarily the [Justice Department] is concerned with the investigation of individual violations of law," he argued, "in the matter of the radical situation . . . intelligent investigations of individuals can be accomplished only by a thorough-going understanding of the situation as a whole."

64 *Thus was born what later would become the FBI:* On the 1908 creation of the Bureau, see Lowenthal, pp. 3–9, and Theoharis (2000), pp. 2–3.

65 *"They had a good time . . .":* Summers, p. 32.

65 *"wraith-like, grim-faced spinster":* Theoharis and Cox, p. 105

65 *"It was about this time . . .":* Demaris, p. 7.

65 *George F. Ruch:* see Whitehead, p. 331.

65 *Bureau . . . staff had ballooned:* Data on staff size from Theoharis (2000), p.4.

65 *"[M]any of the special agents . . .":* Memorandum upon the work of the Radical Division, October 18, 1919, NARA RG 65, in Emma Goldman papers.

66 *Edgar . . . courted the Lusk Committee in New York State:* see, for instance, letter from B.I. Special Agent W. M. Doyar to Lusk Committee staff,

October 7, 1919 ("I respectfully request that your Committee communicate with Mr. J. E. Hoover, Special Assistant to the Attorney-General,
Department of Justice, Washington, D.C., who is now in charge of such
matters"), Lusk Committee files, Albany.

66 *less than two minutes . . . normally would take hours* : see Report of The Radical Division of the Department of Justice, in Palmer hearing, June 1920,
p. 166.

66 *"has probably accumulated a greater mass . . ."*: AG Annual Report, 1919, p. 13.

67 *Edgar . . . complained . . . Frank Burke:* Memorandum from Hoover to
Burke, September 11, 1919; LC collection.

69 *"Everything illegal necessitates integrity . . ."*: Goldman (1910, 1917).

70 *"I feel guilty to be at large . . ."*: Boyer & Morais, p. 199.

70 *"Here in America we can sweep . . ."*: see *New York Times*, June 21, 1919.

7. REDS

71 *"A new soul, a new life . . ."*: Lloyd, Convention Impressions, p. 4.

71 *"The American Communist Party, . . ."*: Gitlow (1939), p. 39.

72 *"[T]he red flag was . . ."*: Francis Irving testimony. Lloyd trial, NYPL, p. 414.

72 *"Lloyd, in my opinion, possesses the ability . . ."*: Report of Agent Abelman,
March 19, 1919. NARA, RG 65, M1085, file OG86163.

73 *"A tall, strong-featured elderly . . ."*: Gitlow (1939), p. 7.

74 *"These Russian Federationists . . ."*: Lloyd, p. 3.

75 *"petty bourgeois, moderate, hesitant, . . ."*; *"[I]t is necessary to destroy . . ."*;
"Revolutionary Socialism does not propose . . .": Gitlow (1919).

75 *Lloyd . . . $650 check . . . to Fraina :* Robert Howe testimony. Lloyd trial,
NYPL, p. 557.

75 *"John Reed had about 50 . . ."*: Report on Communist Conventions to Military Intelligence, Chicago, by unnamed agent, September 5, 1919,
NARA, RG 165, in Emma Goldman papers, Delaware.

76 *"If you do not sit down . . ."*: Charles Egan testimony, Lloyd trial, NYPL, p. 452.

76 *"You are Right Wing enemies . . ."*: Gitlow (1939), p. 30.

76 *"One cannot help wondering . . ."*: Lloyd, p. 1.

76 *"Delegates and visitors rose . . ."*: Gitlow (1939), p. 47.

76 *"the whole crowd petty political intriguers . . ."*: Lloyd, p. 3.

76 *"whose whole demeanor gave . . ."*: Gitlow (1939), p. 33.

77 *"overthrow of . . ."*; *"conquest of . . ."*; *"capture of . . ."*: see Communist
Labor Party platform, in Post hearing, April 1920, p. 154, and Lloyd Trial,
NYPL, p. 517.

77 *"Bolshevik, bolskevik, Bolshevik, bang! . . ."*: In *People v. Lloyd*, 136 N.E.
505, 1922, p. 516.

77 *Lloyd . . . floated $380 . . . for railway tickets:* Howe testimony, Lloyd trial,
NYPL, pp. 567–568.

78 *"minor disagreements . . ."* Memorandum Upon Work of the Radical Division, October 18, 1919, NARA, RG 65, in Emma Goldman Papers,
Delaware.

79 FN: *Documents released from the Russian State Archives:* see "Parliamen-
tarism, Soviet Power, and the Creation of a Communist Party of America:
Thesis of the Executive Committee of the Third International," 1919, in
CPA-USA collection, LC.

79   *Edgar . . . recognized . . . "Left Wing Manifesto.":* One of the first people to visit the offices of *The Revolutionary Age* and buy a copy in July had been Clarence Converse, an undercover agent for the Lusk Committee, which passed it over to Edgar

79   *"[Lloyd] stated that the Department of Justice . . .":* Report of Agent Abelman, March 19, 1919. NARA, RG 65, M1085, file OG86163.

79   *"I am attaching hereto a speech . . .":* Memorandum from Hoover to Creighton, July 24, 1919. NARA, RG 65, M1085, file OG86163.

80   *"It is my intention to endeavor . . .":* Memorandum Upon Work of the Radical Division, October 18, 1919, NARA, RG 65, in Emma Goldman papers, Delaware.

80   *"If such a decision . . .":* Memorandum Upon Work of the Radical Division, October 18, 1919, NARA, RG 65, in Emma Goldman papers, Delaware.

8. STRIKES

83   *"There is no right . . .":* Murray, p. 132.

84   *Newark special agent . . . I.W.W. had sent agitators to Boston:* see Report of Radical Section, September 12, 1919, NARA, RG 65, in Emma Goldman papers, Delaware.

84   *"the most energetic and intelligent . . .":* Allen, p. 45.

85   *"Lenine Red . . ."; "Strike is Part of . . .":* Los Angeles *Times*, September 18, 1919; *Atlanta Constitution*, September 28, 1919.

85   *"the seizure of all property, . . .":* *New York World*, November 7, 1919. A United States Senate committee demanded that Foster come to Washington, D.C., at the height of the strike, and the senators used the opportunity to grill Foster in public session about his radical writings, including statements he'd made that workers should "bring about the revolution by the general strike" and "not be held back . . . by the capitalist code of ethics, duty, honor, patriotism," and that "government as we know it will shrivel up and die." "Those are not my views now," Foster finally insisted. Sitting next to Samuel Gompers at the witness table, Foster squirmed noticeably at one point as a senator read aloud from an essay Foster had written about Gompers's own union, the A.F.L., ridiculing its leaders as "hordes of dishonest officials and labor fakirs. These men must go." Edgar, who attended the hearing, wrote of the performance: "his answers were most evasive and created a very unfavorable impression." Report of the Radical Division, October 3, 1919, p. 12, NARA, RG 65, in Emma Goldman papers, Delaware. On the hearing itself, see *Boston Globe* and other newspapers, October 4, 1919.

85   *Gompers . . . worried . . . Russian-style socialist front:* see Gompers, pp. 212–213.

85   FN: *"to keep his hands off . . ."* : see Report on Communist Conventions to Military Intelligence, Chicago, by unnamed agent, September 5, 1919, NARA, GR 165, in Emma Goldman papers, Delaware.

85   *Haywood . . . sent agitators . . . Ohio . . . Pennsylvania :* Report on Communist Conventions to Military Intelligence, Chicago, by unnamed agent, September 5, 1919, NARA, RG I65, in Emma Goldman papers, Delaware.

85   *"HALF MILLION WORKERS . . ."; "crush the capitalists.":* Murray, p. 142.

85   *"Radicals are taking . . ."; "I want the advocacy . . .":* *New York World*, October 19, 1919.

86 "[I]t appears that there . . ."; "[A]s soon as the Negro . . .": Report of the Radical Division, October 3, 1919, pp. 3,4, and 10, NARA, RG 65, in Emma Goldman papers, Delaware.

86 FN: *Newspaper reports described* . . . : see *Omaha Herald* and *New York World,* October 29 and 30, 1919.

9. PARTNERS

88 "[C]onferences were immediately held . . .": Memorandum Upon Work of the Radical Division, October 18, 1919, NARA, RG 65, in Emma Goldman Papers, Delaware.

89 "no evidence in the accompanying . . .": Memorandum from Post to Caminetti, July 21, 1917, in Emma Goldman papers, Delaware.

90 "operating wide open . . ."; "Unfortunately they enjoy . . . .": Report on Communist Conventions to Military Intelligence, Chicago, by unnamed agent, September 5, 1919, NARA, RG 165, in Emma Goldman papers, Delaware.

90 "According to the records . . .": Memorandum to Caminetti from H. McCllelland, April 25, 1919, in Emma Goldman papers, Delaware.

90 Caminetti . . . sent . . . report to Secretary Wilson: Memorandum from Caminetti to Secretary Wilson, April 26, 1919, in Emma Goldman papers, Delaware.

91 "Emma Goldman and Alexander Berkman are . . .": Memorandum from Hoover to Creighton, August 23, 1919, NARA, RG 60, file 186233-13, in LC collection.

91 Emma RG 65, in Emma Goldman papers.

91 "As these cases are of importance . . .": Caminetti to Wilson, August 29, 1919. See also letter from Creighton to Caminetti, August 25, 1919. Both from Emma Goldman papers, Delaware.

91 "Mr. Caminetti immediately took steps . . .": Memorandum on Conference with Caminetti, NARA, RG 65, M1085, file OG-374213.

92 "a simultaneous raid . . .": Report of Radical Section, September 12, 1919, NARA RG 65, in Emma Goldman papers, Delaware.

92 "The plan that comes to my mind . . ."; "It is needless to say . . .": Letter from Hoover to Caminetti, October 30, 1919, NARA, RG 85, file 85-54235/36.

10. THROMBOSIS

96 "Never have I seen the President . . .": Tumulty, p. 439.

96 Palmer . . . the president . . . two formal private appointments: see memoranda to the president of July 12 and August 21, 1919, in Wilson papers, LC.

97 "revolution in the air—. . .": Confidential Memoranda and Notes, July 26, 1919, Lansing papers, LC.

97 "We will be faced . . .": Confidential Memoranda and Notes, September 1, 1919, Lansing papers, LC.

98 "It would be the irony . . .": Wilson to E.G. Conklin [undated], in Knock, p. 19.

98 "I am not interested in the President . . .": Tumulty, p. 438.

98 FN: "Mr. Lansing, you may rest assured . . .": Tumulty, p. 444.

99 "You read the papers . . .": Smith, p. 101.

99 "Alarming rumors . . .": Letter from Palmer to Morris, November 3, 1919, in Link et al., volume 63, p. 608.

100 *"I went over the whole situation . . ."*: New York Times, October 31, 1919, in Link et al., volume 63, p. 608.
100 *"The strike is a violation . . . "*: see New York Times, November 6, 1919.
100 *"not only unjustified . . ."*; *"No one believed . . . "*: Smith, p. 110.
100 *"The proposed strike, if carried . . ."*: New York World, October 30, 1919.
100 Coal Strike *. . ."*; *"Apathy of Members . . ."*: Los Angeles Times, November 2, 1929; Murray, p. 158.
100 *"The people want a showdown . . . "*: New York Times, November 2, 1919.
100 *"There are men in this country . . ."*: New York World, November 7, 1919.

11. NEW YORK

102 *"My dear little Edgar"*: Letter from Mother to Hoover, October 9, [1905], Hoover Center collection.
103 *Military Intelligence . . . plan to defend . . . New York*: see Bendersky, pp. 127–128 and 130.
103 *"[He] took a dim view . . ."*: Toledano, p. 42.
104 *"[T]here had been a clash . . ."*: Report upon New York Trip, October 10, 1919, JEH-GPO, NARA, RG 65, in Emma Goldman papers, Delaware.
105 *"As a matter of fact . . ."*; *"None of the speakers . . ."*: Report upon New York Trip, October 10, 1919, JEH-GPO, NARA, RG 65, in Emma Goldman papers, Delaware.
106 *"This office has given its entire attention . . ."*: Memorandum Upon Work of Radical Division, October 18, 1919, NARA, RG 65, in Emma Goldman papers, Delaware. Among other things, in preparation for the case, Edgar already had telephoned several Justice Department lawyers who had faced Goldman in prior cases, pulled records from her 1917 Espionage Act trial and the probes into her citizenship, and examined her articles from Mother Earth, her books and speeches, her interviews from prison, and even copies of personal financial records and scrapbooks provided by some of Goldman's former friends. He traveled to Atlanta, Georgia, in September to attend the deportation hearing of Alexander Berkman held at the federal prison there, and, during Goldman's final weeks in prison, he screened her personal mail for evidence. See, for instance, Report by Hoover on Immigration Hearing in Deportation Case of Alexander Berkman, held at the Atlanta Penitentiary, September 25, 1919, and letters from Hoover to Caminetti, September 15, 1919, and to McGlassen, September 23, 1919, all in Emma Goldman papers, Delaware.
106 *"I am a 'revolutionist' . . ."*: see government brief excerpted in the Washington Post, December 22, 1919.
106 *"His naturalization seems . . ."*: Memorandum from John Hanna, Department of Justice, to the Secretary to the Attorney General, September 23, 1919, NARA, RG 60, in Emma Goldman papers, Delaware.

12. EMMA

107 *"Miss Goldman do you swear to tell . . . "*: A full transcript of the Emma Goldman deportation hearing held at Ellis Island on October 27 and November 12, 1919, is in the Emma Goldman papers, microfilm reel 63. The original copy from NARA has been missing for over twenty years. Apparently, it was removed to make a copy, perhaps for the Goldman papers, and never returned to the files.

109 *"In St. Louis we were almost mobbed . . ."*: Goldman (1931), Chapter 50, p. 1.
109 *"The whole United States Government . . ."*: Goldman (1931), Chapter 50, p. 3.
109 *"I did not want to be . . ."*: Goldman (1931), Chapter 50, p. 7.
109 *"I found the inquisitors sitting . . ."*: Goldman (1931), Chapter 50, p. 8.
110 *"Miss Goldman, are you an Anarchist? . . . .This alien has refused . . ."*: Emma Goldman deportation hearing, October 27 and November 12, 1919, p. 52, in Emma Goldman papers, Delaware.
110 *"If the present proceedings are . . ."*: Emma Goldman deportation hearing, October 27, 1919, Emma Goldman papers, Delaware.
111 *"distinctive personalities, . . ."*: Report on Dinner for Emma Goldman and Alexander Berkman by Doris Henry and Betty Thompson, October 27, 1919, NARA, RG 65, in Emma Goldman papers, Delaware.
111 *"the majority were Russian . . ."*: Report on meeting at Hotel Brevoort, October 27th, 1919, from Margaret Scully, to Lusk Committee, Lusk Committee files, Albany, and in Emma Goldman papers, Delaware.
111 *"We had opposed the plan . . ."*: Goldman (1931), Chapter 50, p. 10.
111 *"In the isolation and loneliness . . ."*: Goldman (1931), Chapter 50, p. 1.
111 *"To the Dep't of Justice men . . ."*: Memorandum from Inspector C.L. Converse to Captain W.L. Moffatt, Military Intelligence, on "Anarchist Dinner given to Emma Goldman and Alex Berkman at Hotel Brevoort, N.Y. City, October 27, 1919," NARA, RG 165, in Emma Goldman papers, Delaware.
111 *"Her statement was handed out . . ."*: Report of the Radical Division of the Department of Justice, in Palmer Hearing, June 1920, pp. 169–170.
111 *"In view of information . . ."*: *"[T]his bureau will leave no stone . . ."*: Letters from Hoover to Caminetti, November 7, 1919, and from Caminetti to Hoover, November 8, 1919, both in Emma Goldman papers, Delaware.
112 *"Full information regarding . . ."*: Letter from Burke to Caminetti, October 10, 1919, NARA, RG 85, file 85-54235/36.
112 *"affidavits setting forth the names . . ."*: Letter from Hoover to Caminetti, October 30, 1919, NARA, RG 85, file 85-54235/36.
112 *"It is the desire of the Bureau . . ."*: Letter from Hoover to Caminetti, November 3, 1919, NARA RG85, file 85-54235/36.
112 *"The [Immigration] Bureau is prepared . . ."*: Letter from Caminetti to Hoover, October 31, 1919, NARA RG 85, file 85-54235/36.
112 *"Proceed at once."*: Letter from Hoover to Caminetti, November 3, 1919 (handwritten note by Caminetti in bottom corner), NARA RG 85, file 85-54235/36.
112 *"in the belief, . . . that Mr. Hoover could secure . . ."*: Memorandum from Acting Ellis Island Commissioner Uhl to Caminetti, November 18, 1919, NARA, RG 85, file 85-54235/36.

13. THE FIRST RAID

114 *"When . . . our backs were turned, . . ."*; *"[I] informed these men . . ."*: Statement of Agent Frank Francisco, May 28, 1920, in Palmer hearing, June 1920, pp. 100–101.
115 *"Out in the hall everybody"*: *New York Times*, November 8, 1919.
115 *"upon reaching the head . . ."*: Statement of Agent Edward Anderson, May 28, 1920, in Palmer hearing, June 1920, p. 102.

115 *"a few detectives came in . . ."*: Statements of Varfolmet Ischenko, November 19, 1919, and Nicaoli Melikoff, November 21, 1919, in Twelve Lawyer Report, p. 19. See also the statements of agents Harry C. Leslie and Frank Francisco disputing these account, in Palmer hearing, June 1920, p. 103.

115 *"struck me on the head . . ."*: Statement of Mitchel Lavrowsky, November 21, 1919, in Twelve Lawyer Report, p. 18; see also Post (1923), p. 32.

116 *"A number of those in the building . . ."*: New York Times, November 8, 1919.

116 *"a twelve-inch steel jimmy . . ."*; *"a cut scalp at least"*: New York World, November 9, 1919.

116 *"Every man caught . . ."*: New York Times, November 11, 1919.

117 *"[The lead agent] brought a rope . . ."*: Statement of Peter Muzek, May 18, 1920, in Twelve Lawyer Report, pp. 13-14.

117 *"bandaged heads . . ."*: Chicago Daily Tribune, November 9, 1919.

117 *"We're going back to Russia . . ."*: Boston Herald, November 9, 1919.

118 *"Ladies and gentlemen: Government and police . . ."*: New York World, November 10, 1919.

118 Union of Russian Workers . . . *routinely gave . . . membership card* : Post (1923), pp. 24–25.

119 *"[T]hose found were hustled . . ."*: New York World, November 10, 1919.

119 *"Oh, many of them tore up . . ."*: New York World, November 10, 1919.

120 *"I have repeatedly requested . . ."*: Letter from Hoover to Caminetti, November 7, 1919, NARA, RG 85, file 85-54235/36.

120 *"I am sending this merely . . ."*: Letter from Hoover to Caminetti, November 7, 1919, NARA, RG 85, file 85-54235/36.

120 *"The [Immigration] Bureau is checking . . ."*: Letter from W. W. Peters (for Caminetti) to Hoover, November 7, 1919, NARA, RG 85, file 85-54235/36. Caminetti claimed later that, originally, he had understood he would need to supply only about seventy to eighty warrants for the raids that day instead of the final 220. See letter from Caminetti to Hoover, November 11, 1919, NARA, RG 85, file 85-54235/36.

121 *"I would appreciate it . . ."*: Letter from Hoover to Caminetti, November 8, 1919, NARA RG 85, file 85-54235/36.

121 Newark . . . *five pistols: three revolvers and two automatics*: see also Palmer hearing, June 1920, p. 48.

121 *"Red flags, guns, revolvers, . . ."*: New York Times, November 8, 1919. Later that week, they announced discovery of another bomb factory in the basement under the Russian Peoples House, with containers of TNT, muriatic acid, sulphuric acid, ammonia hydrate, and glycerine sulphate."The most deadly and most dangerous assortment of explosives and bomb ingredients I have seen in many a year," Inspector Owen Eagan said, describing it. See New York Times, November 27, 1919.

121 "PLANNED TO BOMB . . . " "PLOT TO KILL . . . ": New York World, November 9, 1919.

121 *"Proof that Lenin himself . . ."*: New York Times, November 12, 1919.

121 *"the most dangerous piece of propaganda . . ."*: New York Word, November 10, 1919.

121 *"What should be our means . . ."*: New York Times, November10, 1919.

122 Palmer . . . promised *"no let-up"*: New York World, November 11, 1919.

122 *"This is the first big step . . ."*: New York Times, November 8, 1919.

122 *"It is gratifying . . ."*: *Washington Herald*, November 9, 1919.
122 *"I am just as good an American . . ."*: For court rulings and Lewis's statement, see *New York World* and other newspapers, November 9, 1919, and Murray, pp. 160–161.
123 *"Mr. Wilson's political leadership . . ."*; *"considerable number . . ."*: *Washington Herald*, November 9, 1919.

14. CENTRALIA
125 *"The I.W.W. expected trouble . . ."*: *New York Times*, November 13, 1919.
125 *What . . . happened . . . is not clear*: I.W.W. leader Bill Haywood portrayed the legionnaires as the aggressors: "nearing the end of the parade it is said that twenty-five or thirty men broke ranks and started toward the I.W.W. hall, shooting into the building and smashing the windows. The men inside were forced to resort to the first law of nature—the preservation of life." See "Raids, Raids, Raids" by Haywood, in NARA, RG 60, file 187701.
126 *Wesley Everett*: Some newspapers misidentified him as "Brick" Smith, a local I.W.W. official, in the days after the attack. See, for instance, the *Los Angeles Times*, November 12, 1919, and the *New York Times* and *Atlanta Constitution*, November 13, 1929.
126 "RED SNIPERS . . . "; "NORTHWEST ROUSED . . . ": *Atlanta Constitution*, November 12, 1919; *New York Times*, November 13, 1919..
126 *"We must smash every un-American . . ."*: Text of the advertisement is from telegram from W.M. Short, president, Washington State Federal of Labor to Labor Secretary W.B. Wilson, November 17, 1919, in NARA, RG 175, file 13/177.
127 *"the failure of the Federal government . . ."*: *Los Angeles Times*, November 14, 1919. Similarly, an American Legion town meeting in Spokane voted to telegram Washington and demand federal action against "every alien propagandist of revolutionary and subversive doctrine," blaming the violence on "Teachings of class war and class hatred by I.W.W." See telegram to Secretary of Labor from Spokane American Legion, November 19, 1919, NARA, RG 85, file 85-54235/36.
127 *"the result of a long series . . ."*: *Los Angeles Times*, November 14, 1919.
127 *"A dangerous state of public excitement . . ."*: Message to Palmer is included in telegram from W.M. Short, president, Washington State Federation of Labor to Labor Secretary W.B. Wilson, November 15, 1919, NARA RG 175, file 13/177.
127 *"an act of cold-blooded, ruthless barbarity . . . ,"*; *"[T]he American people now are . . .'"*; *"Too long have . . ."*: Confidential Memoranda and Notes, November 13, 1919. Lansing papers, LC.
127 *"If you can obtain for me . . ."*: Memorandum from Hoover to Fisher, December 4, 1919, LC collection.

15. CRIMINAL COURT
128 *charged him with "criminal anarchy"*: see court proceeding, November 10, 1919, Lusk Committee files, Albany.
129 *"The Communist Labor Party has a kitchenette . . ."*: Report of New York Agent "B.B.," October 14, 1919, in Emma Goldman papers.
130 *"Cossack methods . . ."*: *The Christian Science Monitor*, November 11, 1919.

130 *"I hold that the Communist Party has declared . . ."*: New York Times, November 12, 1919.

131 *"peaceful writings . . ."*: New York Times, November 14, 1919.

131 *"clearly guilty"*: Decision of city magistrate McAdoo, November 14, 1919, in Lusk Committee files, Albany.

133 *"In addition to . . ."*: Palmer hearing, June 1920, p. 25.

16. HARVARD

133 *"As a matter of fact . . ."*: Post hearing, April 1920, p. 232.

136 FN: *"Felix had two hundred . . ."*: Frankfurter and Lash, p. 30.

137 *"Every once in a while . . ."*: Frankfurter and Lash, p. 29. "[G]ood people began to worry about this terribly dangerous man Frankfurter," Frankfurter himself said of it later on. Frankfurter (1960), p.169.

137 *"The utilities sought 'to get' Mooney"*: Boyer and Morais, p. 196.

138 *"[Y]ou have taken, and are taking, . . ."*: Roosevelt to Frankfurter, December 19, 1917. Frankfurter papers, LC. Before this incident, Frankfurter had developed a friendly rapport with Roosevelt. But it turned icy when Roosevelt at the start of World War I asked Frankfurter to sign a loyalty oath as an example to other hyphenated Americans and Frankfurter refused. See Frankfurter (1960), pp.168–169.

138 *"An interesting little man . . ."*: Lash (1971), p. 214; Frankfurter and Lash, p. 24.

138 *Frankfurter . . . Poland . . . plight of Jews* : "A thousand Jews were killed in Vilna when the Poles took it. In Lida the death roll was in proportion and so all through the country that the Poles are taking back from the Bolsheviks," Frankfurter reported to President Wilson in a letter through Gilbert Close dated May 22, 1919.The warnings went unbelieved. See also letters from Frankfurter to Wilson, April 29, May 8, May 14, and May 20, 1919, and letters from Wilson to Frankfurter of July 31, May 1, May 13, May 16, and May 24, 1919, all in Wilson papers, LC.

139 *"The only explanation considered possible . . ."*: Memorandum for the Chief, Positive Branch, from M. Churchill, Director of Military Intelligence, October 2, 1919, in NARA, RG 165. Regarding Brandeis, see, NARA, RG 165.

139 FN: *Military Intelligence . . . shadowed Brandeis:* see Memoranda from H.A. Strauss to Director of Military Intelligence on "Zionist Movement," September 13, 1919, and from H.A. Strauss To Director of Military Intelligence on "Zionist Movement," September 13, 1919, both in NARA, RG 165.

139 *"What are you worried about?" . . ."*: Frankfurter (1960), p. 170.

139 *"They are gunning . . ."*: Parrish, p. 120.

139 *"People meet him, . . ."*: Frankfurter and Lash, p. 29.

139 *"three hundred percent kosher"*: Frankfurter (1960), p. 175.

139 *"I dare say I shall be called . . ."*: Parrish, p. 121.

140 *"The last two years . . ."*: Boston Daily Globe, November 12, 1919.

140 *"What's this Communist meeting . . ."*; *"Sanity and goodwill . . ."*: Parrish, p. 122.

140 *"As soon as he bounces . . ."*: Parrish, p. 6.

140 *"Of course it won't be comfortable . . ."*: Parrish, p. 120.

17. POST

142   *Harry Weinberger . . . simple case* : see letter from Weinberger to Caminetti, November 26, 1919, in Emma Goldman papers, Delaware.

142   *"a bright boy . . . shrewd, careful . . ."*: Report on meeting at Hotel Brevoort, October 27th, 1919, from Margaret Scully, to Lusk Committee, in Lusk Committee files, Albany, and , Emma Goldman papers, Delaware.

142   *"Whether or not I liked . . ."*: Post (1923), p. 16.

143   *"There are various kinds . . ."*; *"At one extreme . . ."*: Post (1923), pp. 14–15.

144   "I fairly devoured . . ." Post (unpublished) p. 239.

144   *"The Public . . ."*; *"A Journal of . . ."* : see generally Candeloro (1974), p. 113.

145   *"From the moment that our country plunged . . ."*: Post (unpublished), p. 331 et seq.

145   *Post arranged for Darrow*: see letter from Darrow to Post, August 30, 1917, NARA, RG 85, file 54235/36.

145   *"I believe in individual freedom . . ."*: Transcript of Sam Miller/Schulim Melamed hearing, Chicago Illinois, October 5, 1917, in NARA RG 85, file 54235/36, 2-4.

145   *Darrow argued . . . then-attorney general . . . Gregory, agreed . . . Wilson . . . ordered*: see Brief in case of Schulim Melamed by Clarence Darrow, undated, 1918; Memorandum from the Attorney General to the Secretary of Labor, February 23, 1918; and Memorandum by W.B. Wilson to the Commissioner General of Immigration, April 6, 1918, all in NARA RG 85, file 54235/36.

146   *"[S]he is one of those disbelievers . . ."*: Post (1923), pp. 15–16.

146   *"After conference pending final decision . . ."*: Post's note is at the end of letter from Weinberger to Caminetti, November 26, 1919, in Emma Goldman papers, Delaware.

146   *"if Tolstoy himself . . ." "Why not substitute the name Jesus Christ . . ."*: Undated report titled "Alexander Berkman and Emma Goldman Deportation," apparently by Harry Weinberger, in the Emma Goldman papers, Delaware.

18. FREE SPEECH

147   *"Dear Justice Holmes, And Now . . ."*: Letter from Frankfurter to Holmes, November 12, 1919, inMennel & Compston, p. 75.

148   "one of the most impressive . . .": Baker, p. 488.

148   *"Get down, you damn fool . . ."*: Baker, p. 151.

148   *Lochner v. New York*: The Courts' opinion is at 198 U.S. 45 (1905).

149   *"My son, it was a good piece . . ."*: Baker, pp. 454–455.

149   *"I want you to promise . . ."*: Baker, p. 487.

149   *"very strong feeling that Pound . . ."*: Frankfurter and Lash, p. 29.

149   "books of an agitating tendency.": Baker, p. 519.

149   *"The most stringent protection . . ."*: From *Schenck v. United States*, 249 U.S. 47, 1919, at 52.

150   *Holmes . . . sending Eugene V. Debs to prison*: see *Debs v. United States*, 249 U.S. 211 (1919).

150   FN: *"Lincoln . . ." "laboring, with some effect . . ."*: Letter from Lincoln to Erastes Corning, May 19, 1863, in Simon, p. 251.

150 *Judge Learned Hand . . . critiques:* Hand, for instances, argued that Holmes's test "[could] serve to intimidate many a man who might moderate the storms of popular feeling"; see Baker, p. 527.

150 *"How about the man who gets up . . .":* Chafee (1919), p. 944.

150 *"[Holmes] is inclined to allow . . .":* Letter from Chafee to Judge C. F. Amidon, September 30, 1919, in Irons, p. 1211.

151 *"Congress certainly cannot forbid . . .":* Abrams v. United States, 250 U.S. 616, at 628 (November 10, 1919).

151 *"[W]hen men have realized . . .":* Abrams v. United States, 250 U.S. 616, at 630 (November 10, 1919).

152 *"The time for going . . .":* Letter from Holmes to Frankfurter, December 4, 1919, Mennel & Compston, p. 78.

152 *"Felix is safe. . . .":* quoted in Lash, p. 30.

19. THE BUFORD

156 *Schorr . . . clients . . . wanted to go back to Russia:* see Memorandum from Uhl to Caminetti, November 18, 1919, NARA RG 85, file 85-54235/36.

156 *Soon, they began refusing to speak:* on the "talk strike," see letter from Hoover to Caminetti, November 25, 1919, NARA RG 85, file 85-54235/36.

156 *"Expedite fullest possible extent . . .":* Caminetti telegram to field, November 10, 1919, in letter from Caminetti to Hoover, November 11, 1919, NARA RG 85, file 85-54235/36.

156 *"[T]he next time they . . .":* Letter from Hoover to Caminetti, November 25, 1919, NARA RG 85, file 85-54235/36.

156 *"for a conference with Mr. Hoover":* Memorandum by Inspector W. J. Peters, December 4, 1919, in NARA, RG 85, file 85-54235/36.

157 *"I was informed by Mr. Hoover . . .":* Memorandum from Caminetti to Abercrombie, December 20, 1919.

157 *"This latter arrangement would eliminate . . .":* Letter from Hoover to Caminetti, December 24, 1919, NARA, RG 85, file 85-54809.

157 *"the proposed vacation . . .":* Letter from Hoover to Colonel A.B. Cox, Military Intelligence, December 16, 1919, in LC collection.

158 *"I decided that if Sasha . . .":* Goldman (1931), Chapter 51, p. 3.

158 *"It seemed preposterous"; "No ordinary assemblies, these":* Goldman (1931), chapter 50, p. 12.

158 *"Labor should make an organized demand . . .":* Report by New York agent "B-B," November 21, 1919, NARA, RG 65, in Emma Goldman papers, Delaware.

159 *"Would I had the power and means . . .":* Report by Chicago agent Royal Allen, December 1, 1919, NARA, RG 65, in Emma Goldman papers, Delaware.

159 *"Get up now!":* Goldman (1931), Chapter 51, p. 5.

159 *"slender bundle of high-charged . . .":* Vaile statement from *Congressional Record,* January 5, 1920, in Hoover scrapbook, NARA, RG 65, Director's Official Records and Memorabilia, Box 1.

159 *"I wouldn't trust you . . .":* Whitehead, pp. 48–49.

160 *"Meaning my head, I suppose":* Vaile statement in *Congressional Record,* January 5, 1920, in Hoover scrapbook, NARA, RG 65, Director's Official Records and Memorabilia, Box 1.

160   *"We'll come back. . . ."*: Whitehead, p. 48.
160   *"Merry Christmas, Emma"*: Whitehead, p. 48.
160   *"Oh, I suppose you've given me . . ."*: Vaile statement in *Congressional Record*, January 5, 1920, in Hoover scrapbook, NARA, RG 65, Director's Official Records and Memorabilia, Box 1.
160   FN: *"At least, Hoover was fair"*: see Toledano, p. 45
161   *Buford . . . fifty-one anarchists . . .* : Data on *Buford* deportees from Post (1923), p. 27.
161   *"To my amazement I learned . . ."*; *"If he were . . ."*: Goldman (1931), Chapter 51, 1.

20. DEMANDS

166   *two packages from . . . Mr. Hoover . . . 2,718 deportation warrants* : see letters from Hoover to Caminetti, December 22, 1919, in NARA, RG 60, file 202492-6, and December 24, 27, 31, 1919 and January 2, 1920, in NARA, RG 60, file 205492-10.
166   *"All warrants for arrests . . ."*: Letter from Hoover to Caminetti, December 22, 1919, NARA, RG 60, file 202492-6.
166   *"exactly similar""both being pledged . . ."*: Letter from Hoover to Caminetti, December 24, 1919, NARA RG 60, file 205492-10; and letter from Caminetti to Hoover, December 24, 1919, NARA, RG 60, file 202492—15.
167   *"1. I am a SPECIAL AGENT . . ."*: Sworn statement of agent Daniel O'Connell re: Boris Belada, December 27, 1919, in NARA, M1085, file OG 378656.
167   *"so flimsy that he refused . . ."*: Post (1923), p. 78.
168   *Palmer . . . insisted . . . agents be given another chance:* see letter from Caminetti to Hoover, December 24, 1919, in NARA, RG 60, file 202492—15.
168   *"As the deportation of . . ."*: Letter from Hoover to Camietti, December 26, 1919, NARA RG 85, file 85-54235/36.
168   *"The country was wild . . ."*: Abercrombie testimony, Palmer hearing, 1921, p. 403.
168   *"Although the Department of Labor . . ."*; *"I feel . . . that it is due . . ."*: Letter from Wilson to Palmer, December 30, 1919, NARA, RG 60, file 205492-275.
169   *"permitting these persons to be released . . ."*: Letter from Palmer to Wilson, January 2, 1920, NARA, RG 60, file, 205492. Note initials JEH:MH in top left-hand corner.

21. FINAL PLANS

171   *Edgar . . . start smoking cigarettes:* see Margaret Fennell interview in Demaris, p. 7.
171   *dictaphone listening devices . . . bugged the local Cigar Makers Union:* Williams (1979), pp. 16-17.
171   *Military Intelligence . . . West Coast offices:* see telegram from Lieutenant Colonel Wrisley Brown to Intelligence Officer, San Francisco, California, December 6, 1920, NARA, RG 165.
171   *"[I]t was apparent that . . ."*: see Report of Special Agent M. F. Blackmon, December 2, 1919, NARA M1085, file OG 382153. See also letter to

Hoover, November 29, 1919, and Memorandum to Hoover from GFR, November 20, 1919, in NARA, M1085, file OG 382153.

172 *"Abercrombie called to ask . . ."*: Calendar, January 2, 1920, Lansing papers, LC.

172 *"America's foreign relations . . ."*: *New York Call*, January 30, 1920, in Hoover scrapbook, NARA, RG 65, Director's Official Records and Memorabilia, Box 1.

172 *Louis Fraina*: On Fraina incident, see (1) memorandum to Ruch from M. J. Davis, December 15, 1919, (2) memorandum to Hoover from Ruch, January 20, 1920, and (3) statement of Peterson taken on July 31, 1920, all in NARA, M1085, file OG 381320; Palmer testimony, Post hearing, June 1920, pp. 51–53; and Draper, pp. 227–232.

173 *"His practice has been, . . ."*: Memorandum from Hoover to Creighton, December 4, 1919, NARA, M1085, file OG 377465.

173 *written complaint about Schorr*: see (a) memorandum from Hoover to Creighton, December 4, 1919, and (b) letter from Stone to Uhl, November 13, 1919, both in NARA, M1085, file OG 377465.

174 FN: *"Investigative Records relating to German . . ."*: see *Investigative Case Files of the Bureau of Investigation, 1908–1922: National Archives Microfilm Publications, Pamphlet Describing M1805*: National Archives and Records Service, Washington, D.C., 1983.

174 *"I would appreciate an early . . ."*: Letter from Hoover to Caminetti, in Coben, p. 223; Theoharis and Cox, p. 63.

175 *"at the beginning"; "as soon as . . ."*: Rule 22 text in Abercrombie testimony, Palmer hearing, 1921, p. 398.

175 *"telling the truth in most instances . . ."*: Memorandum from Caminetti to Abercrombie, December 30, 1919, in Preston, p. 218.

175 *"I approved [the rule change] . . ."*: Abercrombie testimony, Palmer hearing, 1921, p. 399.

175 *The Red Dawn . . . Proletariat and Petit-Bourgeois . . . I.W.W.: The Greatest Thing on Earth*: Reading list is from letter from Hoover to Durham, January 7, 1920, NARA, RG 60, file 205492.

22. CHICAGO

176 *"The Reds in this country, . . ."*: *Chicago Tribune*, June 2, 1920.

177 *"Hoyne is nobody's man . . ."*: *Chicago Tribune*, March 28, 1919.

177 *White Sox . . . World Series . . . fix*: On the 1919 baseball scandal, see Pietrusza, chapter 12.

177 *"My dear sir—. . ."*: *Chicago Tribune*, October 2, 1939.

178 *local businessmen . . . $40,000*: On the fund, see *Chicago Herald and Examiner*, January 2, 1920.

178 *Palmer . . . letter . . . Hoyne*: Letter from Palmer to Hoyne, in *Chicago Tribune*, January 3, 1920.

178 *"We are not cooperating . . ."*: *Chicago Tribune*, January 2, 1920.

179 *"Yesterday morning I received . . ."*: *Chicago Tribune* and *Boston Globe*, January 1920.

179 *"[W]ithout any doubt,"*: *Chicago Tribune* and *Boston Globe*, January 2, 1920.

179 *Hoyne's file . . . Old German 383427*: see NARA, M1085, file 383427.

23 THE BIG RAID

181   New York . . . Times Square: see New York Times, January 1, 1920.
181   twenty-seven towns in New England : On these raids, see generally Williams (1979), pp. 20 and 21.
182   Elore Hungarian Daily . . . Eugene Neuwald: see Johnson, p. 362, and New York Call, January 5, 1920.
182   "In my case, . . .": Panunzio, p. 335.
183   "because the algebraic formulas . . .": Jane Addams, Peace and Bread, quoted in Post (1923), p. 127, and Chicago Tribune, January 3, 1920.
183   "We are going to get them . . .": Chicago Tribune, January 2 & 4, 1920.
183   "black eyes, cut lips, bruised faces, . . .": Chicago Tribune, January 9, 1920.
184   "[T]he backbone of . . .": New York Times, January 5, 1920.
184   "His principles are not . . .": Ellis, pp. 35–38.
186   "The Socialists are loyal and patriotic men, . . .": New York Times, March 16, 1920.
186   Bill . . . by . . . . Congressman Martin Davey: For Palmer's statement on it, see New York Times, January 5, 1920.

24. CHAOS

189   "On the evening of the arrests . . .": Letter from Burke to Kelleher, December 27, 1920, in Palmer hearing, 1921, p. 12; and Twelve Lawyer Report, pp. 37–41.
190   "dope fiend": Letter from Hoover to Caminetti, January 2, 1920, NARA, RG 60, file 205492.
190   163 from New York City, 66 from Boston, 41 from Philadelphia . . . : see letters from Hoover to Caminetti January 3 (three separate letters on Boston, New York, and Philadelphia) and January 4 (on Grand Rapids and St. Paul), 1920, all in NARA, RG 60, file 205492.
190   "I desire to bring to your immediate . . .": Hoover to Caminetti, January 3, 1920, NARA, RG 60, file 205492.
191   "I fear that their imprisonment . . .": Letter from O'Brien to Skeffington, January 8, 1920.
191   "Remember the bombs, . . .": Williams (1979), p. 24.
191   "Chains and handcuffs . . .": Boston Herald, January 4, 1920.
191   "crying hysterically . . .": Boston Evening Globe, January 3, 1920.
192   Detroit agents . . . warrants for 145 . . . 101 more warrants: Letters from Hoover to Caminetti, January 7 and 9, 1920, both in NARA, RG 60, file 205492.
193   Philadelphia . . . Moyamensing Prison: see Kane testimony, Palmer hearing, 1921, p. 296.
193   Ellis Island . . . over the region: Caminetti sought additional housing, but War Department officials refused to house communists at harbor forts, Governor's Island. See letters to Caminetti from Uhl, January 9, 1920, and from Major General Harvey Jersey, January 19, 1920. in NARA, RG 85, file 85-54809.
193   "It was midwinter . . .": Recht, Chapter XIII, p. 10.
193   "cleaned as frequently as . . .": Report from Uhl to Caminetti, February 26, 1920, NARA, Labor, 85-54809.
193   Mike Marzinik: On the Marzinik case, see Recht testimony in Palmer hearing, 1921, pp. 376–377; Recht, Chapter XIII, pp. 10-11, and "The

Party Outlook," an unsigned editorial from *Communist Labor,* February 25, 1920.

194 *"concentration camp":* This reference is from the *New York Times,* January 5, 1920.

194 *"Some five hundred men . . .":* Recht to Wilson, January 15, 1920, in NARA, RG 85, file 85-54809.

194 *"The problem of how to communicate . . .":* Recht, Chapter XIII, p. 23.

194 *Recht sent a man . . . only to have him barred:* see telegram from Recht to Caminetti, January 29, 1920, NARA RG 85, file 85-54809.

194 *"[m]any of the subjects taken . . .":* Hoover to Caminetti, January 6, 1920, NARA, RG 60, file 205492.

194 *"I am informed that the attorneys . . .":* Hoover to Caminetti, January 7, 1920, 1920, NARA, RG 60, file 205492.

195 *urgent wires from Baltimore, Detroit, and Jacksonville:* see Hoover to Caminetti, January 7, 1920, NARA, RG 60, file 205492.

195 *"young men and single . . .":* Hoover to Caminetti, January 6, 1920, NARA, RG 60, file 205492.

195 *Skerron . . . "organizing and collecting funds":* Hoover to Caminetti, January 13, 1920, NARA, RG 60, file 205492.

195 *National Surety Company . . . Maryland Casualty Surety Company: New York Call,* January 7, 1920.

195 *Recht . . . Abercrombie . . . Hartford, Connecticut:* see letters from Recht to Abercrombie, January 8, 1920, and from Harry Edlin to Abercrombie, January 15, 1920, in NARA RG 85, file 85-54809.

195 *Communist Labor Party . . . bailed out:* see "The Party Outlook" in *Communist Labor,* February 25, 1920.

196 *Edgar offered to supply . . . photostat copies:* Hoover to Caminetti, January 10, 1920, NARA, RG 60, file 205492.

196 *"Care should be exercised . . .":* Memorandum from Caminetti to field offices, December 31, 1919, NARA, RG 85, file 85-54235/36.

196 *"The Department of Justice man . . .":* Bachrach testimony, Palmer hearing, 1921, p. 688.

25. LLOYD

198 *"Mr. Lloyd told me . . . that . . .":* Sadler testimony, Lloyd trial, NYPL, p. 424.

198 *"[F]or every person deported . . .";* *"The revolution [will] come . . .";* *"Violence is the only way":* Sadler testimony, Lloyd trial, pp. 425, 428–429, 433.

199 *"Those who take up . . .":* Chicago Herald and Examiner, January 5, 1920.

199 *"There is a warrant out . . .":* Sadler testimony, Lloyd trial, NYPL, pp. 435-436.

199 *"But that doesn't matter . . .":* Chicago Herald and Examiner, January 5, 1920.

199 *"I would do this on my own . . .":* Chicago Tribune, January 7, 1910.

26. HEARINGS

202 *"thought that it was in a confidential way . . .":* Bachrach testimony, Palmer hearing, 1921, pp. 688–689.

202 *Italians . . . learn . . . music and read English:* see Bachrach testimony, Palmer hearing, 1921, pp. 692–693.

203 *"The [Party chief] told me . . .";* *"You see, we recognize . . .":* Panunzio, in Palmer hearing, 1921, pp. 330–332.

204 *"Palmer's Bid for Presidency . . ."*: *New York Call*, January 3, 1920.
204 *"I am obliged to take . . ."*: Letter from Kane to Wilson, January 12, 1920, in 1921 hearing, p. 346.
204 *"the present activity against alien radicals . . ."*: *New York Times*, January 23, 1920; and *New Republic*, March 31, 1920, in Johnson (1958), p. 362.
204 *"The police, acting upon instructions . . ."*: Letter from Seattle Commissioner Henry M. White to Caminetti, January 26, 1920, NARA, RG 85, file 85-54809. Generally on Seattle situation, see letters from Hoover to Caminetti, January 12, 13, and 22 1920, in NARA, RG 60, file 205492.
205 *"Habeas Corpus petition filed . . ."*: Telegram from Boynton to Palmer, January 13, 1920, NARA, RG 60, file 205492-163.
205 *habeas corpus*: An earlier *habeas* case stemming from the January raids had been filed in Boston on behalf of Peter Frank, a prisoner detained on Deer Island who was an American citizen and therefore outside the immigration laws, but Justice Department lawyers had responded by releasing Frank along with a second American citizen named John Waglignoro, and the cases were dropped.
206 *"But they are not half as dangerous . . ."*: Anderson speech in *Boston Globe*, January 13, 1920.
206 *"Forward at once . . ."*: Telegram from Palmer to Assistant U.S. Attorney Lewis Goldberg, January 16, 1920, NARA, RG 60, file 205492-163.

27. TRIUMPH
207 *"[Debate] teaches one to control . . ."*: in Toledano, p. 41.
208 *Edgar . . . spoke to congressmen*: see, for instance, letter from Hoover to King, January 7, 1920, NARA RG 60, file 205492.
208 *Edgar . . . traded letters . . . H.L. Mencken*: Letters from Mencken to Hoover, January 8, 1920, and Hoover to Mencken, January 12, 1920, LC collection, NARA, RG 60, file 202600, in LC collection.
208 *"There is enough first-class . . ."*: Ellis, pp. 35–38.
209 *"furnished to you . . ."*; *"Men Like this Would Rule You"*: Twelve Lawyer Report, pp. 66–67. See also *The Nation*, February 14 and March 6, 1920.
209 *"an integral part of the first congress . . ."*: Quote is from case brief, in *New York Times*, January 4, 1920, in Hoover scrapbook, NARA, RG 65, Director's Official Records and Memorabilia, Box 1.
209 *"a struggle [that] must go on . . ."*: from brief quoted in *New York World*, January 4, 1920, in Hoover scrapbook, NARA, RG 65, Director's Official Records and Memorabilia, Box 1
210 *"Then why is it necessary . . ."*: Account of hearing is from *New York Times*, January 22, 1920.
210 *"From the quotations . . ."*: Decision of W. B. Wilson, *In re Preis*, January 23, 1920, in Post hearing, April 1920, pp. 150–151. Delighted at the outcome, Edgar agreed for the first time to give a full, detailed, on-the-record interview to a newspaper reporter, one from the *New York Times*. "Deportation hearings and the shipment of the 'Reds' from this country will be pushed rapidly," he told him. "Second, third and as many other 'Soviet arks' as may be necessary will be made ready as the convictions proceed." He explained how Secretary Wilson's ruling made 3,000 of the pending cases "perfect," as he put it, matching the facts to the law with mathematical precision. See *New York Times*, January 27, 1920.

211   "I am endeavoring . . ."; "likewise any interesting . . .": Hoover to Frank
       Stone, NARA RG 60, file 205492-226.
211   Buttons . . . pictures of Lenin, Trotsky, Liebknecht: Hoover to Frank Stone,
       January 24, 1920, NARA, RG 60. File 202600, in LC collection.
211   "For the blood . . .": This poem is attached to letter from Hoover to
       Caminetti, January 23, 1920, in NARA, RG 85, file 85-54809.
212   "This poem is so indicative . . .": Hoover to Caminetti, January 23, 1920,
       NARA, RG 85, file 85-54809.

28. CHEATED

213   "I consider your opinion . . .": Palmer to Wilson, January 27, 1920, NARA
       RG60, file 205492-380.
214   "There is no other portion . . .": Wilson to Palmer, February 2, 1920, NARA,
       RG60, file 205492-385.
214   Rule 22 . . . Wilson . . . changing the rule back: Memorandum from
       Caminetti to All Commissioners of Immigration in Charge, January 27,
       1920, NARA, RG 85, file 85-54654/378.

29. DARROW

218   "advocated . . . the duty, . . .": New York State criminal anarchy statute,
       Penal Code, Article XVI, section 160 et seq.
218   Attorney for the Damned : Lincoln Steffins, Darrow's one-time law partner,
       coined this expression describing Darrow. See Weinberg, p. xv.
219   "He was an intelligent . . .": Darrow, p. 58.
219   Darrow, p. 190.
219   "I do not believe Faust . . .": Chicago Daily Tribune, January 22, 1918.
220   "I am not holding up . . .": Chicago Daily Tribune, December 1, 1918.
220   "Darrow impressed on juries . . .": Stone, p. 355.
220   reformers . . . found his cynicism infuriating: For instance, when Darrow's
       friends threw a birthday banquet for him in April 1918 and his turn
       came to speak, Darrow said of why he fought so hard for the underdog.
       "I have always had a consciousness that I was doing it to amuse myself. . . .
       I have lived a life in the front trenches, looking for trouble. . . . There, for
       a short time, you really live. It is hard, but it is life. Activity is life." See N
       Tierney, p. 303.
220   "Life drifts on . . .": Letter from Darrow to Field, December 1919, Field
       papers, Chicago.
220   "I rather gathered from . . .": Gitlow transcript, Albany, pp. 25–26.
221   Rorke . . . convictions . . . two other "criminal anarchists": The other con-
       victed anarchists, Carl Paivio and Gust Alonen, were prosecuted for pub-
       lishing what the Lusk Committee staff called a "rabid anarchist sheet"
       called Luokkataistelu," and were the only other prior contested convictions
       under the statute at this point. See Archibald Stevenson, "Search War-
       rants and Prosecutions," pp. 2 and 5, in Lusk Committee files, Albany.
222   "a threat of revolution . . . sparked headlines: such as "Fear Strike of Reds" in
       the Chicago Daily Tribune, January 23, 1920.
222   "The most important point . . .": Darrow article is quoted in memorandum
       from R. E. Joseph to Tolson, June 24, 1936, p. 2, in Darrow file, FBI FOIA
       Reading Room.

222 "He was not enthusiastic . . ."; "Well, I suppose . . .": Gitlow, pp. 69–70.

223 "Peace will come . . .": New York Times, August 9, 1918.

223 FN: "I talked with the President . . ."; "Mitchell Palmer . . . plead that Debs be freed": Chicago Daily Tribune, December 27, 1918; and letter from Darrow to Palmer, July 29, 1919, and Palmer's memorandum to the president, July 30, 1919, in Wilson papers, LC.

223 "The bolsheviki are conducting . . .": see "Bolshevism," by Clarence Darrow, in Chicago Daily Tribune, February 16, 1919.

224 "In addition to . . ."; "I do not feel . . .": Gitlow transcript, Albany, p. 266.

224 "An audience never . . .": Gitlow, p. 72.

224 "Mr. Gitlow, you are not . . .": Gitlow transcript, Albany, pp. 268–269.

224 "What is capitalism?": Gitlow transcript, Albany, p. 271.

225 "No, sir, he has no right . . .": Gitlow transcript, Albany, p. 273.

225 "Again the defendant . . .": Gitlow transcript, Albany, pp. 278–279.

225 "It was obvious . . ."; "Upon my insistence, . . .": Gitlow, pp. 71–72.

225 "The defendant here . . ."; "There is nothing strange . . .": Gitlow transcript, Albany, pp. 279–285.

226 "It is a creed . . .": Gitlow transcript, Albany, p. 315.

226 "As long as men speak . . .": Gitlow transcript, Albany, p. 286.

226 "I am not afraid . . .": Gitlow transcript, pp. 311–313.

226 "If [Abraham] Lincoln . . ."; "I ask you, gentlemen . . .": Gitlow transcript, Albany, pp. 326–328.

227 "Darrow did not even want . . .": Gitlow, p. 73.

227 "It was believed . . .": New York Times, February 6, 1920.

227 "[I]t's a hell of a world . . .": Letter from Darrow to Field, February 13, 1920, Field papers, Chicago. Note that this letter is misdated 1912, but its reference to the communist trial clearly places it in 1920.

227 1,400 people, . . . state sedition laws . . . convict about 300: Data from Murray, p. 234.

228 "It is highly important . . .": Letter from Hoover to Hurley, March 4, 1920, in LC collection.

30. PATERSON

229 "[L'Era Nuova] might truly . . .": Letter from Hoover to Caminetti, February 11, 1920, NARA, M1085, file OG 341761.

229 "Courage is [a] mental . . .": Letter from Hoover to Butterton, November 11, 1971. NARA, RG 65. Director's collection.

230 "Just as official vigilance . . .": New York Times, February 16, 1920.

230 "the tamed lion hatches . . .": In Palmer hearing, June 1920, p. 540.

230 "I was present . . .": Hoover to Caminetti, February 18, 1920, NARA, RG 60, file 205492.

231 "It is well known . . .": Report on Radical Division, October 10, 1919, Emma Goldman papers, Delaware.

231 "Link Raid Evidence . . ."; "Red Raids Yield . . ."; "Bomb Plot . . .": Newark Evening News, February 16, 1920; New York Times and Los Angeles Times, February 17, 1920.

232 Edgar . . . Clarence Converse: see letter from Hoover to Converse, April 22, 1920, NARA, RG 60, file 202600.

232 "I personally was present during . . .": Letter from Hoover to Caminetti, March 1, 1920, LC collection.

232 *"I told Caminita at the outset . . ."*; *"He has a boy . . ."*: Memorandum from Hoover to Flynn, March 8, 1920, pp. 1 and 4, in NARA, RG 65, M1085, file BS 211793.

233 *"[W]e were followed . . ."*: Report ofSpecial Agent Joseph Barbara, March 31, 1920. NARA, RG 65, M1085, file OG 383301.

31. CANDIDATE

234 *"America Must be Up . . ."*: *Leslie's Illustrated Weekly Newspaper*, February 24, 1920.

234 *"I am strong for reducing . . ."*; *"We cannot deny . . ."*; *"All my political life . . ."*: *Chicago Daily Tribune* and *New York Times*, March 11, 1920.

234 *"[T]he pendulum . . ."*: *Atlanta Constitution*, March 11, 1920.

235 *"Probably they won't starve"*: Letter from Campbell to Frank Burke, March 29, 1920, with clip from *St. Paul Daily News*, March 23, 1920. NARA, RG 65, M1085, file OG-341761.

235 *Favors . . . Alien Property Custodian*: For instance, for campaign treasurer, he named J. Harry Covington, a former Maryland Congressman who had received over $46,000 in legal fees from Palmer's wartime office. His New York campaign captain, John J. Fitzgerald, had received $37,000 in fees, and his Illinois manager, Roger Sullivan, had profited by purchasing a German-owned beer company seized by Palmer during the World War. See Coban, p. 247.

32. DOUBLE CROSS

238 *Post's . . . meetings . . . Lincoln Steffens . . . George Andreytchine*: On Hoover's investigation of Post, see Candeloro, p. 48.

238 *Edgar feared the worst*: Hoover had been complaining all though January about the Labor Department's slowness in producing warrants and other problems, and John Abercrombie sent him a formal apology over the Department's inability to handle the workload. See letter from Abercrombie to Hoover, February 6, 1920, NARA, RG 60, file 202600.

239 *Edgar . . . arrangement with Caminetti*: see Hoover to Caminetti, February 2, 1920, in NARA, RG 85, file 85-54809, and Hoover to Caminetti, March 16, 1920, in LC collection.

239 *Edgar sent Caminetti . . . forty-one prisoners*: Hoover to Caminetti, March 22, 1920, in LC collection.

239 *Caminetti . . . Post had snubbed him*: see memorandum from Post to Caminetti, March 22, 1920, in NARA, M1085, file OG 341761. Secretary Wilson, too, had complained about the arrangement. See Wilson to Caminetti, February 6, 1920, in NARA RG 85, file 85-54809

239 *"wholly inimical to . . ."*; *"I must say that . . ."*: Hoover to Caminetti, April 6, 1920, NARA, RG 60, file 205492.

239 *By . . . March . . . a flood*: see, for instrance, Hoover to Caminetti, April 3, 1920, in NARA RG 85, file 54809, saying: "I have received quite a number of letters from you informing me of the cancellation of warrants in certain cases. However, in some of these cases, no mention is made of the jurisdiction or city in which the alien was apprehended and the hearing held."

239 *"There was never any real fighting"*: Anna Kienast interview in Demaris, p. 6.

240 *"His favorite breakfast . . ."*: Margaret Fennell interview in Demaris, p. 6. The dog, named Spee Dee Bozo, was born in July 1922, placing this story slightly after these events.

33. BOSTON

241 *"Expert on Reds . . ."*; *"directed all the activities . . ."*: respectively from the Boston American, and Boston Post, both April 7, 1920, and in Hoover scrapbook, NARA, RG 65, Director's Official Records and Memorabilia, Box 1.

241 *"Man Here Who Directed . . ."*: Boston Evening Globe, April 7, 1920.

242 *"You knew these people . . ."*: For the trial proceedings in Boston, the most readily-available transcript was that published daily in the Boston Globe, relied upon here. Boston Evening Globe, April 7, 1920.

242 *"You will answer that . . ."*: Boston Daily Globe, April 7, 1920.

243 *Mitchell Palmer to send his top radical expert . . .*: Mitchell Palmer had foreseen the possibility of problems like this and earlier had telegraphed Boynton to ask for a two-week delay in the trial so he could travel from Washington and attend it personally, at least on its opening day, but the judge rejected the request. See telegram from Palmer to Boynton, April 2, 1920, in NARA M1085, file OG 378656.

243 *"I'll take great pleasure in getting . . ."*: Boston Daily Globe, January 13, 1920.

243 *"He has lost his head . . ."*: Letter from Everts to Wilson January 13, 1920, in Boston Daily Globe, January 14, 1920. Wilson's response refusing to remove him is in the Boston Daily Globe, January 21, 1920

244 *"I am very much interested . . ."*: Boston Daily Globe, April 8, 1920.

244 *"liberal views,"*: Washington Herald, April 8, 1920, in J. Edgar Hoover's Scrapbooks, RG 65.

244 *"Despite his boyish looks, . . ."*: Boston Post, April 14, 1920, in Hoover scrapbook, NARA, RG 65, Director's Official Records and Memorabilia, Box 1.

245 *"I wanted to say that no disrespect . . ."*: Boston Evening Globe, April 7, 1920.

245 *"whose wits were reinforced . . ."*: Boston Daily Globe, April 8, 1920.

245 *"On the evening of the arrests . . ."* For full text of the letter from Burke to Kelleher, December 27, 1919, see Palmer Hearing, 1921, p. 12, and Twelve Lawyer Report, p. 40.

246 *"Lawyers especially . . ."*: New York Law Journal, April 18, 1919.

247 *"pinkish-red necktie"* : Boston Record, April 7, 1920, in Hoover scrapbook, NARA, RG 65, Director's Official Records and Memorabilia, Box 1.

248 *"If possible you should arrange . . ."*: Letter from Burke to Kelleher, December 27, 1919, in Palmer hearing, 1921, p. 12.

249 *Goldberg . . . back to Boston and testify*: see Memorandum to Hoover, unsigned, GFR-MMP, April 14, 1920, in NARA, M1085, file OG 389244.

34. TRUSS

250 *Post had gotten down to business*: Post got a request to come to Boston and testify in the habeas suit before Judge Anderson that month, but turned it down. See Katzeff to Post, April 8, 1920, NASRA RG 85, file 85-54809.

251 *"could not have been worse . . ."*: Gengarelli, p. 177.

251 *"I undertook to clear . . ."*; *"I went, in any case . . ."*: Post hearing, April 1920, p. 69.

252   *"At first I scrutinized all . . ."*: Post (1923), pp. 188–189.

252   FN: *"Exclusionary Rule . . . in federal courts:* see Boyd v. United States, 116 U.S. 616 (1886), and Weeks v. United States, 232 U.S. 383 (1914).

252   *Supreme Court . . . deportations not to be criminal trials:* see, for instance, Fong Yae Ting v. United States, 149 U.S. 698 (1893); The Japanese Immigrant Case, 189 U.S. 86 (1902); Yick Wo v. Hopkins, 118 U.S. 356; Whitfield v. Hanges 222 FR 745 (1915).

252   *"On the deportation of aliens . . ."*: Letter from Holmes to Frankfurter, December 21, 1919, in Mennel and Compston, p. 80.

253   *Thomas Truss :* Post claimed he first heard about Truss from a lawyer on Caminetti's staff who had recommended Truss be released, but who said that Caminetti overruled him and reassigned the case to another lawyer who changed the outcome. Post hearing, April 1920, p. 69.

254   *"Examination of this record . . ."*: For full text of Truss opinion, see Twelve Lawyers Report, p. 60, and excerpts Post hearing, April 1920, pp. 75–78, and Boston Globe, April 10, 1920.

254   *"[A]s this case appeared . . ."*: Post (1923), p. 204.

254   *"disregarding every principle . . ."*: Truss opinion, in Twelve Lawyer's Report, p. 61.

254   *"working men of good character . . ."*: from Boston Globe, April 10, 1920.

254   *"Will Deport Only . . ."*; *"Official Speaks . . ."*: New York Times and Christian Science Monitor, April 10, 1920.

254   *"I hardly know how . . ."*: Post to Bryan, April 7, 1920, in Post papers, LC.

35. PLAIN WORDS

256   *"They were well treated, . . ."*: Report to Palmer from Creighton, May 17, 1920, p. 20, in NARA, M1085, file BS 211793.

256   *Flynn persuaded Salsedo . . . stay at . . . Park Row:* Also being held at this office was Luduvico Caminita, the L'Era Nuova leader, here from Ellis Island. See Palmer to Post and Post to Palmer, March 8, 1920, in NARA, RG 60, file 205492.

257   FN: *Cannone . . . "damned liar" . . . "son of a bitch":* see affidavit of Walter Nelles (Cannone's attorney), April 18, 1920, in Twelve Lawyer Report, pp. 31–32.

257   *"Salsedo was shown . . ."*: Creighton to Palmer, May 17, 1920, p. 16, NARA, M1085, file BS211793.

36. REACTION

258   *Thomas Truss: Edgar recognized . . . name:* see Hoover to Caminetti, January 9, 1920, in NARA, RG 60, file 205492.

258   *Mrs. Truss . . . coal . . . money to feed the children:* see report from agents White and Doyas, January 12 and February 3, 1920, in NARA, M1085, file OG 382296.

259   *"The raids . . . certainly met . . ."*: Memorandum from Hoover to Burke, February 21, 1920, pp. 4, 6, 7 in NARA, RG 60, file 186701-14.

259   *"We have never reached . . ."*: Report from agent J. F. McDevitt, December 16, 1920, in NARA, M1085, file OG 379228.

260   FN: *"absolutely opposed . . ."*: see Gengarelly, p. 139; Martin, p. 209.

259   *"rare evil . . . flatly at variance . . ."*: O'Brian text in Palmer hearing, 1921, pp. 781–788; quotes from p. 783–785.

260   *"Information received from confidential . . ."*: Report from agent Seib, March 5, 1920, NARA, M1085, file OG 384125.

260   *"[I]t is my opinion that . . ."*: Congressional Record, April 12, 1920, pp. 5551 et seq.

261   *"Sunday Sports Bill Signed"*: Boston Evening Globe, April 2, 1920.

261   *Americans than fretting over Reds*: There were other signs, too. For instance, in Albany that spring, New York Governor Al Smith vetoed a package of bills sponsored by the Lusk Committee to ban the Socialist Party, require loyalty oaths from teachers, and create a detective branch costing $100,000 of taxpayer money to investigate sedition and anarchy. His veto stuck, though these bills were all passed again the next year and signed into law by Smith's successor as Governor, Nathan Miller: Murray, p. 238.

262   *"We have been warning . . ."*: Washington Star, April 12, 1920.

37. IMPEACHMENT

263   *"seemed mentally all right . . ."*: Palmer's description is from Desk Diary of Robert Lansing, April 14, 1920, in Link et al., volume 65, p. 188.

264   *"I felt it well to put . . ."*: from Diary of Josephus Daniels, April 14, 1920, in Link et al., volume 65, p. 187.

264   *"Were I in Washington . . ."*: Tumulty, p. 442.

264   *"I received . . . a letter from the President . . ."*: Lansing to Burleson, February 10, 1920, Burleson papers, LC.

264   *"I outlined to [the president] . . . "*:See, for instance, New York Times, February 14, 1920.

264   FN: *"At the President's request . . ."*: E. Wilson to Burleson, January 28, 1920, Burleson papers, LC.

265   *"The President's silence . . ."*: Diary of Colonel House, January 31, 1920, in Link et al., volume 64, p. 347.

266   *"Palmer said if Post . . ."*: Diary of Josephus Daniels, April 14, 1920, in Link et al., volume 65, p. 187.

266   *"This is an experiment . . ."*: Diary of Josephus Daniels, April 14, 1920, in Link et al., volume 65, p. 187.

266   *"[The President] told Palmer . . ."*: Diary of Josephus Daniels, April 14, 1920, in Link et al., volume 65, p. 187.

266   *"Cabinet officers declared . . . "*; *"It did him good"*: Boston Globe, April 24, 1920.

266   *"In a word, this is . . ."*; *"The basic agitation . . ."*; *"People said I was . . ."*: Christian Science Monitor, April 15, 1920.

267   *"just a plain, ordinary strike . . ."*: Boston Globe, April 17, 1920.

267   *Palmer . . . spread . . . . message*: see for instance, Desk Diary of Robert Lansing, April 14, 1920, in Link et al., volume 65, p. 188, recounting Lansing's conversation with Palmer that week, recalled: "He told me Louis F. Post prevented action against radicals."

267   *"We have there in the Department of Labor . . ."*: Congressional Record, April 14, 1920, pp. 5671–5672.

268   *Edgar . . . turned his agents loose on Louis Post*: Candeloro, p. 48.

268   *"Old German file for Louis Post . . ."*: see entries under Post in NARA, RG 65, M1085.

268	"*Ruling in Truss case by* . . .": Telegram from Palmer to Boynton, May 4, 1920, NARA, RG 60, file 200600.The question was raised by Boston U.S. Attorney. Boynton in Telegram from Boynton to Palmer, April 27, 1920, NARA, RG 60, file 205492.

268	"*Assistant Secretary of Labor Post,* . . .": Hoch testimony, Post hearing, June 1920, p. 6.

268	"*This young man, Hoover* . . . .": Tincher testimony, Post hearing, June 1920, p. 24.

268	"*it is frankly admitted* . . .": Siegel testimony, Post hearing, June 1920, p. 27.

268	"*Cabinet Clash May Force Out* . . .": *Washington Herald*, undated clipping in NARA, RG 65, M1085, file OG 339909.

269	"*Mitchell Palmer talks too much*": Diary of Dr. Grayson, May 1st, 1920, in Link et al., volume 65, p. 242.

38. COMMUNIST LABOR

271	*Post . . . freed . . . CLP members:* see Memorandum from Post to Caminetti, March 27, 1920, and Caminetti's response to Post, March 31, 1920, in Post hearing, April 1920, pp. 15–15. Post had even freed Gaspare Cannone, the suspect in the June 2 bombing case, on $1,000 bail, ignoring Edgar's pleas to raise it to $5,000. See letter from Hoover to Caminetti, April 22, 1920, in NARA, M1085, file OG 383301.

271	*figured to be another kangaroo:* The rupture between the Justice and Labor Departments had become visible at several levels by this point. In mid-April, for instance, Edgar learned that a Labor Department inspector had interrogated a Justice Department agent about the "methods" used in the January raids, suggesting Labor had not been involved. Edgar demanded an explanation, though Caminetti apparently never gave him one. See Hoover to Caminetti, April 17, 1920, LC collection.

271	"*A more lawless proceeding* . . .": *Boston Globe*, April 22 and 23, 1920.

271	*Edgar . . . incriminating statements from the CLP's charter:* For the case, see "Status of the Communist Labor Party under the Act of Congress Approved October 16, 1918," in Palmer hearing, June 1920, pp. 375–377.

271	"*a band of cut throat aliens* . . .": *New York Times* and other papers, April 25, 1920.

272	*Swinburne Hale:* Hale's appearance was arranged by the American Civil Liberties Union. The Communist Labor Party later disavowed his representation, the reasons unclear. see Gengarelli, p. 193, and sources therein.

272	"*an unjustifiable misconception* . . .": *New York Tribune* and *Boston Globe*, April 25, 1920; *Christian Science Monitor*, April 23, 1920.

273	"*Criticism of the methods* . . .": *Boston Globe*, April 25, 1920.

273	*Louis Fraina :* Just a month earlier, in March 1920, Hoover had received reports from Military Intelligence placing Fraina in Mexico, possibly creating a Bolshevik cell there. See Hoover to Churchill, February 4, 1920, in NARA, RG 60, file 205492, and Hoover to Hurley, March 25, 1920, in NARA, RG60, file 202600, and LC collection.

273	"*Are you prepared to prove* . . .": *New York Times* and *Boston Globe*, April 25, 1920.

274	"*call upon [you] publicly* . . .": *New York Times* and *Boston Globe*, April 25, 1920.

274   "Makes Hot Reply . . ."; "Charge Made . . .": Boston Globe, and New York
       Tribune, both April 25, 1920, in Hoover scrapbook, NARA, RG 65,
       Director's Official Records and Memorabilia, Box 1.
274   "If the American people . . .": Memorandum opinion of William B. Wilson
       in re: Carl Miller, May 5, 1920, in Post hearing, April 1920, p. 155.
274   THE BULLY BOLSHEVIK: Undated clipping in Hoover scrapbook, NARA, RG
       65, Director's Official Records and Memorabilia, Box 1.

39. GAGGED

277   "If an impeachable . . .": Letter from Wilson to Frankfurter, April 17, 1920,
       Frankfurter papers, LC.
278   "free love" or divorce-on-demand: Testimony of Congressman Tincher, Post
       hearing, April 1920, p. 26.
278   Emma Goldman . . ."worthy of full credence": Testimony of Congressman
       Johnson, Post hearing, April 1920, p. 37.
278   "She was a woman . . .": Post hearing, April 1920, p. 235.
278   "In my opinion, the public . . .": Johnson testimony, Post hearing, April
       1920, p. 5.
279   "Post, they say, . . .": New York Times, May 2, 1920.
279   "I cannot believe . . .": Letter from Post to Campbell, May 4, 1920, in Post
       hearing, April 1920, pp. 57–58; see also Christian Science Monitor and
       Boston Daily Globe, May 5, 1920.
280   "reiterated that the committee . . .": Boston Daily Globe, May 5, 1920.
280   "the committee never intended . . .": Christian Science Monitor, May 6, 1920.
280   William Howard Taft . . . agreed with Post's logic: New York Times, May 2,
       1920, in Candeloro, p. 50.
280   "Mr. Post has kept his head clear . . .": The Survey, April 28, 1920, in Post
       papers, LC.
280   "On Behalf of Louis Post": New Republic, April 28, 1920, in Post papers, LC.
280   George Peabody . . . stand firm: Letter from Peabody to Post, May 3, 1920,
       Peabody papers, LC. In Candeloro, p. 50.
280   "Blue-eyed, large-toothed, and bald . . .": Washington Times, January 5,
       1915, in King papers, LC.
281   "gentlemen interested . . .": Letter from Ralston to Walsh, April 16, 1920,
       in Gengarelly, p. 202.
281   "vicious and uncalled for attacks . . .": ibid.

40. SALSEDO

282   Salsedo . . . suicide: see Report of Special Agent Crystal, May 25, 1920, in
       NARA, M1085, file BS211793.
283   Flynn . . . convince one newsman . . . Donato: see New York World, May 4,
       1920.
283   "every physical clue . . .": Creighton to Palmer, May 17, 1920, p. 19, in
       NARA, M1085, file BS211793.
283   "Everybody is laughing . . .": Boston American, May 4, 1920, in NARA,
       M1085, file OG 120964.
294   "Red Plot Fell Flat": in Gengarelly, p. 222.
284   "I desire that you communicate . . .": Letter from Hoover to Stone, May 3,
       1920, LC collection.

285   *"I find in my files . . ."*: Letter from Hoover to Charles B. Walsh, May 6, 1920 (re: Johnson), LC collection.
285   *"By all means . . . ,"*; *"Wohle is right."*: Letter from Hoover to Charles B. Walsh, May 6, 1920 (re: Schwartz), LC collection.
285   *"I find in the files . . ."*: Letter from Hoover to Charles B. Walsh, May 6, 1920 (re: Olgin), LC collection.
286   FN: *The 1920 Annual Report . . . searches on . . . passport . . . applications*: [see 1920 Report, p. 168; 1921 Report, p. 133].
287   *"I see no impropriety . . ."*: Holmes letter to Harvard Liberal Club, January 12, 1920, in, among others, *New York Times*, January 13, 1920.

41. DAY IN COURT

289   *"short shaggy dark haired . . ."*: *New Republic* quoted in Post (1923), pp. 247–250.
290   *"I hope the chairman . . ."*: Post hearing, April 1920, p. 61.
290   *"often at variance . . ."*; *"[he] had no such authority"*: Post hearing, April 1920, p. 69.
290   *"The commissioner general [Caminetti] . . ."*: Post hearing, April 1920, Post, p. 162.
291   *"With all these sweeping raids . . ."*: Post hearing, April 1920, p. 71.
291   *"Not the slightest"*: Post hearing, April 1920, p. 240. Along this line, late in the hearing, Post briefly raised the matter of the Andrea Salsedo suicide while in Justice Department custody, though to insist that Salsedo had never been handed over to the Immigration Bureau, as his warrant required. See Post hearing, April 1920, p. 221.
291   *"I am glad to know . . ."*: Post hearing, April 1920, p. 70.
291   *"I think, Mr. Chairman, some people . . ."*: Post hearing, April 1920, p. 160.
292   *"I do not believe in the overthrow of law . . ."*: Post hearing, April 1920, pp. 202–203. See also *Congressional Record*, April 12, 1920, pp. 5553–5554.
292   *case involving . . . Ivan Dudinsky*: Post hearing, April 1920, pp. 175–188. For Hoover's request for higher bail in Dudinsky's case, see letters from Hoover to Caminetti, March 27, 1920, NARA, RG 60 file 205492, and April 23, 1920, NARA, RG 60, file 202600.
292   *"Evidently the bail demanded . . ."*: Post hearing, April 1920, p. 189.
292   *"I was about to say . . ."*: Post hearing, April 1920, p. 79.
292   *"Will you permit me . . ."*: Post hearing, April 1920, p. 83.
292   *"Suppose you give names"*: Post hearing, April 1920, p. 232.
292   *"Mr. Post has been ready . . ."*: Post hearing, April 1920, p. 84.
293   *"I was speaking of the time . . ."*: Post hearing, April 1920, pp. 254–255.
293   *Johnson kept his mouth shut* : When Johnson tried to interrupt Post during his explanation of a case on the second day of testimony, Chairman Campbell cut him off. "That will be taken up at the proper time," he said, and Edward Pou, the ranking Democrat, agreed: "Suppose we let Mr. Post go on and make his statement now, without interruption, unless it becomes absolutely necessary." Post hearing, April 1920, p. 174.
293   *"I suppose we are all anarchists . . ."*: Post hearing, April 1920, p. 197.
293   *"Mr. Secretary, your political convictions . . ."*: Post hearing, April 1920, p. 242.
293   *"There is just one other question . . ."*: Post hearing, April 1920, p. 248.
294   *"Whatever else we have done . . ."*; *"No; we are still within . . ."*: Post hearing, June 1920, p. 263.

294   *"Post hurls broadside . . ."*: *Spokesman-Review* quoted in Post (1923), p. 245.
294   *"Mr. Post said it was his duty . . ."*: *Christian Science Monitor*, May 8, 1920.
294   *"I am glad that my recent experiences . . ."*: Letter from Post to William E.
      Dodd, May 11, 1920, Dodd papers, LC, in Candeloro, p. 50.
294   *"Agitated gentlemen kept going . . ."*: *New Republic* article in Post (1923), pp.
      247–250. See also Hoover's written report to Palmer on the hearing,
      Hoover to Palmer, May 25, 1920, in Gentry, p. 97.

42. PAYBACK

295   *"This may interest you Palmer." "The issue is . . ."*: These flyers are attached
      to a letter from Hoover to Shern, May 8, 1920, in NARA, M1085, RG
      379228.
296   *Southern Pacific Railway . . . oil-rich public lands*: On this case, see Pin-
      chot to Palmer, January 9, 1920, in Walsh Papers, NYPL.
296   *Louisiana sugar . . . protecting profiteers*: Rules Committee Chairman Phillip
      Pitt Campbell went further and suggested this investigation could lead to
      impeachment. "The only action that can be taken at this time, if the rule
      is adopted, is to call the attorney general before the judiciary committee
      and let him explain his action," he told the House. See *Chicago Daily
      News*, March 5, 1920.
296   *unions sick of . . . strikebreaking*: On American Federation of Labor, see *New
      York Times*, June 8, 1920; on American Labor Party and Central Federated
      Union, see *Washington Post*, May 9, 1920.
296   *"A well-informed gentleman . . ."*: Huddleston statement in Post (1923), p. 231.
296   *"Should you desire . . ."*: Campbell to Palmer, May 11, 1920, in Palmer
      hearing, June 1920, pp. 3–5.
297   *Ralston . . . thirteen questions for . . . Palmeri*: Ralston also sent a separate
      list of questions for Caminetti citing specific cases of prisoners being held
      without hearings or whose recommended releases had been overruled or
      ignored. See letters to Campbell from Ralston, May 13, and May 21, 1920,
      in Post hearings, April 1920, pp. 266–268.
297   *"I place these in your hands . . ."*: Hoover to Ahern, May 8, 1920, NARA,
      M1085, file OG 379228. See also Williams (1981), p. 568.
297   *"Forward detailed report . . ."*: Telegram from Burke to Kelleher, May 13,
      1920, in NARA M1085, file OG 1209064.
297   *"I would appreciate . . ."*: Hoover to Churchill, May 13, 1920, NARA, Jus-
      tice, 202600; and LC collection.
298   *"Please personally make investigation . . ."*: Telegram from Burke to Kelleher,
      May 20, 1920, in NARA M1085, file OG 120964.
298   *files on Felix Frankfurter: . . ."Dr. Crouch is intensely Socialist . . ."* : see
      memos to Hoover from Colonel A.B. Coxe by W.W. Hicks, May 15, 1920,
      and from Colonel A.B. Coxe by W.W. Hicks, May 13, 1920, with attached
      "Report on Visit to Headquarters of Interchurch World Movement,
      Monday, March 22, 1920." In NARA, M1085, BSF 207588.
298   *"The League conducts . . ."; "An effort is being made . . ."*: Report of agent
      Kemon, May 19, 1920, NARA, M1085, file OG 120964.
299   *"Mr. Pope [the bank vice president] stated . . ."*: Report from agent Kemon
      June 2, 1920, NARA, M1085, file OG 378228.
299   *"the National Popular Government . . ."*: Report of Agent Reid, June 3,
      1920, NARA M1085, file OG 378228.

299   *"still voicing opposition . . ."*: Letter from Kelleher to Burke, Attention of J. E. Hoover, Esq., May 26, 1920, NARA, M1085, file OG 120964.
300   *"[A]n unexpected request . . ."*: Letter from Hoover to Arthur B. O'Keefe, May 20, 1920, LC collection.

43. Not Guilty

301   *"How do you plead?"*: New York Times, May 11, 1920.
303   *"a typical radical Irishman"*; *"thickset—lop-sided . . ."*: The Liberator, September 1920, p. 14, in Darrow papers, LC.
303   HOYNE ONLY HOPE IN MAYOR'S RACE, in Chicago Daily Tribune, March 23, 1919.
303   *"a Tolstoyan nonresistant . . ."*;*"I want to repeat . . ."*: Letter from Lloyd to Darrow is from report of agent M.F. Burger,January 4, 1918, in NARA, M1085, file OG 86163.
304   *"I believe in a government . . ."*; *"Why, that is almost . . ."*: Stone, p. 370.
304   *"That is my flag . . ."*; *"I want him to be . . ."*: People v. Lloyd, 304 Illinois 23 (1922), at 68 and 72.
305   *"You want to get rifles . . ."*: Lloyd speech from People v. Lloyd, 304 Ill. 23, 1922, at 67.
305   Palmer . . . the real enemy: Darrow that week also told a meeting of the International Ladies Garment Workers Union that Palmer was trying to discredit labor by "reports such as the May Day scare, which had no foundation in fact," and urged them to beat him "in a political way." New York Times and Los Angeles Times, May 4, 1920.
305   *"You might as well ask . . ."*; *"on his neck at . . ."*: Chicago Daily Tribune, May 11, 1920.

44. Twelve Lawyers

306   *"I'm in this typically . . ."*: Frankfurter to Holmes, April 19, in Mennel and Compston, p. 86.
306   *"the man who went before . . ."*: Hillman quote in letter from Kelleher to Burke, May 26, 1920, in NARA, M1085, file OG 120964.
307   *"Those of us having the matter . . ."*: As a sample of Ralston's cover letter, see Ralston to Walsh, May 19, 1920. Walsh papers, NYPL.
307   *"Under the guise . . ."*: Twelve Lawyer Report, p. 3.
309   *"to whose courageous reestablishment . . ."*: Twelve Lawyer Report, p. 8.
308   FN: *Frankfurter had known Louis Post:* On relationship between Post and Frankfurter, see Frankfurter (1960), p. 173, and letter from W. Wilson to Frankfurter, April 17, 1920, Frankfurter papers, L.C.
308   *"Hale & Ralston have spent . . ."*: Letter from King to Walsh, May 23, 1920, in Walsh papers, NYPL.
308   *"[W]hy the thing . . ."*: Chafee testimony, Palmer hearing, 1921, p. 167.
309   *"would have ended . . ."* *"If a company of soldiers . . ."*: Wigmore, p. 554.
309   *"The poor man . . . ,"* *"I'm rather sad about . . ."*: Frankfurter to Holmes, April 19, in Mennel and Compston, p. 86.
309   *"The clash between 'fear'. . . ."*: Frankfurter to Holmes, April 19, in Mennel and Compston, p. 86.
309   *"The venture has been . . ."*: King to Hale, June 8, 1920, in Walsh papers, NYPL.

309 *"a 'gut shot'!"*: Walsh to Walter Nelles, Walsh papers, NYPL, in Gengarelly, p. 220.

311 *were well managed, smoothly run, and humane*: For instance, the Boston office claimed that it sent an agent to visit wives and children of six prisoners said to be suffering poverty because of the husband's imprisonment and in each case made sure a local charity was helping them. Letter from Hoover to Latimer, March 24, 1920, NARA, M1085, file OG 378656

45. PALMER

313 *"I declare these charges . . ."*: Palmer hearing, June 1920, p. 5.

313 *"For peace they would sacrifice . . ."*: Palmer testimony, pp. 13, 15, 18, 19.

314 *"If there is any doubt . . ."*: Palmer hearing, June 1920, p. 27.

314 *"hailed the advent . . ."*; *"My own life is . . ."*; *"one or two isolated cases . . ."*: Palmer hearing, June 1920, pp. 34–35, 50–51.

314 *"was absolutely in error . . ."*; *"men of splendid character . . ."*: Palmer hearing, June 1920, pp. 48–49.

315 *"I do not know . . ."*: Palmer hearing, June 1920, p. 74.

315 *Are you going to believe . . ."*: Washington, *Evening Star*, June 2, 1920.

315 *"We find several . . ."*; *"I have difficulty . . ."*: Washington, *Evening Star*, June 2, 1920. Palmer's language in the hearing transcript differs slightly: "These gentlemen declare in their statements that they make no argument in favor of any radical doctrine as such . . . but they appear here simply as sworn counselors at law, sworn to defend the Constitution itself, and yet three or four of them have appeared as counsel for the Communist Labor Party at hearings before the Secretary of Labor, apparently although we find the Communist Labor Party repudiating their appearance and declaring that they did not represent the party as counsel, which indicates pretty clearly that they were there because they believed in the communist ideas and desired to defend them everywhere." Palmer hearing, June 1920, p. 75. Palmer never disputed the newspaper version.

315 *"I think the public is entitled . . ."*: Palmer hearing, June 1920, p. 209.

315 *Post . . . Palmer's "secret-service auxiliary"*: Post (1923), p. 268.

316 *Rules Committee . . . not to take any action*: Chicago Daily Tribune, June 3, 1920.

316 *"Indeed . . ."*: Murray, p. 249.

316 *"If Attorney General Palmer . . ."*: New York Evening Post, in Post, p. 271.

316 *"Palmer's defense . . . compounded of false testimony"*: Memorandum for the Signers of the Report on the Department of Justice, from Hale, undated, July 1920, Walsh papers, NYPL.

46. POLITICS

321 *dance card*: Theoharis & Cox, p. 33.

321 *"I think he regarded women . . ."*: Fennell interview in Demaris, p. 8.

321 *"If I ever marry . . ."*: in Summers, p. 32.

321 *"America's present need . . ."*: Harding quotes from Murray, p. 261.

322 *"the vigorous malpractice . . ."*: Republican Platform, 1920, from The American Presidency Project.

322 *"[T]oo much has been said . . ."*: Harding quotes from Murray, p. 261.

322 "Since the nomination of Coolidge, . . .": Atlanta Constitution, June 14, 1920.

322 "Whoever nominated Harding . . .": Washington Post, June 14, 1920.

323 "redolent with flowers . . ."; "One is greeted . . .": from Coban, p. 259.

323 Edgar . . . three days in San Francisco . . . convention hall . . . forty-five minutes: see Hoover statement in New York Times, September 24, 1920, in Hoover Scrapbooks, 1913–1972; NARA RG 65, Director's Official Records and Memorabilia, Box 1.

323 "[Palmer's] friends have been . . .": New York Times, June 30, 1920.

323 "secret agents": Boston Daily Globe, June 27, 1920.

323 "official favoritism . . ."; "Here he is . . .": Boston Globe, June 27, 1920.

324 "McAdoo has been to see . . .": Diary of Charles Lee Swem, May 17, 1920, in Link et al., vol. 65, p. 291.

324 "Every family visit . . .": Tumulty, pp. 496 and 497.

324 "Exactly, hence his nomination . . .": Memorandum by Carter Glass, June 19, 1920, in Link et al., vol. 65, p. 435.

324 "In such circumstances . . .": Grayson diary entry, March 25, 1920, in Coban, p. 253.

325 "a brilliant man, a great orator . . .": Coban, p. 261.

325 "All these charges . . .": Coban, p. 254.

325 "You are quoted . . ." "May we respectfully . . .": Telegram from Frankfurter and Chafee to Palmer, June 3, 1920. NARA, RG 60, file, 205492-666.

325 "utterly false charges": Telegram from Palmer to Frankfurter, June 4, 1920 NARA, RG 60, file 205492.

325 shady courtroom tactics in . . . Boston: Palmer's statement is from the Boston Post, June 4, 1920, in NARA M1085, OG 389244.

325 "A mob is a mob . . .": see telegram from Boston Acting Special Agent in Charge Hanrahan, June 23, 1920, in NARA, M1085, file OG-389244.

326 FN: "nothing but a negligible . . .": Letter from Anderson to Walsh, April 26, 1922, in Walsh papers, LC.

326 "the hydra-head . . . "; "True Americanism . . .": Christian Science Monitor, July 1, 1920.

326 Our forces . . .": New York Times, July 1, 1920.

327 "The Palmer managers . . .": Boston Daily Globe, July 4, 1920.

327 "[Mr. Palmer] is not willing . . .": Boston Daily Globe, July 6, 19120.

328 Helena, Montana: On this stop, see memorandum from Hoover to Assistant Attorney General Stewart, July 19, 1920. NARA, RG 60, file 202600-67-9, in LC collection.

328 "I have just returned . . .": Hoover to Lamb, July 13, 1920. NARA, RG 60, file 202600-337.

47. VERDICT

329 "Do you see the defendant . . .": Gitlow trial, NYPL, pp. 144–145.

330 "If we cannot overthrow . . .": People v. Lloyd, 304 Illinois 505 (1922), at p. 542.

330 "Gas was left flowing . . . .": Weinberg(1957), pp. 155, 169.

332 "these twenty cowards"; "Is this cowardly cripple . . .": Chicago Daily Tribune, July 28, 1920.

333 the "Black Sox: On the 1919 baseball scandal, see Pietrusza, Chapter 12.

333 "The state's attorney . . .": Chicago Daily Tribune, July 29, 1920.

333 *"Throngs filled the courtroom. . . .": Chicago Daily Tribune*, July 31, 1920. Shortly before Darrow began his summation, his clients handed him a group letter insisting they still adhered to the Communist Labor Party platform and the "Left Wing Manifesto," and insisting the defense be conducted without "repudiation" of either document. Darrow agreed. See *The Liberator*, August 1920, pp. 13–14, in Darrow papers, LC.

333 *"[T]hey have been called cowards . . ."*: Weinberg, p. 124.

334 *"Here are twenty men . . .": The Liberator*, August 1920, p. 14, in Darrow papers, LC.

334 *$40,000*: On prior disclosure of the fund, see *Chicago Herald and Examiner*, January 2, 1920.

334 *"the Beau Brummel . . ."*; *"Someone must have told . . ."*; *"I object, your Honor . . .": The Liberator*, August 1920, pp. 14–15, in Darrow papers, LC. See Weinberg, p. 167.

335 *"I urge you to stand . . ."*: Weinberg, pp. 170, 172.

335 *"Like Francis Scott Key . . ."*: Comerford's summation from *Chicago Daily Tribune*, August 3, 1920.

336 *"we were certain . . .": The Nation*, August 20, 1920, p. 186.

336 *"This is our country . . ."*: Weinberg, p. 172.

336 *"Obviously, in such a state . . .": The Nation*, August 20, 1920, at 186.

337 *"I lose a $10 hat . . .": Chicago Daily Tribune*, August 3, 1920.

337 *"Every one knows that Mr. Hoyne . . .": Chicago Daily Tribune*, September 6, 1920.

337 *"People are getting . . ."*; *"I wish I was . . ."*: Darrow to Field, Thanksgiving Day, 1920, in Field papers, Chicago.

48. EMPIRE

338 *"high-minded . . ."*; *"Yet there are matters . . .": Washington Post*, September 28, 1920.

339 *charges that Palmer . . . released . . . prisoners, granted pardons*: On these complaints, by Chicago lawyer William Armstrong, see *New York Times*, July 8, 1920.

339 *"Was there a Red outbreak . . ."*: Kenyon committee testimony in *Los Angeles Times*, September 24, 1920.

339 *"All I can say is that . . ."*: Hoover denial in *New York Times*, September 24, 1920, in Hoover scrapbook, NARA, RG 65, Director's Official Records and Memorabilia, Box 1.

340 *"I might state that . . ."*: Hoover to Alvin Kuhn, August 10, 1920, NARA, RG 60, file, 202600.

340 *"In going over the personnel . . ."*: Hoover to James A. Horton, Solicitor, Post Office Department, September 16, 1920, NARA, RG 60, file 202600.

340 *"[T]he Department, as far as . . ."*: Stewart to Hoover, November 5, 1920, NARA, RG 60, file 202600.

340 *"not only ultraradical activities . . ."*: AG Annual Report, 1920, p. 173.

341 *Red Cross . . . prisoner swap*: see letter to Palmer from Third Assistant Secretary of State Merle-Smith, July 23, 1920, NARA, RG60, file 202600-343.

341 *diplomat in Rotterdam, Holland*: see Hoover to Hurley, August 20, 1920, NARA, RG 60, file 202600-377.

341 *"[to] attempt to return . . ."*: Hoover to Hurley, September 30, 1920, NARA, RG 60, file 202600-432.

341 *"That A. Mitchell Palmer . . ."*: Newspaper clipping from August 18 in NARA, RG 60, file 202600.

342 *Protocols of the Elders of Zion:* see letters from Hoover to Hurley, May 5, 1920, and to Carter, July 8, 1920, both at NARA, RG 60, file 202600.

342 *591 . . . found deportable . . . only a handful actually . . . shipped:* see Murray, p. 251, and AG Annual Report, 1921, p. 129.

342 *"I have several communications . . ."*: WWG to Hoover, August 27, 1920, NARA M1085, file OG 341761.

342 *"I would . . . appreciate a suggestion . . ."*: Hoover to Assistant AG Stewart, October 12, 1920, NARA, M1085, file OG 341761.

343 *Red crackdown had succeeded:* In another sign, Edgar learned in May 1920 that leaders of the Communist Party, the Communist Labor Party, and the Union of Russian Workers, had secretly discussed merging under the single banner of the Communist Labor Party, relying on Labor Secretary William Wilson's ruling that Communist Labor was not a forbidden group under the 1918 Immigration Act, but they had decided against it out of fear that Edgar's agents would arrest regardless. See memorandum dated May 19, 1920, authorship indicated by initials JEH-GPO in top right corner. NARA, RG 60, file 202600.

343 *"very inactive, and I have been advised . . ."*: Franklin Dodge, Grand Rapids Special Agent in Charge, to Chicago Division Superintendent, November 10, 1920, NARA, RG 65, file 202600-14.

343 *"As a matter of fact . . ."*: Murray, p. 220.

343 *"These raids were very costly . . ."*: Gitlow, p. 65.

344 *"How do I know? . . ."*; *"One of my ancestors . . ."*: Bolle (1996), p. 217.

344 *"Capitalism is untouched . . ."*: Murray, p. 259. On the Wall Street explosion generally, see NARA, M1085, file OG 386228.

344 *Harding won by a landslide:* Women voting for the first time pushed up vote totals from under 19 million in 1916 to over 26 million in 1920, but that didn't stop voter turnout from falling to its lowest level yet in American history. Only 49.2 percent of eligible voters went to the polls, down from over 61 percent in 1916.

345 *the wrecking of . . ."*; *"the conviction of 32 . . ."*: AG Annual Report, 1920, pp. 176, 178.

49. WALSH

347 *"the murderous acts . . ."*: Walsh to Jeremiah Lynch, June 4, 1919, in Walsh papers, LC.

347 *"If you care to address . . ."*: Walsh to W. G. Richards, February 17, 1920, in Walsh papers, LC.

347 *"I am very sure . . ."*: Walsh to John Ford, February 18, 1920, in Walsh papers, LC.

348 *"Walsh was no backslapper . . ."*: Wheeler, p. 103.

348 *Nobody objected:* Senator William King of Utah rose to criticize the Twelve Lawyer Report as biased old news, but never objected to Walsh's motion. See *Congressional Record*, December 10, 1920, p. 150.

348 *"[E]ven the most conscienceless . . ."*: *Congressional Record*, December 10, 1920, p. 150.

349 *Chafee . . . digest of Justice Department law-breaking:* This summary outline

is attached to a note from Chafee to Walsh, January 28, 1921, in Walsh papers, LC.

349 *Francis Fisher Kane . . . Tyrrel Williams:* Walsh from Kane, January 20, 1921, and Williams to Spencer, December 21, 1920, both in Walsh papers, LC.

349 *"The present Attorney General . . .":* For full text, see Palmer hearing, 1921, pp. 98 et seq.

350 *"I would like to ask . . ."; "Is there anything . . .":* Palmer hearing, 1921, p. 5.

350 *"the time has come . . . I have nothing to go on . . .":* Palmer hearing, 1921, pp. 5–6. See also *Boston Daily Globe* and other newspapers, January 20, 1921.

351 *apple cider:* see *Washington Post,* December 19, 1920.

351 *"beer at the [drugstore] . . .": New York Times,* March 18, 1921. See also *New York Times,* March 10, 1921.

351 *"Debs is now approaching . . ."; "Denied. W.W.":* Memorandum from Palmer to the President, January 29, 1921, in Link et al., vol. 67, p. 98.

351 *Mike Marzinik:* On Marzanik, see Recht, Chapter XIII, p. 11, and *Boston Daily Globe,* February 3, 1921.

352 *"It was the Secretary of Labor . . ."; "Who first decides . . ."; "The inspector . . .":* Palmer hearing, 1921, pp. 8–9.

353 *"I do not think that . . .":* Palmer hearing, 1921, p. 15.

354 *"How many search warrants . . . ,"; "I cannot tell you . . ."; "You have no record . . ."; "No, sir."; "No sir; I do not.":* Palmer hearing, 1921, p. 19.

50. STONE

357 *"When he talks to you . . .": Chicago Daily Tribune,* April 27, 1924.

357 *Winthrop Stone:* see file on loyalty case in Stone papers, LC.

358 *"the loose-thinking, wild-talking . . .":* Stone (Conscientious Objector) pp. 266–267. See also Stone to H.K. Kellen, February 25, 1944, in Stone papers, LC.

358 *"[I]t strengthens the opinion . . .":* Letter from Stone to Butler, January 21, 1920. Stone letters, LC.

358 *New York City Bar Association:* Minutes, Annual Meeting of The Association of the Bar of the City of New York, January 13, 1920, p. 217; also in *New York Times,* January 13, 1920.

358 *ban socialists from attending law schools:* see *New York Times,* April 4, 1920.

359 *J. McKeen Cattell:* On Cattell, see Mason, p. 111, plus the Justice Department file on its investigation both of him and of his son for alleged draft evasion, in NARA, M1085, file OG 44840.

359 *"New York is more solicitous . . .": New York Times,* January 26, 1921.

360 *"It appears by the public admissions . . .":* Stone statement is from Palmer hearing, 1921, pp. 279–280.

361 *Wilson . . . group photograph: Washington Post,* February 17, 1921.

361 *"Mr. Chairman, I am sorry . . .":* Palmer hearing, 1921, p. 421.

362 *"[We] had just passed through . . .":* Palmer hearing, 1921, p. 572.

362 *"At that time, in 1919 . . .":* Palmer hearing, 1921, pp. 580–581.

362 *"I would like to have . . ."; "Now, in as far as . . ."; "That is all I care for":* Palmer hearing, 1921, pp. 648–649.

51. SURVIVOR

364 *"I hope it won't turn out . . .":* Boller (2001), p. 94.

364   *"Well, the Senate threw me . . .":* New York Times, March 5, 1920; Smith, pp. 185–186.

366   *"I was no amateur . . .":* Daugherty, p. 21.

366   *"Well, boys, I'll tell ya . . .":* Boller (1996), p. 214.

368   Military Intelligence: Edgar's tie to Military Intelligence Director Marlborough Churchill grew so close around this time that in 1922 they awarded Edgar his own reserve officer's commission.

368   *"return to Washington . . .":* Theoharis, 2000, p. 328.

368   *"The Red agents . . .":* Daugherty, p. 122.

370   *"for amusing Department . . .* : Alexander (II), p. 22.

370   *"I saw Palmer coming out . . .":* Means testimony in New York Times, April 17, 1924.

370   *"If you knew . . .";* *"Publish it . . .":* Dean, p. 149.

52. Fooled

373   *"any system which confers . . .":* Palmer hearing, 1921, p. 280.

373   *"melancholia"* and *"inanition":* Certificate of death of Dickerson Naylor Hoover Sr., April 1, 1926, D.C.

373   *"My mother used to say . . .":* in Summers, p. 24.

373   *"I remember [Edgar] used to take . . .":* Margaret Fennel interview, in Demaris, p. 6.

374   *"Well, I think . . .":* Mason, p. 144.

374   *"I don't know whom . . .":* Mason, p. 150.

375   *"I shall be grateful . . .":* Letter from Stone to Frankfurter, April 7, 1924. Frankfurter letters, LC.

375   *"There can hardly be two . . .":* Letter from Frankfurter to Stone, May 15, 1924. Frankfurter papers, LC.

375   *"Unable to find a man . . .":* Alexander, II, p. 22.

375   *"much like an active . . .":* Atlanta Constitution, December 27, 1924.

376   *"honest and informed . . .":* Willebrandt to Mason, January 31, 1951, in Mason, p. 150.

376   *"Stone doesn't have to go . . .":* Toledano, pp. 70–71; Whitehead, pp. 66–67, Gentry, p. 125.

377   demanding the resignation . . . female . . . employee: see Gentry, p. 120.

378   *"Personally, I always blamed . . .":* O'Brian to Frankfurter, March 27, 1925, Frankfurter papers, LC.

378   *"Young man, I want you to be . . .":* Toledano, p. 71. See also Whitehead, p. 67.

378   *"A secret police may become . . .";* out six concrete operating principles . . . : Memorandum from Stone to Hoover, May 13, 1924. Stone file, FBI FOIA Reading Room.

378   *"Instructions have been sent . . .":* Lowenthal, pp. 298–299. See also New York Times, May 18, 1924.

379   *"I'm surprised you didn't . . . .":* see letter from Nichols to Mason, September 9, 1950, in Stone file, FBI FOIA Reading Room, Toledano, pp. 76–77, and Whitehead, p. 72.

379   *"Everyone says he's too young . . .":* Willebrandt to Mason, January 31, 1951, in Mason, p. 150.

379   *"Young Mr. Hoover . . .":* from Literary Digest, in Toledano, p. 73.

379   Felix Frankfurter complimented it: Letter from Frankfurter to Stone, May 15, 1924, Frankfurter papers, LC.

379 Edgar meet . . . Roger Baldwin: On Baldwin meeting, see Theoharis and Cox, p. 86, Gentry, p. 138.
379 "at a public meeting here, . . .": Memorandum supplied by L.B. Nichols to Dr. Alpheus Thomas Mason, August 8, 1950, p. 9. Stone file, FBI FOIA Reading Room.
379 "Having been appointed . . .": Letter from Hoover to Stone, March 28, 1929, Harlan Stone papers, LC.
379 "As a young man, his . . .": Letter from Stone to Agnes Harvey Stone, April 23, 1946, Stone file, FBI FOIA Reading Room.
379 "removed from the Bureau . . .": Mason, p. 152.
380 He . . . clarified his name: see Theoharis and Cox, p. 56; Summers, p. 34.
380 "I know you want to know . . .": Letter from Frankfurter to Stone, January 22, 1925, Frankfurter papers, LC.

X. LEGACY

386 "Their avowed objective . . .": Recht, Chapter XIII, p. 5.
387 "If I should step . . .": Flynn interview in Boston Daily Globe, May 28, 1922.
387 "Certainly, gentlemen can not . . .": Palmer hearing, 1921, p. 573.
387 "activities of Communists . . .": Memorandum from Hoover to William J. Donovan, October 1924, in Donner, pp. 46–47.
388 "We shall repent in sackcloth . . .": The Nation, August 19, 1920, p. 185.
388 "[I]t is manifest that . . .": Gitlow v. United States, 268 U.S. 652 (1925).
389 the Magnolia: On the Magnolia, see Leo B. Russell to Caminetti, March 21, 1921, and J. J. Davis to Walsh, May 5, 1921, both in Walsh papers, LC.
390 "Four hundred and twenty-seven . . .": Attorney General, 1921, p. 131.
391 FN: Judiciary Committee . . . marathon session: see summary of committee minutes, March 6, 1922, through January 29, 1923, in Walsh papers, LC.
391 FN: Frankfurter concurrence in Dennis v. United States, 341 U.S. 494, at 544; and Volokh generally.
391 Justice Department . . . strict policy: In August of that year, the Justice Department sent a special counsel to Butte, Montana, to investigate labor unrest at the Anaconda copper mines, but when the lawyer recommended prosecuting the prounion Butte Daily Bulletin, Edgar himself demanded he be fired. See memorandum from Hoover to Stewart, December 1, 1920, NARA, RG 60, file,195397-1-27, and related documents in that file.
393 "a matter which . . ."; "Doubtless you know . . .": Letters from Peabody to Walsh, March 16 and 22, 1921, in Walsh papers, NYPL.
394 FN: "Ask Mitchell . . .": Tumulty to Peggy Palmer, March 29, 1924, in Tumulty papers, LC.
394 "There's no evidence . . .": Flynn interview, in Boston Daily Globe, May 28, 1922.
394 Caminetti . . . new message: see Atlanta Constitution, January 16, 1921.
395 "This flood of cheap foreign . . .": Chicago Daily Tribune, January 27, 1921.
395 "Do you want to let . . .": Christian Science Monitor, April 23, 1920.
395 "We do not want to be . . .": Murray, p. 265.
395 "famed Chicago criminal lawyer": Hoover, p. 252.
396 Frankfurter . . . Franklin Roosevelt . . . save his job: see Gentry, p. 157.
396 "I stated I sign . . .": Theoharis, p. 68
396 "My sympathies . . .": Irons, p. 1233.
397 FN: Communist International . . . end their split and merge: see (i) Resolution

of the Executive Committee of the Communist International, August 8, 1920, and (ii) Memorandum to the Communist International from Louis Fraina, August 15, 1920, concerning distribution of the budget, both in CPA-USA collection, LC.

397   *"an ideological system . . ."*: Gitlow to Hoover, June 29, 1951, in Gitlow Papers, UNC.

397   *Gitlow . . . letter to J. Edgar Hoover*: Gitlow to Hoover, June 29, 1951, and Hoover to Gitlow, July 7, 1951, both in Gitlow Papers, UNC.

398   FN: *Hoover helped the American Legion*: see Hoover to Baldwin Robertson, September 17, 1920, mentioning American Legion contact, in NARA, RG 60, file 195397-1.

398   FN: *"among the ablest and best . . ."*: Wilson letter from *Boston Daily Globe*, January 21, 1921.

398   *"If our young men . . ."*: *Washington Post*, November 2, 1924.

398   *Post . . . Sacco and Vanzetti*: see letter from Post to Frankfurter, May 15, 1927. Frankfurter papers, LC.

400   *"Much sedition is heard . . ."*: *New York Times*, March 19, 1919.

400   *"I was sent up . . ."*: *Look*, May 31, 1955, in Gentry, p. 95.

401   *"I must state that I am . . ."*: Hoover to Caminetti, June 15, 1920, NARA, RG 60, file 202600-324.

401   *"I believe that Mr. Palmer . . ."*: Ralston testimony in Palmer hearing, 1921, p. 273.

402   *"Hoover got wind of this . . ."*: Wheeler, p. 243.

402   *"I spoke to Mr. Hoover . . ."*: Letters from Katzoff to Hoover, July 11, 1940, and Hoover to Katzoff, July 24, 1940, in Stone file, FBI FOIA Reading Room.

402   *"After months of such physical proximity . . ."*: Recht, Chapter XIII, p. 28.

403   *"pseudo liberal" . . . "swaydo"*: Gentry, p. 74.

403   *"I am informed . . ."; "My impression is that . . ."*: Letter from to Johnson, in NARA, RG 60, file 202600. The NARA copy is unsigned and no author listed, though it is alongside many letters from Hoover. Whether the letter was actually sent or not is thus unclear.

403   *telegram Frankfurter sent . . . prominent congressman*: see report from agent Grimes, June 5, 1920, in NARA, M1085, file OG 120964, in Williams, p. 574.

403   *"I am in receipt of information . . ."*: Hoover to Hurley, June 10, 1920, NARA M1085, file OG 120964.

403   *"I would advise you . . ."*: Hurley to Hoover, June 11, 1920. NARA, M1085, file OG 120964.

404   *"There is a feeling in . . ."*: Lowenthal, p. 372.

405   *Edgar . . . patron saint for detectives*: "During those dark days [of the early 1920s] the Bureau was but a seedling of the great American oak it is today [and] run by a bunch of ruthless and unscrupulous characters," one recruit recalled being taught in an FBI training class in the mid-1960s. "Youthful as he was, and surrounded by thieves, [our Director] was tempted to resign in favor of entering private law practice," his teacher went on. "But no! The Director chose the path of sacrifice; and electing to forego private wealth and what to *lesser* men are the *pleasures* of life, he dedicated himself instead to the creation of the organization we are proud to serve today." See Ollestad, p. 61.

405 *"Mr. President, there is no . . ."*: from Whitehead, p. 158-159, and Theoharis, p. 15.

406 *"The FBI kept Joseph McCarthy . . ."*: Sullivan quote from Jerome, p. 100.

406 *Mary Pickford:* see Memorandum to Director, FBI, April 17, 1944, regarding "Mary Pickford," in Mary Pickford file, FBI FOIA Reading Room.

407 *"the crime of . . ."*: On Rosenberg case, see Theoharis, 2000, pp. 64–66.

407 *"[He] required that Bureau officials . . ."*: Theoharis, 1991, p. 3.

407 *"One hears in Washington . . ."*: Alexander, II, 1935.

BIBLIOGRAPHY

MANUSCRIPT COLLECTIONS

Chicago, Circuit Court of Cook County:
- William Bross Lloyd case file

District of Columbia Archives (DC):
- Dickinson Naylor Hoover file

Clerk of the Circuit Court of Cook County, Illinois:
- *People v. William Bross Lloyd et al.*

Ellis Island Library
FBI FOIA Reading Room:
- Clarence Darrow file
- Harlan Stone file
- Mary Pickford file

J. Edgar Hoover Center for Law Enforcement (Hoover Center):[*]
- J. Edgar Hoover collection

Library of Congress (LC):
- Clarence S. Darrow papers
- Communist Party of America papers (CPA-USA collection)
- William E. Borah papers
- Federal Bureau of Investigation investigative files (LC collection)
- Felix Frankfurter papers
- J. Edgar Hoover: Personal and Confidential File
- Judson King papers
- Robert Lansing papers
- W. Mitchel Palmer papers (merged with Wilson)
- Louis F. Post papers
- Harlan Stone papers
- Joseph Tumulty papers
- Thomas J. Walsh papers
- Woodrow Wilson papers

---

[*]The Hoover Center is located at the Supreme Council of the Scottish Rite Freemasons, 1733 Sixteenth Street, Washington, D.C.

National Archives (NARA):
- Department of Justice (Record Group 60)
- Department of Labor (Record Group 175)
- Federal Bureau of Investigation (Record Group 65)
- Bureau of Investigation, 1918–1922, microfilm collection (M1085)
- Immigration (Record Group 85)
- Military Intelligence (Record Group 165)

Newberry Library (Chicago):
- Darrow Family Scrapbooks
- Mary Field Parton—Clarence Darrow papers ("Field papers")

New York Public Library (NYPL):
- *People v. William Bross Lloyd* (Lloyd Trial)
- Frank P. Walsh papers

New York State Library and Archives (Albany):
- Lusk Committee files
- *People v. Benjamin Gitlow* ("Gitlow transcript")

New York University, Tamiment Library (NYU):
- Charles Recht papers

University of Delaware (Delaware):
- Emma Goldman papers

University of North Carolina, Charlotte, Library (UNC):
- Benjamin Gitlow papers

SELECTED NEWSPAPERS:

- *Atlanta Constitution*
- *Boston Globe*
- *Boston Herald*
- *Butte Weekly Bulletin*
- *Chicago Herald and Examiner*
- *Chicago Tribune*
- *Christian Science Monitor*
- *Congressional Record*
- *Leslie's Illustrated Weekly Newspaper*
- *Los Angeles Times*
- *New York Call*
- *New York Law Journal*
- *New York Times*
- *New York World*

- *The New Yorker*
- *Newark Evening News*
- *Omaha Herald*
- *Pittsburgh Post*
- *Washington Evening Star*
- *Washington Herald*
- *Washington Post*

GOVERNMENT REPORTS, HEARINGS:

Annual Reports of the Attorney General of the United States for the Fiscal Years 1919, 1920, and 1921. ("AG Annual Report") Washington, Government Printing Office. Submitted December 8, 1919, December 11, 1920, and December 8, 1921.

Attorney General A. Mitchell Palmer on Charges Made Against Department of Justice by Louis F. Post and Others ("Palmer hearing, June 1920"). Hearings before the Committee on Rules, House of Representatives. 66th Congress, 2d Session. June 1 1920.

Charges of Illegal Practices of the Department of Justice ("Palmer hearing, 1921"). Hearings before Subcommittee of the Committee on the Judiciary, United States Senate. 66rd Congress, 3rd Session. January 19 to March 3, 1921.

Investigation into the Destruction of Former FBI Director J. Edgar Hoover's Files and FBI Recordkeeping. Hearing before a Subcommittee of the Committee on Government Operations, House of Representatives. 94th Congress, 1st Session. December 1, 1975.

Investigation of Administration of Louis F. Post, Assistant Secretary of Labor, in the Matter of Deportation of Aliens ("Post hearing, April 1920"). Hearings before the Committee on Rules, House of Representatives. 66th Congress, 2d Session. April 27, 1920 et seq.

Nomination of A. Mitchell Palmer ("Palmer nomination hearing, 1919"). Hearing before Subcommittee of the Committee on the Judiciary, United States Senate. 66th Congress, 1st Session. June 4, 1919 et seq.

Sundry Civil Appropriations Bill for 1920 ("Appropriation hearing, 1920"). Hearings before Subcommittees of House Committee on Appropriations. 66th Congress, 1st Session. June 13, 1919.

CITED ARTICLES, REPORTS, DISSERTATIONS

Alexander, Jack. "Profiles: The Director." *The New Yorker.* (I) September 25, (II) October 2, and (III) October 9, 1937.

Candeloro, Dominic. "Louis F. Post and the Red Scare of 1920." *Prologue; the Journal of the National Archives.* Vol. 11, No. 1. Spring 1979.

Candeloro, Dominic. "The Public of Louis F. Post and Progressivism." *Mid-America: An Historical Review.* Vol. 56, No. 2. April 1974.

Chafee, Zechariah. "A Contemporary State Trial—The United States versus Jacob Abrams et al." *Harvard Law Review.* April 1920.

Chafee, Zechariah. "*Freedom of Speech in Time of War.*" *Harvard Law Review.* June 1919.

Chafee, Zechariah, et al. *Report to the American People upon the Illegal Practices of the Department of Justice.* Washington, D.C.: National Popular Government League. May 1920 ("Twelve Lawyer Report").

Crockett, Sam. *Frankfurter's Red Record.* New Jersey: Christian Educational Association, 1961.

Darrow, Clarence S. *War Prisoners.* Chicago: Maclaskey & Maclaskey, 1919.

Dosik, Jeffrey S. "*Deportation and the Red Scare of 1919–1920.*" Ellis Island Library, Statue of Liberty Ellis Island National Monument Project, 1984.

Dunn, Arthur Wallace. "The 'Reds' in America, From the Standpoint of the Department of Justice." *The American Review of Reviews.* February 1920.

Ellis, William T. "The 'Fighting Quaker' in the Cabinet." *The American Review of Reviews.* January 1920.

Gengarelly, W. Anthony. *Resistance Spokesmen: Opponents of the Red Scare, 1919–1920.* Ph.D. Dissertation, Boston University, 1972.

Gitlow, Benjamin. "The Left Wing Manifesto." *The Revolutionary Age.* July 5, 1919.

Goldman, Emma. "*Anarchism: What It Really Stands For.*" *Mother Earth.* 1910, 1917.

Irons, Peter H. "'Fighting Fair': Zachariah Chafee Jr., the Department of Justice, and the 'Trial at the Harvard Club.'" *Harvard Law Review.* Vol. 94, No. 6. April 1981.

Johnson, Donald. "The Political Career of A. Mitchell Palmer." *Pennsylvania History.* Vol. 25, No. 4. October 1958.

Johnson, Marion. *Preliminary Inventory of the General Records of the Department of Justice.* Washington: National Archives and Records Service, 1981.

Lloyd, William Bross. "Convention Impressions." *The Class Struggle,* November 1919.

Lusk, Senator Clayton R. "Radicalism Under Inquiry: Conclusions Reached after a Year's Study of Alien Anarchy in America." *The American Review of Reviews,* February 1920.

Palmer, A. Mitchell. "Crushing the German Advance in American Industry." *Scribner's,* July 1919.

Panunzio, Constantine M. "*The Deportation Cases of 1919–1920.*" Federal Council of the Churches of Christ, 1921.

Report upon the Illegal Practices of the United States Department of Justice. Washington, D.C.: National Popular Government League, May 1920 ("Twelve Lawyer Report").

Rosenzweig, Paul, and Carafano, James Jay. "*Preventive Detention and Actionable Intelligence.*" *Heritage Homeland Security.* The Heritage Foundation. Legal Memorandum #13, September 16, 2004.

Simons, H. Austin. "*Guilty: the General Strike.*" *The Liberator.* August 1920.

Stone, Harlan F. "The Conscientious Objector." *Columbia University Quarterly.* October 1919.

Volokh, Eugene. "Freedom of Speech and the Constitutional Tension Method." *University of Chicago Roundtable*. Vol. 3. 1996.

Weimer, Douglas R. "A Look Around the Neighborhood." *Cosmos Journal*. 1999.

Wigmore, John H. "*Abrams v. U.S.*: Freedom of Speech and Freedom of Thuggery in War-time and Peace-Time." *Illinois Law Review*. Vol. 14, No. 8. March 1920.

Williams, David. "The Bureau of Investigation and Its Critics, 1919–1921: The Origins of Federal Political Surveillance." *The Journal of American History*. Vol. 68, No. 3. December 1981.

Williams, David. "'Sowing the Wind: The Deportation Raids of 1920 in New Hampshire." *Historical New Hampshire*. Vol. 34, No. 1. Spring 1979.

BOOKS

Allen, Frederick Lewis. *Only Yesterday: An Informal History of the 1920s*. New York: Harper & Row, Publishers, 1931.

Baker, Liva. *The Justice from Beacon Hill: The Life and Times of Oliver Wendell Holmes*. New York: HarperCollins Publishers, 1991.

Barson, Michael, and Steven Heller. *Red Scared! The Commie Menace in Propaganda and Popular Culture*. San Francisco: Chronicle Books, 2001.

Bendersky, Joseph W. *The Jewish Threat: Anti-Semitic Politics of the U.S. Army*. New York: Basic Books, 2000.

Bennett, David H. *The Party of Fear: From Nativist Movements to the New Right in American History*. Raleigh: University of North Carolina Press, 1988.

Boller, Paul F. *Presidential Campaigns*. New York: Oxford University Press, 1996.

———. *Presidential Inaugurations*. New York: Harcourt, Inc., 2001.

Boyer, Richard O., and Herbert M. Morais. *Labor's Untold Story*. New York: United Electrical, Radio and Machine Workers of America, 1955.

Brands, H. W. *Woodrow Wilson*. New York: Times Books, 2003.

Coban, Stanley. *A. Mitchell Palmer: Politician*. New York: Columbia University Press, 1963.

———. *Reform, War, and Reaction: 1912–1932*. Columbia, South Carolina: University of South Carolina Press, 1972.

Collier, Peter. *The Roosevelts: An American Saga*. New York: Simon & Schuster, 1994.

Congressional Directory. Washington: Government Printing Office. December 1918; May 1920; January 1921.

Cowan, Geoffrey. *The People v. Clarence Darrow*. New York: Times Books, 1993.

Cowing, Cedric C. *Populists, Plungers, and Progressives: A Social History of Stock and Commodity Speculation, 1890–1936*. Princeton: Princeton University Press, 1965.

Darrow, Clarence. *The Story of My Life*. New York: Charles Scribner's Sons, 1932.

Daugherty, Harry M. *The Inside Story of the Harding Tragedy*. New York: The Churchill Company, 1932.

Demaris, Ovid. *The Director: An Oral Biography of J. Edgar Hoover*. New York: Harper's Magazine Press, 1975.

Dershowitz, Alan M. *America on Trial: Inside the Legal Battles that Transformed Our Nation*. New York: Warner Books, 2004.

De Toledano, Ralph. *J. Edgar Hoover: The Man in His Time*. New Rochelle: Arlington House, 1973.

Dean, John W. *Warren G. Harding*. New York: Times Books, Henry Holt and Company, 2004.

Donner, Frank J. *The Age of Surveillance: The Aims and Methods of America's Political Intelligence System*. New York: Vintage Books, 1980.

Draper, Theodore. *The Roots of American Communism*. Chicago: Elephant Paperbacks, Ivan R. Dee, Inc., Publisher, 1989, 1957.

Feuerlicht, Roberta Strauss. *America's Reign of Terror: World War I, the Red Scare, and the Palmer Raids*. New York: Random House, 1971.

Fleming, Thomas. *The Illusion of Victory: America in World War I*. New York: Basic Books, 2003.

Foglesong, David S. *America's Secret War against Bolshevism*. Chapel Hill: The University of North Carolina Press, 1995.

Frankfurter, Felix. *Felix Frankfurter Reminisces: Recorded Talks with Dr. Harlan B. Philips*. New York: Reynal & Company, 1960.

Frankfurter, Felix, and Joseph P. Lash. *From the Diaries of Felix Frankfurter*. New York: W.W. Norton & Co., Inc., 1975.

Gengarelly, W. Anthony. *Distinguished Dissenters and Opposition to the 1919–1920 Red Scare*. Lewiston/Queenston/Lampeter: The Edwin Mellen Press. 1996.

Gentry, Curt. *J. Edgar Hoover: The Man and the Secrets*. New York: Penguin Group, 1991.

Ginger, Ray. *Eugene V. Debs: The Making of an American Radical*. New York: The Macmillan Company, 1949.

Gitlow, Benjamin. *I Confess: The Truth about American Communism*. New York: E.P. Dutton & Co., 1939.

Goldman, Emma. *Living My Life*. New York: Da Capo Press, 1931, 1970.

Gompers, Samuel. *Seventy Years of Life and Labor*. New York: E.P. Dutton, Inc., 1925.

Haynes, John E. *Red Scare or Red Menace: American Communism and Anticommunism in the Cold War Era*. Chicago: Ivan R. Dee, 1996.

Hoover, J. Edgar. *Masters of Deceit: The Story of Communism in America and How to Fight It*. New York: Holt, Rinehart and Winston, 1958.

Hoyt, Edwin P. *The Palmer Raids, 1919–1920: An Attempt to Suppress Dissent*. New York: The Seabury Press, 1969.

Jacoby, Susan. *Freethinkers: A History of American Secularism*. New York: Henry Holt and Company, 2004.

Jerome, Fred. *The Einstein File: J. Edgar Hoover's Secret War Against the World's Most Famous Scientist*. New York: St. Martin's Press. 2002.

Kennan, George F. *Soviet-American Relations, 1917–1920: The Decision to Intervene*. Princeton, New Jersey: Princeton University Press, 1958.

Klehr, Harvey, John Earl Haynes, and Fridrikh Igorevich Firsov. *The Secret World of American Communism.* New Haven: Yale University Press, 1995.

Knock, Thomas J. *To End All Wars: Woodrow Wilson and the Quest for a New World Order.* Princeton, New Jersey: Princeton University Press, 1992.

Lash, Joseph. *Eleanor and Franklin.* New York: W.W. Norton & Company, 1971.

Link, Arthur S. et al., editors. *The Papers of Woodrow Wilson* (69 volumes). Princeton, New Jersey: Princeton University Press, 1978.

Lombardi, John. *Labor's Voice in the Cabinet: A History of the Department of Labor from Its Origin to 1921.* New York: Columbia University Press, 1942.

Lowenthal, Max. *The Federal Bureau of Investigation.* New York: Harcourt Brace Javanovich, Inc., 1950.

Mason, Alpheus Thomas. *Harlan Fiske Stone: Pillar of the Law.* New York: The Viking Press, 1956.

McCombs, William F. *Making Woodrow Wilson President.* New York: Fairview Publishing Company, 1921.

Mennel, Robert M., and Christine L. Compston, editors. *Holmes and Frankfurter: Their Correspondence, 1912–1934.* Hanover: University Press of New England, 1996.

Murray, Robert K. *Red Scare: A Study in National Hysteria, 1919–1920.* New York: McGraw-Hill Book Company, 1955.

Novotny, Ann. *Strangers at the Door: Ellis Island, Castle Garden, and the Great Migration to America.* Riverside, Conn.: The Chatham Press. 1971.

Ollestad, Normal. *Inside the F.B.I.* New York: Lyle Stuart, 1967.

Parrish, Michael. *Felix Frankfurter and His Times.* New York: The Free Press, 1982.

Pietrusza, David. *Rothstein: The Life, Times, and Murder of the Criminal Genius Who Fixed the 1919 World Series.* New York: Carroll & Graf Publishers, 2003.

Post, Louis F. *The Deportations Delirium of Nineteen-Twenty.* Chicago: Charles H. Kerr & Company, 1923.

———. "Living a Long Life Over Again." Unpublished manuscript in Post papers, Library of Congress, circa 1925.

Preston, William Jr. *Aliens and Dissenters: Federal Suppression of Radicals, 1903–1933.* Urbana and Chicago: University of Illinois Press, 1963.

Recht, Charles. "A World To Win." Unpublished manuscript in Recht papers, NYU. Undated.

Roosevelt, James, and Sidney Shalett. *Affectionately, F.D.R.: A Son's Story of a Lonely Man.* New York: Harcourt, Brace & Company, 1959.

Schlesinger, Arthur M. Jr., ed. *The Almanac of American History.* New York: Pedigree Books, 1983.

Simon, James F. *Lincoln and Chief Justice Taney: Slavery, Secession, and the President's War Powers.* New York: Simon & Schuster, 2006.

Smith, Gene. *When the Cheering Stopped: The Last Years of Woodrow Wilson.* New York: William Morrow and Company, 1964.

Stone, Irving. *Clarence Darrow for the Defense.* Garden City, New York: Garden City Publishing Co., 1943.

Summers, Anthony. *Official and Confidential: The Secret Life of J. Edgar Hoover.* New York: G.P. Putnam's Sons, 1993.

Theoharis, Athan G., and John Stuart Cox. *The Boss: J. Edgar Hoover and the Great American Inquisition.* Philadelphia: Temple University Press, 1988.

———. *The FBI: A Comprehensive Guide, From J. Edgar Hoover to The X-Files.* New York: The Oryx Press, 2000.

———. *From the Secret Files of J. Edgar Hoover.* Chicago: Ivan R. Dee, 1991.

———. *J. Edgar Hoover, Sex, and Crime.* Chicago: Ivan R. Dee, 1995.

Tierney, Kevin. *Darrow: A Biography.* New York: Thomas Y. Crowell, Publishers, 1979.

Tumulty, Joseph. *Woodrow Wilson as I Know Him.* Garden City, New York: Doubleday, Page & Company, 1921.

Weinberg, Arthur. *Attorney for the Damned: Clarence Darrow in the Courtroom.* Chicago: University of Chicago Press, 1957, 1989.

Weinberg, Arthur, and Lila Weinberg. *Clarence Darrow: A Sentimental Rebel.* New York: G.P. Putnam and Sons, 1980.

Wheeler, Burton K. *Yankee from the West.* Garden City, New York; Doubleday & Company, Inc., 1962.

Whitehead, Don. *The FBI Story: A Report to the American People.* New York: Random House, 1956.

ACKNOWLEDGMENTS

Reconstructing the twisted tale of young J. Edgar Hoover and the Palmer Raids, an episode blurred by eight decades of spin, myth, and often deliberate distortion, was a daunting task, and I simply could not have done it without the generosity and support of many friends and colleagues who stepped in to help at every step. To them all, I give my heartfelt thanks.

Researching this story brought me to some of America's premier research centers, and in each case I benefited from the expertise of staff professionals whose aid and courtesy allowed me to appreciate the treasures over which they presided. My two principal research homes for *Young J. Edgar* were the Library of Congress in Washington, D.C., and the National Archives in Washington and College Park, Maryland. Both these institutions once again proved themselves to be true national gems. At the Library of Congress, I relied heavily on advice and support from the staffs of the Manuscript Room and Law Library whose patience and depth of knowledge were invaluable. At the National Archives, archivists including Fred Romanski, Alan Walker, and Marian Smith came through for me time after time when I needed help in deciphering the complex systems of records from the era. In addition, I thank Jeffrey Dosik, of the National Park Service station at Ellis Island, New York, who gave me the rare opportunity to see long-abandoned sections of that historic site, and shared with me his invaluable insights into the events that transpired there. Similarly, Ray Batvinis of the J. Edgar Hoover Center for Law Enforcement, located in the historic Masonic Temple building on Washington, D.C.'s Sixteenth Street, NW, not only walked me through the center's unique collection, but also gave me insights into the man himself, as well as feedback on the manuscript.

I owe a special tribute to a handful of earlier scholars whose groundbreaking research on J. Edgar Hoover, the FBI, and government crackdowns of the World War I era paved the way for later writers like myself. Two who were particularly generous to me in this process, including providing feedback on the manuscript, were Professor Athan Theoharis of Marquette University, whose multiple books on Hoover and the FBI are indispensable references, and Professor William Preston of the John Jay College of Criminal Law, whose 1963 classic *Aliens and Dissenters* pioneered the review of archival materials from the era. In addition, John S. Cox, who coauthored Theoharis's 1988 volume on Hoover's life, gave me important insights into both Hoover and how he is regarded in the world.

In the actual writing of *Young J. Edgar*, I benefited from the eyes and critiques of many friends and experts who read parts or all of the manuscript, including Ellen Roberts of Where Books Begin; my friends in the Washington Independent Writers History Small Group, Sky Beaven, Lawrence Ellsworth, Cynthia Gayton, Valery Garrett, Steve Hardesty, Clyde Linsley, Lloyd Muller, Patricia Pearson, and Michael Williams; my legal colleagues David Durkin, Robert Hahn, and Phil Olsson at Olsson, Frank, and Weeda, P.C.; and my historian-biographer colleagues Jamie Morris, Jim Robenalt, and David Stewart. Jim Hershberg, the eminent professor of history at George Washington University, and Frank Murphy of the New York City Bar both stepped in at key points to help me fill in the story.

Young J. Edgar is the fourth book on which I have had the pleasure to work with Carroll & Graf Publishers, Inc., and once again I thank them for the care and skill they exercised in handling my work and presenting it to the commercial marketplace. I particularly thank publisher Will Balliett, my editor, Philip Turner (now at Sterling Publishing, Inc.), Betsy Steve, Bill Strachan, Keith Wallman, Adelaide Docx, and the production, graphics, distribution, marketing, and technical teams that contributed to this project. I thank my agent, Jeff Gerecke, who has guided me now through several excellent adventures in publishing, and Gene Taft, my publicist on the book, who played an invaluable role in helping to place it in the public eye.

I once again give a special thanks to my colleagues at Olsson, Frank, and Weeda, P.C., where I practice law in Washington, D.C., without whose support and understanding while I have gone off on my writing escapades none of my books would have been possible. To Honey and Dave—especially for repeated use of the apartment in New York—Phyl and Lewis, all the friend and family who provided moral support when needed, and, of course to Karen, my wife, who has happily put up with the whole thing with love and humor. I thank you all.

INDEX